PHILOSOPHY
AT THE
BOUNDARY
OF REASON

D0947426

PHILOSOPHY AT THE BOUNDARY OF REASON

Ethics and Postmodernity

PATRICK L. BOURGEOIS

State University
of New York
Press

Published by
State University of New York Press, Albany

© 2001 State University of New York

All rights reserved

Production by Susan Geraghty
Marketing by Anne M. Valentine

Printed in the United States of America

No part of this book may be used or reproduced in any manner whatsoever
without written permission. No part of this book may be stored in a retrieval
system or transmitted in any form or by any means including electronic,
electrostatic, magnetic tape, mechanical, photocopying, recording, or otherwise
without the prior permission in writing of the publisher.

For information, address State University of New York Press,
90 State Street, Suite 700, Albany, NY 12207

Library of Congress Cataloging-in-Publication Data

Bourgeois, Patrick L.
    Philosophy at the boundary of reason : ethics and postmodernity / Patrick L. Bourgeois.
        p. cm.
    Includes bibliographical references and index.
    ISBN 0-7914-4821-5 (hardcover : alk. paper) — ISBN 0-7914-4822-3 (pbk. : alk. paper)
        1. Limit (Logic) 2. Philosophy. I. Title.

BC199.L54 B68 2000
190'.9'04—dc21
                                                                    00-026525

10 9 8 7 6 5 4 3 2 1

For
Paul J. Bourgeois,
my twin,
and
Ambrose Wathen, O. S. B.,
my friend

CONTENTS

ACKNOWLEDGMENTS

Thanks are due to the editor of the *American Catholic Philosophical Quarterly* for permission to republish parts of the article: "Semiotics and the Deconstruction of Presence: A Ricoeurian Alternative," published in the *American Catholic Philosophical Quarterly*, vol. 66, no. 3, pp. 361–379.

On a personal note, I would like to express my gratitude to my wife, Mary, for her constant patience, endurance, and support during this lengthy project; and to Patricia Blanchard for her expertise and patience in proofreading this text.

PREFACE

In writing a contribution in 1986 for the *Library of Living Philosophers* on the philosophy of Paul Ricoeur, I concentrated on the central role of the Kantian notion of limit-boundary for Ricoeur's philosophy.[1] In further pursuing this line of thought, I became aware of the central role of this same notion, in one form or another, to continental philosophy today. The related statements of the end of philosophy and of metaphysics, the Kantian role of imagination, and the various and divergent interpretations of that role of the imagination emerged as central to the whole problematic. For it is clear that the stance taken concerning the interpretation of the Kantian imagination determines the direction of recent continental philosophy. At this point, the pervasive influence of Emmanuel Levinas' ethics as first philosophy on such developments became apparent.

Once this project was formulated as a study on *Philosophy at the Boundary of Reason*, the issues of the crossroads of continental philosophy emerged in the light of the role of imagination and limit-boundary, revealing in this context a positive element in postmodern deconstruction. As we shall see in the first chapter, and later in part II, it is precisely the interpretation that is given to the imagination that distinguishes the several directions of development. Thus, the topics of the three parts of this study, working toward a viable ethics today, fall into place: limit-boundary and philosophy; imagination at the crossroads of philosophy; and evaluation, obligation, and practical wisdom in the context of the foundation and principle of ethicomoral philosophy.

My working hypothesis for this entire study, stated in chapter 1, is that, by understanding deconstruction as a philosophy of limit[2] and taking into account its positive element, it is possible to advance an alternative, more viable ethics at the limit-boundary that both takes into account deconstructive reading and passes beyond it. And it is precisely the tension between limit-boundary and extension that allows a revived ethics, cast against the backdrop of Kantian limit-boundary and the extensions beyond them, to take place within the polarity between ethical foundations and moral principle of obligation.[3] It is necessary to confront deconstruction's critique of any such philosophy as a closure that requires deconstruction. We will find that this very critique of closure

can be turned back on deconstruction itself, and that the heart of deconstruction as a philosophy of limit-boundary essentially entails a misunderstanding of time, sign, and trace.

Chapter 1 of this study presents the challenge of postmodern deconstruction to philosophy today, showing how it can be considered a philosophy of limit-boundary and, as such, a type of reading of texts. This
challenge is presented in the fundamental context of the basis of the initial will to believe that we can arrive at logos, meaning, and values in
general, within which deconstruction gives a certain priority to closure
intrinsic to this very process. This priority of closure is seen in its impact
on the ethics of deconstruction as a philosophy of limit-boundary. This
closure has led either to the denial of ethics, deconstructing it so that
nothing but the deconstructive process is left; or to the affirmation of an
ethics of obligation at the core of the deconstructive process, but, as in
the case above, including a denial of the personal ethical relation, whose
possibility/impossibility are entailed in the deconstructive process. And
it is precisely the effort to confront such a challenge that affords the positive opportunity for philosophical growth.

Chapter 2 casts a wider net to encompass the relation of limit to the
end of philosophy, showing how this Heideggerian beginning has led to
the present-day discussion of the possibility of philosophy. It requires a
critical evaluation of the end of philosophy, proclaimed by Heidegger,
and extends to the death of philosophy as it emerges in the Derrida-Levinas dialogue. The purpose of so doing is to ascertain the extent to
which end or death is latent and essential to philosophy itself, and thus
to deepen our focus and eventually, if it is found necessary after a
perusal of Kant's treatment of correlated issues, to adjust the philosophy
of limit-boundary. Thus, in order to further clarify and deepen our discussion concerning limit-boundary and end in their fullness and variation, we must now turn to Kant's notion of limit, boundary, and end,
relate these to the role of the imagination in order to trace in depth the
recent emergence of differing attitudes toward the limit of philosophy.
This is the project of the ensuing chapters, before taking up again the
various recent positions and readings of philosophy, especially regarding sign, language, time, and trace, all of which lurk beneath the surface
as underlying elements.

After delving into the relation of philosophy to boundary, closure,
and end, we will now, in chapter 3, turn to their common backdrop in
Kantian philosophy. This detour will provide a means of clarifying basic
divergences among styles of thinking today that, although different,
come to light in a special way when cast against such a common backdrop. Thus, in presenting several essential points in relation to Kant's
philosophy, a beginning for contrasting and interarticulating these dif-

fering positions comes to the fore. First, these positions can be seen in one way or another to relate to the Kantian imagination, which justifies and requires turning to Kant's view of imagination in coming chapters. Second, since the Kantian doctrine of limit, boundary, and end has served as a backdrop for the entire discussion of the last two chapters, an explication of these will help us along our way to clarify these issues for philosophy today. Third, focusing upon the interrelations of time, imagination, and language in a Kantian context allows us to contrast how this interrelation is appropriated differently by Ricoeur and by Derrida in critical dialogue with Heidegger. Fourth, Ricoeur's entire philosophy, which is of central concern for us in these studies, must at least in some measure be interpreted as containing a post-Hegelian Kantian dimesnion, as he sometimes affirms. And in addition, Ricoeur's philosophy can be seen as a completion, in his own unique fashion, of the Kantian enterprise of imagination.[4] Thus, it becomes necessary for us to turn to some important elements of Kantian philosophy, and to contrast the various recent styles of thinking with this common reference.

In addition, we are able to glean, from a digression with Ricoeur into the contrast between Husserl and Kant, a sharp focus on the solution to the enigma created by the critique of Husserl's ontological omission and Kant's phenomenological deficit. Ricoeur supplies to the Husserlian omission the thinking of Being as limiting at the boundary, thus supplying to phenomenology its needed limit (boundary) and critique essential to such limit-boundary. We can now turn more explicitly to the question of ground in the realm of the practical.

In chapter 4 we turn to Kantian practical philosophy in order to make clear the full significance of Ricoeur's critique and expansion of central Kantian elements in a philosophy of praxis that attempts to interarticulate Aristotelian teleology with Kantian deontology. We first consider the question of Kantian limit and ground in practical judgment, then Ricoeur's expansion of Kantian elements, Ricoeur's own philosophy as a philosophy of limit, returning finally to the relation of his philosophy, precisely as a philosophy of limit, to that of deconstruction. This will make it possible more clearly to understand Ricoeur's integration of the teleological and the deontological in ethics, and the central role of the imagination in his philosophy.

Several paths of inquiry have emerged in this discussion that must be taken up and investigated in the following chapters of part II and part III. The central role of the imagination, again adjusted by Ricoeur from Kant, and in stark contrast to the role of the imagination in deconstruction, makes it necessary to focus at length on the imagination. From this investigation, it will be necessary to turn to the nature of language, sign, and trace, contrasting the views of Ricoeur and of deconstruction, and leading to a discussion on the nature of time and the living present in relation to sign. Finally, after considering these issues the stage will then be set for a full-blown consideration of ethics at the boundary of reason in part III, contrasting Ricoeur's view with those of deconstruction.

As mentioned above, it is necessary for us to detour into this detailed study of Kant's productive imagination as background for further studies of recent philosophical developments rooted in it. For the development of philosophy in the twentieth century is rooted in variations in interpreting the role of this productive imagination of Kant. To renew this discussion at an originary level it is necessary for us to invoke Kant's own doctrine before it is creatively appropriated by his own immediate followers, as well as before it is incorporated into various contemporary projects: a fundamental ontological project or a deconstruction in a clotural reading that do not do justice to Kant's own doctrine. It remains for us now, in chapter 5, to turn to its various roles on the contemporary scene, leading to the depth of divergent paths of development in continental thinking today.[5] During the development of these alternative positions, springing from the role allowed to the imagination, the challenge from deconstruction as developing in dialogue with the phenomenological and semiological traditions will be brought to its depth and intensity, allowing the central issues at stake in ethics today to emerge.

The role assigned to the imagination in recent philosophy is either central, in which case the productive imagination and semantic innovation are paramount, as they are for such thinkers as Paul Ricoeur; or it is not at all central, in which case chance replaces the productive imagination in its centrality, as is the case for Jacques Derrida. Given this disparity in roles of the imagination, chapter 6 will attempt to show how imagination or chance shape the core of these two positions leading to its diverse roles in the constitution of sign and the living present, and thus revealing these positions to be mutually exclusive. I will argue in strong support for the centrality of productive imagination as a legacy from Kantian philosophy, and for semantic innovation rooted in its extension. For what is essentially at stake in this appropriation of the role of the imagination is an innovation of meaning within a viable semantic theory as opposed to an intense and subversive intellectual anarchism, based on a will to believe in the priority of the subversive. A first brief focus on the recent adaptations of the role of the Kantian productive imagination will be helpful to distinguish currents of thought in addressing this limit of thinking.

Thus, it is clear that at least three distinct interpretations of the role of imagination emerge in philosophy at its end-boundary. First, in Heidegger's finitization of reason, the productive imagination is the source of reason itself and, as such, of the limit placed by reason, all of which, in Heidegger's view, are rooted in "primordial time,"[6] bespeaking the closure that must be transgressed—the closure toward the meaning of Being and toward Being itself within language and within time. In this position, as we shall see the Kantian heterogeneity between the sensible and the intelligible is overcome in a common root, the imagination, thus clearly going beyond the Kantian ground of reason and its problematic elements in the realm of practical reason and its ground. Rendering imagination central in this direction of fundamental ontology leads to an "originary ethos" in the context of the truth of being, rendering ethics, like traditional metaphysics and epistemology, secondary as derivative and impersonal.

Ricoeur's manner of dealing with indirect language and the imagination and Derrida's manner of dealing with chance in relation to dissemination and *différance* differ radically from Heidegger's finitization of reason. The postmodern and deconstructive critique of Heidegger transforms his interpretation of the central role of the Kantian productive imagination by subordinating it to chance or to language itself. For the deconstruction of Derrida, the closure results from the propensity to fixate on the effect within the flux of the *différance*, a fixation that prevents the transgressing of philosophy to *différance*, dissemination, and the "play of reason." And Lyotard, rendering the treatment of the sublime in the *Critique of Judgment* as central, seeking to displace any conceptual rule, thus supports invention that displaces the whole "game" over the innovation that makes new moves within the rules of the game. Lyotard extends the indeterminate dimension of the limited role of the reflective judgment of the sublime in Kant's use to a paradigmatic role in thinking, leading to common antilogocentism with Derrida. Thus, there is an attempt on the part of both to supplant the primacy of the Kantian theoretical understanding in its knowing function in favor of a priority of language that renders the human role of imagination passive and secondary to that of the "other."[7] Further, language in their employ loses its semantic priority in favor of semiological priority. There is, however, another way of reaching this other, one that does not go by either of the paths above and one that has not lost original creativity or some role of the understanding other than that in Kant's theoretical knowledge.

If reason is not produced by imagination, then reason itself limits knowledge to experience from above, as already seen, putting the imagination in a central position both in knowledge and in thinking, as it is for Ricoeur. This limit enacted by reason on human knowledge encompasses knowledge within the experience of reality itself, but allows reason to reach beyond the boundary to something of a more far-reaching significance.

What does this say about philosophy at its end? That its end as boundary is transgressed and therefore philosophy becomes thinking in its context of the whole or of completion. But, due to the limit of human experience, and to the quest for the total in thinking (and in action), philosophy will never be completed. Thus, one could perhaps say that philosophy culminates precisely in its attempt to stay attuned to its limited access to the total—to completion, and to "see" or to interpret at this point, its ultimate significance. And is this not what Ricoeur is attempting to do? We must attempt to come to grips now with precisely what the subordination of imagination means. Ricoeur's view of a central role of productive imagination, rooted in his interpretation of the priority of the semantic in language and the unity of language in the sentence, pulls the props out from under Derrida's reduction of the imagination and at once offers a richer and more viable view of language and semantic innovation at the center of his hermeneutic.

Chapter 7 will study the respective roles of trace in the thinking of Derrida and Ricoeur, requiring a thorough investigation of their views of sign, language, and the living present. Derrida's view of trace hinges on his critiques of Saussure's and Husserl's views of sign, as well as on his critique of Husserl's view of the living present, making trace central to language at the core of his deconstruction. It can be seen that Ricoeur's view of language, taking its point of departure from a more radical critique of Saussure and structuralism than that of Derrida, together with his radical critique of Derrida's deconstruction of Husserl's living present, likewise pulls the props out from under Derrida's view of trace by offering a view of the living present and of time that is able to support a richer and more viable view of trace, language, and semiotics. Yet bringing to clear light Ricoeur's critiques of Derrida's understanding of the living present and of phenomenology's view of inner time will, at once, reveals his agreement with Derrida on essential points of a view of trace in a sign system, and with Husserl regarding the phenomenological primordiality of the living present. Although the development in this chapter regarding deconstruction's view of language, time, and the connection between them is critical regarding its interpretation of both time and sign, a positive element emerges as something that cannot be avoided, and that must instruct any future development of thought today.

Thus, Ricoeur's alternative to Derrida's semiological reductionism, and the flux of time as discrete on which it is founded, provides a viable position that does not succumb to the facile distinction of Saussure, nor to Derrida's collapse of signs to the relations of differences within the system and the reduction of language to the play of *différance*. Rather, Ricoeur is able adequately to account for duration and continuity in the living present as the basis for language as discourse and for trace. And Ricoeur's account of the temporal context for understanding language undercuts Derrida's pseudo-alternatives of signs or presence, for the temporal span of the present is neither pure identity nor pure alterity. The present, as thickened by retention and protention, "intends" the future in light of the past. Since the very function of the present is to mean and the very nature of presence requires signs, language and signs are inseparably intertwined with time. Thus, his theory of language as essentially discourse, his distinctions between words and signs and between signs and sentences, in the overall contexts of the new unity of language in the semantics of the sentence, reestablishes some faith in philosophical analysis as having something worthwhile to say about something, even when it deals with an interpretation of language and of texts. While the positioning of signs, or the play of *différance*, can yield a productivity of some kind of meaning, it is not the replacement of the semantic dimension of language as primary. Syntax of any kind exists for the semantic. To invert this is to distort language, to make a mockery of meaning, to reduce meaning to an empty shell, as well as to render meaningless any attempt to communicate this message of inversion.

Chapter 8 can now turn to the contemporary conversation regarding ethics in an attempt to go beyond the impasses presented by recent oppositions arising out of postmodern deconstruction. This opposition is essentially intertwined with the deconstructive interpretation of the role of imagination, language, sign, and lived time. Continuing our investigation regarding the status of these elements in relation to ethics allows to emerge a viable context for seriously reflecting upon and conversing about ethics and morality today. Thus, in the context of the dialogue between Levinas and Derrida, the discussion will turn to several explicit accounts of deconstructive ethics. This chapter will proceed from an analysis and critique of Caputo's poetics of obligation and move to the consideration of the fuller current of deconstruction and ethics. Thus, this chapter will bring into focus the question of a Derridian ethical element, invoking Levinas' view of ethics in the context of double reading and closure. Critchley refers to an "unconditional ethical imperative" as the source of the "injunction that produces deconstruction and is produced through deconstructive reading." He also shows "how the 'concept' of general text and *différance* can be articulated within an ethical problematic,"[8] the central element of which entails the concept of the closure of metaphysics, a concept already seen above. Critchley contends, against a too typical tendency to consider all ethics to presuppose the metaphysics that deconstruction deconstructs, that there is an ethic at the heart of deconstruction.

It will be seen that Caputo, Cornell, and Critchley all, attuned to the

Derrida-Levinas dialogue, put obligation at the heart of deconstruction, but Caputo, following Derrida's hesitance, rejects ethics in favor of a poetics of obligation, while Critchley and Cornell, following Levinas, hang onto the term in their own rejection of virtually the same ethics that Caputo rejects. For my part, I would recognize a positive contribution of deconstruction, and proceed to a further extension of ethics following Ricoeur, who is likewise influenced by Levinas, but in a way entirely different from the way in which deconstruction is influenced by him. For Ricoeur, there is an opening back to the tradition, rather than a cutting away toward a deconstructive clotural reading. We will see that this obligation or duty at the heart of the deconstructive enterprise is not something to be lost sight of, even if it requires an extension beyond the usual sense of ethics. But is it not to be seen as self sufficient, and it is tied to something that would best be brought into a more positive frame of philosophical mind.

Critchley's argument, then, would put an ethical duty at the heart of the deconstructive enterprise: "Rather, I hope to demonstrate that the pattern of reading produced in the deconstruction of—mostly, but by no means exclusively—philosophical texts has an ethical structure: deconstruction 'is' ethical; or, to formulate the same thought less ontologically . . . deconstruction takes place (*a lieu*) ethically, or there is duty in deconstruction (*Il y a du devoir dans la déconstruction*)."[9] Critchley's main point about Levinas' ethics in relation to a more traditionally oriented ethics, even such as that of Ricoeur, is that it reveals a level of primordial ethical experience that is more primordial than, and is presupposed by, those ethical considerations that attempt to reflect on maxims or judgments in relation to social action and civic duty, and that are derived and distinct from that primordial level. Levinas himself does not see his task as one of constructing an ethics. He says, rather, that "I only try to seek its meaning (*sens*)."[10] This primacy for Levinas means the primacy of the face-to-face personal relation.

All of the commentators of deconstruction considered here, Caputo, Cornell, and Critchley, report on Derrida's ethics by entering the discussion between Derrida and Levinas. It seems that Derrida has dialogued with and deconstructed Levinas' ethics in coming to a deconstructive ethics of his own, if the term "ethics" can even be retained. Caputo, in his *Against Ethics*, has opted to stress the "other" to ethics. Ethics presupposes the very metaphysics that deconstruction must deconstruct, which requires the deconstruction of even Heideggian "originary ethos." Yet, although they agree for the most part on the essential points toward an ethics of deconstruction, Cornell and Critchley do not abrogate the term "ethics" or "ethical." They simply transform the word, or deconstruct it. Further, for all of them, and for Derrida, this sense of ethics at the heart of the deconstructive enterprise is a philosophy of limit-boundary, but not necessarily a critical philosophy, which itself would need deconstructing.

All three of the authors mentioned above introduce a new sense of ethics at the heart of the deconstructive enterprise. For Drucilla Cornell this ethical impulse can be easily seen at the heart of her interpretation of this enterprise as a philosophy of limit.[11] As has been seen, Caputo, deconstructing the ethics and the metaphysics on which it is built, reveals the poetic obligation at the heart of deconstruction. And Critchley sees a primordial importance to ethics at the heart of deconstructive or clotural reading. And for all three, it is the role of Levinas' reflections on the ethical relation that takes on significance, especially in the light of the discussion between him and Levinas. The one problem that I have is that Levinas does not seem to enclose all this in terms of language taken to be a system of signs, with each sign functioning as a trace. Caputo seems to address this directly when he discusses the sense of self in terms of personal pronouns. One can deconstruct ethics, arriving thereby at an ethical demand placed on deconstruction itself. That is precisely what emerges in raising the question of ethics in the context of deconstruction understood as a philosophy of limit-boundary: that there is some serious and sincere ethical obligation or responsibility at the heart of the enterprise, already envisioned by Derrida, especially as he deconstructs Levinas. The positive element of deconstruction mentioned throughout these chapters must not obscure its failure as a philosophy of limit that must be brought to light. This chapter considers both the failures in the context of deconstruction's positive contribution mentioned throughout our studies, as well as the extent to which we can even speak of this as ethics.

We can now, in chapter 9, turn to the ethicomoral philosophy of Paul Ricoeur that takes account of these positive elements of postmodern deconstruction, but does not succumb to its demands that lead to its failures. Paul Ricoeur's recent ethicomoral project, culminating in three of the last four chapters of *Oneself as Another*,[12] and extended in *Le Just*,[13] consists in polarizing the ethical philosophies of Aristotle and Kant, and integrating a critically adjusted version of each into a unique and encompassing ethical framework. Within this entire enterprise he likewise develops many opposing polarities that he similarly proceeds to interarticulate and appropriate into a coherent position. One such opposition is that between the exteriority at the heart of the ethical philosophy of Emmanuel Levinas and the interiority of Husserl's transcendental philosophy. And within this context he employs elements of Heidegger's existential analysis of Dasein to flesh out the way of a satisfactory interarticulation, from which he appropriates his own position.

It is within this context that the accusation has been made that Ricoeur is too severe in his critique of Levinas. Although we must concede to this accusation in a qualified way, such an admission must not prevent us from appreciating the fullness and the richness of Ricoeur's contemporary ethicomoral philosophy, especially in the light of the recent contrasting works on deconstruction and ethics.[14] I intend in this chapter to enter this present conversation on deconstruction and ethics by proposing a complex thesis: first, that Ricoeur's critique of Levinas is indeed a bit too severe, but when understood in his own context, the place of this critique in his overall project of an ethicomoral foundation and principle comes to light. It will be seen that a fundamental dimension that Ricoeur wants to supply to Levinas' own position is already contained in it, even though it is in need of further development. This then becomes the context for adjusting Ricoeur's interpretation in deference to Levinas, but without any need to alter Ricoeur's own position. Thus, after investigating Ricoeur's critique of Levinas and briefly defending Levinas' own position, I will attempt to work toward interarticulating the positions of Ricoeur and Levinas, incorporating both the solitude of interiority and the solicitude that Ricoeur incorporates from Heidegger. This leads into the second part of my thesis, arising from the treatment of the first: that Ricoeur, precisely by incorporating an essential element from Levinas, provides a viable ethics as an alternative to postmodern deconstruction.

At the outset, however, it must be admitted that the projects of Ricoeur and of Levinas are entirely different and somewhat opposed. For, from Levinas' point of view, it could be claimed that Ricoeur's whole enterprise fits into the context of totality, thus constituting precisely what Levinas intends to interrupt with infinity. Even in this apparent opposition, however, it must be admitted that Ricoeur's project, always considered to be ethical, has certain explicit affinities with that of Levinas. For Ricoeur has constantly adhered to the need in ethics precisely for Levinas' "face to face," even contending that ethics has its beginning in the second-person recognition of the other's will and freedom. And, on the other side, Ricoeur says that he has not ever assumed Levinas' ontology of totality, showing how Levinas restricts identity to the point that it "results that the self, not distinguished from the I, is not taken in the sense of the self-designation of a subject of discourse, action, narrative, or ethical commitment" (OA, 335). I believe it is here with the notion of totality that the difficulty between them is found. And Levinas' notion of totality in the context of the identity of the self needs to be extended, just as Ricoeur's interpretation of Levinas regarding the place within interiority for an encounter with the Other will be adjusted.

The failure of postmodern deconstruction, as mentioned above, to give a viable account of time and the living present, sign and trace, and philosophy at the boundary of reason, has prompted us in chapter 10 and chapter 11 to turn to the account pursued throughout this study, that of Paul Ricoeur as an alternative. In these last chapters, we mediated this turn to the ethicomoral philosophy of Ricoeur by clarifying the integration of Levinas' face to face, solitude, and infinity into the ethics of Ricoeur. Now, in turning to his ethicomoral philosophy more explicitly, we find it to be fundamentally attuned to the whole western tradition and sensitive to the ethicomoral dimension, as well as to those of the political, the legal, and the religious. His challenging writings on ethics afford the most encompassing and viable ethical framework and principle for facing up to problems in ethics today.

Not withstanding the success in this entire analysis in coming to an ethics that is viable today in spite of radical challenges from postmodern deconstruction, this study concludes by exposing a couple of aporia intrinsic to this entire enterprise, requiring further study. This effort appears, then, as the first word in this enterprise, and not the last.

PART I

Philosophy at the Boundary of Reason

CHAPTER 1

Ethics at the Limit of Reason

INTRODUCTION: THE CHALLENGE
OF POSTMODERN DECONSTRUCTION

The scene of recent ethical discussions is comprised of somewhat disparate conversations. On the one hand applied ethics assumes settled and accepted ethical theory in its attempts to address specific problems and cases, thus proceeding without the guiding light of consistent, well-understood ethical theory. It hence ignores much of the ethical consternation in recent discussions and in the history of philosophy. On the other hand, ethical theory has been challenged not only from within its own ranks by particular conflicting theories, but also by those who would challenge it precisely as theory and then again as ethics. Within this vast conversation, one can see a certain polarity around the poles of which similar types of discussion take place. For there is Alasdair MacIntyre's critique of the Western tradition, and a concomitant return to a quasi-Aristotelian medieval ethics,[1] and in the same camp, the placing of ethics in a different context and level with Heidegger's delving to the originary ethos. MacIntyre and Heidegger, both looking back to the Greek heritage against modern restrictiveness, have recourse to a certain eschatological element in ethics.[2] Then, in extreme opposition to this tendency, the deconstructionists' and postmodernists' proclaim that all ethics of value and moral intelligibility, even those of MacIntyre and Heidegger, have not gone far enough in their respective critiques of the tradition, and have gone too far in their respective closures effecting exclusions. Thus their texts are themselves in need of deconstructive or "clotural" reading[3] deciphering their dislocations and contradictions. And it is in this latter context that the somewhat mitigated deconstructive account of John Caputo[4] fits, with its own ethics of dissemination in opposition even to Heidegger's view of originary ethos. In the spirit of carrying further this conversation, the question can be raised whether any ethics today can be revisited and considered viable. Such is the challenge to ethical philosophy arising out of deconstruction. And this challenge must be taken seriously, avoiding the usual first attempts to dismiss it as some kind of kinky philosophy, resulting in ignoring its important challenge. For it is precisely such a challenge and the consequent dialogues that afford a positive opportunity for philosophical growth and advance.

Once a philosophical movement such as "postmodern" deconstruction has developed to its present state of maturity, it is time to stop ignoring, lampooning, or condemning it, and, rather, to take its challenge to traditional philosophy seriously. If postmodern deconstruction is interpreted as a philosophy at its limit,[5] its positive contribution comes to light better than if an attempt is made at the outset of a critical reflection to depict it as a relativism, nihilism, or skepticism. Taking such a tack allows one to respond more favorably to the positive contribution of deconstruction within a more viable alternative account.

It is necessary at once, however, to face up to the challenge that this thinking poses to the philosophical enterprise itself—a challenge that does not so much deny or annihilate philosophy as much as it shows this enterprise to be derived and secondary, not getting beneath its own so-called foundations. It is thus considered the product of a closure that prevents any serious ethical justice.[6] If the extreme formulation of such a challenge is accepted, the sense in which any ethical philosophy can be considered worthwhile arises. For it would seem that to deconstruct ethics or to engage it in a "clotural reading" involves a fundamental style of thinking at odds with the very project of any usual ethics. Included in this approach is the tendency to deal with all such considerations as a "reading," and thus within some kind of expression of sign or interpretation of language that precludes any approach to virtues, goods, or values expressed or grasped prior to language. Such is the nature of the challenge to ethical philosophy arising out of postmodern deconstruction that must be confronted today.

My working hypothesis for this entire study is that, by understanding deconstruction as a philosophy of limit and taking into account its positive element, it is possible to advance an alternative, more viable ethics at the limit-boundary, both taking into account deconstructive reading as well as passing beyond it. And it is precisely the tension between limit and extension that allows a revived ethics, cast against the backdrop of the tension between Kantian limits and the extensions beyond them, to take place within the polarity between ethical foundation and moral principle of obligation.[7] Further, it is necessary to confront deconstruction's critique of any such philosophy as a closure that requires deconstruction. And finally we will find that the very critique of closure can be turned back on deconstruction itself. It will be found that the heart of deconstruction as a philosophy of limit essentially entails a misunderstanding of time, sign, and trace.[8] We must now turn briefly to the notion of limit in order to show how deconstructive ethics and any revitalized philosophy today fit into that context.

THE LIMIT OF PHILOSOPHY

In focusing on philosophy at the limit, we bring together and correlate two distinct senses of limit: one emerging from Kant's transcendental idealism as the notion of a limit placed by reason, an act of reason limiting knowledge to experience;[9] the other from Peirce's notion of secondness, within interaction, as indicating the "given" that places limit on the projected interpretation in opposition to idealism. It seems to me that both senses obtain, the first from the direction of reason, the second from the "other." And, similarly, deconstruction itself can be considered a philosophy of limit in these two senses. We will see, however, that we must eventually derive a further and more inclusive sense of limit.

I shall begin by following Drucilla Cornell's recasting of this designation of deconstruction as a philosophy of limit in the first sense as a positive effect, exposing the "quasi-transcendental conditions" establishing a system as a system, showing that this very establishment of a system implies a "beyond to it," precisely of what it excludes.[10] This is the other side of the closure, that is, that the system, and any determination of meaning, allows closure and exclusion at the expense of the openness and what is excluded. Thus, deconstruction as a philosophy of limit at the end of metaphysics challenges us to be open to the excluded, thus affording us a "golden opportunity"[11] rather than a crisis of termination. Hence, Cornell's rendition of deconstruction as a philosophy of limit open to the beyond, to unimagined possibilities, is a call for a radical transformation of the present.[12] Deconstruction, then, questions traditional philosophy's ability to get at the "beyond" in its discourse, that is, in its saying of what cannot be said.

The second way of taking limit can likewise be related to deconstruction as a philosophy of limit.[13] Here, in the context of idealism and its system, especially of the Hegelian vintage, one can incorporate C. S. Peirce's notion of secondness in his own opposition to Hegelian idealism. As Cornell says, by secondness Peirce indicates "the materiality that persists *beyond* any attempt to conceptualize it," that is, as that which resists and cannot be entirely rendered in interpretation—that is, reality is not wholly interpretation. It seems here that this notion of limit is no longer the one placed by reason, but rather is from the other—that is, from Kant's unknowable x, but in a far more positive sense than that of Kant, since for Peirce that distinction between noumenal and phenomenal is overcome. Hence it is clear that this Peircean notion of secondness reaches to that other that is beyond our conceptualization and interpretation, thus serving as a limit that is not from reason or understanding as it is for Kant. Rather this is a limit placed on the interpretation of our understanding from the other direction than that considered above. This placing of limit will require further consideration later in this study since it is here that indirect expressions such as symbols become relevant in allowing thought and interpretation beyond the limit of Kant.

Limit as Closure, Clotural Reading, and End

According to some interpreters, the word "limit" carries the same force as closure for Derrida,[14] thus again depicting deconstruction as a philosophy of limit, but with a sharper focus on a certain aspect of deconstruction. Simon Critchley coins the phrase "clotural reading" to depict the kind of activity of closure as distinguished from end, and to distinguish a trivializing of deconstruction with the phrase "deconstructive reading," which he adamantly eschews. Clotural reading entails deciphering a dislocation within a text, dividing it along the split axes of belonging and not belonging to the metaphysical or logocentric tradition. This *clotural* structure of textuality is indicated by the transgression and restoration of closure, both maintained in a nonsymmetrical and nontotalizable relation, "a relation in which the *relata* remain absolute."[15] This *clotural* structure is "provoked" by a *reading* in which two clashing lines of thought open up. The "clotural reading" has two moments that vary according to the text that is being read. First, a general pattern can be delineated: a "repetition of the text's internal exigencies through an act of 'commentary'"; and second, "within and through this repetition, an ellipsis or moment of alterity opens up within the text" that allows a different reading to emerge. It is important to understand that this moment of alterity, as the ellipsis within the text, is grasped only through the first reading leading to the second, thus revealing the need for a double reading. "The ellipsis is the space within repetition."[16] Thus, it is not the case that any reading is possible for a "deconstructive reading," as some opponents of deconstruction like to contend. Rather, the process of clotural reading is rigorous, involving a serious repetition that resuscitates the original impetus or exigency of the text. And, at once, the serious work of this reading brings to the fore the alterity or ellipsis that leads to an entirely other reading, but one making the closure emerge into view. Such a clotural reading puts one in the throes of the closure of the metaphysical tradition, caught in the midst of the logocentric sense and its closure, and thus brings about an interruption of these. It is Critchley's contention that such reading is the context for the emergence of the ethics of deconstruction: for such a reading of a text provokes the suspension of decision between the two alternative readings.[17]

This clotural reading can be seen as a philosophy at the limit in both senses above. First, the sense of limit as openness to the residue in creating a system is the same in the creation or reading of a text. It is precisely the logocentrism expressed by the construction of the text that demands, from the first repetitive reading, that the ellipsis come to the fore, requiring a deconstruction of the text in terms of the alterity that is latent in it. Secondly, the alterity or the other is precisely what defies any interpretation or conceptualization, because it lies beyond any such attempt. Thus, Critchley is correct is taking closure as another expression for limit. We must now turn to reflect further on what is entailed at this initial point of reflection on limit and closure.

If one takes deconstruction as a philosophy of limit in both the senses outlined above, and if it is seen to focus on closure as another way of expressing limit, the question emerges as to whether deconstruction (closure) is the only or the best interpretation of limit. To respond to this question, we must consider further what else is entailed in deconstruction as a philosophy of limit.[18] We must therefore explore the very basis for deconstruction itself and for this alternative way of believing. In doing so, we will reflect in a Jamesian way.[19]

PRIMARY AFFIRMATION AND NEGATION

Logocentrism, especially in its philosophical and scientific expressions, can be seen to contain a latent and subtle affirmation in common with deconstruction. All discovery and meaning, all value and ethics, spring from a will to believe or a certain faith that we can arrive at a logos, knowledge, unconcealment or sense and that we are amidst values that we can grasp and seek. In fact the critical philosophy of modernity arose in the attempt to check and limit reason's self-assurance, especially in the context of the success of science. And when once these have been attained to some degree of sophistication (e.g., in science, in philosophy), we can be thrown back to reflect on the precognitive and prephilosophical level, discovering and accounting more explicitly for that very level within the scope of the enlightening process itself. At this point, deconstruction and its opponents are within the same commitment of belief and are on the same level of discourse, for both admit this coming to knowledge and its claims. It is the status of the logos and knowledge that deconstruction must be seen to dismantle.

It is here that deconstructionists have come to what might be called a quasi conversion, a complete change-about in their way of looking at the whole enterprise, so that the post-Copernican revolution now becomes a postcritical conversion.[20] At this point, following the faith in the sense of logos, there is a complete about-face or transformation in attitude, giving rise to a further interpretation according to which the logos is incapable of doing justice to the unfathomable or to the abyss. It entails a closure of sense, an effect that looses its fluidity.

But the above analysis runs the risk of missing an important point: *the point of agreement between deconstruction and its opponents.* Deconstruction, as we have shown, does not disavow logos or cognition. It simply reinterprets further their sense and value so that both positions, deconstruction and logocentrism, operate in the same basic will to believe in logos, but with a different interpretation of its basic sense. Deconstruction does recognize that logos brings something to light, but this process is seen to have a different and perhaps concomitant negative dimension—that is, closure from the fullness and richness of the flux from which it emerges. It is precisely this will to believe in the logos with a concomitant negative aspect that demands a return to the abyss. Thus, besides a shared belief in the positive achievement of cognition, there is a further differing interpretation of the limitation of sense as opening-closure. There are two distinct attitudes: on the one hand, there is the acceptance of this move as positive openness, and advertance to the need for constant attunement to the opening itself. On the other hand there is the attitude that this commonly accepted move to the logos is really a point of departure for subverting itself due to the closure entailed. This second attitude interprets the move to logos not as primarily openness to, but rather as closedness from. The puzzling element is the contrast in attitudes. Why one and not the other? This question requires a look at two ways of viewing the status of logos itself. And these differing attitudes consider the openness from which the closure of knowledge enters into closure. Such a looking by deconstruction gapes at the opening as tied to the priority of the flux, the richness of the abyss, and the limiting derivativeness and closure of all logos; and leads to the overturning of the so-called logocentrism. Can reflection stand neutral at this point, investigate honestly, and attain some further insight about the negative reading at the limit?

Since there is the common faith in the work of logos and cognition as the positive dimensions of each interpretation, our reflection can certainly try to take a position between the two differing interpretations of closure-opening in order honestly to take both of them into account. To do so, we must begin within this initial shared will to believe in the logos, which is the common basis that leads in two differing directions. From within the process toward logos, it is necessary to admit that there are two distinct and opposed priorities operative. In the first case, one *ultimately* believes that, in spite of the unfathomable dimension of the sense of existence or of the flux out of which all sense emerges, we do arrive in logos at sense, at truth, at values, and that this has a certain priority. Or in the other case, the sense, truth, and value at which one arrives are interpreted to be derivative, constituting a closure (and hence violence), and that the priority is constituted by the closure to the flux, to that which constitutes all this as an effect, and thus is negative. This is a question of the priority of openness to sense, or the priority of closedness (closure) to the residue.

Deconstruction, at least that of Derrida, does not disavow or attempt to abrogate completely, metaphysics or philosophy, nor does it even like the notion of an interruption or complete rupture. For the move is always first to and from logos, then to its deconstruction, because of its closure and limit. Thus, the focal point must be the initial belief in logos; does the claim hold up that the logos of logocentrism and all such enterprises are concomitantly closures, and consequently inevitably lead to their own self-destruction or deconstruction? and that thus we must approach the text with a double reading because of its closure resulting in the unavoidable ellipsis?

It is in clotural reading itself that the logos precisely as closure is first focused upon, and, from there, in the process of this technique of reading, the language of difference emerges, leading beyond the transgression of closure to the alterity of the text! And the alterity is reached due to the ellipsis, which can be discovered by focusing on pivotal words of the text or through the conflict between the author's intentions or declarations and his/her text. The question inevitably arises as to whether anyone attempting to write deconstructively is simply held to silence. And the response is of course negative. The technique in writing is similar to that in clotural reading: one employs the language of metaphysics or logos, making the closure explicit, and thus transforms the metaphysical language into the language of *différance* from which the metaphysical language itself has emerged.

Now the neophyte to this type of thinking will naively ask if it is possible that the first reading of a specific text could be the final reading because this particular text has no ellipsis, no alterity, no way to the emergence of difference. Deconstruction must disavow this possibility in principle because of its belief in and commitment to the priority of the antilogocentrism of the text, of any text, all texts, even its own. And thus the language of *différance* is there to be had by someone sophisticated enough—deconstructive enough—to engage the process, since any statement, in fixing a meaning, enacts a closure to be disclosed and deconstructed.

Again the neophyte might contend that there is nothing the matter with a healthy logocentrism. But deconstruction can then legitimately ask whether this priority of logocentrism is still possible after Freud, Lacan, Foucault, and Derrida. Can we still be so naive as to want to posit the centrality of logos without adverting adamantly to its closure?

At this point the real issue has re-emerged: the priority of logos or, in stark contrast, the priority of closure and its antilogocentrism. And, if any claim is made in favor of antilogocentrism concerning the sciences of language (semiology) and of syntax, even in a new adaptation of syntax, and to psychoanalysis of some kind, this very claim expresses explicitly a subtle faith in logos—in the expressed doctrines of these two inquiries. Can this insight and recourse really settle the issue for deconstruction without putting it once again back into the logos—of these sciences of linguistics or psychoanalysis? Is it possible to approach these two sciences in the way of a text, by cloutral reading that sees the alterity even in those texts that deal precisely with alterity?

This belief of deconstruction in the essential closure of logos giving rise to an ellipsis does contain a partial truth since any logos is limited in that it cannot "say it all." This limit bespeaks the need for constant openness to the flux, to the fullness of existence, but deconstruction goes further by requiring an essential closedness as absolute, concomitant with every logos. I believe that this requirement constitutes an "over-belief"[21] that we need not meet. Thus, the pivotal focus is between a belief in the logos as having priority, admitting at once that it has openness-closure as an aspect, that is, an openness *to* and as such a closure *from*; or belief in the priority of the antilogocentric, so that the closure is absolute, and must be transgressed by a return from the opening to that from which it is an openness-closure. This can be seen partially as the option between the priority of the logocentric or the priority of the antilogocentric; between sense and nonsense; between voluntary and the involuntary; and between philosophy and nonphilosophy.

Deconstruction thus entails more than cognition in its will to believe in cognition. There is a further commitment to the belief in closure intrinsic to such logos and to the priority of this closure over sense, and the priority of the flux. Deconstruction brings excess baggage to the will to believe in logos and cognition. But how is this baggage to be distinguished from the initial will to believe, since it seems to be tied to it as a certain presupposition that is an unquestionable given—that is the way it is. The excess is the demanded and absolutely given belief in the priority of the flux and of the closure supposedly intrinsic to all openness to logos, thus constituting a priority of the nonlogocentric. Hence, the logos inevitably leads to its own downfall because it is exclusive, closive, and emerges from a prior abyss. That is, there is a further belief, even more basic, that all beliefs reveal the initial belief in logos as a bit of an illusion; it reveals itself—this belief in the logos—as itself closed in on itself, and it is from the very movement toward logos itself that this further belief emerges. Hence, for it to emerge, there must be logos, but the latter's natural self-relation is to grasp itself as essentially *inclusive of a closure.* Thus, the belief itself in the logos contains the seeds of its own further evolution toward the priority of its own closure.

The ultimate issue, then, is that the will to believe of deconstruction, while seeming to affirm the logos through which one must pass to reach closure and the beyond, is basically a belief in the absolute status of closure and the priority of the abyss, thus leading to its antilogocentrism. Protesting that their opponents have not grasped their thinking, it is clear that their very protestations reveal an underlying prejudice, as absolute in its claim as it is illusive and unattainable: a belief in the undecidable, the inexpressible, the abyss. And to this it is best to reply with an alternate belief, one that makes sense out of sense, while at once seeing and admitting its limits, but with an openness beyond the initial limit as openness. This limit, then, while initially a certain kind of closure in being open to coming to light, is likewise an openness to its source for constant renewal from that origin in an ongoing process of interpretation. Thus, its openness consists in bringing to light, and, at once, openness toward renewal in its rich source, even though there is closure in coming to sense as limit. Let us now dwell further on certain enigmas raised by postmodern deconstruction. Thus we turn to reflect further with those who speak most explicitly today about deconstruction in terms of limit in ethics to understand more explicitly what is at stake.

DECONSTRUCTIVE ETHICS AT THE LIMIT

The priority given to closure mentioned above must now be seen in its impact on the ethics of deconstruction as a philosophy of limit. For the resistance to system and any closure by deconstruction constitutes the very center of such ethics. In deconstruction, the closure itself has led to the denial of ethics, deconstructing it so that nothing but the deconstructive process is left, including a denial of the personal ethical relation, the possibility/impossibility of which are entailed in the deconstructive process. In a cursory and summary fashion, it becomes clear that recent writers on deconstructive ethics, such as John Caputo, Drucilla Cornell, and Simon Critchley all, attuned to the Derrida-Levinas dialogue, to which we will turn later, put obligation at the heart of deconstruction. Caputo, however, following Derrida's hesitance, rejects ethics in favor of a poetics of obligation, while Critchley and Cornell, following Levinas, retain the term in their own rejection of virtually the same ethics that Caputo rejects. For my part, I would at least partially agree with these efforts, appropriating a positive contribution of deconstruction, and indicate that these authors have pointed to something essential to any responsible attempt at an ethics today, and then move on to a further extension of ethics following the recent writings of Paul Ricoeur, who can be seen as likewise influenced by Levinas, but who develops in an entirely different way what can be called an ethicomoral view. We will see that the obligation or duty at the heart of the deconstructive enterprise is not something to be lost sight of, even if it requires an extension beyond any usual or typical sense of ethics. But it is not to be seen as self-sufficient, and it must be tied to something that would best be brought into a more positive frame of philosophical mind.

Bernasconi, in any context of dealing with deconstruction and the possibility of ethics, is rather consistent in pointing out that the real issue is whether deconstruction enacts the ethical relation. Somewhat in contrast to Cornell's mitigating and benign interpretation of Derrida, he indicates the self-destruction of the ethical relation once it is established.

> Hence in the face of the demand for an ethics, deconstruction can reply, in the course of its reading of Levinas that the ethical relation is impossible and 'the impossible has already occurred' *at this very moment*. In other words, the ethical relation occurs in the face-to-face relation, as witnessed in the demand for an ethics itself, a demand which it is as impossible to satisfy as it is to refuse. To acknowledge this is to submit the demand for an ethics, not to instruction, but to deconstruction. And the *possibility* of ethics is referred, not to its actuality, but to its *impossibility*. This does not mean that writing ethical systems is impossible. Only that the attempt to do so is a denial of the ethical relation, though one which (fortunately) can never be complete; ontology denies the ethical relation when it presents its ethical system, but at the same time gives birth to it afresh in the saying of its said. The impossibility of murder.[22]

Bernasconi admits that deconstruction (at least Derrida's in "Violence and Metaphysics") does seem to preserve the ethical relation, but only in the sense of the thought of the ethical relation, not yet a practice, in its insistence that the *logos* of it is the impossible-unthinkable-unsayable. This, for Bernasconi, is deconstruction's rigorously holding to the limits of thinking. In this context, the ethical enactment lies especially in the refusal of deconstruction to take on the standpoint of critique, thus not passing judgment in its own voice on its own behalf. This does not entirely preclude its finding a voice of its own in its "*saying* of the said, its writerly saying." This limitation of ethics and the ethical relation can be seen to be closer to the limitations of Caputo than to those of Cornell and Critchley. So understood, deconstruction as such, following Bernasconi and Caputo, cannot accept anything of the ethical, even the ethical relation as Levinas interprets it, and must deconstruct it (not merely oppose it) in terms of the nonlogocentrism, the ellipsis, of its own view. The only ethical relation that Bernasconi allows, as also in the case of Critchley, is one with the deconstructive process itself. The ethical relation is not the face to face, and thus, as in that of Heidegger, takes on an impersonal dimension, with a loss of the personal face. Hence, we find Bernasconi and Critchley focusing ethics on the impersonal deconstructive process. Further, we find that Bernasconi and Caputo in that vein want to jettison the term ethics, while Critchley and Cornell risk going somewhat away from the strict script in retaining it in their own senses.

Cornell, on the other hand, affirms the ethical relation, but with her own twist: the philosophy of limit aspires to enact the ethical relationship that cannot be *enacted* in the sense of actualized but only adhered to as an aspiration. Cornell interprets Derrida's dialogue with Levinas as in the service of the ethical relation. For her, deconstruction as a philosophy of limit clearly guards the trace of otherness as exterior to the self-same while deconstructing Levinas' formulation of the ethical as beyond metaphysics. She continues: "Indeed, I read Derrida to warn Levinas against the potential violence to otherness inherent in his own understanding of the ethical, a warning that itself can be understood to be inspired by an ethical desire, as much as it can be read to embody the 'truth' that there is beyond-the-undecidable."[23]

Cornell goes further (109) and emphasizes the close relationship between Derrida and Levinas as that is evident once the philosophy of limit is read ethically. The philosophy of limit read ethically, as Cornell wants, does not as such simply put us into the abyss of skepticism and irrationalism, but, rather, exposes ethical "transcendence" beyond the same. Against Levinas, Derrida shows us that the same is not a totality closed in upon itself. It is clear, then, that the Derrida-Levinas dialogue (Levinas deconstructed and Derrida supplemented from Levinas) have provided an obligation after ethics, or, for some, an ethics of deconstruction, which is novel, innovative, and positive in its impact on postmodern discussions of ethics.[24]

The move toward such postmodern ethics was begun by Heidegger's now famous treatment in the "Letter on Humanism" where Heidegger considers ethics as such to denigrate the proper dignity of Dasein in its special role in the truth of Being. Heidegger has missed completely the sense of ethics, especially in this very response to Jean Beaufret regarding an originary ethics rooted in the truth of being. For it is here that his ethics emerges as impersonal and ontological, and it is an "ontology without morals," an "ontology of the Neutral."[25] Dasein is closed in on itself in the sense that it is not related to infinity or to the Other. Its deficiency or inauthenticity must consist in some relation to itself, resulting in the diminuated and defective ethics mentioned above. This is not a personal ethics, nor is it one that reaches the Other, but rather a dimension of Dasein's relation to Being in the emergence of the truth of Being for Dasein—at most an originary ethics within that relation. And as Peperzak so eloquently and precisely expresses this:

> The idea of a debt or guilt toward others than the self is excluded from this thought. By the absence of a true alterity that could question and accuse *Dasein*'s freedom, that is, by the absence of an ethical 'principle,' the Heideggerian perspective belongs to a tradition the barbarous depths of which were shown by Nazism. When Heidegger criticizes the essence of technology, he forgets that the source of modern evil, such as it was manifested in Nazism, is found at a depth that lies deeper than the realm of technology. Alluding to certain expressions found in Heidegger's later works, Levinas sketches the portrait of a pagan existence rooted in mother earth and prone to exploitation—very different from the sober existence of availability for the needs of others. The individuals are immersed in the *physis* that encompasses them like elements of its unfolding.[26]

Let us now turn to a broader consideration of the limit of philosophy, relating it to what has come to be called the death or end of philosophy. This further consideration broadens the focus to essential implications of the limit of philosophy, and prepares the way for focusing explicitly on the precise question of limit and end in the critical philosophy of Kant, the ultimate source of much of the present-day conversations.

CHAPTER 2

Death, End,
and Limit of Philosophy

INTRODUCTION

Ethics at the limit-boundary of reason must now be considered in relation to the end and death of philosophy, the proclamations of which we have recently become so accustomed. Postmodern deconstruction follows Heidegger in opening discussion to this broader question of the nature, extent, and possibility of any philosophy today. Turning to this expanded context allows a deepening of philosophy at the limit. This chapter will require a critical evaluation of the end of philosophy proclaimed by Heidegger and expand to the death of philosophy as it emerges in the Derrida-Levinas dialogue. The purpose in so doing is to ascertain the extent to which end or death is latent and essential to philosophy itself, and thus to deepen our focus. Eventually, if it is found necessary after a perusal of Kant's treatment of correlated issues, we may find it necessary to adjust our view of philosophy at the limit.

My contention is that continental philosophy today, if it is to emerge as at all viable, must take account of the positive elements of postmodern deconstruction, while at once offering itself in a different relation to the tradition. We have already considered the very basis of the commitment to sense and meaning, comparing these two differing developments of philosophy attentive to its limit and extension beyond them. And it is precisely the tension between limit and extension that will allow us, in the present chapter, to bring to the fore the breadth and depth of this discussion on limit, death, and end, thus preparing the ground for looking more deeply into the Kantian influence on the present-day discussion. This broadened focus on the Kantian influence in turn makes way for the possibility of an ethicomoral philosophy within a polarity between ethical foundations and moral principle of obligation.[1]

HEIDEGGER: DEATH AND END OF PHILOSOPHY

One of the most influential appropriations of the Kantian limit, boundary, and end is that of Heidegger, whose debt to Kierkegaard on this issue is obvious, although too little admitted. Heidegger's treatment of death and end in *Being and Time* has a certain parallel treatment in the later works. For, in the beginning, borrowing from Kierkegaard's *Concept of Dread* and appropriating it into his own ontological context, Heidegger characterizes death as caught up in the hermeneutical situation of Dasein. As such, it is the structure of Dasein that brings forth one direction of its possibilities in refocusing in order to get the whole of Dasein's presuppositional totality into view. And it is here that he characterizes Being toward death as the Being (of Dasein) toward the possibility of no longer having possibilities. This Being toward the end, or the possibility of no longer having possibilities, he characterizes as the essential finitude of Dasein. And by the same token, in the later writings, he characterizes philosophy in similar terms as being at its extreme possibility, that is, as being toward the possibility of no longer having possibilities, thus bespeaking the essential finitude of philosophy. At the end of his lectures on Nietzsche, he has come close to this formulation: "But then what does it mean, 'the end of metaphysics'? It means the historical moment in *which the essential possibilities* of metaphysics are exhausted. The last of these possibilities must be that form of metaphysics in which its essence is reversed."[2] And immediately before this, he has indicated a resurrection of metaphysics: "The end of metaphysics that is to be thought here is but the beginning of metaphysics' 'resurrection' in altered forms; these forms leave to the proper, exhausted history of fundamental metaphysical positions the purely economic role of providing raw materials with which—once they are correspondingly transformed—the world of 'knowledge' is built 'anew'."[3]

According to some of his followers and critics, it is in this context that Heidegger interprets philosophy to be at its end, not as an Aristotelian finality of a biological fulfillment as maturity, nor in the Hegelian sense of *Vollendung* as completion or perfection, but rather in the sense of a long-lasting ending process. As in the early work, death and end accompany Dasein throughout its entire life as an ontological possibility, indeed, precisely as its possibility of no longer having possibilities, so too now, this essential finitude, as the ending of a long history of metaphysics, is at its end, not as its perfection, fulfillment, or culmination, but rather, as at its *Verendung*, its end. The process of reason goes on, but now humbled and brought down to earth, so that it is no longer the grandiose quest of Being in the tradition of metaphysics or of the Hegelian Absolute. It is, to the extent that it is still viable, the process of bringing to light from unconcealment the Being of an epoch, the event and its *Ereigniss*. Heidegger has indeed come to grips with the limits of philosophy once reason is finitized and sensibilized as evinced in its process of unfolding. In this effort to fathom the depths of what he

has found, he comes close, but not acceptably so, to postmodern deconstruction's adherence to the process of deconstruction below logocentrism and its so-called closure (limit) and he finds the opening to the
abyss as the *Abgrund*. What still remains unclear in this account is the
contrast between *Vollendung* and *Verendung*. We must further clarify
what precisely these mean for Heidegger.

Vollendung *and* Verendung

The Hegelian sense of *Vollendung* as philosophy's reaching its end in the
sense of culmination is the self-recognition in the absolute otherness.[4]
For Hegel it is possible to grasp the whole or the true as system in the
absolute. The absolute is attained in this completion (*Vollendung*) in the
system, where the end of philosophy has the sense of completion as perfection. Perhaps some have been too inclined to contrast Heidegger's
sense of end as *Verendung* with this sense of *Vollendung*, which he does
indeed oppose, yet it must be remembered that Heidegger mentions
some sense of *Vollendung* too.

We all too easily understand the end of something in the negative
sense as a mere stopping, as the lack of continuation, perhaps even as
decline and impotence. In contrast, what we say about the end of philosophy means the completion of metaphysics (*die Vollendung der
Metaphysik*).[5] Heidegger goes on in that same text to say, "However,
completion [*Vollendung*] does not mean perfection [*Vollkommenheit*] as
a consequence of which philosophy would have to have attained the
highest perfection at its end." Heidegger further makes clear precisely
what he intends by end in stating: "The end of philosophy is the place
[*Ort*], that place in which the whole *of* philosophy's history is gathered
into its most extreme possibility [*in seine ausserst Moglichkeit*]. End as
completion means this gathering [*Versammlung*]."[6] Thus the end of philosophy is being gathered into an end as an extreme possibility, rather
than as perfection [*telos*], contrasting completion with the Hegelian
sense of perfection (*Vollkommenheit*).

There are affinities between this use of end and that in *Being and
Time*, for both uses invoke extreme possibility, the possibility of no
longer having possibilities. In this present case, in the latest writings, this
extreme possibility applied to philosophy draws the sense of end away
from the sense of perfection and culmination and brings it to is possibility as finite, as no longer having possibilities. Does this not in the present
context mean to stand at this point of finitude and take up the task of
thinking? As for Kant, one thinks at the boundary. Once philosophy has
realized its possibility of no longer having possibilities and this as its own
authenticity, as is the case with Dasein in *Being and Time*, it requires

embracing this finitude, and thinking from there. Is Heidegger saying anything other than this? Does Heidegger ever abandon the project of thinking Being? I do not think so! This is precisely the point of condemnation from postmodern deconstruction, that he has not moved sufficiently into the abyss beyond closure, thus moving away from the project itself of thinking Being at the boundary, and shepherding it into language. As Sallis has so well indicated, after philosophy comes to completion in Hegel, Heidegger completes it again, starting anew, but now from its radical center.[7] What Heidegger has inserted into Hegel's system is the essential dimension of finitude, requiring the recasting of end as completion in the Hegelian sense. And for Heidegger, this brings temporality to front stage, as that upon which Being is ultimately projected. As Sallis so well says: "This end is also the beginning (*arché*) in the sense that it generates the entire series, that is, makes possible all the other projections; it is the source which overflows toward them. Indeed, the pre-ontological understanding that informs Dasein's everyday comportment is simply a matter of perpetually drifting along in the flow from this source. Philosophy, on the other hand, requires that one turn against the flow and swim upstream."[8] In a sense for Heidegger philosophy is the attempt to somehow withdraw back into the beginning, that the end is tied to this withdrawal to the beginning; that the end "generates the entire series" so that the whole path of philosophy, indeed, its entire undertaking in history, emerges from this finite temporality. This means that philosophy must reach its pre-ontological beginning, a task requiring much effort. Heidegger, for one, has noted the intense difficulty of this enterprise. And once attained, the task of the thinking of Being at the end of philosophy emerges. Heidegger continuously attempts, after *Being and Time*, considering his "misunderstanding of the question of Being,"[9] to bring it and philosophy to completion as gathering.

One can truly say that Heidegger throughout his works has been writing about philosophy at its end or limit from his first indication of it as essentially a temporal enterprise of a finite Being-there. It is precisely at this point of focus that philosophy achieves self-understanding as the process of attunement at this limit. For it is this emergence or unconcealment of Being in the very process of thinking Being caught up in its own unfolding. It is here that one can see how *Vollendung* and *Verendung* come together in Heidegger's sense of end, that at its completion in tradition or history, philosophy ends in culminating precisely in its task of beginning in thinking. Thus it is culminated precisely at its limit, at its end, at which point thinking passes beyond philosophy. In a sense then philosophy has to be left behind, and the task of thinking Being in its process of emergence through its own possibility of no longer having possibilities must be taken up.

Heidegger, in the work cited above, "The End of Philosophy and the Task of Thinking," indicates that this text is his attempt, "undertaken again and again ever since 1930, to shape the question of *Being and Time* in a more primal way."[10] In the 1973 preface to the fourth edition of *Kant and the Problem of Metaphysics,* Heidegger indicates the decisive motivation for this Kant book as the "misunderstanding of the Question of Being presented in *Being and Time,*" which he says was apparent in 1929.[11] The seeds for the end of philosophy are contained in this hindsight admission. For if Heidegger's attention is drawn to the chapter on schematism, and he indeed "glimpsed therein a connection between the problem of Categories, that is, the problem of Being in traditional Metaphysics and the phenomenon of time," we see the role of time at the center of the question, but now apparently in a way different from that in *Being and Time*. Perhaps it is necessary to recall that Kant attempts to get away from metaphysics as "dogmatic twaddle,"[12] moving to understand metaphysics precisely as critique in order for it to be considered science. He then interprets the ground of metaphysics so considered to be metaphysics in general, entailing thinking at the boundary concepts as the mark between two fields, as will be seen in the next chapter. In Heidegger's move toward schematism and the centrality of imagination and time, and in his attempt to finitize reason, what happens to the ground, to the critique as such, that, in Kant's terms, sees reason limiting knowledge, thus revealing the place of metaphysics in general and as science? Heidegger's move here somehow puts Being in such a relation to time and to ground that it more clearly leads to the end of metaphysics, precisely in the way of his coming out of Kant, made clear in the Kant book and in his confrontation with Cassirer. If, indeed, the categories are derived from time, then metaphysics is at its end.

The phrasing of the parenthetic statement—"Categories, that is the problem of Being"—says something important about Heidegger's understanding of the relation between Kant's categories and the traditional metaphysics' sense of being. In Heidegger's so explicitly mentioning, ". . . the decisive motivation for the publication of the Kant book: the misunderstanding of the Question of Being presented in *Being and Time,* which had already become clear in 1929," attention is drawn to this misunderstanding, which plagued him throughout the rest of his writings. The nature of this misunderstanding, in the light of the later *Kant and the Problem of Metaphysics* regarding the question of Being, must be related to the connection seen between the categories (Being in traditional metaphysics) and time, of Being and time, so that, if he misunderstood this relation so basic to the whole project of *Being and Time,* this turn is a radical shift or deepening in his thinking. And our present concern is the impact it has on his view of the end of metaphysics and the role of the imagination. The question of the traditional concept of metaphysics requires clarification as central to the issue of this entire enterprise on Kant and the laying of the foundation of metaphysics, especially in the light of Kant's epistemological priority that Heidegger subverts.

Concerning the concept of metaphysics found in Kant, Heidegger says: "The horizon from within which Kant saw metaphysics and in terms of which his ground-laying must be fixed may be characterized roughly by means of Baumgarten's definition: 'Metaphysica est scientia prima cognitionis humanae principia continens.' Metaphysics is the science which contains the first principles of human knowledge."[13] This definition clearly confirms Kant's epistemological prejudice in that for him metaphysics is basically reduced to an epistemological foundation and enterprise. Metaphysics as critique justifies the basic (a priori) elements of knowledge, and metaphysics in general focuses upon the ground of that in the boundary concepts as ground. Also, judging from the fact that Heidegger expands the fourth German edition (which this volume translates), does he move further in the re-understanding of the question of Being later?

The end of Western metaphysics is explicitly contained in the following statement by Heidegger in *Kant and the Problem of Metaphysics*:[14]

> The point of departure in reason has thus been broken asunder.
>
> With that Kant himself, through his radicalism, was brought to the brink of a position from which he had to shrink back.
>
> It implies: destruction of the former foundation of Western metaphysics (spirit, logos, reason).
>
> It demands a radical, renewed unveiling of the grounds for the possibility of metaphysics as natural disposition of human beings, i.e., a metaphysics of Dasein directed at the possibility of metaphysics as such, which must pose the question concerning the essence of human beings in a way which is prior to all philosophical anthropology and cultural philosophy.[15]

Deconstruction emerges logically from this, delving beyond the logocentrism of the Western tradition.

Heidegger is essentially correct in his critique of the epistemological emphasis of Kant's critical philosophy and his overly narrow—epistemological—understanding of metaphysics. For it is clear in any serious perusal of Kant's critical works that Kant is indeed laying the foundation of metaphysics, but precisely in a critical philosophy and with a specific (narrow) understanding of metaphysics as seen above. But Heidegger goes too far in his repetitive retrieval of Kant, or in trying to show how Kant is actually, in the unsaid of the said, laying the foundation of

metaphysics in any way that compromises the famous Kantian epistemological priority.

Returning to the focus on "The End of Philosophy and the Task of
Thinking," in the light of the above, one can conclude that, since shortly
following the publication of *Being and Time*, Heidegger has constantly
returned to the attempt to shape the question of *Being and Time* in a
more primal way, which means, as he himself asserts, "to subject the
point of departure of the question . . . to an immanent criticism."[16] The
critical question here seems to entail, according to Heidegger, the extent
to which the critical question of the matter of thinking belongs to thinking. The task now, in contrast to that of *Being and Time*, deals with the
question of what it means that philosophy in the present age has entered
its final stage. What task is reserved for thinking at the end of philosophy? And Heidegger here comes under fire from postmodern deconstruction for not going far enough in dealing with these questions. But
he does go a long way in their direction, as is clear from the fact that
Derrida and Levinas have followed Heidegger down this same path. Heidegger focuses on the notion of end, *Vollendung,* as gathering. Yet, in
disavowing end as completion or perfection of metaphysics, Heidegger
indicates that there is no criterion for evaluating the perfection or completion of an epoch, that each epoch has its own necessity and that thus
the right to this kind of evaluation does not exist. That contention gives
rise to serious problems, for criteria are used in the latent decision within
a culture for one philosophy obtaining more sanction than another, such
as postmodern deconstruction versus another stance toward philosophy.
But for Heidegger, we simply have to "acknowledge the fact that a philosophy is the way it is. It is not our business to prefer one to the other,
as can be the case with regard to various *Weltanschauungen.*"[17] The end
of philosophy becomes the place in which the "whole of philosophy's
history is gathered in its most extreme possibility."[18] Thus, we return to
what we have claimed earlier, that this later development, though
rethought in a more elusive context here, is somewhat similar to the
point made in *Being and Time*, that this is Being toward the extreme
possibility, that is, of no longer having possibilities, in the sense of the
essential finitude of thinking Being, due to its radical temporality. The
only sense of completion retained here, if at all, is its sense as gathering.
Thus, philosophy reaches its end as gathering, which is much the same
as reaching its origin. For, this end is much like that which generates a
whole series, and in that sense is its end and beginning. This is why Heidegger wanted to refocus on the point of departure of *Being and Time*.

We must still pursue further with Heidegger, even at the expense of
belaboring the point, what precisely he considers the task reserved for
thinking at the end of philosophy, not yet made clear, especially if we

are to grasp the emergence of postmodern deconstruction from this task. For it can be seen that both Derrida and Levinas and their followers have deep roots in this project, even though they all pride themselves on going beyond Heidegger in deconstructing his thinking as still to some extent caught within the web of logocentrism.

Heidegger indicates several points of importance for the task of thinking. At the very end of his famous "The End of Philosophy and the Task of Thinking," he continues the questioning begun after *Being and Time* concerning a better formulation of the question of Being, now in terms of Opening and Presence. He concludes this essay with the statement: "The task of thinking would then be the surrender of previous thinking to the determination of the matter of thinking."[19] But there is an element brought in before this concluding remark. Heidegger has come to the opening, but no longer alone and merely as such. It is the opening as an opening of self-concealing.[20] He states a little later that the very question about the task of thinking is made questionable in asking about this task. It is in this context, that of the unthought, that he again refers to the "more and more urgent" attempts, since *Being and Time*, to ask about a "possible task of thinking at the end of philosophy."[21] The "binding character" or commitment of thinking is grounded in the "bond" between Being and thinking. And it is precisely aletheia as unconcealment that must be thought "as the opening which first grants Being and thinking and their presencing to and for each other."[22]

We have seen for Heidegger that the end of philosophy brings on the new beginning, not of philosophy, but rather of thinking, taking us back to the time before philosophy as such, to Parmenides and Heraclitus, and likewise, in relation to the history of metaphysics, to the gathering of thinking. We have seen above that the end (*Vollendung*) means that it is complete in the sense that it has run the course of its possibilities inherent in its essence, it has "unraveled all of its potentialities."[23] Can we not perhaps surmise that in a sense the famous "overcoming" of philosophy is a mode of its possibility of no longer having possibilities, as its death? For Heidegger, this is a certain resurrection or transformation, but one in which philosophy is supplanted or re-placed. It is truly the case for Heidegger that thinking arises out of the end or death of philosophy. It should be admitted that the seeds of postmodern deconstruction are already embryonically contained in this thinking arising at the end of philosophy precisely as a departure from the *ratio*, the reason, of the philosophical tradition. Heidegger some time ago, even in the very first of his writings, has to some extent abrogated reason, just as Cassirer has accused him of doing in the famous 1929 confrontation over the Kant book.

There is a paradox that must be faced at this point: on the one hand,

Heidegger moves away from the term "philosophy," telling us that we need less philosophy and more thinking: "It is time to wean ourselves of the habit of overestimating philosophy and therefore of demanding too much of it. What is necessary in the present time of world need is less philosophy but more of the attentiveness of thought."[24] On the other hand, later in *Was ist dass, die Philosophie?* he retains a certain sense of philosophy in relation to thinking Being in the following remark:[25] "This corresponding is a speaking. It is in the service of language. What this means is difficult for us to understand today, for our current conception of language has undergone strange changes. As a consequence, language appears as an instrument of expression. Accordingly, it is considered more correct to say that language is in the service of thinking rather than that thinking, as co-respondence, is in the service of language. Above all, the current conception of language is as far removed as possible from the Greek experience of language. To the Greeks the nature of language is revealed as the logos."[26] Here we see Heidegger referring philosophy to language as logos, which becomes *ratio*. Is this a contradiction from what we mentioned above, in his attempt to overcome philosophy and his turn away from ratio, logos, reason? Heidegger here characterizes philosophy precisely as a distinctive manner of saying[27] (*als eine aus-gezeichnete Weise des Sagens ist*).[28] And thus he moves to the specific kinship between thinking and poetic creation, due to their respective relations to language: "Between these two there exists a secret kinship because in the service of language both intercede on behalf of language and give lavishly of themselves. Between both there is, however, at the same time an abyss for they 'dwell on the most widely separated mountains'."[29] And this thinking he has already characterized as: "*Das Seiende als solces bestimmt das Sprechen in einer Weise, dass sich das Sagen abstimmt (accorder) auf das Sein des Seienden.*" That is, "The being [Seiende] as such determines speaking in such a way that saying is attuned (*accorder*) to the Being of being."[30] Thus one can see the correlation between being and speaking, and between Being and saying. In being's coming to be spoken and thus determined, the saying is attuned to Being. Thus, in speaking of things, one can be attuned to the saying of Being. And he goes on: "Correspondence is necessary and is always attuned, and not just accidentally and occasionally. It is an attunement. And only on the basis of the attunement (*disposition*) does the saying of correspondence obtain its precision, its tuning."[31] And it is the Being of the being that calls forth and appeals in the correspondence. Thus, what must be made clear is that, although Heidegger has been seen in the context of the end, limit, and death of philosophy, to aim at an overcoming of philosophy and of metaphysics, sometimes identifying philosophy with metaphysics in the tradition, it is necessary to admit that he has another sense of philosophy as the thinking of Being, which is what even in the later writings, he is adamant to foster.[32] Now that we have considered the limit and end of philosophy for Heidegger, we must turn now to a further consideration of deconstruction as a philosophy of limit in relation to end and death.

POSTMODERN DECONSTRUCTION:
DERRIDA AND LEVINAS

Derrida's entire philosophy, just as that of Heidegger, is written in some sense at the end of philosophy. The very beginning of Derrida's essay "Violence and Metaphysics" bears this out, for it begins with a serious reflection on death and philosophy.[33] At once, however, it brings into focus the equally pervasive and more extreme position of Levinas regarding the end of philosophy, but in contrast both to Derrida's own view and to that of Heidegger. In this context, let us recall that Levinas, at least in *Totality and Infinity,* considers such questions as the end of philosophy to be still caught in the totality, which he wants to interrupt. Derrida moves in a critical commentary and interpretation, as a first phase of a deconstructive reading, out of the closure of the text in going beyond Levinas' own intention. He does, however, fail to focus on the relation of Levinas especially to thinkers such as Hegel and Heidegger for whom the end of philosophy is significantly central, and both of whom have had a powerful influence on Levinas, as Bernasconi indicates.[34] This influence must not, however, be thought to mitigate Levinas' extreme position.

Although for both Heidegger and Hegel the realization of the historical nature of philosophy is significant in their respective views of the end of philosophy, they view this end quite differently, even though the historical nature of philosophy requires, for both, that philosophy lose its naiveté about itself. Bernasconi indicates that for Hegel and Heidegger this historical dimension of philosophy requires that its true subject matter, hitherto hidden, is now accessible in the history of philosophy. However, for Hegel it is the Absolute, and for Heidegger it is Being (*Sein*). Bernasconi interprets the end of philosophy in terms of the transformation of thinking now brought to remembrance from its previous concealment. "For Hegel, now that thinking has attained its element— 'pure self-recognition in absolute otherness'—it becomes possible to apprehend the whole, hence the true, as system. It is only in the completion (*Vollendung*) of truth in the system that the absolute is attained. The end of philosophy means its completion as a fulfillment, as perfection."[35] For Heidegger, in contrast to this completion as a fulfillment, it is rather when the thinker finds that his task of thinking within the philosophical tradition is to think Being that a certain end is achieved. This task entails a certain quasidisruption in overcoming philosophy, and is the completion of a destiny, an end, in the sense that the tradition has run its course. Thus, we again see, as above, that Heidegger does not consider the end of philosophy as a cessation, death, or termination, a sense completely alien to Heidegger's thought but, rather, in terms of *die Vollendung* understood in the sense of a gathering of philosophy, entailing the gathering of thought when the furthermost possibilities of philosophy in its finitude have been exhausted. It is in this sense that the end of philosophy entails a new beginning.

Derrida highlights precisely this context in *Positions* when asked about the possibility of overcoming metaphysics. In answer to this question, Derrida establishes that one does not cross from one center to another in transgression. Rather, the closure is an ongoing one, or, better, a limit that is "always at work."[36] Thus, it is not the case of entering into a domain, exposing its closure, and moving outside of it. There is no opposition between outside and inside. Rather, there is the process of limit at work, of closure and transgression. And this is the sense in which Derrida can be seen to have some affinity with Heidegger's notion of end of philosophy as considered above, for neither of them take this end as a cessation or finish of philosophy.[37]

Thus, it must be seen that closure is to be distinguished from end, in that closure entails the activity of bringing something to its end. *Cloture*, then, stressing this dynamic of action, is a limit in the sense of delimiting an area inside the closure, as well as delimiting the outside of the closure. In this sense of limit, deconstructive or clotural reading involves the dynamic process of limit, in the sense of "leaving each text *on the limit* between belonging and not belonging to the tradition."[38] As seen above regarding clotural reading, and in the sense of the process of closure and of limit, to engage the closure of metaphysics or of a text is already to have engaged in their deconstruction.

We have already seen in chapter 1 that Derrida, in the early 1960s, prefers closure to end, since, for him, there can be no "sudden passage" beyond philosophy, as there is for Levinas. Bernasconi interprets Heidegger's use of the term *Verendung* to correspond basically with the term closure (cloture). According to Bernasconi, the reading of texts for both of them shows the play of presence and absence at work in metaphysics, in texts, especially relating to the ambiguity of certain words central to the text. "Heidegger refers it to the concealment at the heart of truth, the lethe in aletheia, that reverberates through language at the end of philosophy as a ringing of silence (*Gelaeut der Stille*). Derrida gives it a variety of names, including that of difference. A 'saying not-saying'—a phrase Heidegger uses to characterize 'another possibility of saying,' a possibility other than that offered by metaphysics—aptly describes Derrida's own way with language, where books are not (will not have been) books, prefaces are not prefaces, and philosophy is not philosophy."[39] Thus, the decisive figure for Derrida's thinking of the end of philosophy is Heidegger, precisely because Heidegger's history of being "provides the essential model governing Derrida's relation to previous thinking exhibited in his deconstructive readings."[40]

In now turning to Levinas, we must note that there is one central contrast between these two thinkers that must be emphasized at the outset. Although Derrida and Levinas agree on the issue of the break with logocentrism, Derrida insists that one must still borrow one's resources from logocentrism, even from metaphysics,[41] thus adhering to the term closure and refusing to declare the rupture or interruption of philosophy.[42] Levinas, however, insists on an interruption and a break with metaphysics, with philosophy, and with the tradition.

Levinas

Levinas' attitude toward the end or limit of philosophy is perhaps the most extreme, even in comparison to that of Derrida and Heidegger. And yet it is extremely important for us to confront that very position, since he especially, and not only Heidegger and Derrida, has something essential to contribute that none of the others offer, when all is said and done on this topic. And it goes without saying that Heidegger and Derrida will be found to have something to contribute also, some of which will overlap with that of Levinas, and some of which is proper to them and not to Levinas.

Levinas' stark contrast to Derrida is emphasized in the beginning of *Otherwise than Being and Beyond Essence*, where he asks: "Should we not think with . . . caution of the possibility of a conclusion or a closure [*fermeture*] of the philosophical discourse? Is not its interruption its only possible end?"[43] Now, this notion of interruption goes beyond its role in Heidegger's thought, in the "disruption of the thinker's vocation to name being," and insofar as it is an excess not explicable in terms of what has gone before it. And rupture and excess, for Derrida, are never decisive ruptures. The notion of the rupture with philosophy and with ontology goes further for Levinas than for any of these others. For him, it entails the break with ontology in favor of an ethics of the face-to-face relation as first philosophy, and not an ethics of the tradition, any more than it entails the philosophy of the tradition. By contrast, Heidegger, followed in some sense by Derrida, has turned to a certain priority of the truth of Being over any ethics. And Derrida, to the extent possible, has turned to the language of the presence of Being, or to the closure of Being in order to have a point of departure for a double reading, one of which is deconstructive or clotural. We will see that this constitutes a vast difference for Levinas precisely because this notion of rupture or interruption of philosophy and of ontology, in deference to the face to face, is able to speak of transcendence, of the infinite, and of the singular other person who calls forth an obligation. And, it must be stated, the ethical relation of the face to face, and the imperative that it entails, and, as such, enacts, is not an ethics of the tradition, which he sees this face to face as surpassing and transgressing. This must be emphasized as a unique contribution of Levinas, one that should not be too glibly dismissed, reduced, or deconstructively read. It should be mentioned that, although he accepts and incorporates the "face to face" of Levinas, Ricoeur somewhat opposes Levinas' interpretation of the interpersonal relation. Ricoeur's positions must eventually be faced since it is the best case of ethics at the limit, and since, in this Ricoeurian context, I want to accept more of Levinas' position than Ricoeur allows for in his own appropriation. Further, it will be found that Ricoeur is too severe in his critique of Levinas.[44]

There is another aspect of this irruption in philosophy that should be briefly brought to light.[45] For Levinas, the rupture entails a separation from totality, from the tradition, from solicitude, from communality, ending up in solitude. There is a further separation between this solitary one and the Other whose face irrupts onto the scene in the face-to-face relation. Levinas, especially in *Totality and Infinity*, must emphasize the exteriority of the Other or suffer its collapse into the totality as has happened with the tradition of philosophy. Thus, in order to maintain transcendence, he must highlight, even hyperbolize, this exteriority and separation so that transcendence and complete alterity of the Other are not jeopardized.

It has been our purpose here to see the extreme expression of the end of philosophy as interruption, which is required to maintain transcendence of the face to face. As will be seen later, it must be admitted that, in spite of some critiques, such as that of Ricoeur, Levinas must keep a tension alive between the exteriority of the face and the interiority of totality, or there is no transcendence. Yet interiority must contain a capacity or a possibility for a relation with that Other, or such an irruption in totality and in the solitude of the separation is not possible. But the opposition enacted by Levinas' treatment of rupture has not yet been completed, for Levinas speaks explicitly of going "beyond the limit," "exceeding of limits," "without limits."

The alterity of the other cannot be that which limits the same for Levinas, for that would place the other and the same within the common horizon of totality, and the other would not be truly other, but, rather, would be reduced within the totality to the same. As not limiting the same, the other is "other with an alterity constitutive of the very content of the other."[46] Further than this, one can speak of "without limits" for Levinas, but within the context of the existent. It is interesting that Levinas considers the "without limit" of infinition to be that of the existent, beyond Being:

> To be infinitely—infinition—means to exist without limits, and thus in the form of an origin, a commencement, that is, again, as an existent. The absolute indetermination of the *there is*, an existing without limits, is an incessant negation, to an infinite degree, consequently an infinite limitation. Against the anarchy of the *there is* the existent is produced, a subject of what can happen, an origin and commencement, a power. Unless the origin had its identity, infinition would not be possible. But infinition is produced by the existent that is not trammeled in being, that can, while remaining bound to being, take its distance with regard to being: infinition if produced by the existent that exists in truth.[47]

We must pursue this notion of infinition in relation to infinity and limit.

For Levinas, the "idea of the infinite" and the production of the "infinite entity," are inseparable, "for it is precisely in the disproportion between the idea of infinity and the infinity of which it is the idea that this exceeding of limits is produced." It is this idea of the infinity that is for Levinas the mode of being or the infinition of infinity. The infinition of infinity (not a pre-existing infinity) is "produced as revelation, as a positing of its idea in me." Thus, for Levinas, the separate being "fixed in its identity, the same, the I nonetheless contains in itself what it can neither contain nor receive solely by virtue of its own identity." It thereby clearly contains more than it is possible to contain. Levinas' *Totality and Infinity*, while focusing essentially on exteriority and separation as indicated by its subtitle, yet presents subjectivity, the same, totality as welcoming the Other in the context of hospitality, bringing to consummation the idea of infinity. Levinas uses this enterprise as getting beyond the limited definition of consciousness as intentionality, since "knowing qua intentionality" presupposes this idea of infinity, which does not entail adequation as does intentionality.

Levinas aims in *Totality and Infinity* to defend the view (reminiscent somewhat of Kant's *Critique of Judgment*) that infinity and perfection exceed conception, overflowing the concept.[48] These ideas of infinity and perfection do not reside within the same, and thus, as seen above, are not mere negations. Rather, the idea of infinity designates "a height and a nobility, a transcendence" that mere negation of the imperfect or limit cannot attain. The crux of the issue, the ambiguity, if not aporia, is contained in the statement that "[t]ranscendence designates a relation with a reality infinitely distant from my own reality, yet without the distance destroying this relation and without this relation destroying the distance, as would happen with relations within the same; this relation does not become an implantation in the other and a confusion with him, does not affect the very identity of the same, its ipseity."[49]

For Levinas, the "beyond philosophy" is already in philosophy. Bernasconi points out that the procedure whereby Levinas passes from experiences within the totality back to the rupture that conditions the totality exhibits how and in what sense Levinas supposes that one can pass beyond philosophy. Bernasconi quotes Levinas: "Without substituting eschatology for philosophy, without philosophically 'demonstrating' eschatological 'truths,' we can proceed from the experience of totality back to a situation where totality breaks up, a situation that conditions the totality itself. Such a situation is the gleam of exteriority or of transcendence in the face of the Other. The rigorously developed concept of this transcendence is expressed by the term infinity."[50] Just as we have seen that totality must have the seeds of transcendence to the Other, so here, this requires an alternative account of history that inscribes this possibility, and not a continuous history (of philosophy) any more than that of Heidegger or Derrida. Bernasoni calls it the "history of the face"[51]—not that the face has a history, but that it ruptures history from within just as, in the history of Being, Being ruptures the history of philosophy as an excess that at the same time conditions that history. "The phrase history of the face is disruptive."[52]

As we have already stated, the rupture with philosophy has been emphasized by Levinas in a sense that does not obtain for Heidegger or Derrida. For it represents the overcoming of the priority of ontology to which they, too, remain in some sense subject, preventing them from adhering to a priority of the ethical as first philosophy. And, as Bernasconi puts it so well, the "contribution of the history of the face would be to invite us to recognize the ethical where we would not otherwise expect it."[53] Heidegger and Derrida are still subject to the priority of ontology for which they efface the ethical, each within a different demand, but leading to a subordination of ethics to the impersonal ontological realm. This contrasts with and indicates the importance of the ethical relation in Levinas' ethics, for which neither Heidegger nor Derrida allow.

I do not consider Derrida's way of deconstructively reading Levinas to do justice to Levinas' thought. It seems to me that Levinas wants to account for the enactment of the ethical relation, deriving ethics from it. But this is not an ethics of the tradition, but rather an ethics of the face to face and the imperative that it entails, and as such, enacts, thus surpassing and transgressing the tradition. Hence, to point out the impossibility of the ethical relation is not to deconstruct, but rather to distort in deconstructing, and thus to miss the full positive impact of Levinas' message. It is clear, then, that deconstruction as such cannot accept—go along with—anything of the ethical, even the ethical relation as Levinas has it, and must deconstruct it, rather than oppose it, in terms of the ellipsis, the nonlogocentrism of its own view. Thus, the only ethical element that deconstruction allows is the deconstructive process itself, not falling into critique, and not deciding between alternative interpretations: that is, not having a voice.

Let us recall, in this text, Heidegger's response about ethics to Jean Beaufert. In accord with his own path of thinking, Heidegger could not provide the ethics that was requested, but rather, leads the way to the truth of Being and in that context fosters an originary ethics. Here, for deconstruction, ethical possibility is contrasted with its impossibility, both of which are within the totality, and thus do not reach beyond the closure. For Levinas, the ethical relation gets beneath or ruptures that, reaching to the infinite, which infinite Derrida does not like.

While it is true that deconstruction cannot enact the ethical relation, this inability cannot be applied to Levinas' view without great distortion. This is clearly the case, as we have already seen, because Levinas could simply be saying that the interiority or totality, which tends to close in on itself as the tradition has done (according to him), already contains the capacity, the possibility for the other. And the encounter with the other has already been seen to have occurred in the world and in some sense in interiority. And the interruption shows that it cannot be a closed totality, or that it should not be. While this does break the absoluteness of the totality, it is the tension within the totality that Levinas leaves operative, preventing the totality from being absolutized.[54]

We must also keep in mind two points: first, that the two terms of Levinas, interiority and exteriority, must be external to each other; and yet that interiority contains a capacity for a relation with the other, as seen above.[55] And this latter is precisely the point that Ricoeur will be seen to interpret in too extreme a way. For he attributes this, and the more extreme way in which Levinas expresses the alterity and the holding of one a hostage, to the fact that Levinas speaks hyperbolically in dealing with the complete externality of the other, which is at least partially true, and is compensated for, in Levinas' writings themselves, by the fact that totality and interiority should be interpreted as capable of responding to the Other, even in its alterity. Ricoeur is, however, a bit extreme, for his own purposes, in his rendition of these elements of Levinas, as we will see in chapter 7.

What does ethics at the limit of reason look like? Is this too Kantian a focus on such enterprises as ethics, or, a fortiori, as philosophy in general? If one takes deconstruction as a philosophy of limit, in both of the senses outlined above in chapter 1, if it is seen to focus on closure as another way of expressing limit, and if deconstructive reading entails the sense of clotural reading outlined above as a process of transgressing, is it possible to bring this to bear in ethics only in the manner expressed above? Certainly these are the kinds of questions that give rise to the present reflection, and lead to the formulation of an hypothesis: that some ethics is viable today only insofar as it confronts these very questions in terms of the views giving rise to them: that the philosophy that helps most in dealing with ethics in terms of these questions, without succumbing to their allure uncritically, is that style of philosophy of limit embraced by Paul Ricoeur. And it must be confronted with and distinguished from, and then perhaps expanded in terms of, the deconstructive style of thinking precisely as a philosophy of limit. And since Ricoeur considers himself a post-Hegelian Kantian at least in some small sense, and since Kant epitomizes the very enlightenment of modernity to which both deconstruction and Ricoeur are so adamantly opposed, this present work must reach back to that great philosophy which initially posited this philosophy of limit.

Thus, it is clear that this theme of "ethics at the limit of reason" places us at the heart of the development of contemporary thinking and all of its major protagonists: postmodern deconstruction in relation to Heidegger, Husserl, Kierkegaard, Nietzsche, and Ricoeur and his relation to the same, and to most contemporary styles of thinking. Keeping our theme ever in mind, we will focus on the development of a coherent possibility of ethics today, capable of dealing with actual ethical living and its moral problems rather than remaining limited to esoteric thinking irrelevant to life; and encompassing the whole tradition of philosophy latent in our present, but taken up actively in an interpretation that must confront the whole sweep of philosophy at the limit of reason.

Thus, in order to further clarify and deepen our discussion concerning limit and end in their fullness and variation seen above, we must now turn to Kant's notion of limit, boundary, and end, relate these to the role of the imagination in order to trace in depth the recent emergence of differing attitudes toward the limit of philosophy. This is the project of the ensuing chapters, before taking up again the various recent positions and readings of philosophy, especially regarding sign, language, time, and trace, all of which lurk beneath the surface as underlying elements.

CHAPTER 3

Limit, Critique, and Reason

INTRODUCTION

After delving, in the last chapter, into the relation of philosophy to limit, closure, and end, we will now turn to their common backdrop in Kantian philosophy. This detour will provide a means of clarifying basic differences among styles of thinking today that, although different, come to light in a special way when cast against such a common backdrop. Thus, in presenting several essential points in relation to Kant's philosophy, a possibility for contrasting and interarticulating these differing positions comes to the fore. First, these positions can be seen to relate in one way or another to the Kantian imagination, which requires turning to Kant's view of imagination in coming chapters. Second, it should be obvious that the Kantian doctrine of limit, boundary, and end served as a backdrop for the entire discussion of the last two chapters. Hence an explication of these will help us along our way to clarify these issues for philosophy today. Third, focusing upon the interrelations of time, imagination, and language in a Kantian context allows us to contrast how this interrelation is appropriated differently by Ricoeur and by Derrida in critical dialogue with Heidegger. Fourth, Ricoeur's entire philosophy, which is of central concern for us in these studies, can at least in some measure be taken as a post-Hegelian Kantianism, as he sometimes affirms. And in addition, Ricoeur's philosophy can be seen as a completion, in his own unique fashion, of the Kantian enterprise.[1] Thus, it becomes necessary for us to turn to some important elements of Kantian philosophy, and to contrast the various recent styles of thinking with this common reference.

These reflections cannot simply dwell on the traditional Kantian doctrine. For, today, it is necessary to address the myopic hermeneutic focus of Heidegger, who, in his preoccupation with his own fundamental question, is attentive to Kant's texts with a view (i.e., a pre-ontological orientation) toward appropriating Kant's doctrine into his own questioning. Heidegger cannot be legitimately faulted for doing so, since this is his explicitly stated intention in interpreting Kant, and since for Heidegger the ontological question *is* the structure of Dasein. In contrast, our interest is to unravel the Kantian doctrine, with its enigmatic fullness, allowing to come to light the possibilities in it of divergent directions in relation to the interpretation of the role of the transcendental imagination. Before turning to basic issues in Kant concerning the contrast between traditional metaphysics and critique, and the question of ground, and in order fully to clarify the natural predisposition and the end of reason, it is necessary first to clarify a consistent distinction of Kant between boundary and limit.

KANT'S LIMIT [*DIE GRENZE*] AND BOUNDARY [*DIE SCHRANKE*] OF REASON

We now turn explicitly to address Kant's enigmatic treatment of the relation between limit and boundary, leading to some points about end and ground. It must be recalled, however, that these operate for Kant within the radical distinction between the phenomenal and the noumenal realms, a gap that has been breached in most contemporary philosophy. Such radical adjustments call for reinterpretations of these fundamental notions and their functions as limit and boundary. For their basic nature, function, and use in Kantian philosophy have been too little understood for us to pass over a reflection on them here. And altering these in relation to the revamping of the phenomenal-noumenal distinction also entails the adjustments in the functions of the roles of reason, understanding, imagination, sense, and even of knowledge and thinking, the pervasive significance of which shall be investigated only in the later chapters of this study. The fundamental Kantian elements to be clarified here are the notion of end in relation to limit and boundary, the ground of knowledge, and the roles of these in the Heideggerian project of retrieval.

The fundamental context of Kant cannot be lost: to show the limits of reason by way of critique, manifesting the limiting function of reason itself; to guard the bounds of our reason with respect to its empirical use and to set a limit to its pretensions, revealing the principles as the limitation on the use of reason to possible experience; and to show the limits and boundaries of metaphysics, and in this context, its ground. This limiting use of reason reveals its role in avoiding a too typical "dogmatic twaddle"[2] in traditional metaphysics. In the process, the claim that mathematics and natural philosophy admit of limits and not bounds, and that metaphysics leads towards bounds in the dialectical attempts of pure reason must be clarified in this light.

For Kant, the importance of the distinction between limit (*die Schranke*) and boundary or bound (*die Grenze*) cannot be exaggerated, since it enters essentially into his theory of critique. And, as such, it thus fits into the core of his whole project to critique metaphysics and the project of reason in its speculative and theoretical enterprise as well as in its practical and moral orientation, thus delimiting knowledge as he interpreted it. In order to render this distinction clear in his various accounts, a rather common and prosaic contemporary example is in order.

Perhaps a good example of the distinction between limit and boundary is that of a sport such as basketball, soccer, or football in each of which the boundary marks the legitimate field of play, separating it off from the rest of the field or context. The legitimate play of the sport, football for instance, must take place within the field of play, that is, within the limits of the field, so that the boundary lines mark the limits within which the sport is played and advanced. And likewise, it must take place within the time frame designated by the rules. To further complicate the sport, football in our example, the boundaries are transgressed for a purpose, for an advantage in the game, that is, invoking the limit to stop play—that is, to get a time-out and thus better use the time of play, since the legitimate play takes place only within the limit (in this case, both of time and space). Now, as in the case for a priori elements of knowledge, these rules of the game are set down before any particular game, and constitute the legitimate play for winning the game. Thus, as the boundary marks the limit within which the sport is played, so too with Kant's limit-boundary, the boundary marks the limit in relation to understanding in knowledge. Yet the understanding is not limited to experience for its entire field of play, but to that play in knowledge, according to its "rules," the limit set by the boundary must be heeded. Thus is delimited the basic sense of boundary and limit in their chief sense employed by Kant.

It would be a bit narrow and absurd to think of the rules of football, for example, as employed in the 1999 Superbowl in Miami at the end of January, to be adequate rules to apply to life in general or even to other activities. Likewise, for Kant, the principles of the understanding constitutive for knowledge that is objective afford the rules and limits for the use of reason to possible experience, and cannot become transcendent, employed as limits of the possibility of things in themselves.

Kant further refers to boundary as something positive and to limit as something negative (PFM, 101, 109). Bounds or boundary includes the sense of something beyond the bound, so that both sides have a space, so to speak. There are two fields of play, a field within the limits of knowledge and a field beyond the limits of knowledge, that the boundary admits. But limit is entirely negative, showing the limits within which the play occurs, the field of play within which the game (knowledge) is played, and beyond which it cannot venture for legitimate knowledge. These negations affect a quantity insofar as it is not absolutely complete. It is conditioned and is led to another conditioned, and cannot ever arrive at the unconditioned. In a subtle way, the understanding grasps both fields, aware that experience is limited to appearances. Thus, understanding must assume that there are things in themselves, noumena, as an empty space for us. That which bounds experience and knowledge to experience lies outside the limits of that field, and is the "field of the pure beings of the understanding" (PFM, 109). Thus, reason uses the one field to bound the other within its limits.[3]

It is clear, then, that this basic distinction between limit and boundary is fundamental to Kant's entire enterprise, playing an essential part in metaphysics as science and in general. We must now turn to the natural disposition (*Naturanlage*) in humans for metaphysics and the illusions that must be avoided in further clarifying this distinction.

THE NATURAL PREDISPOSITION TO METAPHYSICS AND THE END OF REASON

Since Heidegger and Cassirer, some sense of the metaphysical orientation of Kant's project is generally admitted today, overcoming the narrow and exclusively epistemological interpretation of the Neo-Kantians. In Heidegger's and Cassirer's orientations, the role of reason vis-à-vis the limit, boundary, and ground have become pivotal, and eventually, as we will see, the imagination becomes central in this discussion. In this context, the "objective boundary" (PFM, 110) of experience must be discussed in the context of the subjective possibility of metaphysics as the "natural predisposition" of human reason to metaphysics and to some end of reason. And it is also necessary to have as the backdrop of this discussion the "original proposition" (PFM, 110), which Kant considers to be the *résumé* of the whole *Critique*: "Reason by all its *a priori* principles never teachers us anything more than objects of possible experience, and even of these nothing more than can be known in experience" (PFM, 110). It is precisely the critical task of reason in philosophy to make knowledge stay within its limits. This critical task, however, keeps bumping against a natural predisposition of reason, in its dissatisfaction with such limits, and with the incompleteness of its limited enterprise, to move beyond these limits. In fact, this temptation entails the end of reason. But rather than getting lost in this tendency to "fallacious metaphysics," let us further investigate the natural ends of this disposition to transcendent concepts (PFM, 111).

Kant finds that the conflicting commands of pure reason, to avoid all transcendent judgments of pure reason, and, in contrast, to proceed to concepts that lie beyond the field of its immanent (empirical use), can subsist together at the boundary of the permitted use of reason precisely because this boundary belongs to both fields, that of experience and that of the beings of thought. Kant shows that these ideas of reason mark the bounds of human reason, and at once warn us not to extend knowledge of experience boundlessly as if nothing but world remained for us to know, and, on the other hand, not to transgress the bounds of experience and to think of judging about things beyond them as things in themselves. And Kant contends that we stop at this boundary "if we limit our judgment merely to the relation which the world may have to a Being whose very concept lies beyond all the knowledge which we can attain within the world" (PFM, 105).

"For we then do not attribute to the Supreme Being any of the properties in themselves by which we represent objects of experience, and thereby avoid *dogmatic* anthropomorphism; but we attribute them to the relation of the Being to the world and allow ourselves a *symbolical* anthropomorphism, which in fact concerns language only and not the object itself" (PFM, 105–106). If Kant were to consider such a symbolic to have a reference, then he would have to admit going beyond language, and indeed dissolving his distinction of the noumenal/phenomenal, which, although alien to Kant's view, is precisely how the later tradition adapted his doctrine. Since language, and indirect expressions such as symbols, metaphors, and narratives, do refer in some way, even if to reveal real possibilities in the world, the radical distinction between phenomenal/noumenal is mitigated if not entirely overcome, the boundary transgressed in a new way, and thinking has a new dimension not envisioned by Kant, and indeed, is set on its way. Perhaps one should in this context accept Kant's limits placed on the claims for objective knowledge, but make allowance, with the indirect language of symbol and analogy, for an indirect knowledge emerging from that language. This would mean that indirect language does say something about something, but indirectly and through a glass darkly. It means that this is not the same manner of predication, but yet is one that is to be taken seriously. Ricoeur, with his vast developments of indirect language in symbols, metaphors, and narratives, has gone a long way in extending and completing the Kantian project, but we cannot help but ask whether he has indeed gone far enough. For is it not possible to have such indirect language address more than the latent and ultimate spirit and desire, and reach beyond human experience, but not in the normal mode of predication? Perhaps this is where we will have to take a hint from postmodern deconstruction and especially from Levinas to expand on Ricoeur's views to make full sense out of indirect language in metaphysics and in religious language. This issue will have to be pursued further in a later chapter, dealing with the world of the narrative text.

Kant says that we are compelled to consider the world "*as if*" it were the work of a Supreme Understanding and Will. He contends that, in so saying, he is really saying nothing more than that a "watch, a ship, a regiment, bears the same relation to the watchmaker, the shipbuilder, the commanding officer as the world of sense (or whatever constitutes the substratum of this complex of appearances) does to the unknown," and that we do not hereby know anything as it is in itself but only as it is for us, that is, in relation to the world of which we are part (PFM, 106).

For Kant, such cognition by analogy does not signify an imperfect similarity of two things, but rather a perfect "similarity of relations between two quite dissimilar things." "By means of this analogy, however, there remains a concept of the Supreme Being sufficiently determined *for us*, though we have left out everything that could determine it absolutely or *in itself*; for we determine it as regards the world and hence as regards ourselves, and more do we not require" (PFM, 106). Kant contends that we can get a notion of the relation of things, such as the Supreme Being, which are "absolutely unknown" to us (PFM, 106, fn. 1). In explaining this facet of analogy Kant employs the analogy between the juridical relation of human actions and the mechanical relation to moving forces. Just as a person can do nothing to another person without giving the right to do the same in return, so too, no mass can act with its moving forces on another mass without thereby occasioning the other to react equally against it. Although right and moving force are entirely different, there is a complete similarity in their relation. So, we come back to the fundamental point made above, that it is not the two things that are similar, but the relations.

Now, reason must set boundaries to the understanding as regards both these fields (PFM, 109), for experience does not bound itself, but rather, has bounds set entirely outside itself: "That which bounds it must lie quite without it, and this is the field of the pure beings of the understanding. But this field, so far as the *determination* of the nature of these beings is concerned, is an empty space for us. . . ." Because a boundary is positive, belonging to both sides bound, it is an actual cognition that "reason only acquires by enlarging itself to this boundary, yet without attempting to pass it because it there finds itself in the presence of an empty space in which it can conceive forms of things, but not things themselves." Having the boundary to the field of the understanding set by something that is otherwise unknown to it is still cognition.

That is, this setting of the boundary is a cognition, not anything extending beyond to the space beyond. Here, the cognition of reason, not confined within the sensible nor straying beyond it, limits itself to the relation between "that which lies beyond it and that which is contained within it" (PFM, 109). What is of importance here is that he considers this a cognition, but one limited to the *relation* between the "within" and the "without" of the boundary.

Kant goes on to point out that natural theology is "such a concept at the boundary of human reason." And this natural theology is "constrained" to "look beyond this boundary to the Idea of a Supreme Being (and for practical purposes, to that of an intelligible world also), . . . in order to guide the use of reason within it according to principles of the greatest possible (theoretical as well as practical) unity" (PFM, 110). Kant is quick to prevent these from being interpreted in a determinative way, indicating that they do not determine anything relative to the pure being of the understanding, thus determining something beyond the world of sense. That is, this is not a constitutive concept nor is there an object of or beyond experience that it determines. Looking beyond the boundary to the idea of a Supreme Being does not at all aim at determining anything relative to this pure being of the understanding, thus determining something that lies beyond the world of sense. "For this purpose, it makes use of the reference of the world of sense to an independent reason as the cause of all its connections. Thereby it does not just *invent* a being, but, as beyond the sensible world there must be something that can be thought only by the pure understanding, it determines that something in this particular way, though only of course by analogy" (PFM, 110). Kant has not come up with a Being responsible for the things in themselves. Rather, he has taken the world of sense, thought as the unity of phenomena, in relation to the Idea of thought, by way of analogy. Keeping in mind what Kant means by analogy, it is clear that it involves a relation of similarity between pairs of dissimilar things, as indicated above. Thus, there is nothing known in this analogy, but for thought, some sense is made for reason looking within itself for unities, indicating to us the nature of the concept and its limits. It focuses on the relation between that which is within the bounds and that which is without, and thus the cognition of the relation alone and not of something beyond it.

Hence, it is clear that for Kant, although reason is limited in the use of principles to the objects of possible experience, nothing more can be known of these. Further, reason is not prevented by this limitation from "leading us to the objective boundary of experience, namely, to the relation to something which is not itself an object of experience but is the ground of all experience" (PFM, 110). Although reason does not teach us anything beyond the boundary about the thing in itself, it does instruct us about its own complete and highest use in the field of possible experience.

The Seduction of Understanding and Reason

Returning to the context of the understanding and its categories constitutive of the objectivity of knowledge, there is, according to Kant, something "seductive" (PFM, 62) about the very nature of these concepts of understanding, tempting us to claims beyond their limits. For they are *independent* of experience, not arising out of experience, yet they contribute *necessity* and *universality* to knowledge, which does begin with experience; and further, they do not contain anything of sense experience and would *seem* to be applicable to things in themselves. Thus it would seem that the concepts of understanding have a deeper meaning and importance than that of their empirical use. As Kant puts this, the understanding is seduced to "inadvertently add for itself to the house of experience a much more extensive wing, which it fills with nothing but beings of thought without ever observing that it has transgressed with its otherwise legitimate concepts the bounds of their use" (PFM, 63). It is precisely the task of a critique to deal with this seduction resulting from a natural tendency of reason, and to mark the bounds of the two fields, one of experience and the other of the beings of thought, and not to allow any transcendent use of concepts as though they were applicable to objects or to possible objects.

This aberration of understanding begins quite "innocently and modestly" (PFM, 64), first in the derivation of a priori cognition, then in losing sight of the limits to experience. While imagination can be forgiven for not keeping within the limits of experience since that indulgence stimulates it from a too common lethargy, the understanding cannot be so forgiven since it must be depended upon *to assist reason in setting bounds* to such productions of the imagination. In expounding the question "How is metaphysics in general possible?" Kant confronts the fact that reason can never satisfy itself with the empirical limits in the use of pure understanding, which is limited to possible objects of experience, as conditioned, to their appearance, and which never reaches the totally unconditioned that is the domain of reason. The requirement for such concepts of totality, completeness, and unity goes beyond the concepts of the understanding, limited to their immanent use. "Every single experience is only a part of the whole sphere of its domain, but the absolute totality of all possible experience is itself not experience. . . . Whereas the concepts of reason aim at the completeness, that is, the collective unity of all possible experience, and thereby transcend every given experience. Thus they become *transcendent*" (PFM, 76). These ideas of reason, which are neither constitutive of knowledge nor have objects of experience, carry an *inevitable* illusion, while the illusion of the concepts of understanding are only *likely* to mislead. We see that Kant considers this distinction between the concepts of understanding (as categories) and the concepts of reason (as ideas) to be most important to clear up the misconception of the role and nature of metaphysics in dispelling the illusions of understanding and especially of reason. All such illusions consist in "holding the subjective ground of our judgments to be objective" (PFM, 76).

This then is the crux of the matter. Kant considers the distinction between these two fields to be the most important for his critical enterprise of the *Critique of Pure Reason*. It is precisely the distinction between limit and boundary and the disparity in their specific functions and roles that is significant in relation to the natural drive of reason to metaphysics. For critique has revealed the concepts of understanding that constitute knowledge as objective. But the limits within which knowledge transpires in relation to experience of sense necessarily reveal the role of boundary. It opens the other domain or field that cannot be known objectively, and yet that is so pivotal to the metaphysical enterprise, especially for critical philosophy in dealing with the question of the possibility of metaphysics in general and as a science. And the predisposition to metaphysics in us by nature has this end—that the transcendental ideas reveal not only the "bounds of the pure use of reason, but also the way to determine them" (PFM, 102). Now, Kant states that the limits pointed out in those paragraphs (33 and 34) are "not enough after we have discovered that beyond them there still lies something though we can never know what it is in itself. For the question now is, What is the attitude of our reason in this connection of what we know with what we do not, and never shall, know? This is an actual connection of a known thing with one quite unknown (and which will always remain so), and though what is unknown should not become in the least more known—which we cannot even hope—yet the concept of this connection must be definite and capable of being rendered distinct" (PFM, 103). Thus, we come to think the noumenal, an immaterial being, a world of understanding, and a Supreme Being, which as things in themselves, allow reason to find "completion and satisfaction which it can never hope for in the derivation of appearances from their homogeneous grounds, and because these actually have reference to something distinct from them (and totally heterogeneous), as appearances always presuppose an object in itself and therefore suggest its existence whether we can know more of it or not" (PFM, 103).

Seduction of Reason and Its Dialectic

In this context Kant raises the illusive question of the "natural ends intended by this disposition to transcendent concepts in our nature" (PFM, 110–111) since what lies in nature is intended for some useful purpose. Thus even such a natural disposition to transcendent concepts must serve a useful purpose. For Kant, it is understood that such an undertaking is of a "doubtful nature" and only conjecture, "like every speculation about the ultimate ends of nature" (PFM, 111). In spite of this, Kant considers this inquiry to be allowed since the question is not one of the objective validity of metaphysical judgments, but rather of our natural predisposition to them, and as such, belongs to anthropology and not metaphysics.

It is of critical importance to understand what Kant is clarifying in this context: that while the Ideas of reason do not teach us something positive in the knowledge of soul, nature, or God, they do destroy the "narrowing assertions of materialism, of naturalism, and of fatalism," and more importantly, they give "scope for the moral Ideas beyond the field of speculation" (PFM, 112). This is his account of the natural predisposition of reason—that is, if it can be considered positive, this natural predisposition of reason leads to a place for moral ideas that are "beyond the field of speculation." Kant, in a rather tenuous statement, contends that the aim of this natural tendency to produce metaphysics is to "free our concepts from the fetters of experience and from the limits of the mere contemplation of nature" in order to open a field of objects for the pure understanding, not reached by sensibility, in order that "practical principles may be assumed as at least possible" (PFM, 111).[4]

For Kant, such a practical value given to a speculative science belongs outside the bounds of this science. Therefore, he must consider it to be a mere "scholium," and not a part of the science, but certainly belonging within philosophy, "especially of philosophy drawn from the pure sources of reason, where its speculative use in metaphysics must necessarily be at one with its practical use in morals" (PFM, 112). This leads to what has become extremely significant in our discussion in the confrontation between Heidegger and Cassirer—a point on which they both agree, that is, the positive employment of the dialectic of Kant. For Kant himself indicates for us this positive use. He refers to "the unavoidable dialectic of pure reason" as a natural tendency that deserves to be interpreted not as a mere illusion to be removed, "but also, if possible, as a natural provision as regards its end, though this task, a work of supererogation" that cannot "justly be assigned to metaphysics proper" (PFM, 112). Kant considers dealing with this question to belong to a second scholium, "which has a greater affinity for metaphysics" (PFM, 112).⁵

Yet, more central to the issues of the critique of knowledge, Kant affirms that the transcendental ideas show how to determine the bounds of the pure use of reason. He adds, however: "Such is the end and the use of this natural predisposition of our reason, which has brought forth metaphysics as its favorite child, whose generation, like every other in the world is not to be ascribed to blind chance but to an original germ, wisely organized for great ends"⁶ (PFM, 102, 131). And Kant, as we have seen, points out that the end and use of what he calls the "natural predisposition" of our reason, placed in us by nature, is "to point out to us actually not only the bounds of the pure use of reason, but also the way to determine them" (PFM, 113). Kant believes that he has fully exhibited metaphysics, in its subjective possibility, as it is given in its natural predisposition and in the essential end of its pursuit. And he contends that the natural use of this predisposition of our reason, without the discipline arising from a scientific critique to bridle and sets limits to it, involves it in transcendent and conflicting dialectical inferences. In spite of this "fallacious metaphysics," it is worth investigating the problem of finding out the natural ends intended by this disposition to transcendent concepts in our nature, since everything lying in nature must be intended for some useful purpose.

Thus it must be seen that the natural disposition of reason to metaphysics, as actual, is dialectical and illusory and that critique establishes metaphysics as a science, giving metaphysics a respectability and at once overcoming all "dogmatic twaddle" that occurs when metaphysics is oblivious to critique. We return to the important account of the last sentence of the conclusion of this *Prolegomina*: "And thus I conclude the analytical solution of the main question which I had proposed: 'how is metaphysics in general possible?' by ascending from the data of its actual use, as shown in its consequences, to the grounds of its possibility" (PFM, 113). What are these grounds of its possibility? Are not these in the relation or connection between the two fields, that of experience and that of mere thought—the unknown, the void (PFM, 103)? Is not the boundary between the two fields, in its positive dimension, and in its determinate meaning, the ground of metaphysics?

Kant concludes this "Conclusion" to the *Prolegomena* by insisting on ascending to the grounds of the possibility of metaphysics. The ground of its possibility is that with which he has dealt in the context of the "objective boundary" of experience as the relation to the ground of experience. This boundary, as something positive, can lead to an actual positive cognition "which reason itself acquires by enlarging itself to this boundary" (PFM, 109). Thus, this *cognition*, belonging to reason, sets a boundary to the field of understanding, even though it is otherwise unknown. Kant refers to this as the ascending to the grounds of its (metaphysics) possibility. Let us reflect further on the relation between this possibility of metaphysics and the ground of metaphysics.

In the context of the question of how metaphysics is possible as a science, Kant indicates that as a natural disposition, metaphysics is actual, but, if considered by itself, is dialectical and illusory. This natural illusion accounts for the fact that metaphysics has trouble getting just and lasting approbation. For Kant the solution to this question, arrived at only after a laborious road of inquiry, is rather simple. Critique, alone establishing metaphysics as a science, exhibits the whole stock of a priori concepts, their divisions according to various sources, sensibility, understanding, and reason, and exhibits a complete table of them in a complete system. Hence, the possibility of metaphysics as a science consists in a critique, and we spurn anything less. Kant observes that after it is appreciated, it becomes clear that critique is to common metaphysics of the schools as chemistry is to alchemy. Furthermore, before the development of his critical philosophy, metaphysics has not existed as a science (PFM, 117).

But does this not mean that metaphysics as science, as critique, is grounded in the boundary as the possibility of metaphysics in general? Hence, it is precisely the boundary as ground that is more fundamental than the enterprise of critique. Is not that what renders it possible? What is the relation between "discussing the possibility of metaphysics" and "laying the foundation of metaphysics"? But if Kant considers the possibility of metaphysics in terms of its ground (for metaphysics in general), and the ground in terms of the relation between the two fields . . . bordered by the boundary, is this not close to Heidegger's laying the foundation of metaphysics? It is interesting that Heidegger simply ascends more directly to Being of beings of experience as such a ground of metaphysics. So Heidegger, accepting the basic thrust of Kant, recasts it within his own situated question, that is, the Being question, but, true to Kant, has remained faithful to certain natural tendencies to metaphysics, and to the need to go to ground.

THE GROUND OF KNOWLEDGE
AND THE FOUNDATION OF METAPHYSICS

Limit and Ground

The connection between limiting and grounding by reason has to be considered in the light of the epistemological and ontological intentions, and how they becomes separated today in philosophies of limit without ground. How are each of these perspectives entailed in relation to the critical enterprise of Kant, then appropriated and redirected by Heidegger against the Neo-Kantians, and dealt with by Ricoeur and the postmodern deconstructionists? It is in dealing with these interrelated questions that greater clarity comes to the enterprise of reason in establishing limits and in thinking at them, and at once, reveals the central issue of the differing interpretations of the Kantian imagination. The importance of Kantian philosophy and the development from it in the two decades following the publication of the third *Critique*, especially the role of the imagination, for the differing and conflicting philosophies constituting continental philosophy, especially that which has crossed into the United States, has by now become apparent. Before turning to focus on the central role of the imagination in these various paths coming from Kant, it is necessary to reflect further on the Kantian limit function of reason in relation to critique, the relation between limiting and grounding as functions of reason, and the relation of critique to the phenomenology of Husserl.

It is clear from the above discussion that in Kant thinking itself reflects on the sense of the categories beyond their empirical usage where they are schematized for cognition. This reflection, prescinding from cognition, is a justification of the ideas of reason. Thus the illusion of reason in attempting to make its ideas have an object of experience must be overcome through a critique of transcendental illusion, as has been seen. Further, this speculative orientation of reason, rooted in the drive on the part of reason to find unity and totality, is the outgrowth of the tendency to found, although in a limited way, the knowledge of understanding.

Heidegger is correct, however, and Ricoeur at least in part concurs, in critiquing the epistemological emphasis of Kant's critical philosophy and his overly narrow—epistemological—understanding of metaphysics. Yet Heidegger overextends his own hermeneutical situation in his *Kant and the Problem of Metaphysics* in interpreting Kant as actually, in the unsaid of the said, laying the foundation of metaphysics in the direction of Heidegger's own fundamental ontology. For it is clear from a serious perusal of Kant's critical works that Kant is indeed laying the foundation of metaphysics, but precisely in a critical philosophy, which entails a certain epistemological priority. In the light of what will be seen of Ricoeur and the postmodern deconstructionists, the question of revamping the epistemological priority of Kant, and, indeed, even of Husserl, should not be limited to the ontological reading of Heidegger. For Kant, even within a critical philosophy, can be seen in his own way to lay the foundation of metaphysics in transcendental critique, one of whose essential tasks is to justify the objectivity of knowledge, but at once to show the limits of metaphysical claims to knowledge. And this enterprise is grounded in the thinking of the boundary concepts, which in the Heideggerian turn, become Being.

How we appropriate this attempt today will depend on what we bring to the enterprise: the Being-question first and foremost for Heidegger; a more ontic encompassment for Ricoeur; the Neo-Kantian orientation of Cassirer; or the postmodern deconstructive orientation. While it is the case that Kant actually lays the foundation of metaphysics as a science precisely in the *Critique*, which is largely an epistemological enterprise, Heidegger, in his retrieval of Kant, not only subverts this basic orientation of Kant, but likewise collapses the entire enterprise of reason into finitude and temporality. He thus derives practical reason from imagination, hence reducing morality strictly to a matter of temporal concrete historical existence, tendencies to which Ricoeur and Cassirer do not succumb.

It is necessary to remember that Kant, in attempting to move away from metaphysics as "dogmatic twaddle," understands metaphysics precisely as critique for it to be considered a science, and reaches toward its ground in the boundary concepts as the mark between two fields, which constitutes metaphysics in general. In Heidegger's move of ontological transformation toward schematism and the centrality of imagination and time, and in his attempt to finitize reason, what happens to the *ground*, to the *critique* as such? Heidegger's move in his retrieval of Kant must be considered to have put Being in its relation to time and to ground in such a way that it more clearly leads to the end of metaphysics, precisely in the way of his coming out of Kant, made clear in the Kant book and in his confrontation with Cassirer. If, indeed, the categories are derived from time, then metaphysics is in some sense at its end, as was seen in the last chapter. The critical difference between Heidegger's turn in the *Kant and the Problem of Metaphysics*, distinguishing him from the direction from Kant and consequent philosophies of Cassirer, Ricoeur and others, centers precisely here on the derivation of the categories. For as Heidegger begins the further and ongoing questioning of the formulation of the question of Being after *Being and Time*, he focuses more on primordial time in relation to the schematism, and the consequent role of the productive imagination in relation to originary time. As we will see, it is precisely here that Cassirer challenges his interpretation of Kant and his consequent ontology. It is also the place of Ricoeur's ongoing critique of Heidegger sustained for decades, for whom it is chimerical to hope to derive the categories from time.

In the Davos *Hochschule* lectures, Heidegger already lays out the project consummated immediately after in *Kant and the Problem of Metaphysics*, in which he interprets Kant's *grounding and founding* faculty as the transcendental imagination: "the ground for the possibility of a priori synthetic knowledge is the transcendental power of imagination . . . this (root) is indicated by the fact that pure sensibility and pure understanding lead back to the power of imagination—not only this, but to theoretical *and* practical reason in their separateness and their unity."[7] This move back to a tendency of philosophy evolving shortly after Kant's publication of the third *Critique*, diverging from Kant's own position, is precisely what postmodern deconstruction has followed. And the end of Western metaphysics is further and explicitly contained in Heidegger's statement in the "Appendices" to the fourth edition of *Kant and the Problem of Metaphysics*, in the claim that the point of departure in reason has thus been broken asunder from reason:[8] "destruction of the former foundation of Western metaphysics (spirit, *logos*, reason)." Deconstruction comes logically from this, delving beyond the logocentrism of the Western tradition. Heidegger continues: "It demands a radical, renewed unveiling of the grounds for the possibility of metaphysics as natural disposition of human beings, that is, a metaphysics of Dasein directed at the possibility of metaphysics as such, which must pose the question concerning the essence of human beings in a way which is *prior to* all philosophical anthropology and cultural philosophy."[9]

Cassirer and Heidegger

As we have already seen for Kant, while the understanding in the use of the categories for objective knowledge involves the conditions of possible experience, reason is unsatisfied with the conditions, and of its nature seeks beyond them to the unconditioned, thus reaching beyond the entire sphere of objectivity and of constituting things for objective knowledge. Thus, the finite operation of reason in knowledge exhausts only one element in the use of understanding. Cassirer wants to emphasize in this context what Heidegger slights, the infinite of understanding: "The understanding is, however, infinite in so far as the absolute totality in the synthesis of conditions belongs to its peculiar and essential task. In virtue of this requirement that reason places before the understanding, the latter is for the first time completely aware of its own nature and boundlessness. If it appears to be bound by its relation to the transcendental imagination of sensibility and thus to finitude, the understanding participates in the infinite through the no-less-necessary relation to the pure ideas of reason. For the latter can be symbolically represented."[10]

In the second *Critique* and in the writings on the moral law, Kant shows that the Idea of freedom requires the certainty of the supersensuous determination of rational being.[11] Cassirer affirms what we have seen in Kant, that thus the rational being for Kant is placed in two distinct and separate orders, the phenomenal and the noumenal as the sensible and intelligible orders; and that this separation means that all human existence and all human activities are to be measured by two completely different modes of orientation and judgment.

Cassirer's main objections to Heidegger's interpretation and appropriation of Kant's fundamental problematic center around the following essential issues. First, Cassirer accuses Heidegger of giving too much importance to the imagination, cutting off the infinite of Kant, and thus deriving the categories from temporal existence; further, he denies the role Heidegger attributes to schematism and considers the Heideggerian problem of temporality and human existence to be alien to Kant; finally, he considers Heidegger to have missed the focal point of Kant—as completed in the "Transcendental Dialectic," in the *Critique of Practical Reason*, and in the *Critique of Judgment*. Cassirer says:

> And here lies the essential objection that I have to make against Heidegger's interpretation of Kant. While Heidegger tries to relate and indeed to trace back all faculties of knowledge to transcendental imagination, the only thing left to him is the one frame of reference; namely, the framework of temporal existence. The distinction between phenomenon and noumenon is effaced: for all existence belongs now to the dimension of time and thus to finitude. But this removes one of the foundation stones on which that position must collapse. Nowhere does Kant contend for such a monism of imagination. Rather, he insists upon a decided and radical dualism, the dualism of the sensuous and intelligible worlds. For his problem is not the problem of being and time but rather the problem of "is" and "ought," of experience and Idea.[12]

Cassirer denies the "subjective" aspect of schematism, accusing Heidegger of superimposing his own fundamental ontology upon Kant's thought. Here perhaps Cassirer misses something phenomenological that needs to be supplied to Kant, as we shall see. He wants rather to emphasize the focal point of Kant's system as completed in the transcendental dialectic, in the *Critique of Practical Reason* and in the *Critique of Judgment*. Although he does not agree with Kant's interpretation of the role of his "transcendental dialectic," Heidegger, as seen above, emphasizes the importance of its positive content as ontology, that is, for uncovering the problem of Being in the Transcendental Logic in a decisive manner.[13] Even precisely within the context indicated by Cassirer, of the denial of the noumenal/phenomenal distinction and restriction to temporality, Heidegger has appropriated the demands of reason for unity and totality in regard to the understanding, and of the dialectic in relation to the analytic.

In spite of the exclusively ontological intent of the Kant book, Heidegger has overstated his case, leaving him vulnerable to these criticisms that he neglects to consider the entirety of Kant's project in assigning priority to the role of schematism. In his review of the Kant book in 1930, Cassirer remarked: "Schematism stands at the beginning of Kant's metaphysics and constitutes, as it were, the entrance to it. But its real content is developed only on the other side of that entrance."[14] While determined to establish the incongruity between phenomenology and Kant's thinking, Cassirer's intention to preserve the systematic relation of reason, understanding, and imagination is actually more appropriately fulfilled by pursuing an alternative path that comes to fruition in Ricoeur's use of phenomenology. Thus, Cassirer's criticism sets the stage for that of Ricoeur, yet both of them perhaps have a myopic attitude toward epistemology in overlooking the possibility of transforming epistemology at a more basic, experiential level. By the same token, Ricoeur, by re-affirming the importance of an "epistemic" and the ontic level of reflection, actually confirms the viability of seeking a "middle way" between phenomenology and Kantianism.[15]

This discussion will now more sharply establish the contrast between Heidegger and Ricoeur by considering their differing views of the roles of the imagination and schematism.

Heidegger's Retrieval of the Unthought of Kant

As we have seen, Ricoeur sets himself apart from Heidegger in regard to several essential issues by denying that the transcendental imagination is the root of understanding and sensibility, and in challenging the derivation of the categories from the schemata and time. These were precisely the innovations that distinguished Heidegger's attempt, in *Kant and the Problem of Metaphysics,* to elicit the unthought dimension of transcendental philosophy, particularly by establishing the centrality of the imagination over against reason within Heidegger's hermeneutical situation. With regard to the transcendental imagination Ricoeur stresses the independence and spontaneity of understanding and reason, thereby preventing the imaginative synthesis from being totally foundational even if it is a synthesis of sense and understanding. It achieves a synthesis while not being the "common root" of the elements brought together, and mediates between the finite and the infinite on the level of knowledge. Heidegger, by contrast, roots practical reason in the transcendental imagination, and ultimately, in primordial time.

Ricoeur further contends that the derivation of the categories from the schemata reduces knowledge to receptivity, to finitude, and to letting appear, thus falsifying spontaneity, activity, and the infinite element. For him, purely intellectual relations determine time, rather than evolve from time. Yet he has insisted on the essentially noetic aspect of the section of the *Critique of Pure Reason* on the schematism and the noematic aspect of the section on the deduction of the principles. But Ricoeur, in agreeing with Heidegger here, has evidently not agreed with regard to the levels, types, and relations of the noetic activity in his appraisal of fundamental ontology in *Fallible Man*. In focusing upon the synthesis between the finite and the infinite in knowledge on the theoretical level, Ricoeur considers the categories to be derived from a level above the finite, giving more importance to the understanding and the infinite. Heidegger, by contrast, derives the structures of knowledge from the transcendental imagination interpreted as a more basic unity. In Ricoeur's view, agreeing with Cassirer, the transcendental imagination deals only with the introduction to the Kantian metaphysical problems.

Ricoeur carefully considers the implications and exclusions of Heidegger's account of temporal existence, according to which all possibilities belong to the dimension of time and thus to finitude. The distinction between phenomenon and noumenon is effaced without qualification or reference to indirect expressions. Yet the contrast with Heidegger on the above points, and the central focus by Ricoeur on the Dialectic, the *Critique of Practical Reason*, and the *Critique of Judgment*, again in agreement with Cassirer, must not be allowed to dismiss Heidegger's indication of the importance of incorporating the positive content of the Dialectic. As Heidegger himself recognized in countering an analogous, though earlier objection raised by Cassirer, "By reason of my interpretation of the *Dialectic* as ontology, I believe that the problem of Being [*Sein*] in the Transcendental Logic, seemingly only negative in Kant, is really a positive problem."[16] Precisely within the context of denying the phenomenal-noumenal distinction, and of affirming *temporality as a limit*, Heidegger has recast the demands placed by reason on the understanding for unity and totality.

Within the accepted limits, Heidegger cannot simply uphold reason's ideas of the *Unconditioned*—of the cosmos, of self, and of God. In light of finite, temporal existence, he has redefined the kind of totality, unity, and transcendence that is demanded by reason. This demand for totality is most aptly expressed in Heidegger's view of the world and care, now radically finitized and temporalized. For Heidegger, the sensibilization of reason involves the temporalizing of the meaningful and referential totality of world and Dasein. Dasein's totality is grasped properly only within the hermeneutical situation of Being-toward-death and of Being-toward-birth, which brings its totality fully into the fore-comprehension of care. In this way, the unified totality of historical exis-

tence comes to light, and the world in its worldhood arises as the defini-
tive project of finite transcendence. Thus, it is seen how Dasein's Being
is distinguished by transcendence in a way that reveals the world as the
source of the Kantian notion of a totality and that thereby undercuts the
phenomenon-noumenon distinction. A further implication in Heidegger's manner of overcoming that distinction is the recasting of the relation between the theoretical and practical dimensions, now unified at the
deeper ontological level, attempting thus to reconcile the Kantian conflict between freedom and nature within the context of the finite totality
of Being-in-the-world. Yet another implication of Heidegger's temporalizing reason must be further investigated in the context of Ricoeur's criticism and interpretation, and that implication involves the relation of the
understanding to the infinite, as seen above.[17]

Although Kant's analysis of temporality is central to the philosophies of both Heidegger and Ricoeur, its role in each philosophy throws
into focus their essential philosophical differences. Originary time or
temporality is more central to Heidegger's philosophy than it is even for
that of Kant, becoming the primordial ontological structure of human
existence and the horizon for the inquiry into Being. In contrast, for
Ricoeur, although time is an essential condition of human finitude and
must be dealt with pervasively throughout his philosophy, culminating
in poetics and narrative, it does not have the same centrality as in Heidegger's reductive philosophy. Ricoeur has, however, continued to be
attuned to Heidegger's view of time, although his own basic view has
not radically changed in its evolution from the first part of *The Philosophy of the Will.* This fundamental role and sense of time in Ricoeur's
philosophy must now be discussed.

Ricoeur, as a post-Hegelian Kantian philosopher, preserves the a
priori character of Kant's philosophy, while maintaining an interpretation of temporality according to which it is not ontologically centered in
the constitution of human existence as it is for Heidegger. In fact, temporality is not, for Ricoeur, the essential unity of human "nature" nor
does it preclude the synthesis between finitude and infinitude, but,
rather, is subordinate to the human "essence." In this view, he strongly
opposes Heidegger's interpretation. Ricoeur's objections to Heidegger's
philosophy will be seen further to bear great similarity to Cassirer's criticisms of Heidegger analyzed above, which thus will greatly illuminate
the difference between Ricoeur and Heidegger especially concerning
such central Kantian issues as time, imagination, and reason. And it is
precisely here that the focus for divergent paths from Kant emerge: in
the direction of Heidegger and later postmodern deconstruction; and in
the direction of Cassirer and Ricoeur; and all of these somewhat reminiscent of the late-eighteenth- and early-nineteenth-century debates

between idealism and romanticism, which in some sense come from the manner of interpreting the role of the imagination in Kant's, especially after the publication of the third *Critique*.

The Time of Narrativity

It is worth repeating that Ricoeur agrees substantially with Cassirer's 1929 critique of Heidegger's appropriation of Kantian philosophy: that the derivation of the categories cannot be from time, nor can the imagination and time be the origin of the understanding. Although he places the imagination in a central place, it is crucial to the application of the categories but not to the origin of time, given the primacy of reason. Ricoeur insists, against Heidegger, upon a nontemporal dimension belonging to the essential aspects of man. As we have already seen, Ricoeur rejects Heidegger's view of the role of the transcendental imagination and the "genesis of the categories from the schemata,"[18] which, according to him, is not an adequate origin of a well-formulated notional order. Yet, despite the reservations toward Heidegger's interpretation of schematism that Ricoeur and Cassirer share, the most telling divergence lies in a common need to restore the dimension of the infinite and the eternal, although for Ricoeur within the concrete context provided by phenomenology. Thus, for Ricoeur the essential structures of intelligibility, which for Kant consisted of the categories, are themselves to be critically expanded to mark the "practical synthesis" of the infinite and the finite, thereby indicating a nascent tendency in the person to seek the absolute and the eternal in terms of both faith and action.

In this way Ricoeur, although considering temporality to be essential to human existence and not allowing a temporal derivation or origin of the categories, has left room for the possibility of speculative philosophy rooted in the categories. And he criticizes Heidegger for having excluded this option. Ricoeur accepts the essentially temporal character of human existence provided the basic ontological structures, rather than strictly finite, are considered to be a synthesis of finitude and infinitude. Thus, Ricoeur's phenomenological method uncovers originary time, but not as the essential unity of human existence. He is then led to criticize Heidegger's too quick move to the unity of man, and for placing the unity so quickly in temporal existence.

In two recent works,[19] Ricoeur brings together time with the semantic innovation of the productive imagination and schematism. Narrative fiction[20] takes on a central role because by means of it" . . . we re-configure our confused, unformed, and at the limit mute temporal existence."[21] The culmination, however, of the relation of time and narrative is reached within Ricoeur's project as a whole when the "refiguration of time by narrative" is achieved, when "referential intentions of the historical narrative and the fictional narrative *interweave*. Our analysis of the fictive experience of time will at least have marked a decisive turning point in the direction of the solution of this problem that forms the horizon of my investigation, by providing something like a *world of the text* for us to think about, while awaiting its complement, the *life-world of the reader*, without which the signification of the literary work is incomplete."[22]

In these same later works Ricoeur considers his analysis of Heidegger to do justice to the "originality that a phenomenology founded upon an ontology and that presents itself as a hermeneutic can boast of."[23] He refers here to Heidegger's founding his phenomenology on an ontology of Dasein and of Being-in-the-world, in which temporality is "more subjective" than any subject and "more objective" than any object since his ontology is not bound by any subjective/objective dichotomy. Ricoeur stipulates that Heidegger's originality consists in a "hierarchization of levels of temporality or rather of temporalization."[24] He considers one invaluable result of Heidegger's analysis to be its having established, with a hermeneutic phenomenology, "that our experience of temporality is capable of unfolding itself on several levels of radicality, and that it belongs to the analytic of Dasein to traverse them, whether from above to below, in the order followed in *Being and Time*, from authentic and mortal time toward everyday and public time where everything happens 'in' time, or from below to above, as in *The Basic Problems of Phenomenology*."[25] He further considers the direction in which the range of temporalization is traversed to be less important than the hierarchization of temporal experience.[26]

Ricoeur is particularly interested in thinking about death and eternity at the same time. "The most serious question this work may be able to pose is to what degree a philosophical reflection on narrativity and time may aid us in thinking about eternity and death at the same time."[27] Accordingly, he wishes to uphold the possibility of man's redemption within the wake of eternity, while avoiding the reification of that notion which Heidegger and Nietzsche previously have criticized. The visions of eternity grasped in the mythic beginning of the world and in the narrative message of the Kingdom yield the occasion for man's initiation into a higher level of existence, the fulfillment of the regulative idea originally proposed by Kant. More attention must now be given to the aporia of lived and cosmic time, which Ricoeur addresses in the three volumes of *Time and Narrative*.

Ricoeur's *Time and Narrative* is constructed around the aporetic of time witnessed in the accounts of internal time and reaching an "extreme degree of aporia"[28] in phenomenology, a consideration raised initially by Augustine whose treatment of time presented the aporia of internal time, and later developed by Husserl and Heidegger.[29] Ricoeur is insistent on the inadequacy of this account to deal with cosmic time. And it is precisely this aporia between phenomenological time and cosmic time that history, with its manifold connections, brings together, bridging the gap between internal time and cosmic time, thus opening the way for the interweaving of history and fiction on refigured time as a way of addressing the aporia and of transforming faulted existence through the imaginative variation worked on time by fiction, but with an application to some aspect of the real. For fiction is not entirely separated from the real, just as history is not devoid of the imaginative.

Historical time, then, bridges the chasm between internal time and cosmic time by means of its connections: calendar time is the first of the connectors, joining astronomical time with human institutions, harmonizing "work with days and festivals with the seasons and the years. It integrates the community and its customs into the cosmic order."[30] The second connector, the notion of the sequence of generations, shown in the transmission of biblical curses and blessing from generation to generation, results from the connection between lived time and biological time that underlies it and connects it with astronomical time. This grounding of lived time on biological time "is thus added to the *inscription* of lived time upon astronomical time."[31] The third connector is implied by history's recourse to documents and monuments. Here Ricoeur appropriates the sense of trace employed by F. Simiand in defining history as knowledge by traces. Because of its mixed nature, the trace, according to Ricoeur, is a connector between lived time and physical time. The trace exists as such now, but it is a remnant or a vestige of something from another world as, for instance, documents or monuments. Further, it is a remnant, a vestige, a window to something that was in a past world. As Ricoeur says, "A trace, then, is a present thing which stands for (*vaut*) an absent past."[32] Or, it is also both "a remains and a sign of what was but no longer is."[33] For Ricoeur, the trace's double allegiance to different temporal orders is an original phenomenon that Heidegger's account, focusing on having-been of Dasein, does not adequately account for.

Ricoeur's strongest articulation of the critique of the phenomenology of time, coming to grips with the primordial time of Heidegger, constitutes a serious critique of Heidegger's limitations regarding time that cannot be ignored. Thus, it might prove instructive to follow Ricoeur's critique of the phenomenology of time further, beginning with his perceptive insights on Augustine's analysis especially in relation to Husserl's phenomenology of time, and then turning to the limits of Heidegger's valuable contribution.

Although it is phenomenology that intensifies the aporia of time, it is in Augustine's *Confessions* that the aporetic of time is initially sketched in terms of the paradox of the triple present (present of the past, present of the future, present of the present)[34] in terms of the paradox of *distentio animi* and of the *intentio*; and in terms of the paradox of the originality of the present vis-à-vis the eternal present. Ricoeur considers Husserl's famous doctrine of time to prolong the Augustinian paradoxes. In the same vein Ricoeur extols the achievements of *Being and Time* of Heidegger, that the principle of temporalization is sought out within the structure of care that allows for distinguishing time on different levels.

But by this very advance, phenomenology creates aporias. Ricoeur considers this failure to cover the problematic of time adequately in its entirety to have begun with Augustine's attempt to derive the Aristotlian cosmic from the distention of the soul: "the simple distention of the soul hit up against Aristotelian reef: referring time to movement and to the root of movement, the accomplishment of the unaccomplished of *phusis*."[35] Similarly, the Husserlian attempt to deal with time as a pure experience by putting aside objective time "strikes another reef, that Kantian one: it is from Kant that we learned that time as such is invisible, that it could not appear in any living experience that it is always presupposed as the condition of experience, and from this fact could only appear indirectly on objects apprehended in space and according to the schemata and the categories of objectivity." According to Ricoeur, it is this constraint that shows why even the internal time-consciousness borrows its structure form this objective time that the reduction holds in suspense. Even and especially Heidegger's treatment of time, with its levels of temporalization, reveals most completely this inability. "But this very effort comes up against *the other* of phenomenological time: the 'popular' concept of time, made up of an infinite series of indifferent nows. Even the most decentered level of temporality—within-time-ness—where the 'in' of being in time is highlighted, never rejoins the 'ordinary' time which is simply removed from the phenomenological field by the allegation of an enigmatic leveling of the 'in' of 'within-time-ness.'"[36] Ricoeur considers Heidegger's attempt to include the history of time from Aristotle to Hegel in this ordinary time to be in vain. For Ricoeur, there is a disproportion between time that we unfold in living and time that envelops us everywhere.

Heidegger's account does not take into consideration the "heterogeneous temporal orders" to which the trace, as an original phenomenon, belongs. Ricoeur asks the crucial question of Heidegger's attempt to deal with this in terms of having-been and within-time-ness: "For how does *Dasein* interpret its having-been-there if not by relying on the autonomy of marks left by the passage of former humans? Heidegger's failure to understand the phenomenon of the trace reflects the failure of *Sein und Zeit* to give an account of the time of the world which has no care for our care."[37] Ricoeur goes on to show how the trace, as an element with history, crosses the gap between internal time and cosmic time.

Further, this critique is parallel to a broader critique of Heidegger's hermeneutic considered above. Although Ricoeur is exemplarily respectful of Heidegger's hermeneutic ontology and the primordial time that it reveals, he must supply an hermeneutic that does more than Heidegger's hermeneutic. In allowing the text a certain distanciation from its situation of origin, and focusing on it in a quasi-independence of the reader, Ricoeur has pointed out in hermeneutics something similar to what he is pointing out here regarding time, that is, the need adequately to deal with that which is not reducible to the having been of Dasein in the temporal extases. For no matter how much effort is exerted to consider the mode of being of Dasein, and the past as derivative from the temporality or historicality of Dasein, the fact remains that there is still something past that is independent of human existence and Dasein's temporality and historicality—that other of which the trace serves as a trace of . . . as, for example, with the historical documents, monuments, and implements that have no world remaining and no Dasein that is familiar with them. This requires, in fact demands, a reconstruction by imagination and intelligent interpretation and explanation, before being appropriated into the familiarity of human existence. This is the same domain that is entered through a critique of Heidegger regarding the inadequacy of the internal time of phenomenology and his own primordial time that cannot encompass cosmic time.

This critique shows clearly how Heidegger's perspective must be recognized in its limits regarding time and hermeneutics, especially concerning that which is not reducible to care. While it can well be replied that the primordial relation of Dasein to Being demands the prior attunement to Being and to time, that response is inadequate to deal with the otherness of cosmic time and of texts. Now that the importance of distinguishing Heidegger's and Ricoeur's conflicting views of time has become evident, we can now turn to the expansion of Kant in terms of an insight from Husserlian phenomenology; and an expansion of Husserlian phenomenology in terms of an insight from Kant.

Ricoeur, Kant, and Husserl

As will be seen clearly in a later chapter, the differing attitudes toward Husserlian phenomenology by Ricoeur and other postmodern thinkers puts them in a different stance toward the whole philosophical enterprise, in spite of certain similarities. Thus, it is necessary to consider the relation between phenomenology as foundational philosophy and a philosophy of limit. And the best entrance is to focus precisely on the expansion of Husserlian phenomenology in terms of Kantian boundary philosophy; and the expansion of Kantian philosophy in terms of Husserlian lived experience and its subject.

Ricoeur's position, as seen above, can be interpreted to be somewhat between those of Heidegger and Cassirer in their debate over the epistemological and the ontological. What must be done is to integrate this mediation between Kant and Husserl, interpreting Kant with a quasi-ontological thrust, in spite of his dominant epistemological rendition; and interpreting Husserl's phenomenology in relation to limit, in spite of his lack of such a critique. Ricoeur says, regarding this ontological thrust: "When this revolution (Copernican) is not reduced to the *questio juris*, to the axiomatization of Newtonian physics, it is none other than the reduction of particular beings to their appearance in the *Gemut*. With the guidance of a transcendental experience of the *Gemut* it is possible to grasp the features of the Kantian phenomenology."[38] This has taken place, following Ricoeur, in the general context of interpreting the Copernican Revolution as a quasireduction, loosely considered (and for my purposes, better loosely considered as mentioned above), which, when shaken loose from an overcommitment to the strict objectivity of scientific knowledge, reveals the *Gemut* precisely as Kant's unavoidable recourse to something other than the narrowness of his own allowance: the empirical ego as phenomenal self, and the transcendental unity of apperception as the unity of the "I think." And in a way parallel to Kant's omission of the *Gemut* is Husserlian ascesis regarding the ontological substrate of the phenomenon in his initial act of reduction, which itself yields lived experience, as well as conceals, in Husserl's use of it, any ontological dimension.

And it is precisely the extrapolation in the direction of the *Gemut* in Kantian critique and in the direction of the ontological in relation to the Husserlian reduction that allows a bringing of Kant and Husserl into the same domain of discourse, as will now be made clear. Ricoeur wants certainly to open in Kant a further dimension of the subject or of subjectivity than that offered within Kant's dichotomy: "The whole epistemological conception of objectivity tends to make the 'I-think' a function of objectivity and imposes the alternatives to which we referred at the outset. Either I am 'conscious' of the 'I-think' but do not 'know' it, or I 'know' the ego, but it is a phenomenon within nature. This is why Kant's phenomenological description tends toward the discovery of a concrete subject who has no tenable place in the system. However, Kant moves in the direction of this subject whenever he moves toward originary time at work in the judgment by means of the schematism" (KH, 185), a central point highlighted by Heidegger in his statement of the misunderstanding of the Being question in *Being and Time* that initially gave rise to the Kant book of 1929. Ricoeur considers Kant to broach this subject in determining the existence of things as correlative to my existence. Ricoeur quotes Kant: "I am conscious of my own existence as determined in time . . . consequently the determination of my existence in time is possible only through the existence of actual things which I perceive outside me."[39] Ricoeur points out that Kant escapes this dilemma "every time he proceeds to a direct inspection of the *Gemut* (mind). The very term, *Gemut*, so enigmatic, designates the 'field of transcendental experience' which Husserl thematizes" (KH, 180–181). Ricoeur thus is able to bring something of Husserl to Kantian philosophy, understanding the requirement from within Kant's own texts on the *Gemut*, which Kant does mention and seems to require more than he admits. Such an expansion allows this *Gemut* to be interpreted in terms of Husserl's thematization of the field of transcendental experience. Of course, it goes without saying that Kant would not have any clue of the sense of "transcendental experience," a strictly Husserlian notion, and one that Kant excludes in principle. Yet Ricoeur certainly is correct in this expansion of Kant here, because this enigma, so radical to Kantian philosophy, can indeed be expanded upon in terms of a fuller sense of the self, one that can be set on its way by an initial reflection on Husserl in this manner. And as clearly stated, this is basically what the Copernican Revolution brings to light when it is not reduced to the "axiomatization of Newtonian physics": it is no other than the "reduction of particular beings to their appearance in the *Gemut*" (KH, 181). Kant, according to Ricoeur, attempts to resolve this problem by linking existence to the "undetermined empirical intuition" prior to organized experience. Thus, Kant says: "Existence is not yet a category" (B 423). Ricoeur considers this extracategorical existence to be the very subjectivity without which the 'I-think' would not merit being called first person. He suggests that perhaps this is the existence of *Gemut*, the mind "Which is neither the I-think as principle of the possibility of the categories nor the self phenomenon of psychological science, but rather the mind which is offered to transcendental experience by the phenomenological reduction" (KH, 187), thus rounding out a Kantian inadequacy by means of a phenomenological largess.

The ontological intent of the *Critique* distinguishes it from phenomenology. The *Critique* is not limited to the internal structure of knowledge, but rather investigates the limits of knowledge. "The rooting of the knowledge of phenomena in the thinking of being (*être*) which is not convertible into knowledge gives the Kantian *Critique* its properly ontological dimension. To destroy this tension between knowing and thinking, between the phenomenon and being, is to destroy Kantianism itself" (KH, 186). This claim by Ricoeur must be interrelated and reconciled with Kant's statements about the possibility of metaphysics as a science, and in general. It seems to me that Kant thought of his ground as strictly epistemological, that is, as an epistemological ground of knowledge, where knowledge is limited, and metaphysics, which studies only the transcendental in a critique, is confined within the priority of the epistemic. We have already considered the extent to which this way of formulating the Kantian orientation to ontology is permissible. Ricoeur too, within limits, agrees with the Cassirer-Heidegger debate, where they seem to agree on a more positive interpretation of the dialectic of Kant than that provided by Kant.

Ricoeur is more explicit than either Heidegger or Cassirer in his efforts to enlarge critical philosophy and transcendental phenomenology by one another. He wants to first take account of the function of the positing of the thing-in-itself in relation to the inspection of phenomena as Kant sees it. He says: "In spite of the impossibility of knowledge of being, *Denken* still can be interpreted as positing being as that which limits the claims of the phenomena to make up ultimate reality. Thus, *Denken* confers on phenomenology its ontological dimension or status. One can trace this connection between a deception (regarding knowledge) and a positive act of limitation throughout the *Critique*" (KH, 186–187). Thus, what Ricoeur has achieved is an adherence to Kantian restriction regarding knowledge, yet included the ontological dimension of the phenomenon for phenomenology in the thinking as limiting, and as positively positing being, in the Heideggerian sense.

The significance of the representation (*Vorstellung*) comes to light as revealing the aspect of the object "for us" as distinguished from that "in itself," to which we have no access. "'Our whole intuition is *only* the representation of the phenomenon. The things that we intuit are not in themselves as we intuit them.'"[40] Thus from the outset there is this split between the for-itself and the for-us, since the representation does not give access to the in-itself. This dimension extends to space and time, which, as a priori and transcendental, makes the object possible, and does not come to us from the outside and from the object, so to speak. This dimension of space and time lends itself to the notion of transcendental ideality since

> . . . space is nothing outside of the subjective condition (A 28). This bit of fancy expresses what is positive in the negative of our lack of originary intuition. The *Denken* is the positive. It is not reducible to our being-affected and in consequence is not reducible to that 'dependence' of man 'in his existence as well as in his intuition' (B 72) which was

pointed out near the end of the 'Aesthetic.' The *Denken* is what imposes the limit, so that, rather than the phenomenal understanding limiting the usage of categories of experience, it is the positing of being by *Denken* that limits the claim of knowing the absolute. Knowledge, finitude, and death are thus linked by an indissoluble pact which is only recognized by the very act of *Denken* that escapes from this condition and somehow views it from without.[41]

Let us now turn to delve further into some correlated ontological implications regarding Husserl's phenomenology, closing the gap between Kant, thus expanded, and Husserl, to be treated to the same opening process.

Ricoeur, agreeing somewhat with Heidegger as already seen, criticizes the overly epistemological interpretation of Kant by the Neo-Kantians. He thus wants to show that the difference between Husserl and Kant should be located "on the level where Kant determines the ontological status of the phenomena themselves and not on the level of an exploration of the world of phenomena" (KH, 187). Ricoeur is contending that the Neo-Kantians are not radical enough, that they miss the real difference because of their incapacity to grasp that difference in questioning the ontological status of the phenomenon. Does Kant really determine the ontological status of the phenomenon? Since Kant explicitly deals with the metaphysical, it is certainly legitimate to ask about the metaphysical in his critical philosophy, about its "ontological intention" (KH, 175), its limits and its positive expression.[42]

Ricoeur proposes to see how Husserl destroys an "ontological problem-set" that had found its expression in the role of limiting and founding on the part of the thing-in-itself, which then ties the ontological dimension to the critical task of limiting and bounding. "We can then ask whether the loss of the ontological dimension of the object qua phenomenon was not common to both Husserl and his turn-of-the-century Neo-Kantian critics. If so, this would be the reason why they located their dispute in an area of secondary importance" (KH, 175). Ricoeur proposes, after making this point, what becomes one of the pivotal points of his own entire later development, as well as the foundation for his way of approaching the philosophic problems that occupy him. He proposes to reinterpret Husserl's idealism with the guidance of that "sense of limits which is perhaps the soul of the Kantian philosophy" (KH, 176).

"The reduction is the straight gate to phenomenology. But in this very act of reduction a methodological conversion and a metaphysical decision intersect, and just at that point one must distinguish between them. In its strictly methodological intention the reduction is a conversion which causes the 'for-me' to emerge from every ontic positing.

Whether the being (*être*) is a thing, a state of affairs, a value, a living creature, or a person, the *epoché* 'reduces' it to its appearing."⁴³ This reduction leaves out the "ontic positing" that Ricoeur distinguishes from the ontological problem. Ricoeur indicates this metaphysical bias to the reduction in another place, contending that the "reduction strains our links to things only to discover that these links exist prior to any act of consciousness, any reflection which would make of them an object of thought."⁴⁴ It is at this point that the reduction could perhaps be adjusted, so that the ontic positing could or could not be left within the focus, distinguishing ontological from epistemological concerns within the focus of phenomenology, rather than making it an either/or.

Limit, Critique, and the Practical

In making the transition to the philosophical limit of the practical realm of acting or praxis, it is necessary to reconcile two difficult issues for Ricoeur in the appropriation of both Kant and Husserl corrected and expanded in terms of one another. The focal question is how to reconcile the philosophy of limit with the critique of Husserl's ontological omission. It is precisely the philosophy of limit that prevents us from a naiveté about the realm of the thing in itself; and it is the critique of Husserl's ontological failure at the initial phases of the reduction that brings the noumenal back into focus. In this context, as seen above, perhaps Ricoeur remains a bit too Kantian, yet while appropriating essential aspects of Heidegger's initial focus on the phenomenon as already entailing Being. It is in working out this problem that we will find it necessary perhaps to expand on Ricoeur's doctrine, eventually in terms of postmodern deconstruction. Let us now turn to Ricoeur's dialogue with Kant and Husserl concerning the limits of practical reason, which underlies in some way the entirety of his later works.

Ricoeur emphasizes the role of limit in relation to the phenomenon, even early in Kant's first *Critique*, focusing on the fact that Kant constantly affirms that transcendental philosophy stands on the dividing line separating the "two sides" of the phenomenon (A 38), the in-itself and the for-us. And the unconditioned authorizes us to speak of the things "only so far as we do not know them," thus forcing us across the limits (boundary, *die Grenze*) of experience and all appearances (A 38). In thus quoting Kant, Ricoeur shows the direction toward Kant and away from Husserl regarding the realm of the practical, which for Kant takes place largely in the realm that cannot be known. Serving as limit, as seen in the last chapter:

> the in-itself protects knowledge of the phenomena of nature from falling into a dogmatic naturalism. This limiting function of the in-itself

is given its most complete expression in the chapter on the 'Distinction of all Objects into Phenomena and Noumena.' The concept of the in-itself even though 'problematical' (. . . non-contradictory) is necessary 'to prevent sensuous intuition from being extended to the things-in-themselves' (A 254). To be even clearer: 'The concept of a noumenon is thus a merely limiting concept, the function of which is to limit the presumptions of sensuousness' (A 255). Hence, there would be a sort of *hubris* of sensuousness—not, correctly speaking, of sensuousness as such, but of empirical usage of the understanding, of the positive and positivistic praxis of the understanding. (KH, 188)

The distinction between the usage and sense of the categories is important: the usage of the categories in their primary function to limit experience, and their sense, can be used to clarify what Kant understands by the presumption of sensuousness: "It is not reason that is unsuccessful in the 'Transcendental Dialectic'; it is rather sensuousness in its claim to apply to the things-in-themselves" (KH, 188). Thus, one could show how the foundation of knowledge is the thinking of Being, but not in lowering or bringing down to earth this thinking of Being. The two now are together, but knowledge is not advanced in the thinking of Being. "The understanding accordingly limits sensuousness, but does not thereby extend its own sphere. In the process of warning the latter that it must not presume to claim applicability to things-in-themselves but only to appearance, it does indeed think for itself an object in itself, but only as transcendental object" (A 288, B 344). It is essential to come to grips with the Kantian notion of "transcendental object," so enigmatic, so necessary, and so misunderstood.

Ricoeur continues by pointing out that if we are going to use the Kantian doctrine as a guide for interpreting the implicit philosophy of Husserl (and I might add, for his own future philosophy) we need assurance that Kant succeeded in "reconciling this function of limitation with the idealism of his theory of objectivity, such as it is developed in the'Transcendental Deduction.' Is not objectivity reduced to the synthesis imposed on the manifold of sensibility by apperception through the categories?" (KH, 189). It is the thing-in-itself that radically situates the object outside. "The intending of the phenomenon beyond itself is toward the nonempirical object, the transcendental X. This is why Kant balances the texts where objectivity emerges from the separation between my representations and the phenomenon with others, where the phenomena remain 'representations, which in turn have their object (A 109). The transcendental object is 'what can alone confer upon all of our empirical concepts in general relation to an object, that is, objective reality'" (A 109).

Ricoeur interprets the realistic function of intentionality (the object X as "correlative of the unity of apperception") to penetrate through and through the idealistic function of objectifying representations. Further, it is the crucial distinction between *intention* and *intuition*, so fundament to Kant, that is pivotal for understanding this correlation. For, while Kant radically separates from one another the relation to something and the intuition of something, Husserl, due to the ontological lacuna, has no place for such a correlation. Ricoeur says, in regard to this distinction in Kant: "*An object=X is an intention without intuition. This distinction subtends that of thinking and knowing and maintains the agreement as well as the tension between them*" (KH, 189).[45]

This Kantian correlation between the transcendental ideality of the object and the realism of the thing-in-itself has no parallel in Husserlian phenomenology, for, in losing the ontological dimension of the phenomenon, Husserl at once lost the possibility of a meditation on the limits and foundation of phenomenality. As Ricoeur so well says, "This is why phenomenology is not a 'critique,' that is to say, an envisagement of the limits of its own field of experience" (KH, 190). Thus, Ricoeur wants to supply from an expansion on Kant the thinking of Being as the limit to knowing reality. He here follows Heidegger somewhat in going to the pre-comprehension of the existential level, with the limiting thinking of Being, yet he again requires the detour or prolongation on the ontic level, on the level of concrete existence, and this in the domain or realm of the practical. This realm, however, does not extend to theoretical knowledge, but is limited to practical cognition, thus adding nothing to our stock of knowledge as such.

Thus, if recast, the reduction does not have to remove us from being, since, for Ricoeur, the metaphysical, Being, or that which is given cannot be bracketed. And we must add that the reduction can be seen in the light of a certain neutrality, not envisioned even by Ricoeur. It can thus be employed in such way as to allow the bracketing of being, while leaving it operative, and simply focusing, somewhat at will, on the epistemic or on the ontological dimensions of our ontic or concrete existence. The refocus allowed for by the reduction is somewhat arbitrary, avoiding the metaphysical bias of Husserl. But Husserl cannot allow such a possibility since he has completely cut the props out from experience by his failure to distinguish the "problems of being (*être*)" from the "naive positing of particular beings (*etants*) in the natural attitude,"[46] thus not raising the question of Being as such.[47] Ricoeur sees this naive positing as the "omission of the connection of particular beings to ourselves, and considers it to arise from that *Anmassung* (presumption) of sensuousness discussed by Kant" (KH, 190–191). Thus there is a certain implicit metaphysics in the seemingly lack of metaphysics and being in the Husserlian reduction. Furthermore, Husserl has cut off the correlation between the objectivity constituted "in" us and the objectivity "of" the phenomenon (the thing-in-itself?) founding it. This is how Husserl must see the being status as "from" me: "this world that is 'for' me in respect to its sense (and 'in' me in the intentional sense of 'in') is also 'from' (de) me in respect to its Seinsgeltung, its 'being-status.' There-upon the epoche is also the measure of being and cannot be measured by anything else" (KH, 191). The function of reason differs profoundly in Kant and Husserl. For Kant, as has been seen to some extent, intuition refers back to the thinking (Denken) that limits it, while for Husserl, simply thinking refers back to the evidence that fulfills it. "The problem of fullness (Fulle) has replaced that of limitation [boundary, Grenze]" (KH, 192).[48] Husserl has crushed any vestige of the thing-in-itself "which might insinuate itself into presence, decides that the presence of the thing itself is my present. The radical otherness attaching to presence is reduced to the nowness of the present; the presence of the Other is the present of myself" (HK, 192). Kant, with the allowance for the in-itself, has not locked the subject into subjectivity as has Husserl, and thus has allowed the Other to be another person. This is the context for more explicitly focusing on the boundary in relation to practical reason.

We have been able to glean from this digression with Ricoeur into the contrast between Husserl and Kant a sharp focus on the solution to this enigma created by the critique of Husserl's ontological omission and Kant's phenomenological deficit, mentioned throughout this detour. Ricoeur has been able to supply to the Husserlian omission the thinking of Being as limiting at the boundary, thus supplying to phenomenology its needed limit (boundary) and critique essential to such limit-boundary. We can now turn more explicitly to the question of ground in the realm of the practical.

CHAPTER 4

Limit and Ground
in Practical Reason

GROUND OF PRACTICAL REASON

We must now turn to Kantian practical philosophy in order to make clear the full significance of Ricoeur's critique and expansion of central Kantian elements in a philosophy of praxis that attempts to interarticulate Aristotelian teleology with Kantian deontology. We will first consider the question of Kantian limit and ground in practical judgment, then Ricoeur's expansion of Kantian elements and his own philosophy as a philosophy of limit-boundary, returning finally to the relation of his philosophy, precisely as a philosophy of limit, to that of deconstruction. This will make it possible to more clearly understand Ricoeur's integration of the teleological and the deontological in ethics, and the central role of the imagination in his philosophy. It is to Kant's treatment of practical reason that we will now turn.

Pure practical judgment as Kant conceives it in the second *Critique* is a determinative judgment that subsumes a general maxim under the universality of the categorical imperative, and is ultimately grounded in the moral law. For Kant, the will essentially is the power to act according to the representation of law, in contrast with nature, which acts according to laws[1]. Hence, the idea of law is the ground that determines the will of a rational being. And the true function of reason as a practical power, as one that is to have influence on the will, is to produce a will that is good in itself.

In the "Typic of Pure Practical Judgment,"[2] the determinateness of nature becomes a type permitting the universalization through which the will is grounded. The determination of nature becomes a symbol, through the form of lawfulness in general supplied by the understanding, that renders the supersensuous determination of the will. Kant is careful to preserve the purity of practical reason, even in its dealing with action and maxims. This is the same problem that Kant confronts in dealing with the incentive of reason in practical judgment. He consistently maintains the purity of the will and the lack of recourse to intuition, and thus cannot allow the mistaken interpretation of input from the imagination by way of schema. And, at least in part, it is precisely the purpose of this important section on "The Typic of Pure Practical Judgment" to preserve the purity of reason and will in pure practical judgments, while showing how actions relate to the pure practical reason without jeopardizing the purity and a priority of its law.

Kant says expressly in that section: "to the law of freedom which is a causality not sensuously conditioned, and consequently to the concept of the absolutely good, no intuition and hence no schema can be supplied for the purpose of applying it *in concreto*" (CPrR, 71). That is why there is no need for the imagination's contribution to practical judgments in such a reflection on the pure practical reason. Thus, there is a problem with any attempt to interpret a schema or schematization in the pure practical reason: the type does not provide a schematization, but rather a law: "and the understanding can supply to an idea of reason not a schema of sensibility but a law" (CPrR, 71). But this law, Kant admits, is a "natural law" that can be used only in its *formal aspect* . . . the form of *lawfulness in general*. Kant make it clear that it is nature "in its pure intelligible form" (CPrR, 71) that serves as the type of judgment. He even adds: "Only rationalism of judgments is suitable to the use of moral laws, for rationalism takes no more from sensuous nature than that which pure reason can also think for itself, i.e., lawfulness, and conversely transfers into the supersensuous nothing more than can be actually exhibited by actions in the world of sense according to a formal rule of natural law in general" (CPrR, 71). Thus for Kant there is no "sensibilizing" of the moral law, nor any admittance of any element of intuition. Lawfulness of nature comes from the understanding.

It is necessary to invoke here the distinction between pure practical reason and simply practical reason. For reason to be practical, for actions to take place as events in nature, according to the laws of nature, some relation to intuition is needed. But that is an entirely different issue from the one before him in considering pure practical reason in his moral philosophy. In pure practical reason, the analysis of which he is trying to establish in the *Critique of Practical Reason*, there is no such need. Here he is concerned with how the moral law determines the will a priori, and how the will, though morally necessitated, yet not necessitated in its choice, can be determined without the impurity of input from our sensuous human nature. Yet, in contrast, it would seem that he must consider possibilities of action in this context, which would belong to the sensuous, thus presenting a difficulty. For here he is concerned with applying freedom to actions that are possible for humans in the world of sense and thus according to the laws of nature. The status of possibility presents difficulty to a reason and will supposedly *pure*. It is on this possibility that we must focus, for Kant makes a distinction that is crucial to his development here.

In order to deal with this problem adequately, Kant indicates that this subsumption under a pure practical law of an action possible in the world of sense does "not concern the possibility of the action as an event of the world of sense" (CPrR, 71). Rather, this *possibility* is relegated entirely to the realm of understanding and maintains its purity. The lawfulness of nature, serving as a type, and not as a schema for sensibilization, thus, is not a schema of a *case* of action according to a category, but rather a type of a *law* itself, maintaining independence from the sensuous. This determination of the will is through the law alone without any sensuous determining ground. Hence, "the determination of the will through law alone and without any other determining ground . . . connects the concept of causality to conditions altogether different from those which constitute natural connections" (CPrR, 71). It is thus that the understanding supplies the type of the moral law, which entails only the formal aspect, the *lawfulness* of nature.[3]

INCENTIVES AND RESPECT IN PRACTICAL REASON

In the case of the incentives of practical reason and respect, Kant maintains, as expected, the complete purity of practical reason, as he has been seen to do in the above section in the case of the type of practical reason. Here, however, in the treatment of incentives, the difficulty is different. Before, he developed the notion of lawfulness as the type, tying causality of freedom with the law of reason by means of the lawfulness understood as a symbol of nature, and not as a schema. Here, in the case of the incentives, he must find objectively and subjectively something that would move us, a feeling, without jeopardizing the purity of practical reason. Hence, he has to move in the direction of the subjective incentive, while maintaining the purity of practical reason. Thus, he admits a feeling that is not reducible to that of inclination, but is rather independent of experience, a priori, and fixed on the moral law. This is what must be seen now.

According to Kant if there is to be any moral work, then moral law must directly determine the will, and there must be an explicit intention to fulfill the law, that is, the action must be done for the sake of the law. The task for Kant now is to maintain the purity of practical reason while uncovering this subjective determination of the will. Since humans are not necessitated to comply with or obey the moral law of reason, which is morally necessary, the moral law itself must determine from above their contingency of choice, for moral worth of actions. Otherwise a mixture and corrupting element would enter by way of inclinations. And we have already established that such actions, even in accordance with the law instead of for the sake of the law, are not of moral worth. This focus on pure subjective determination of the will centers on incentives, respect, interest, and maxim.

Kant understands by an incentive such a "subjective determining ground of a will whose reason does not by its nature necessarily conform to the objective law" (CPrR, 74). It follows from this understanding that the moral law itself must be the incentive of such a human will, so that thus, the objective determining ground becomes the "exclusive and subjectively sufficient determining ground of action." Thus, even though we humans do not have to do what we morally should do or what is morally necessary, we in effect have our choice (*die Willkür*) subjectively grounded in the moral law, and thus act for the sake of the law. We will do that which is right simply because it is our duty. Other motives cannot be this determining ground, or even enter the picture without risk. Thus, Kant virtually closes off any possibility of motives other than duty or obligation to the moral law entering into the subjective ground of action having moral worth.

What we have so far seen is the negative effect of moral law as an incentive, as checking inclinations, thus giving rise to a feeling of pain.[4] Here Kant goes on to refer to all inclination taken together, the satisfaction of which is called happiness, as constituting self-regard. Self-regard consists of self-love or selfishness (*philautia*) or self-satisfaction or self-conceit (*arrogantia*). While the pure practical law merely checks selfishness, it strikes down self-conceit. Selfishness then becomes "rational self love." Thus, the moral law precisely in this striking down of self-conceit checks any self-esteem resting only on sensibility.

More than this negative effect of the moral law, this law is in itself positive, and, as the form of freedom, it is at once the object of respect for the very reason that, in conflict with the inclinations, it weakens or checks selfishness and strikes down self-conceit. As striking down and thereby humiliating self-conceit, it becomes the object of "the greatest respect and thus the ground of a positive feeling which is not of empirical origin" (CPrR, 76). And this is a feeling that is produced by an intellectual cause, that can be known a priori, and that can be seen as necessary. Thus, the moral law is objectively a cause of respect. Kant wants to go further and show that the moral law is even subjectively the cause of respect, by invoking the fact that the moral law inevitably humbles all humans when they compare the sensuous propensity of their nature with the law. Since it removes the obstacle or resistance to the law, thus acting as a positive assistance to the causality of freedom, this feeling or respect for the moral law can be called a moral feeling. And this moral feeling is produced solely by reason.

Kant moves from the concept of the incentive to that of an interest, to that of a maxim, all coming from the top down in the sense that they are not polluted by the sensuous inclinations. An interest, proper to beings with reason, indicates an incentive of the will insofar as it is presented by reason. And for Kant, the law itself must be the incentive in morally good will, so it follows that the moral interest must be a pure nonsensuous interest of the practical reason alone, since it is an incentive of the will presented by reason. Now, since the concept of maxim rests on that of an interest, the maxim can be morally genuine only if it rests on the interest in obedience to the law. Thus we can see how Kant can say of all three concepts, incentive, interest, and maxim, that they "presuppose a limitation of the nature of the being, in that the subjective character of its choice does not of itself agree with the objective law of practical reason" (CPrR, 82).[5]

And it is precisely here that freedom can be seen in its limiting role. The causality of freedom is determinable through the moral law, and thus freedom as such consists in limiting all inclinations, including self-esteem, "to the condition of obedience to its pure law"[6] (CPrR, 81). For Kant, it is some kind of fanaticism to overstep the limits of reason, and here it would be a moral fanaticism. And what pure practical reason forbids is that we place the moral incentive anywhere else other than in the moral law itself, and that we not place the disposition thus brought into the maxims otherwise than in the respect for this same law. For Kant, pure practical reason "commands that we make the thought of duty, which strikes down all arrogance as well as vain self-love, the supreme life-principle of all human morality."[7]

Thus, for pure practical reason, the principle that grounds determination resides in subjectivity itself, that is, in pure reason giving the moral law. Subjectivity, as ground of determination (*Wille*), gives the moral law, yet also has a power of choice (*Willkür*) to enact the law. But when once the need for pure practical reason is replaced by the concern for actions in the concrete that require a maxim, and a general maxim at that, in order for it to be universalized by being subsumed under the categorical imperative, one has to reflect in a different manner than in the case of the pure practical reason. For what must be considered is how one comes up with the very maxim that is to be subsumed under the moral law through the categorical imperative for actions with moral worth. To fill this gap, we must reflect on the reflective judgment both in its role in theoretical and practical reason, perhaps going beyond Kant's explicit doctrine, but in the present context, remaining true to his doctrine and making sense of it.

REFLECTIVE JUDGMENT

Much of what has preceded, to be completed, entails Kant's rather sophisticated doctrine of the reflective judgment, which he only develops at length in his third *Critique*, but which is required in all three *Critiques* if they are to be rounded out and made relevant to life and to knowledge of the world and nature as we live, act, and produce sciences. For, even in knowledge, Kant rather explicitly indicates the place of the reflective judgment to be at the heart of empirical inquiry in search of the empirical laws of nature. The natural scientist presupposes the reflective judgment in two ways. First and more generally, in order to seek empirical laws, there must be some assumption of a unity to nature that is not accessible to knowledge, and that is required in some sense for there to be any empirical laws of nature. This is the sense in which Kant says: "Particular empirical laws, in respect of what is in them left undetermined by these universal laws, must be considered in accordance with such a unity as they would have if an understanding (although not our understanding) had furnished them to our cognitive faculties, so as to make possible a system of experience according to particular laws of nature."[8] This is a strictly subjective unity, given by our reflection, to regulate our knowledge. And it is the *purposiveness* of nature that we give or supply ourselves, so that we proceed in empirical science as though there were an understanding, not our own, that contained the ground of the unity of the variety of nature's empirical laws. But this concept of purposiveness has its origin solely in reflective judgment, as can be seen in relation to the judgment of the beautiful. This is the assumption in the reflective judgment when it ascends from the particular in nature to the universal, and ascends to further and further unities. For instance, the three laws of motion derived by Kepler, and the laws of earthly dynamics derived by Galileo, are themselves the attempt to ascend to ever more inclusive unities. Both of their efforts, however, are brought to further unity by Newton's universal law of gravity. And all of these assume the unity of nature as a subjective assumption, as a regulative idea of reflective judgment, which says nothing objective about nature itself.

The reflective judgment is distinguished from that of the determinative in that it begins with the particulars and seeks to find the universal. The determinative judgment, in contrast, begins with the universal (law, principle, rule), and subsumes the particular under it, which, as transcendental, furnishes a priori the conditions in conformity with which the subsumption under that universal is alone possible. Thus, the determinative judgment simply subsumes under a given a priori law, and does not need to seek the universal as is the case with reflective judgments.

The reflective judgment, on the other hand, must subsume under a law that is not given, and that must be sought in the reflection upon objects for which we must find and supply the law. Kant affirms in this context a firm conviction: "Since now no use of the cognitive faculties can be permitted without principles, the reflective judgment just in such cases serves as a principle for itself,"[9] as we have seen in the cases above. And this principle must serve as a "mere subjective principle for the purposive employment of our cognitive faculties, i.e., for reflection upon a class of objects."[10]

And although the first two *Critiques* have been mainly concerned with determinative judgments, theoretical and practical, it is clear from the above that the reflective judgment has been in the background, as seen for theoretical knowledge, and as can be seen now in the case of practical reason. At first it seems that in the realm of the practical, the reflective judgment is not at all involved, since there is no use of the imagination in such pure practical judgments. For, such a judgment, according to Kant, is a determinative judgment that subsumes a maxim under universality itself, the moral law. In the case of the pure practical judgment, then, the imagination is not entailed at all, and the judgment borrows from understanding the lawfulness of nature in general, as seen above. There is no schematization involved. The determinateness of nature thus becomes the type through which we formally judge.

Keeping this use of lawfulness in the realm of pure practical reason in view, and distinguishing the pure from the simply practical reason, prevents gross misrepresentations of Kant's moral philosophy and the pure practical reason. If we want to critique his moral philosophy, and we do, we must first understand it as it is, and not reduce it to some simplistic moral philosophy of subsuming our particular actions under moral law by the categorical imperative. For Kant nowhere wants to do so. What he subsumes is general maxims, which themselves serve as the general universals for the subsumption of lesser maxims, which need such subsumption. To reach down to particular actions, Kant would be the first to admit the need for further general maxims, which serve as mediators between actions and the maxims universalized in the use of the categorical imperative. For instance, I cannot universalize the rather subjective maxim for anyone and everyone that it is moral for me to develop my skills to become the best philosopher I can. I must take a different maxim for that universalization: all of us should develop our skills to the best of our ability. That I should become the best philosopher that I can is a maxim for me and not to be as such universalized. Then, under the universalized maxim, that all should develop their skills, this other maxim for me is subsumed, and the particular actions under it.Thus, one must take care to distinguish properly as Kant himself does between pure practical reason, the main concern of the second *Critique*, and practical reason and action, which, as not pure, entails what is excluded from pure practical reason as pure, and as determined by the moral law. There is for Kant no direct determination of concrete action in pure practical reason, but only of general maxims. Thus, there is no sensibilization of pure practical reason or of the moral law. Yet practical judgment requires a preliminary teleologically guided reflection arriving at concepts that formulate aspects of situations in the phenomenal world. The place of maxims in moral judgment parallels that of empirical and specific laws of nature in cognitive judgment, as long as one keeps in mind that this holds only for the general maxims and not particular ones for particular individuals. Thus, one can say that the formulation of maxims that express actions under moral consideration presupposes teleological orientation. And for this we can see the parallel need for reflective judgment. For in this reflective judgment, the particulars are subsumed under a rule, and the moral agent is looking for the general moral rule or maxim that can hold not only for him, but also for all. The general maxim must therefore be able to be subsumed under the universal law, or be universalizable according to the categorical imperative.

The manner of this treatment leads to Ricoeur's manner of expanding on Kant, yet we have remained, I think, entirely faithful to Kant's own meaning. The above doctrine is true to a strict interpretation of Kant, correcting a naive interpretation according to which particular actions are universalized, which is contrary to Kant's doctrine and makes a mockery of his view. But this strict Kantian doctrine is not put forth as though it does not require critique and expansion. For that is precisely the intent of our focus: to go beyond Kant following the direction of Ricoeur, and, in doing so, to appropriate postmodern deconstructive insights, while redirecting our vision according to a different basic option.

In the context of the pure practical reason, considered above in relation to the practical reason, it is necessary for us now to turn to the distinction Kant makes in "The Dialectic of Pure Reason in Defining the Concept of the Highest Good," where Kant makes a distinction in the concept of the highest good. It has been seen that the sole determining ground of the pure will is the moral law, which itself is merely *formal*. As such, it requires that only the form of the maxim be universally legislative, abstracting from all material aspects and thus from any object of volition. Thus, no object of the will nor any material aspect, can be seen as having any determining ground of the pure will, which can come only from the moral law given by pure reason. "One sees from the Analytic that when we assume any object, under the name of good, as the determining ground of the will prior to the moral law, and then derive the supreme practical principle from it, this always produces heteronomy and rules out the moral principle" (CPrR, 113). This heteronomy is reintroduced, however, when consideration is opened, as it was above, to practical reason as such, without limiting it to pure practical reason. Before turning to the definition of the highest good in chapter 2 of this "Dialectic of Pure Practical Reason," Kant adds an insight regarding pure practical reason, relating the concept of the highest good to the moral law. Here the highest good is still included within *pure* practical reason, and as an object of will only under this guise. For Kant, "it is self-evident not only that, if the moral law is included as the supreme condition in the concept of the highest good, the highest good is then the object, but also that the concept of it and the idea of its existence as possible through our practical reason are likewise the determining ground of the pure will." He attributes this to the fact that this moral law that is included and thought in this concept of the highest good *as its "supreme condition*," and includes no other object, determines the will as required by the principle of autonomy. Kant wants to make sure that there is no possibility of being misunderstood as contradicting himself here, where he allows the concept of the highest good into the picture of determination of the will, but only as included within the moral law in its conception. The moral law is included and thought in this very concept of the highest good, so that in determining the will, it is really the moral law alone that determines the will. With this point firmly made, he now turns to the distinction necessary to the proper understanding of the highest good, a distinction that will allow us to incorporate a relation of Aristotelian virtue ethics of happiness with that of Kantian obligation, given some adjustments to Kantian pure doctrine.

Kant shows here that happiness and virtue are two specifically different elements of the highest good, both included in the concept of the "highest good," and in a way not entirely alien to Aristotle and the later tradition, but interpreted, of course, now within Kant's own limits. The highest can mean both the "supreme" (*supremum*) or the "perfect" (*consummatum*). The "highest" (the supreme) is the unconditional condition, "the condition which is subordinate to no other (*originarium*)"; and the "perfect" is the "whole which is no part of a yet larger whole of the same kind (*perfectissimum*)."[11] It follows that virtue is on the side of the highest good, the supreme condition as the supreme good, and what makes us worthy to be happy. But for the entire object of will, the perfect or complete object, happiness is required. Now Kant goes on to add that (CPrR, 117) this highest good is a synthesis of concepts and known a priori. Since this is an a priori necessary synthesis, and not derivable from experience, the deduction of this concept must be transcendental. "It is a priori (morally) necessary to bring forth the highest good

through the freedom of the will: the condition of its possibility, therefore, must rest solely on a priori grounds of knowledge" (CPrR, 117).
Now Kant, as is well known, resolves the conflict of the antinomy
regarding the highest good by the distinction of the two worlds, the phenomenal and the noumenal, in which the moral human being exists.
Thus in the interrelation between happiness and virtue, causality cannot
be relegated merely to the phenomenal, but must also take into account
the realm of freedom and its causality. "But not only since I am justified
in thinking of my existence as that of a noumenal in an intelligible world
but also since I have in the moral law a pure intellectual determining
ground of my causality (in the sensuous world), it is not impossible that
the morality of intention would have a necessary relation as cause to
happiness as an effect in the sensuous world; but this relation is indirect,
mediated by an intelligible Author of nature" (CPrR, 115). Now that we
have seen how Kant is adamantly consistent to maintain the purity of
practical reason and its determination, we can return to the question of
practical reason and limit, recalling that Kant refers to a certain extension of cognition in this realm.

LIMIT AND PRACTICAL REASON

Kant is particularly keen to warn us about two transgressions of the limit
of practical reason: first, in this realm of thinking ourselves in the world of
understanding, we cannot try to enter by intuition or sensation, for sense
is limited to appearances as has already been mentioned, and has no access
to the things themselves, and thus cannot have access through any intuition
to the world of thought; and second, we cannot borrow any object of the
will, that is, a motive, from the world of understanding, for that would also
constitute a transgression of the limit, and make a claim to grasp something
that we cannot know.[12] For Kant, then, we must be careful about the manner in which we speak of the world of understanding, even in this practical realm. For it is only a "point of view which reason finds itself compelled
to take outside the appearances in order to *conceive itself as practical*,
which would not be possible if the influences of the sensibility had a determining power on man, but which is necessary unless he is to be denied the
consciousness of himself as an intelligence, and consequently as a rational
cause, energizing by reason, that is, operating freely."[13] This allows us only
to *think* it as formal conditions, but not at all in regard to a definite object
belonging to the laws of nature in the sensible world. Thus Kant allows for
two systems of laws: that of the mechanism of nature belonging to the sensible world; and that of the intelligible world, the "whole system of rational beings as things in themselves."[14]

Kant often refers to the practical reason as thinking itself into the world of understanding, but without breaching the limit as such as long as it makes no claim to have entered it by intuition or sensuous receptivity. This preserves the limitation of cognitive faculties involved in (pure) practical reason to the understanding, with no recourse to imagination. The world of sense does not give any laws to reason in determining the will, and is positive only in this single point that this freedom as a negative characteristic is at the same time conjoined with a (positive) faculty and even with a causality of reason, which Kant designates a will, namely, "a faculty of so acting that the principle of the actions shall conform to the essential character of a rational motive, that is, the condition that the maxim have universal validity as a law."[15]

Kant, in the same section, "The Extreme Limit [*Grenze*] of Practical Philosophy," warns against another transgression of the limit in practical philosophy. Since explanation is limited to "that which we can reduce to laws the object of which can be given in some possible experience,"[16] and since freedom cannot be so reduced to the laws of nature and hence cannot be expressed as objective reality in any possible experience, it cannot be explained. Kant has often affirmed in his practical philosophy that freedom is a necessary hypothesis of reason as a presupposition of the moral law. In fact, in the preface to the *Critique of Practical Reason,*[17] Kant states that freedom, "among all the ideas of speculative reason is the only one whose possibility we know a priori. We do not understand it, but we know it as the condition of the moral law which we do know." Kant goes on later in the preface to state this as the enigma of the critical philosophy: "which lies in the fact that we must renounce the objective reality of the supersensible use of the categories in speculation and yet can attribute this reality to them in respect to the objects of pure practical reason" (CPrR, 5). He is quick to make it clear, however, that a thorough analysis of the practical use of reason prevents us from claiming any extension of our knowledge to the supersensible, and provides no "theoretical determination of the categories" (CPrR, 5). Kant goes on to address what is meant in attributing reality to these concepts: an object is so attributed to them insofar as they are contained in the necessary determination of the will a priori; or "because they are indissolubly connected with the object of this determination." The inconsistency is dissolved because this entails a different *use* of these concepts than that entailed by speculative reason. And in the last paragraph of the *Groundwork of the Metaphysics of Morals*, Kant emphasizes these different uses of reason: "The speculative use of reason *in regard to nature* leads to the absolute necessity of some supreme cause of the *world*; the practical use of reason *with regard to freedom* leads also to absolute necessity—but only to the absolute necessity *of the laws of action* for a rational being as such" (GMM, 131, Paton). Now, while it is an essential principle for these uses of reason to push to the consciousness of necessity, it is an equally essential limitation of reason that it cannot have insight into necessity except on the basis of a condition, so that it seeks ultimately the unconditionally necessary, "and sees itself compelled to assume this without any means of making it comprehensible—happy enough if only it can find a concept compatible with this presupposition" (Ibid.). Kant is thus defending the incomprehensibility of the basic elements of moral philosophy, for he sees that we cannot make comprehensible the absolute necessity of the unconditioned practical law, the categorical imperative. Thus, he concludes this work with the statement: "And thus, while we do not comprehend the practical unconditioned necessity of the moral imperative, we do comprehend its *incomprehensibility*. This is all that can fairly be asked of a philosophy which presses forward in its principles to the very limit [boundary, *zur Grenze der menschlichen Vernunft*] of human reason" (GMM, 131, Paton). Kant is here putting his humble cards on the table regarding the bounds of practical reason, and the bounds of philosophy, for this treatment of the practical and freedom is central to the whole edifice of his critical philosophy. We can now see how, within this limit, Kant limits explanation in relation to the incentive in practical reason. Since for Kant, "where determination according to laws of nature ceases, there all *explanation* ceases also," it is just as subjectively impossible to explain how humans can take an interest in the moral law as to explaining the freedom of the will.[18]

RICOEUR AND LIMIT

Paul Ricoeur has consistently unfolded his philosophy within the keen awareness of, and attunement to, the Kantian philosophy of limits, yet without reducing his philosophy to that of Kant. This is the context of his creative reinterpretation of the Kantian limit idea that, as such, does not provide an object of experience and is not constitutive of knowledge, but that can serve a regulative role in directing reason to totality and to completion regarding what is unconditioned.[19]

When referring to Ricoeur's thought as a philosophy at the limit, however, it would be a distortion not to mention the correlate, extension (*Erweiterung*) beyond the limit, and Ricoeur's basic extensions of Kant's own later extensions, to which deconstruction responds quite differently, if at all. It is noteworthy that deconstruction as a philosophy of limit does not pay attention even to Kant's own extensions of limit, to which Ricoeur adverts in the process of extending beyond them. Thus,

in contrast to deconstruction, for Ricoeur limit and extension are correlated. There are two contexts relevant for our discussion where Ricoeur
extends upon Kantian elements, themselves extensions:[20] first, regarding
freedom in its connection to the law in practical philosophy in relation
to theoretical philosophy that receives a practical extension beyond its
limitation within the antinomy of pure reason; and, second, in the *Critique of Judgment*, by means of the reflective judgment, which "performs, precisely, an extension of judgment."[21] Now we turn to Ricoeur's
pursuit of the movement of extensions further than Kant.

First, Ricoeur admits reproaching Kant for having constructed his
second *Critique* on the model of the first, by applying to the practical
field the distinction between the transcendental and the empirical, without taking into account the structures proper to human action."[22]
Ricoeur's critique of Kant and his own contemporary vision reveals a
harmony between man and nature, overcoming the modern antinomy
between freedom and nature or necessity by means of an enriched nature
in man and man in nature. For instance, his adjustment in the Kantian
doctrine on the antinomy between nature and freedom can be summa-
rized this way: first, sensibility must be capable of a relation to willing
as a motive for decision that *inclines without compelling*; second, a
rational principle must be capable of touching me in a way analogous to
that of sensible goods. Indeed, for Kant, as seen above, respect is a *sui
generis* feeling of subordination of the will to a law without any other
intermediary influence on sensibility, so that, in respecting its own rationality, the will receives nothing, but spontaneously produces the feeling
of respect in itself, thereby restoring sovereignty to reason.[23] Ricoeur, in
another place, observes: "Respect, as a practical feeling, posits a limit to
my ability to act," still close to the Kantian context of respecting humanity as an objective end, as an end that I should never act against.[24] In
expanding the function and role of respect to parallel that of the transcendental imagination in the cognitive synthesis, Ricoeur also changes
the role of duty from the strictly Kantian role. Rather, for him the relation between motive and project is far more inclusive if liberated from
such a Kantian ethical a priori. In a way that entails the possibility of
man as bodily comportment, Ricoeur also considers desire to be a
motive or a value and not only a cause.[25] Such spontaneities can incline
without compelling the will and thus serve as a basis for decision without mitigating active freedom as human and receptive. To recast the
Kantian relationship between freedom and necessity in phenomenological terms, Ricoeur speaks of the reciprocity between the voluntary and
the involuntary. Given this experiential focus, he dispenses with the need
to postulate freedom as a cause in the strictly Kantian sense. Indeed, for
him the whole of the voluntary in all three of its moments must be recep-

tive to the involuntary as already human and therefore as liberated from a causal language that is reductive of motive, powers of action, and life. Lived nature, which includes the weddedness of man to nature both within and outside himself, the lived body, and lived existence reveal a freedom in being-in-the-world that does not separate man from the lived world and lived nature, but, rather, bespeaks a quasi-unity of existing man with the world and within himself or herself.

Second, because of the above, Ricoeur considers the formalism of duty to be introduced too early into the split between desire and obligation, as a "consequence of the dualism between the principle of obligation and the fact of desire."[26] The third point to which Ricoeur turns now, following from the two already spelled out, is that his claim for the primacy of the teleology of living well is due to his assignment of a positive place to desire in the structure of human action, as just mentioned. And this desire he does not interpret as a replica of sensible receptivity in the theoretical order. Fourth, Ricoeur now suggests that his analyses of semantic innovation in metaphorical and narrative contexts enlarge the field of the third *Critique*, but at the cost of his "refusal to distinguish between reflective judgment and determinant judgment, a refusal expressed in the recognition of the function of redescription or, better yet, of refiguration, performed by all the innovating and, in this sense, poetic forms of discourse. One can legitimately see in this function of refiguration an extension of the Kantian theory of productive imagination beyond the region assigned to it by the theory of reflective judgment."[27] Some of these points must be explored further.[28]

Appropriating Kant's doctrine, Ricoeur contends that objective knowledge is the labor of understanding (*Verstand*), but understanding does not exhaust the power of reason (*Vernunft*) that remains the function of the unconditioned. This distance and this tension between reason, as the function of the unconditioned, and understanding, as the function of conditioned knowledge, finds an expression in the notion of limit that for Kant is not to be identified with boundary, as we have so clearly seen. This concept of "limit" does not primarily imply that our knowledge is limited, but, rather, that the quest for the unconditioned puts limits on the claim of objective knowledge (the thinking of Being limits the knowledge of object). "'Limit' is not a fact, but an act,"[29] meaning that in its quest for the unconditioned, reason actively puts limits to the claim of objective knowledge to become absolute. Ricoeur, however, wants to give to the limit-concept of Kant a less negative function than this prohibition addressed by reason to the claim of objective knowledge to absolutize itself. Rather, for Ricoeur, the "empty" requirement of an Unconditioned finds a certain fulfillment in the indirect presentation of metaphorical language, which says what things are like rather than what things are, and that the "is like" implies an "is not."[30] And in contrast to deconstruction, Ricoeur wants to advert to a further and deeper opening, rather than fixate on the closure of the opening.

At this point it must be asked whether Ricoeur has adequately addressed the positive element of deconstruction, and whether he has overcome modernity. To the second question, it must be stated that Ricoeur has opposed modernity all the way back to his first formulation of the theory of symbolic, showing that the fullness of sense of existence and experience cannot be exhaustively and adequately articulated at the conceptual level, that there is always a residue, a remainder to be deciphered, that the fullness of sense is always elusive. For Ricoeur there has always been a dynamic and living tension between the level of logos and that of the richness and fullness of experience, between the *Ursprung* of experience and the *Logos* of rationality. He does not, however, go the distance with deconstruction in opting for the chaos, for the undecidable, for the primacy of the flux. Ricoeur's whole effort is to keep alive the tension between the direction toward logos and the fullness and richness of experience. In this sense he opposes the enlightenment and modernity without losing sight of their gain, yet overcoming their deficiency.

Due to his expansions on the Kantian philosophy at the limit, Ricoeur is able to interarticulate the moral, as encompassing the articulation or actualization of the ethical aim in norms characterized at once by a "claim to universality and by an effect of constraint"[31] with the "ethical" as encompassing the aim of an accomplished life. Following from his critique of Kant's practical reason and freedom, as seen above, and due to the expansion of Kantian themes, Ricoeur is able to turn in a positive way to a priority of the teleological, putting into place the evaluative element of Aristotelian ethics to subtend the moral imperative of Kant and deconstruction. This might seem to be diametrically opposed to deconstruction, but there is another aspect of this move.

Ricoeur's inclusion of certain positive elements of deconstruction is manifest in his recent treatment of the alterity of cosmic time and in his appropriation of the alterity that the face to face actualizes beyond interiority. In the latter case, Ricoeur appropriates the face to face developed by Levinas in the context of the tension that he sees between inwardness stressed by Husserl and exteriority emphasized by Levinas.[32] Thus, in these appropriations of a certain positive element of deconstruction, Ricoeur's rich and full treatment of ethicomoral philosophy, entailing the points above, emerges as one of the most viable ethics today.

In rejoining the discussion of deconstruction and limit, by turning now to the philosophy of Paul Ricoeur as a viable and positive alternative to present-day deconstruction, several preliminary points must be clarified. First, how this philosophy fits into the option discussed in chapter 1, and, second, how his philosophy at the limit relates to limit as we have interpreted it. Turning to the first point, it can be seen that Ricoeur's entire philosophy is attuned in a special, unique way to the openness, fullness, and richness of existence, where concrete sense is expressed, and to which he often in the past alluded in terms of the surplus or fullness of sense and of existence. And, although his thought is anchored in such a richness and abyss, he never wavers in his faith or option in making sense out of experience and existence, but a sense ever attuned to the creative process and to the ongoing re-creation that subtends all thinking, knowledge, action, and interpretation. Thus, in turning to a more explicit development of Ricoeur's position in terms of these focuses and questions, we will be able to shed more light on the issues as we go along, and reveal an astonishing contemporary philosophical thought sophisticated enough to encompass the problems issuing from deconstructive thinking without buying into the belief in the priority of the closure intrinsic to logos. And it is my contention, as a working hypothesis, that this thought is far more appropriate to the issues focused upon, making sense where deconstruction deconstructs. One has the feeling throughout that Ricoeur is addressing something that resonates with our own experience and with our reflections on that experience, and thus provides a fitting alternative, not oblivious to closure or to the need for constant creative openness and reinterpretation. I have to admit, however, that his thinking, although accounting for the positive element of deconstruction, differs from deconstruction on vital points.[33] He will be seen briefly to disagree basically with the antilogo-centrism of deconstruction. I shall now reflect further with Ricoeur on these issues, beginning with a focus on the second point mentioned above.

It seems to me that both senses of limit treated above obtain in his philosophy. As will become clear throughout the discussion on his philosophy, Ricoeur clearly appropriates the Kantian limit placed by reason on the use of the categories in experience for knowledge. And in the second sense of limit, he sees the double expressions (symbols and metaphors) as modes of accessing for which Kant did not explicitly allow. There is still an ambiguity here, however, as to whether and to what extent this is really a limit placed from the other in Peirce's sense seen above. Indirect expressions, especially symbols, are his way of extending beyond the Kantian limit; and further, his changes in Kant's view of reflective judgments, productive imagination, and schematism, now seen in a full philosophy of action that requires a hermeneutic, will be the path to fulfilling the second sense of limit. And Ricoeur clearly, in his later writings, comes to grips precisely with the other as other.[34]

Ricoeur employs limit in a way that includes both senses mentioned above, but with a distinctive difference. He remains strict in interpreting the Kantian sense of limit against any tendency to Hegelian totalization in appropriating the Hegelian sense of freedom as actualization against Kant's too formal sense of freedom. And against Kant, Ricoeur allows the use of indirect language, that is, beginning with symbols, then metaphors and narrative, as ways of expressing the boundary, and as an indirect way of access to the so-called noumenal that does not at all constitute knowledge, but affords a way to think, not within or without, but at the boundary.[35] It is now finally necessary to face explicitly the critique of his philosophy by deconstruction mentioned above.

A DECONSTRUCTIVE CRITIQUE OF RICOEUR

Deconstruction challenges Ricoeur's attempts to address time and narrative, proposing that there might be other ways in which language resolves the aporiae of time if the closure of language and of time is interpreted differently or is deconstructed.[36] It is clear that deconstruction (here, David Wood) has opted for a view of metaphor, and, indeed, of language as such, which calls for an interruption, rather then a synthesis, within a view of language as a system of signs. This critique by deconstruction makes sense only if one ignores or disagrees with Ricoeur's view of the semantic priority in language and continuity in time.[37] By extension, the same critique, in a more general way, could be made of Ricoeur especially in the context of his ethicomoral position in that he operates within the closure of language, tradition, institutions, and so on, following the clotural reading discussed above. He is in need of being deconstructed in terms of the ellipsis necessarily to be found, according to the belief of the deconstructionist, in his texts, by means of the double reading. But that technique, already seen to presuppose itself as absolutely given without reason and simply in a belief that we have considered to be misguided, is a bit supererogatory. Ricoeur does not allow for such an ellipsis, which itself absolutely presupposes a priority of the flux, but, rather, only for a sort of an imbalance due to the fullness of meaning in experience and existence. His belief, however, and admittedly only a belief like that of deconstruction, favors making sense in making sense; values in evaluating; and responding to the face of the other responsibly and personally. Yet, as has been seen, two points of contact have emerged: first in Ricoeur's affinities for Levinas' face to face, suffering, and responsibility; and his allegiance to the alterity of time. Finally, in this context I must mention one last point: Ricoeur's view of reading a text, reconfiguring and appropriating its world, thus expanding and fusing one's own horizons, provides a healthy and compelling alternative to clotural reading, and is far more rewarding and insightful, leading to richer Being-in-the-world.

In conclusion, we have responded with both a yes as well as a no to the underlying limit of deconstruction as a philosophy of limit. The yes: to alterity, to the "other" to which any phenomenological heritage must be opened, and a limited yes to the closure of logos, as seen above. And the no: to the priority or deference given to closure intrinsic to logos and its openness; and to any reduction to a naive view of values, time, sign, and language.[38] But there is a *latent contradiction* in deconstruction between the positive element, which I have stressed, and the negative element that needs critique: the positive element reintroduces with force the "other"; but its account of the flux, of time, of sign, of consciousness, and of language eliminates any possibility of experiencing or accessing that other, as shall become fully clear in the ensuing chapters. For such a deconstructive consideration, leading to alterity, is much like the modern account of sense experience in cognition. Perception was broken down to sense experience, which was further decomposed into impressions within a conscious flow considered to be discrete because of the point-like instant now. Against this reductionistic view, the philosophical return to lived experience brought back into view the holistic human perspective.

Likewise with deconstruction, the tenuous human ground or foundation is reduced, drawing away from the lived experience of time and language. Rather, attention is directed to the alterity of the undecidable, of the unnameable and, in another context, of retention and protention as other than the instant now, and in language from the semantic to the syntactic. Language is no longer considered to be saying something in a discourse: rather, language (*la langue*) is interpreted strictly in terms of signs in diacritical relations, the meaning of which comes to be from the placing of such signs, from the syntax, all happening according to chance: thus, the ardent antihumanism at the core of such a reduction. And it is in this context of alterity from which obligation emerges, from the impersonal cloaked with the quasipersonal. The discreteness of time so interpreted, the process of which is meant to sustain a set of signs in diacritical relations of differences rooted in *différance*, emerges as an effect from a further time as alterity, the other time producing these effects, including protentions and retentions, and "without why."[39] These are said to undergird as effects, phenomenological priority in experience, semantic priority in language (*le langage*), the lived present, and the personal. The fundamental point at issue is whether the deconstructive turn in moving against such elements provides a view of time and sign in language able to sustain anything about saying something to someone, or other than silence. Further, it seems that obligation and responsibility, even as taking place in the collapse of reason, and without why, must be constituted in lived experience, just as any meaningful communication involving language must have continuity to sustain a viable view of language to which trace is so important.

Several paths of inquiry have emerged in this discussion that must be taken up and investigated in the following chapters. The central role of the imagination, again adjusted by Ricoeur from Kant, and in stark contrast to the role of the imagination in deconstruction, makes it necessary to focus at length on the imagination. From this investigation, it will be necessary to turn to the nature of language, sign, and trace, contrasting the views of Ricoeur and deconstruction, and leading to a discussion on the nature of time and the lived present in relation to sign. Finally, after considering these issues the stage will then be set for a full-blown consideration of ethics at the limit of reason in part III, contrasting Ricoeur's view with those of deconstruction considered in the part I.

PART II

Imagination at the Boundary of Reason

CHAPTER 5

Imagination at the Boundary

INTRODUCTION

In a special way today, when the emphasis on the end of metaphysics puts the very possibility of philosophy into question, the interpretation given to the role of the imagination, especially of the productive imagination, can shed light on the philosophical enterprise for the future. Into whatever form it evolves, continental philosophy, to be viable and adequate, must confront head-on the challenge from postmodern deconstructive thinkers. It is our purpose to dwell on this challenge now in the light of the role of the imagination in relation to ethicomorals and to assess its positive contribution to recent thinking. Then, we will present in part III a philosophy at the limit-boundary of reason as one of the most innovative and fruitful currents of contemporary thinking in ethics. A first brief focus on the recent adaptations of the role of the Kantian productive imagination will be helpful to distinguish currents of thought in addressing the limit-boundary of thinking in relation to the imagination.

At least three distinct interpretations of the role of imagination emerge in philosophy at its end-limit. First, in Heidegger's finitization of reason, the productive imagination is the source of reason itself and, as such, of the limit placed by reason, all of which, in Heidegger's view, are rooted in "primordial time,"[1] bespeaking the closure that must be transgressed—the closure toward the meaning of Being and toward Being itself within language and within time. In this position, as we shall see, the Kantian heterogeneity between the sensible and the intelligible is overcome in a common root, the imagination, thus clearly overcoming the Kantian ground of reason and its problematic elements in the realm of practical reason and its ground. Rendering imagination central in this direction of fundamental ontology leads to an "originary ethos" in the context of the truth of being, rendering ethics, like traditional metaphysics and epistemology, secondary as derivative.

A second distinctive role, one arising out of Heidegger's proclamation of the end of philosophy, and from a postmodern and deconstructive critique of Heidegger, transforms Heidegger's interpretation of the central role of the Kantian productive imagination by subordinating it to language or chance, thus radically adjusting the nature of the end of metaphysics. For the deconstruction of Derrida, the closure results from the propensity to fixate on the effect within the flux of the *différance*, a fixation that prevents the transgressing of philosophy to *différance*, dissemination, and the "play of reason." And Lyotard, rendering the treatment of the sublime in the *Critique of Judgment* as central and paradigmatic, seeking to displace any conceptual rule, thus supports *invention,* which displaces the *innovation* in the "game" that makes new moves within the rules of the game. He extends the indeterminate dimension of the limited role of the reflective judgment of the sublime in Kant's use to a paradigmatic role in thinking, leading to an antilogocentrism in agreement with Derrida. Thus there is an attempt on the part of both to supplant the primacy of the Kantian theoretical understanding in its knowing function in favor of some priority of language that renders the human role (of imagination) passive and secondary to that of the "other." Further, language in their employ loses its semantic priority in favor of semiological priority.

But there is yet another way of appropriating the imagination in relation to "closure," one that does not go by either of the paths above and one that has not lost original creativity, yet takes into account the input from the *other* at the boundary. If reason is not produced by imagination, then reason itself from above limits knowledge to experience, putting the imagination in a central position in knowledge as it is for Cassirer, Marcel, and Ricoeur. And with the famous phenomenal/noumenal distinction overturned, this limit enacted by reason on human knowledge encompasses knowledge within the experience of reality itself, but allows reason to reach beyond the boundary to something of a more far-reaching significance, as it does in the philosophies of both Marcel and Ricoeur. And in the second sense of limit-boundary seen in chapter 1, the "other" acts also as a limit, supplementing the role of reason in limiting and setting the boundary.

During the development of these alternative positions in philosophy today springing from the role allowed to the imagination, the challenge from deconstruction as developing in dialogue with the phenomenological and semiological traditions will be brought to its depth and intensity, allowing the central issues at stake in ethics today to emerge. To clarify fully the alternative possibilities, the problematic role of the imagination in Kant's philosophy, together with the interpretation given to this role by later thinkers,[2] must be brought to light.

KANT'S PRODUCTIVE IMAGINATION

In turning to the role of the imagination for Kant, it is helpful to recall a few fundamental points in each of the three *Critiques* especially focusing upon the transcendental and productive imagination rather than on the empirical and reproductive role. In the first *Critique* the role of the imagination, of central importance for theoretical knowledge no matter how the first or second editions are read, one of the problematic elements is precisely the relation between imagination, as psychological reproductive and as transcendental productive, and reason's act of limiting. In the Kantian context of thinking, reason thinks (*Denken*) in line with the sense of the categories beyond their empirical usage, which thinking is at once a critique of transcendental illusion as well as a justification of the ideas of reason.[3] Here Kant does not seem to consider the imagination to be involved, but rather sees the understanding moving toward the unconditioned.

In the second *Critique*, as seen in chapter 4, pure practical reason does not require the imagination in its determinative judgment, but rather reason, will, and understanding: "A schema is a universal procedure of the imagination in presenting a priori to the senses a pure concept of the understanding which is determined by the law; and a schema must correspond to natural laws as laws to which objects of sensuous intuition as such are subject. But to the law of freedom (which is a causality not sensuously conditioned), and consequently to the concept of the absolutely good, no intuition and hence no schema can be supplied for the purpose of applying it *in concreto*. Thus the moral law has no other cognitive faculty to mediate its application to objects of nature than the understanding (not the imagination); and the understanding can supply to an idea of reason not a schema of sensibility but a law."[4] This is what Kant calls the law of freedom. As we saw in chapter 4, there is symbolization rather than a schematization, and the understanding supplies lawfulness of nature in general. Kant only allows a type of the lawfulness of nature, the form of lawfulness in general in sensible nature, rather than sensuousness and the imagination, to serve as the type of an intelligible nature.

And in the third *Critique*, the role of the imagination becomes prominent—some even say Kant returns to the primacy of the imagination of the first edition of the first *Critique* from which he so acutely withdrew in the second editions.[5] But there is somewhat of an ambiguity here. The role of the imagination becomes central for the aesthetic judgment of taste and especially of the sublime. But in those instances the context is not at all that of objective knowledge, but rather that of the subjective realm. One of our specific interests in this third *Critique*, seen in chapter 4, is the relation between the determinative judgment and reflective judgment in practical reason, which inevitably broaches the question of the ground of practical reason and pure practical reason, that is, not that of determinative judgment, but rather, that of reflective judgment.[6]

According to some, there seems to be an "unresolved conflict"[7] in Kant between the primacy of imagination established in the first edition of the first *Critique* and the primacy of limiting reason re-established in the second edition. Kant's followers, idealists and some romantics, resolved the supposed conflict by simply conflating reason and imagination in favor of the imagination. The idealists tended to put the faculties of the mind under the productive imagination, so that Heidegger was not the first to extol the centrality of the productive imagination. Fichte claims that all syntheses of subjectivity, even those of reason, are due to the productive imagination. And Schelling makes the productive and synthetic imagination the organon and pinnacle of all philosophy.[8]

Rather than an "unresolved conflict," this seems to be simply a redirection of Kantian transcendental philosophy by his followers who, especially after the third *Critique*, no longer wanted to follow his direction of transcendental idealism. And Heidegger enters this dispute precisely at this point.

Is it possible that there is a certain sense in which both can be maintained, following in his own ontological direction: the centrality of productive imagination and the centrality of limiting reason? The centrality of limiting reason means that reason sets limits beyond which knowledge cannot pass, but that can be considered as boundaries with another side, and beyond which practical cognition, with no addition to theoretical cognition, does extend; and the centrality of imagination in the constitution of the subject . . . as in the reflective aesthetic judgment . . . where the imagination's work is limited to the subjective. And this latter can be rendered helpful to human understanding—or interpretation—only via a hermeneutic dimension of method. This throws into focus the centrality of productive imagination, not only in its function in theoretical knowledge, but also in a philosophy attuned to poetics of any kind. But it does not compromise the limits, beyond which we can go in practical cognition by Kant's own strict admission. Yet recent poetics, with the addition of the indirect access through indirect language, including the recent focus on narrative, succeeds in bringing about an understanding of this extension that Kant did not have available, yet that he made possible by his own development of the role of the productive imagination and its role in the judgments of taste and especially of the sublime.

In order more adequately to explore the contemporary role of the imagination in human cognition, desire, and feeling, it is necessary to retrieve the place of this power in the whole of the Kantian critical philosophy, interpreting from the direction of Kant's position rather than from our own stance today. While it is true that we have indeed already seen that it has a central place in Kant's attempt to ground metaphysics, neither its role nor the interpretation of Kant's attempt to lay the foundation of metaphysics need be reduced to the project depicted by Heidegger as that of Kant, for that Heideggerian interpretation is meant to fit Kant's whole project into the hermeneutic situation and project of Heidegger, within the context of the fundamental question of Being, which, at this time for Heidegger, is entailed within the very ontological structures of Dasein. In contrast to that rendition, the more one clarifies the Kantian doctrine in terms of his own world and meaning, the richer the possibilities to place the imagination in our own situated stance. This undertaking is in stark contrast to that of Heidegger, yet learning from both the Heideggerian project and from that of deconstruction, which renders one of the most austere critiques of Heidegger, while buying into his unique presupposition.

Into whatever form it evolves, continental philosophy, to be viable and adequate, must confront head-on the challenge from postmodern deconstructive thinking as well as give evidence of incorporating its positive element. It is our purpose now to focus on the challenge seen in part I in the light of, and in relation to, the role of the imagination, assess its positive contribution to recent thinking, and eventually, in the following chapters, to present a philosophy at the boundary of reason as one of the most important currents of contemporary thinking.

The brief focus on the recent adaptations of the role of the Kantian productive imagination have gone a long way to help us to distinguish currents of thought in addressing the limit of thinking in relation to the imagination, where we saw briefly at least three distinct interpretations of the role of imagination emerge in philosophy at it end-limit. To all of these, the role of the productive imagination, adapted in one way or another from that of Kant, is significant, even if from the point of view of its absence. It is this productive role that must be seen in its complexity and simplicity.

Kant makes clear certain fundamental points regarding imagination in his *Anthropology*[9] that, in spite of some alterations in his *Critique of Pure Reason*, remain in tact. First, imagination intuits an object without its presence. It is an active power of making present.[10] It is thus passive as sense, but active as making present. This imagination is productive and reproductive, depending on whether it produces or reproduces based on a prior sense intuition in which the content is already given. As Sallis says, the imagination is "either productive-original-intentive or reproductive-derivative-recollective."[11] *The Critique of Pure Reason* makes it clear that the difference between these two functions of the imagination is the difference between a psychological and a transcendental faculty. The productive imagination, transcendental in its function, gives itself its object rather than merely recalls some previous empirical experience as reproductive imagination does.

What Kant means to indicate by transcendental in this context is that it preconditions our very experience of the world as the hidden condition of all knowledge, that it grounds the objectivity of the object in the subjectivity of the subject rather than in some transcendent order beyond human experience. The only kind of object that it can give to itself instead of receiving through experience must be intuited a priori independently of affection, which holds only for the a priori forms, space and time. Thus, productive imagination must bring forth originally spatial and temporal form. (Since this is not an infinite creation, this productive function of transcendental imagination gives itself its form, but must receive the material element, the sense content.) The productive is distinguished from the reproductive imagination precisely in that the former gives itself the form of the object and does not only reproduce a previous form. "*Imagination* is the faculty of representing in intuition, an object that is *not itself present*."[12] It is important to remember that the productive imagination gives form to a manifold of intuition. While the transcendental imagination forms time by forming the manifold of pure intuition through transcendental schematism, reproductive imagination presupposes that formed time and thus presupposes the function of the transcendental imagination: hence Ricoeur's emphasis on this productive function of the imagination instead of the reproductive role. Thus, the transcendental imagination, rather than making present an absent object, makes possible the very objectivity of knowledge.

It seems that Kant is giving a hint that militates against the interpretation, even in the first edition, which gives too much weight to the role of the imagination at the expense of the understanding. For he indicates in the preliminary remark in section 2 of the second chapter of the Transcendental Deduction of the Categories (CPR, 131) that he must first "prepare" the reader rather than to "instruct" at this point. He goes on to say that "Systematic exposition of these elements of the understanding is first given in Section 3, immediately following. The reader must not therefore be deterred by obscurities in these earlier sections. . . . They will, as I trust, in the section referred to, finally give way to complete insight." That section 3 to which Kant refers deals with "The Relation of the Understanding to Objects in General, and the Possibility of Knowing Them *A Priori*," in which the elements for which the reader is prepared are presented "in systematic interconnection" (CPR, 141).

In this exposition of the three subjective sources of knowledge, sense, imagination, and apperception, it is clear that even in the first edition of the first *Critique* Kant envisioned the foundational character of understanding as apperception.[13] It is this transcendental unity of apperception that is the condition and ground of the other unities, as Kant clearly states, still in the first edition. "The transcendental unity of apperception thus relates to the pure synthesis of imagination, as an *a priori* condition of the possibility of all combination of the manifold in one knowledge" (CPR, 142). But Kant adds a rather enigmatic remark, in relation to what has just been exposed: "But only the *productive* synthesis of the imagination can take place *a priori;* the reproductive rests upon empirical conditions. Thus the principle of the necessary unity of pure (productive) synthesis of imagination, prior to apperception, is the ground of the possibility of all knowledge, especially of experience" (CPR, 142–143). Is this a contradiction to what has just been explicated concerning the grounding character of transcendental apperception? The key phrase in that statement is "prior to apperception," thus meaning that the ground unity of Intuition is the pure unity of pure productive synthesis of imagination. And the ground for this unity is the transcendental unity of apperception, which itself is the ground of all that precedes it. He actually uses the same expression "the ground of the possibility of all knowledge" in the very next paragraph in relation to transcendental apperception, which could be allowed to confuse the matter even further. However, instead, everything falls into the place envisioned in Kant's understanding of the interrelations of these unities of imagination and of apperception, each of which is seen to be necessary for knowledge if that next paragraph is read carefully. And, in the next paragraph, Kant gives the direction of the process of knowledge: "In the understanding there are then pure *a priori* modes of knowledge (*Erkenntnisse)* which contain the necessary unity of the pure synthesis of imagination in respect of all possible appearances. These are the *categories*, that is, the pure concepts of the understanding" (CPR, 143). A little earlier, Kant has stated, in a review of this point, that "Since this unity of the manifold in one subject is synthetic, pure apperception supplies a principle of the synthetic unity of the manifold in all possible intuition" (CPR, 142). He adds, making the relation rather obvious: "The transcendental unity of apperception thus relates to the pure synthesis of imagination, as an *a priori* condition of the possibility of all combination of the manifold in one knowledge" (CPR, 142). In the footnote to the paragraph before the one just quoted, Kant explicitly states: "But all empirical consciousness has a necessary relation to a transcendental consciousness which precedes all special experience, namely, the consciousness of myself as original apperception. It is therefore absolutely necessary that in my knowledge all consciousness should belong to a single consciousness, that of myself" (CPR, 142 fn.).

Kant concludes that there must be an *objective ground*, comprehended a priori, antecedently to all empirical laws of the imagination, "upon which rests the possibility, nay, the necessity, of a law that extends to all appearances—a ground, namely, which constrains us to regard all appearances as data of the senses that must be associable in themselves and subject to universal rules of a thoroughgoing connection in their reproduction" (CPR, 145). This objective ground of association of appearances he calls their *affinity*. It is only found in the principle of the unity of apperception. "That the affinity of appearances, and with it their association, and through this, in turn, their reproduction according to laws, and so [as involving these various factors] experience itself, should only be possible by means of this transcendental function of imagination, is indeed strange, but is none the less an obvious consequence of the preceding argument. For without this transcendental function no concepts of objects would together make up a unitary experience" (145–146).

Kant affirms that a

pure imagination, which conditions all *a priori* knowledge, is thus one of the fundamental faculties of the human soul. By its means we bring the manifold of intuition on the one side, into connection with the condition of the necessary unity of pure apperception on the other. The two extremes, namely sensibility and understanding, must stand in necessary connection with each other through the mediation of this transcendental function of imagination, because otherwise the former, though indeed yielding appearances, would supply no objects of empirical knowledge, and consequently no experience. Actual experience, which is constituted by apprehension, association (reproduction), and finally recognition of appearances, contains in recognition, the last and highest of these merely empirical elements of experience, certain concepts which render possible the formal unity of experience, and therewith all objective validity (truth) of empirical knowledge. These grounds of the recognition of the manifold, so far as they concern *solely the form of the experience in general*, are the *categories*. Upon them is based not only all formal unity in the [transcendental] synthesis of imagination, but also, thanks to that synthesis, all its empirical employment (in recognition, reproduction, association, apprehension) in connection with the appearances. For only by means of these fundamental concepts can appearances belong to knowledge or even to our consciousness, and so to ourselves. (CPR, 147)

He goes on to state that the "unity of apperception is thus the transcendental ground of necessary conformity to law of all appearances in one experience" (148).

It is important to focus on Kant's limit here: that even with the pure intuition, the categories do not give us knowledge of things; but rather only for the *possibility* of *empirical knowledge*. "Our conclusion is therefore this: the categories, as yielding knowledge of *things*, have no kind of application, save only in regard to things which may be objects of possible experience" (CPR, 162). This states the limits within which the categories are employed.

Kant goes on to state that

> [t]he above proposition is of the greatest importance; for it determines the limits [*die Grenzen* boundary] of the employment of the pure concepts of understanding in regard to objects, just as the Transcendental Aesthetic determined the limits [*die Grenzen* boundary] of the employment of the pure form of our sensible intuition. Space and time, as conditions under which alone objects can possibly be given to us, are valid no further than for objects of the senses, and therefore only for experience. Beyond these limits they represent nothing; for they are only in the senses, and beyond them have no reality. The pure concepts of the understanding are free from this limitation, and extend to objects of intuition in general, be the intuition like or unlike ours, if only it be sensible and not intellectual. . . . Only *our* sensible and empirical intuition can give to them body and meaning [*Sinn und Bedeutung*]. (CPR, 163)

FIGURATIVE SYNTHESIS

Intuition's a priori synthesis of appearances Kant calls figurative (*synthesis speciosa*), distinguishing it from the synthesis that is thought in the mere category in respect of the manifold of an intuition in general (*synthesis intellectualis*). These syntheses are *transcendental*, taking place a priori, and conditioning the possibility of other a priori knowledge (CPR, 164–165).

> Now since all our intuition is sensible, the imagination, owing to the subjective condition under which alone it can give to the concepts of understanding a corresponding intuition, belongs to *sensibility*. But inasmuch as its synthesis is an expression of spontaneity, which is determinative and not, like sense, determinable merely, and which is therefore able to determine sense *a priori* in respect of its form in accordance with the unity of apperception, imagination is to that extent a faculty which determines the sensibility *a priori*; and its synthesis of intuition, conforming as it does to the *categories*, must be the transcendental synthesis of *imagination*. This synthesis is an action of the understanding on the sensibility; and is its first application—and thereby the ground of all its other applications—to the objects of our possible intuition. As figurative, it is distinguished from the intellectual synthesis, which is carried out by the understanding alone, without the aid of the imagination. (CPR, 165)

THE PRODUCTIVE IMAGINATION
IN ITS AESTHETIC FUNCTION

It might be beneficial to begin our reflection on the aesthetic function of the productive imagination by contrasting it with the reproductive and other productive functions of the imagination. It has been seen above that the reproductive function is bound by empirical laws of association, and that the productive imagination is bound, in the sense of determined, by categories of the understanding. In a sense, then, neither of these functions enjoys freedom. The aesthetic function of the productive imagination is free in the sense that empirical laws or categories do not determine it. But it has to be seen that the freedom differs among its various manifestations: in the judgment of beauty, in the judgment of the sublime, and in its use in making fine art.

In the judgment of beauty, the imagination is somewhat bound by the form of the object about which the judgment is made, since the form of the object is a limitation. It is free, however, in relation to the understanding, since, as stated, there is no concept and thus no determinate relation, but only an indeterminate relation. Now in the case of the judgment of the sublime, it is precisely the formlessness and unlimitedness of the object that gives rise to awe, so that there is not this limitation or bond with the form of the object; and there is the orientation to that which is beyond our world, beyond our sensibility, reaching to the ideas of reason. But again it is a relation of indeterminateness. We must examine this aesthetic judgment further.

Thus, it is clear that the aesthetic judgment of the beautiful does not enjoy the same free play as does the judgment of the sublime, or as those of sheer fancy. In the *Prolegomena*, Kant has stated that the imagination can be forgiven such flights into fancy, but not the understanding, which must adhere to limits. Here, it should be clear that there is a distinction between the imagination given to such fancy, not bound to the form of objects of experience, and that of the aesthetic judgment of the beautiful, which is so bound. Thus, this latter function of imagination is free, but it relates to the form of the object, as well as enjoys an indeterminate relation to the understanding and its principle of conformity to law in general. Since the imagination is a faculty of sense, it needs the understanding in this relation for there to be a judgment, not a concept of the understanding, but rather only its principle of conformity to law in general. Thus, the imagination (in the judgment of beauty) is not free in reference to two relations: first in its relation to the form of the object; and second, in its relation to the principle of conformity to law in general. Now this is clearly a subjective, universal judgment, but not employing any objective law or category. That is, anyone should, on seeing this object, be able to judge it to be beautiful. Kant invokes a "common sense" (*ein Gemeinsinn*) in this relation, but not in the usual sense of *sensus communis* of the medieval philosophy, which is an inner sense unifying what is given in external senses. Rather, for Kant, the common sense is employed to distinguish the "universal" principle of aesthetic judgment of the beautiful from a logical principle, that is, the common sense is the presupposed commonness bringing about the judgment: this is the effect of the free play of the cognitive powers in their harmony, which can and should be experienced by all on the occasion of experiencing this particular beautiful object. Thus, there is a sort of necessity of assent on the part of all, which Kant calls "exemplary." The judgment is regarded as an example of a universal rule that one cannot state, so that when I state that this object is beautiful, I am claiming that all ought to describe it as beautiful.

In order to contrast the free play of the judgment of the sublime with that of the beautiful, it is necessary to consider briefly the differences between the two. Kant, in focusing on these differences, first refers to their agreements: that they both please in themselves, and neither presupposes a judgment of sense or a judgment logically determined, but rather, a judgment of reflection. Also, they are both singular judgments even though they "announce themselves as universally valid for every subject," in the feeling of pleasure and not in the cognition of an object. But we must also see the "remarkable differences" between these two types of aesthetic judgment.[14]

Now these differences must be elaborated upon, since they become the significant focus for Lyotard, and since the entire enterprise becomes significant for Ricoeur's expansion of the role of the productive imagination of Kant. First, the beautiful is connected with the form of the object, consisting in having definite boundaries, while the sublime is found in a formless object, so to speak, so that boundlessness is represented in it, and totality is thought, entailing the ideas of reason considered as the faculty of indeterminate ideas of totality. And this brings us to the paramount difference: "Thus the beautiful seems to be regarded as the presentation of an indefinite concept of understanding, the sublime as that of a like concept of reason."[15] But the main difference between them Kant indicates as the fact that the sublime does violence to the imagination. On the apprehension of an object, what excites the feeling of the sublime appears in its form "to violate purpose in respect of judgment, to be unsuited to our presentative faculty, and . . . to do violence to the imagination; and yet it is judged to be only the more sublime."

Kant makes an important point about the "independent natural beauty" as making us see a "technique of nature" analogous to art, thus overcoming a closed and absolute nature as purposeless mechanism. This conjures up the principle of the purposiveness as a regulative and subjective principle, extending our concept of nature without extending our cognition of natural objects, so that nature can be considered as art and not merely as mechanism. Kant concludes, which will become important later: "Hence, we see *that the concept of the sublime is not nearly so important or rich in consequences as the concept of the beautiful*; and that, in general, it displays nothing purposive in nature itself, but only in that possible use of our intuition of it by which there is produced in us a feeling of a purposiveness quite independent of nature."[16] Thus, because of this separation of the sublime from purposiveness of nature, and the fact that it only involves a purposive use that imagination makes of its representation, Kant considers the theory of the sublime a "mere appendix" to the aesthetic judging of that purposiveness.

We must not, however, underestimate the importance of this transition from the beautiful to the sublime, for it is here that Kant shows how he has "circumscribed the creative role of the imagination."[17] And it is the sublime that challenges the human mind to unfathomable depths, in shattering form and limits. This inadequacy of the images of the imagination drives it toward reason, toward the totality of the realm beyond its own. Thus the artistic imagination can serve as a symbol that directs us toward the "mind's supra-sensible province." Something becomes sublime, or rather, elicits the sublime in us, to the extent that it produces symbols analogous to the ideas of reason, which means something that our mind cannot actually grasp, drawing us to the awareness of something great in the mind itself.

Productive Imagination in the Production of Works of Art

We must now consider the ramifications of the productive imagination in the actual production of a work of art according to Kant, a view that has become paramount since then, even if the original script was not often followed. For us, it is necessary to decipher Kant's own view before giving in to the temptation to expand beyond it, since this study considers divergent paths from that doctrine. It is already clear that undertaking entails the productive imagination in its aesthetic function considered above, and precisely as a case of reflective judgment in contrast to a determinative judgment.

It will be helpful to include in our scope of consideration the Kantian distinction between mechanical and aesthetic arts. Mechanical art is depicted to be art "which is adequate to the *cognition* of a possible object" and "performs the actions requisite therefore merely in order to make it actual." The *aesthetical* art "has for its immediate design the feeling of pleasure." Thus there is a need to distinguish pleasures to see precisely where this kind fits. There are two kinds of pleasure, which come about in two ways: first, the *pleasant* whose purpose is that the pleasure accompanies the representations of the object as mere sensations; and second, "if they are regarded as *modes of cognition*" (CJ, 148). Kant explains this latter further by centering it on purposiveness without purpose, and the culture of the mental powers.

"Beautiful art is a mode of representation which is purposive for itself and which, although devoid of [definite] purpose, yet furthers the culture of the mental powers in reference to social communication" (CJ, 148). It must be emphasized with Kant again that the aesthetic pleasure is derived from reflection, that it is the harmony among the faculties that gives rise to the feeling of pleasure, distinguishing it as a pleasure of reflection and not one of mere sensation (the pleasant). Thus the "standard" for beautiful art is reflective judgment rather than sensation. The fact of this derivation from reflection is entailed by the "universal communicability" of this pleasure (CJ, 148). In the development of his theory of fine art, the theory of aesthetic judgment of the beautiful is quite apparent, with its essential elements coming into play. Thus it must be clear that to understand fine art and how it is produced, the conditions that make us judge a thing to be beautiful are essentially entailed, which has been presented in the Analytic of the Beautiful. Thus we can see the essential role of the productive imagination working in both.

Leading up to his famous treatment of the production of the work of art, Kant presents in paragraph 43 important distinctions and points for recent re-appropriations of this doctrine, especially in distinguishing the production of a work of art from mere play. In distinguishing art from handicraft, which is employed not because it is pleasant, but rather for its effect, wages, in contrast to art as pleasant and purposive as play. The significance of the end of this treatment is Kant's distinction of the art production as work from mere play, invoking a sort of mechanism or compulsion essential to handicraft, but now revealed as pre-required for art production. Kant shows clearly that for the artist or for the production of fine art there must be a backdrop of knowledge presupposed for this particular fine art: for instance, the poet must have a good knowledge of languages, and if classical, of the classical disciplines as prerequisite for his production. As Kant so tersely expresses this: "But it is not inexpedient to recall that, in all free arts, there is yet requisite something compulsory or, as it is called, mechanism, without which the spirit, which must be free in art and which alone inspires the work, would have no body and would evaporate altogether: e.g. in poetry there must be an accuracy and wealth of language, and also prosody and measure. [It is not inexpedient, I say, to recall this], for many modern educators believe that the best way to produce a free art is to remove it from all constraint, and thus to change it from work into mere play" (CJ, 147). This insight, as Kant so well puts it for the end of the eighteenth century, is quite relevant today, especially in the case of some tendencies in postmodernism. For there we see the attempt to sidestep constraints, and thus do precisely what Kant warns against when he refers to spirit, without such compulsory element, as having "no body" and as evaporating altogether. So, postmodernism, in some of its adherents, has done just that by not only decentering the subject, but by subverting its role altogether, yielding to some force of language or chance, as we will see in later chapters.

Continuing our discussion of the productive activity in the production of the work of art, there is a subtle and relevant point that becomes apparent in Kant's rigorous attempt to distinguish beautiful art from nature. It seems for Kant that beautiful art must look like nature even though we are conscious of it as art, as a product of art. It appears like nature in that it can be seen in agreement with rules that make it become what it ought to be, yet there is no trace of the rule capturing or hampering the artist. This insight springs from the difference between nature according to the rules of the categories and art as entailing, not a rule or a concept of understanding, but rather the general lawfulness or purposiveness of understanding without being hampered by the strict and specific rule. Thus, Kant can say that beautiful art looks like nature, even though we are acutely aware of it precisely as art.

At the heart of his treatment of the production of fine art is Kant's famous and enigmatic doctrine of genius as the (producer) productive capacity of fine art in paragraphs 46–51, culminating in paragraph 49. The first tentative and inadequate articulation of genius is that it is the talent of giving the rule to art, but this is obviously insufficient because one must be careful of the rule and the talent as well. Kant goes on to define genius as "the innate mental disposition (*ingenium*) *through which* nature gives the rule to art" (CJ, 150). (*Genie ist die angeborne Gemütsanlage [ingenium], durch welche die Natur der Kunst die Regel gibt*).[18] In Kant's sense, beautiful art must be considered as a product of such genius. This reveals something of the productive imagination that is of great interest to us. In further explaining genius, Kant is drawn to tie it down and at once to free it. For it is first *original* as a talent, an *ingenium*, an innate ability, one not taught or learned, of producing that for which "no definite rule can be given." It is, however, tempered or bridled, in that the unbridled imagination in fancy can produce total nonsense, while genius produces fine art, which itself must serve as models that are exemplary, as seen above in the context of the necessity of everyone's agreeing that a particular product is beautiful. Now the function of "exemplary" is also manifest in the other direction, not in aesthetic judgment, but rather, in its actual production on the part of genius. In this production, the imagination is tied down, although minimally in not jeopardizing its free play by tying it to a rule or concept. Thus, genius is the inborn mental disposition through which nature gives the rule to art, all things above considered.

In the next paragraph, 47, Kant clarifies a glaring ambiguity in the above account of genius regarding the rule prescribed by a quasinature in the artist, or by the natural disposition endowed by nature for the prescription of such a rule. Kant is aware of the obvious care necessary to further stipulate that this is not a precept or a formula, for then the aesthetic judgments of the beautiful would be determinative judgments according to rules, which he cannot admit. The rule must hence be "abstracted from the fact, i.e., from the product" (152), so that others might imitate its aesthetic production, but not copy it, according to their own innate talent. "The ideas of the artist excite like ideas in his pupils if nature has endowed them with a like proportion of their mental powers" (152). But again Kant does what we have already seen. He emphasizes that even beautiful art, basically distinguished from mechanical art, still does have a modicum of the mechanical element that can be followed as rules, since in such art some purpose must be conceived. If there were not this element, it would not be the product of art, but rather of *chance* (CJ, 153).[19] While the artist who merely copies produces art with no soul or animating principle, in contrast, the artist who throws off all relation to rule produces fancy and nonsense that is not fine art at all, and to whom Kant refers as "shallow heads."

At the outset of his famous paragraph 49, Kant attributes to genius, as the productive capacity of the imagination in producing fine art, the enigmatic and illusive power of spirit (*Geist*). This is the very animating principle of the mind (*im Gemüte*), the very faculty of presenting aesthetic ideas (*als das Vermogen der Darstellung asthetischer Ideen*) (CJ, 157).[20] In the process of unfolding the sense of the aesthetical ideas the fuller sense of genius and artistic production of the productive imagination in relation to the other powers will become clearer. For the aesthetic idea is the product of the imagination in the interplay of other elements, and a rather enigmatic interplay. The aesthetic idea is "that representation of the imagination [*Vorstellung der Einbildungskraft*] that occasions much thought, without however any definite thought, that is, any *concept*, being capable of being adequate to it" (CJ, 157). Hence, this aesthetic idea can not ever be made completely intelligible in language. It is the counterpart of a rational idea. Thus, while the rational idea is one to which no intuition, or representation of the imagination, is adequate, the aesthetic idea is a representation of the imagination to which no concept can be adequate.

Kant focuses on the productive imagination as the power of producing from the material given us by "actual nature" a quasi-second nature, by which we "remold experience, always indeed in accordance with analogical laws, but yet also in accordance with principles which occupy a higher place in reason" (CJ, 157). He is quick to point out that these principles are laws that are just as natural to us as the ones by which understanding comprehends empirical nature. Thus, there is the freedom that is not jeopardized, yet there is the relation to law without which genius in unbridled and produces sheer fancy or nonsense. We feel the freedom from the empirical laws of association that bind the empirical employment of the (reproductive) imagination, "so that the material supplied to us by nature in accordance with this law can be worked up into something different which surpasses nature" (CJ, 157). And this material by means of which spirit animates the soul puts the mental powers purposively into swing, that is, "into such a play as maintains itself and strengthens the mental powers in their exercise" (CJ, 157).

In explaining the aesthetic ideas as ideas, Kant clarifies to some extent precisely what they are. These representations (*Vorstellungen*) of the productive imagination are called ideas in part because they strive or reach to something beyond the bounds of experience, seeking to approximate to a "*presentation [einer Darstellung]* of concepts of reason" (CJ, 157, 247) or intellectual ideas. In this striving, they give to the intellectual ideas the appearance of objective reality. They are called ideas also because no concept can be fully adequate to them as internal intuitions. Poets venture to "realize to sense, rational ideas of invisible beings, the kingdom of the blessed, hell, eternity, creation, etc." (CJ, 157). And in dealing with things of experience, such as death, vices, love, fame, and so on, the poet uses the imagination in emulating "the play of reason in its quest after a maximum, to go beyond the limits of experience and to present them to sense with a completeness of which there is no example in nature" (CJ, 158). Kant contends that it is in the case of the poet that the faculty of aesthetical ideas manifests itself in its "entire strength," and then adds that it is properly a talent of the imagination. The focal point now has become the aesthetic ideas, which must be dealt with at greater depth, if not clarified further, to the extent that is possible while remaining faithful to Kant's doctrine.

This further account of the aesthetic idea in relation to concept and presentation allows us to begin by focusing first on the representation (*einer Vorstellung*). This representation of the imagination itself presents or exhibits a concept and is placed under that same concept. Now, when this very representation, provided for that concept, prompts more thought than it is possible to comprehend in a definite concept, thus enlarging aesthetically the concept itself in an unbounded fashion (*auf unbegrenzte Art*),[21] the imagination is then creative, bringing reason, as the faculty of intellectual ideas, into motion. This representation (*Vorstellung*) gives rise to more thought, which thought does belong to the concept of the object, than can be grasped or made clear in it. Thus, for Kant it is precisely the *creativity of the productive imagination that prompts reason into action in the process of aesthetically enlarging the concept, and the representation gives rise to thought that cannot be adequate for the concept, as seen above.*

This aesthetic idea, as a representation (*Vorstellung*) of the imagination associated with a given concept, is also bound up with a multiplicity of partial representations as forms that do not constitute the exhibition of a given concept, but are merely supplementary representations expressing the concept's implications and its kinship with other concepts. These partial representations "are called (aesthetical) *attributes* of an object whose concept as a rational idea cannot be adequately presented" (CJ, 158). Thus, such a representation adds to the concept "much ineffable thought, the feeling of which quickens the cognitive faculties, and with language, which is the mere letter, binds up spirit also" (CJ, 160).

In concluding that it is the imagination and understanding that constitute genius, Kant distinguishes the distinct roles of the understanding in aesthetic production from that in cognition. In the aesthetic point of view, the imagination does not submit to a concept, but rather is free to "furnish unsought, over and above that agreement with a concept, abundance of undeveloped material for understanding, to which the understanding paid no regard in its concept, but which it applies, though not objectively for cognition, yet subjectively to quicken the cognitive powers and therefore also indirectly to cognitions" (CJ, 160). This indirect contribution to cognition is by way of quickening the cognitive powers.

Kant comes now to recharacterize genius as properly consisting in:

> the happy relation [between these faculties], by which ideas are found for a given concept; and, on the other hand, we thus find for these ideas the expression by means of which the subjective state of mind brought about by them, as an accompaniment of the concept, can be communicated to others. The latter talent is, properly speaking, what is called spirit; for to express the ineffable element in the state of mind implied by a certain representation and to make it universally communicable, . . . this requires a faculty of seizing the quickly passing play of imagination and of unifying it in a concept (which is even on that

account original and discloses a new rule that could not have been inferred from any preceding principles or examples) that can be communicated without any constraint [of rules]. (CJ, 160–161)

Kant attempts to clarify the interrelation of the faculties functioning in the aesthetic idea considered above in another way. He points out that the forms, as approximate representations of the imagination, which do not constitute the presentation of the given concept, but only "express the consequences bound up with that concept and its relationship to other concepts" are what he calls "aesthetic attributes of an object whose concept as a rational idea cannot be adequately presented" (CJ, 158). It is as a rational idea that this concept cannot be adequately presented. And these forms do not constitute the exhibition or presentation of the concept itself, but, rather, are supplementary representations (*Nebensvorstellungen*) expressing the concept's implications and its kinship with other concepts. These aesthetic attributes yield or furnish an aesthetic idea, substituting for or taking the place of the logical presentation for that rational idea. Its proper function, however, is to quicken or enliven (*beleben*) the mind by opening up for it a "view into an immense realm of kindred presentation."[22]

Thus, genius is seen to be a talent for art in which rules clearly determine the procedure. And, as such a talent, it presupposes a determinate concept of the product as its purpose and hence presupposes understanding. But "it also presupposes a representation (although an indeterminate one) of the material, i.e. of the intuition for the presentment of this concept, and, therefore, a relation between the imagination and the understanding." This genius shows itself more in the "enunciation or expression of aesthetical ideas which contain abundant material" for accomplishment of the proposed purpose in a presentment of a definite concept than in actually accomplishing that purpose in a presentation; and consequently it "represents the imagination as free from all guidance of rules and yet as purposive in reference to the presentment of the given concept" (CJ, 161). Finally "the unsought undesigned subjective purposiveness" in the free harmony of the imagination with the lawfulness of the understanding "presupposes such a proportion and disposition of these faculties as no following of rules, whether of science or of mechanical imitation, can bring about, but which only the nature of the subject can produce" (CJ, 161). The product given rise to by such genius is an "example" for another kindred spirit or genius in whom is awakened a like productivity, and hence shows that the work of genius is truly "exemplary."

Link between Aesthetics and Morals

In leading to his conclusion that the beautiful is the symbol of the morally good, Kant dedicates more than half of paragraph 59 to the "presentation" of concepts to the imagination in the dynamics of symbol and analogy in contrast to that of schemata. In this contrast, he focuses on the mode of presentation of concepts in each, showing especially the uniqueness of symbolic presentation, which does not entail schemata, but rather a following of the procedure for providing the schemata to intuition. It is clear that, in these processes, all intuition supplied to concepts a priori are either schemata or symbols. Each of these contains the presentation of the concept, but each in its own way. The schemata entails the direct presentation of the concept, while the symbol is an indirect presentation of the concept, by means of an analogy, with the judgment exercising a "double function" (CJ, 197), one that applies the concept to the object of a sensible intuition, and then "applying the mere rule of the reflection made upon that intuition to a quite different object of which the first is only the symbol. In this latter, even empirical intuitions are employed.[23] Thus, for Kant, presentation, as "*subjectio sub adspectum*" or sensible illustration, what he calls *hypotyposis*, comes about either as schematical or as symbolic. Elaborating further on the symbolic than done immediately above, we can now add that this symbolic has an intuition supplied with which "accords a procedure of the judgment analogous to what it observes in schematism, that is, merely analogous to the rule of this procedure, not to the intuition itself, consequently to the form of reflection merely and not to its content" (CJ, 197). Thus Kant finds it necessary to distinguish his use of symbol from a misuse of it by logicians according to whom it is distinguished from intuition rather than from a mode of intuition.

Symbol and Analogy

Kant's aesthetic, especially the production of fine art works, has come to focus on the role of symbol as central to the process involving the relation between the ideas of reason and the aesthetic ideas, as seen above. It remains for us to delve further into the nature of symbol and analogy, which he has placed in such a central role and which has come to play such an important role for later developments from Kant. This is especially the case with Cassirer and Ricoeur, but not irrelevant to that of Heidegger, as manifest in such works as the *Letter on Humanism* and in the works on art and that of postmodern deconstruction, as will be seen in later chapters.

Kant's example in giving an account of a symbol is that of a monarchical state represented by a living body if it is governed by laws that spring from the people, and by a machine (such as a hand mill) if governed according to the individual, absolute will of an autocrat. Thus Kant bases his idea of symbolism on analogy, which means that the similarity is between the relation between two relations, and not between objects. For the second example, it is not the question of the hand mill that is similar to a despotic state. Rather, the relation between the hand mill and its causality, that is, how it operates, is related to the relation of the state to its causality, that is, the causality of the despotic will as absolute cause. And the question arises about what are the points of analogy between the aesthetic and the moral judgments, or between the beautiful and the morally good, which justify our looking on the beautiful as a symbol of the morally good, keeping in mind that what is similar is the relation between two relations, each entailing the relation between two objects. In his own example, the first relation is that between the monarchical state and its government by the laws of the people, and the living body and its rules of operation; and the second relation is between the monarchical state and its government by the will of the autocratic monarch, and the hand mill and its causality. The first relation he calls a living body, and the second relation he calls a machine.

Kant points out that our language is filled with such indirect presentations that are symbolic in spite of the fact that this matter has not been adequately analyzed before now. Such expressions of indirect presentations do not contain the proper schema of concepts as stated, but rather symbols for reflection. Now we can return to the question of the beautiful as the symbol of the morally good.

The main and obvious link between them is in the law given by each. In the faculty of the judgment of the beautiful, not considered by itself along the lines of empirical judging according to empirical laws, the law is given to itself by itself in respect of the "objects of so pure a satisfaction" (CJ, 199). This comes about in a way similar and parallel to reason giving law to the faculty of desire. So, just as reason gives the law to itself (*Selbstgesetzgebung*), to the faculty of desire (to the practical reason, to the will), so here, the faulty of judging gives itself the law, the subjectively based purposiveness as a regulative concept of reflective judgment. Thus, again we see the relation of similarity between two relations, and in this the beautiful is the symbol of the morally good. But this is not sufficiently clear in its ramifications, and Kant draws it out further, although in the aforementioned, he is not clear at all. In going further, Kant indicates explicitly that it is in this "supersensible ground" that the theoretical faculty and the practical faculty are bound together in unity, in a "way which, though common, is yet unknown."[24]

There are four points to this analogy. First, they are similar because they both please immediately; the beautiful pleasing in reflective intuition, the morally good in the concept. Again the beautiful pleases apart from any interest; and though the morally good is indeed bound up with an interest, it does not precede the moral judgment but follows it. Further, they each entail a relation between law and freedom; in the aesthetic judgment of the beautiful, the freedom of the imagination is experienced as in harmony with the lawfulness or purposiveness of the understanding, while in the moral judgment the freedom of the will is thought to be in harmony with itself in accordance with the moral law of reason. And finally, the subjective principle for judging the beautiful is represented as universal, so that everyone must see it as beautiful even though it is not knowable in any concept; and the objective principle of morality is also universal. Thus, the moral judgment is constituted by the grounding of our maxims on the universality of principles.

It has been necessary for us to detour into this detailed study of Kant's productive imagination as background for further studies of recent philosophical developments rooted in it. For the development of philosophy in the twentieth century is rooted in variations in interpreting the role of this productive imagination of Kant. To renew this discussion at an originary level it has been necessary for us to invoke Kant's own doctrine before it is creatively appropriated by his own immediate followers, as well as before it is incorporated into various contemporary projects: a fundamental ontological project that does not do justice to Kant's own doctrine; or a deconstruction in a clotural reading. It remains for us now to turn to its various roles on the contemporary scene, leading to the depth of divergent paths of development in continental thinking today.[25]

CHAPTER 6

Imagination:
Postmodern Deconstruction
and Ricoeur

INTRODUCTION

The role assigned to the imagination in recent philosophy has become extremely significant, for it is either central, in which case the productive imagination and semantic innovation are paramount, as they are for such thinkers as Paul Ricoeur; or it is not at all central, in which case chance replaces the productive imagination in its centrality, as is the case for Jacques Derrida. Given this disparity in roles of the imagination, this chapter will attempt to show how imagination or chance shapes the core of these two positions, leading to its diverse roles in the constitution of sign and the living present, and thus revealing these positions to be mutually exclusive. I will argue in strong support for the centrality of productive imagination as a legacy from Kantian philosophy, and for semantic innovation rooted in its extension. For what is essentially at stake in this appropriation of the role of the imagination is an innovation of meaning within a viable semantic theory as opposed to an intense and subversive intellectual anarchism, based on a will to believe in the priority of the subversive. A first brief focus on the recent adaptations of the role of the Kantian productive imagination will be helpful to distinguish currents of thought in addressing this limit of thinking.

Ricoeur's manner of dealing with indirect language and the imagination and Derrida's manner of dealing with chance in relation to dissemination and *différance* differ radically from that of Heidegger's finitization of reason. The postmodern and deconstructive critique of Heidegger transforms Heidegger's interpretation of the central role of the Kantian productive imagination by subordinating it to chance or to language itself. For the deconstruction of Derrida, the closure results from the propensity to fixate on the effect within the flux of the *différance*, a fixation that prevents the transgressing of philosophy to *différance*, dissemination, and the "play of reason." And Lyotard, rendering the treatment of the sublime in the *Critique of Judgment* as central, seeking to displace any conceptual rule, thus supports invention that displaces the whole "game" over the innovation that makes new moves with the rules of the game. Lyotard extends the indeterminate dimension of the limited role of the reflective judgment of the sublime in Kant's use to a paradigmatic role in thinking, leading to a common antilogocentrism with Derrida. Thus, there is an attempt on the part of both to supplant the primacy of the Kantian theoretical understanding in its knowing function in favor of a priority of language that renders the human role of imagination passive and secondary to that of the "other." Further, language in their employ loses its semantic priority in favor of semiological priority. There is, however, another way of reaching this other, one that does not go by either of the paths above and one that has not lost original creativity or some role of the understanding other than that in Kant's theoretical knowledge.

If reason is not produced by imagination, then reason itself limits knowledge to experience from above, as already seen, putting the imagination in a central position both in knowledge and in thinking, as it is for Ricoeur. This limit enacted by reason on human knowledge encompasses knowledge within the experience of reality itself, but allows reason to reach beyond the boundary to something of a more far-reaching significance.

For Ricoeur, in this context of limit, the objectivity of the theoretical is surpassed in the notion of the fullness and excess of meaning in existence to which access is gained in a reflection attuned to existence in such a way as to bring it to thought, and without jettisoning understanding and imagination. For Ricoeur, existence eludes any problematical treatment, for it is irreducible to that consideration. It is not univocal, but ambiguous because of its fullness. Expressing this in the first person, I cannot abstract myself from the concrete fullness of my own being. Rather, I am precisely what (who) is being reflected upon. On this level there is an ontological exigency at the heart of human existence that should prevent me from closing myself off into the problematic and the objective. And it is on this level that the "you," the other person, is encountered in presence. If reflection were to allow itself to begin other than with this realization, that is, the presence of the other, it would not be possible to get the "other" precisely as person back into reflection. This presence is closely linked to availability or readiness for the other (*disponibilité*). The unavailable person is not *really there* for the other, but maintains a certain closedness and distraction toward something else.

In this context, Ricoeur seems to admit the need for an indirect access to the question of the whole, in thinking beyond the boundaries of knowledge and of problematic reflection. In fact, most of his reflection on existence and being takes place within a certain domain going beyond the boundaries of the Kantian limit—that is, the total and full existence beneath and beyond the realm of a strictly theoretical reflection—the domain of existence, which for Kant must remain unknowable. And Ricoeur constantly speaks of the need for indirect language of myth, symbol, metaphor, and narrative in general in order to prevent idolatrizing that which is reflected upon here. Must not the philosopher admit that we cannot really free ourselves from some key images—for example, that of heaven as the abode of the blessed—provided that she/he shows that these images are bound up with the conditions of existence that belong to a wayfaring creature, and that they cannot accordingly be considered as literally true.

Derrida, in stark contrast, follows Heidegger's finitization of reason, but goes further, and instead of centralizing the role of imagination, subordinates it to chance, rendering it more passive than creative. And, like the late-modern idealists, he tends to reduce everything to the same status under the sway of chance, thus eliminating the creativity so central for Ricoeur. In spite of Derrida's critique of structuralism and of de Saussure, he himself succumbs to the allure of the sciences of sign, ending up in a semiological reductionism that strips away meaning, reference, and persons involved in discourse. He, rather, favors diacritical relationships in language as a system of signs with the concomitant loss of words as words, as will be seen in the next chapter.

Derrida's shift of focus from the imagination to chance originates from his critiques of de Saussure's and Husserl's views of signs as well as from his critique of Husserl's view of the living present,[1] making chance and trace central to writing at the core of his deconstruction. It is for this reason that he refers to artistic or imaginative discourse as a "floating signifier" or a "wild card which puts play into play."[2] And the imagination is limited at best to its reproductive function,[3] serving to yield indeterminacy and ambivalence into discourse in a move away from logocentrism. This move from logocentrism and phonocentrism and the extension of the notion of writing means that the imagination's role has dissolved into the textual play of undecidability. The world becomes a never-beginning, never-ending text where "everything is reflected in the medium or speculum of *reading-writing without breaking the mirror*." It becomes clear from the above consideration that, in order adequately to understand deconstruction, the significance of its substitution of chance for the central role of productive imagination must be understood, for this shift in the role of play marks not only a distinctive thought, but a fundamentally different attitude from that which places the imagination in a central position, and opts for a philosophical thinking at the end of philosophy. The option of chance at the core of a doctrine of dissemination and the view of the living present as effect, both of these within the primacy of a unique syntactics, spills over into an entirely different doctrine than one for which imagination is central, for which semantics of discourse takes precedence over syntax, and for which the unity of the sentence on the semantic side is far more fundamental than the unity of a sign in relation to others in the system.[4] By contrasting these differing roles of chance and imagination and their respective philosophies, the fundamental motif leading to one or the other emerges into light: on the one hand, a thought arbitrary to its core, in which the human act of thinking, grasping, and imagining is left, like a ship in a tumultuous sea with no other control over the sail or rudder except the haphazard capriciousness of the elements; and on the other hand, a philosophy of limit in the context of reason's demand for infinity and completeness. And it is a fundamental option that sets the basic directions of these two courses of thought—an option for chaos engulfing any effort toward sense, where sense transpires in the context of spacing, of lettering, and of words in positions; or an option for a sense and light arising out of what could be called the fullness of the sense of existence. It is Ricoeur who plots this latter course in terms of a hermeneutic of existence at the limit of reason. We will now further investigate Derrida's use of chance in place of the imagination.

DERRIDA AND CHANCE

In the famous "Double Session" of *Dissemination* Derrida begins with an enigma right at the outset, by raising the question, rhetorical in his posing, of "what is literature"? His sense of mimesis is not at all like the threefold mimesis made so famous by Ricoeur, as (pre)figuration, configuration, and refiguration. Rather, Derrida finds that two enigmas already place him at the core of his own deconstructive process and its priority given to writing, which itself obliterates any question of the "real" in literature, thus effacing the difference between truth and the imaginary. Both are equally the results of a process of basic writing going on in a quasi-independence from anyone, and thus distinguished from mere mimetic writing, to which we are usually confined in thinking, speaking, or writing about writing. And his question, "what is literature?" hardly gets posed as such, for he does not let it get off the ground as a question with a fixed sense, but rather as an enigma that unfolds in a deconstructive process, or better, in the process of self-deconstruction. As we will see more explicitly in the next chapter, Derrida's view of language in relation to differences and *différance* puts the status of truth, the real, and the imaginary in literature on the same level of derivation from *différance* in writing.

What is at stake here is that in a certain sense, everything is derived from writing in such a way that there is no origin, no presence, no imitation, and therefore, no hard-and-fast fixed distinction between truth and imaginary. Both are derivative from and effects of dissemination. The shift is toward text and textuality and away from a centrality of subjects and their imagination. The distinction between the reproductive imagination, which requires a form to be repeated, and the productive imagination, which gives the form, falls apart in that they are both derivative from that which is "beneath" presence, which they both presuppose, as is clear. And with the example of the multifaceted "lustre,"[5] which looms so large in the "Double Session," Derrida reinforces the breakdown of the distinction between the image and the thing, the signifier and the referent or the signified, the imitation, and the reality.

Thus, it is the case that all else is condemned to some kind of presence, whether it is the mimesis of imitation of the tradition, or the productive imagination as the source and origin against the imitation and copy views: all are equally effects employing presence, even the romantic idealism of the post-Kantian era. Thus, it is clear that Derrida and postmodern deconstruction cannot be reduced to the alternative thinking of Heidegger, who centralizes the Kantian productive imagination, now within an ontological questioning. For Derrida considers that to entail a view of presence of its own kind, witnessed especially in the later writings of Heidegger.

We have seen that the boundary between the imaginary and the real has been deconstructed, thus giving rise to the figure of play, where there is no question of truth or reality. We must consider the consequences of this deconstruction of the imagination, of the metaphysical distinction between the imaginary and the real, following Kearney.[6] First, we can no longer legitimately ask the question about what literature is. We have seen that Derrida, even at the beginning of the "Double Session," was a bit enigmatic and cagey about writing about the question, stating that "I don't quite have the gall to say plumb straight out that it is reserved for the question 'what is literature?', this question being henceforth properly considered a quotation already, in which the place of the 'what is' ought to lend itself to careful scrutiny, along with the presumed authority under which one submits anything whatever, and particularly literature, to the form of its inquisition—this double session about which I will never have the militant innocence to announce that it is concerned with the question 'what is literature,' will find its corner BETWEEN [ENTRE] literature and truth, between literature and that by which the question 'what is?' wants answering."[7] A question of this kind supposes that there is some "essence" of imagination that would distinguish it from a real world existing beyond it or before it. But Derrida's extended notion of writing includes *everything* so that the opposition between imagination and reality dissolves into the textual play of undecidablity from which nothing escapes. As Kearney says, the world becomes a never-beginning, never-ending text "where 'everything is reflected in the medium or speculum of reading-writing *without breaking the mirror.*' This implies, furthermore, that the question *what is literature?* is also meaningless. We can no longer speak of a decidable being of literature, one that might be distinguished from some notion of 'truth' which it is supposed to imitate (as copy) or create (as origin). Literature is a product, and is therefore *both* true *and* false. And following the deconstruction formulation, this also means it is *neither* true *nor* false."[8]

We likewise cannot ask about who it is who imagines. Once the notion of an origin of meaning has been done away with, it makes no sense to speak of a transcendental or existential subject who produces or reproduces images. This does not mean that there is no "I" of discourse, but, rather, that it simply indicates the personal pronoun in language. But that is on another tier, secondary to writing in the basic sense, that undercuts discourse as a derived realm. In this passage, it becomes clear that it is a misfocus in a Derridian context to be overly concerned with the distinction between productive and reproductive imagination, since it makes no difference. The author or writer and the reader fall back into quasi-oblivion, since what is important is the substitution. There is no *author* or reader as some decidable identity existing outside the text, no human center from which the imaginary emanates: "Father and son, author and reader, mirror each other in a textual interplay of mutual dispossession."[9] Derrida himself reflects this sentiment in stating in reference to the reader:[10]

> But who is it that is addressing you? Since it is not an 'author,' a 'narrator,' or a 'deus ex machina,' it is an 'I' that is both part of the spectacle and part of the audience: an 'I' that, a bit like 'you' . . . functioning as a pure passageway for operations or substitutions, is not some singular and irreplaceable existence, some subject of 'life,' but only, moving between life and death, reality and fiction, etc., a mere function or phantom.

Finally, the question *how does one escape from parody?* cannot be asked since there is no escape. The imagination that is deconstructed into parody of itself as an ongoing process of copying, and so on, abandons all recourse to the metaphysical opposition between inner and outer. There is no way out of the cave of mirrors, for there is nothing outside of writing. All is text. This is a serious dethronement of the imagination from its lofty perch of Heideggerian focus, and before that, of the romantics and idealists of the nineteenth century, and, finally, of Sartre and of Ricoeur. It is in this context that this is the deconstructive sense of philosophy at the limit or end, as considered in chapter 1, not in the sense of being completed, but of the postmodern order of perpetual allusion. This analysis has made it clear how the claim can be made that Derrida substitutes chance (moira), under the influence of Heidegger's stress on moira, for the imagination.[11] We must now connect these points to the emphasis on the absolute of passage.

This phrase, "*the absolute of passage*," entails Husserlian temporalization or the living present. And, as will be seen in the following chapters, this living present with its retentions and protentions is derived rather than primary. Second memory, to which retentions are relegated according to this Derridian script, takes on central importance. Thus, the living present is a derivation or an effect produced from second memory. Therefore, the three implications of historical passage must be rooted in it. This absolute passage means for Derrida first that empirical genesis conditions transcendental structure and simultaneously that transcendental structure conditions empirical genesis. The living present is the structure or form of all experience, of all temporal geneses, from which objects or structures come. Thus the living present is simultaneously constituting and constituted. Like that of any structure, the completeness of the living present's structure can only be approximated because it too can be infinitely iterated. In turn, however, because the *telos* can only be approximated, the *arché* recedes. The living present, like historicity, contains a reciprocal implication of end and origin.

Lawlor contends that the absolute *of* passage means first that all sense arises out of a series or iteration of singular, factual, or empirical events; and that, conversely, an iterable structure cannot come about through an arbitrary series. The series itself must have presupposed some structure as its guide, so that structure conditions genesis, and genesis conditions structure. Thus, this absolute of passage means linguistic iteration and likewise implies the reciprocal implication of end and origin. The passage of writing is the absolute, the absolute, however, "of a Danger."[12]

Derrida's interpretation in *Speech and Phenomena* takes him in the direction of space, distance, discontinuity, and mediation as prior to temporalization, duration, continuity, and especially the living present. And his diacritical view of language and the role of trace make the rupture from dialectic and from distanciation complete for Derrida. Lawlor indicates that Derrida goes further in separating *différance* from dialectic and from imagination in *Dissemination* and, in particular, in "The Double Session," where he clarifies the nondialectical notion of dissemination. "Disssemination is a genesis based not in temporalization and imagination, but rather in spacing and the aleatory. For Derrida, chance alterations are radically discontinuous, totally unexpected, even though they are based in the continuity of a minimal form such as a letter."[13]

For Derrida, the emphasis is taken away from the imagination and put on chance, dissemination, and *rhythmos*. Lawlor again correctly indicates that according to Derrida Mallarmé's genius is not imagination but chance; dissemination is *rhythmos*.[14] "For difference is the necessary interval, the suspense between two outcomes, the 'lapse of time' between two shots, two rolls, two chances. Without its being possible in advance to 'decide' the limits of this sort of propagation, a different effect is produced each time, an effect that is therefore each time 'new' [*neuf*], a game [*jeu*]of chance forever new, a play of fire [*feu*] forever young [*jeune*]—fire and games being always, as Heraclitus and Nietzsche have said, a play of luck with necessity, of contingency with law. A hymen between chance and rule"[15] (Dissemination, p. 277). For Derrida, necessity is not the negation of chance, but the affirmation of it. Dissemination, as Derrida says, "*affirms* the always already divided generation of meaning. Dissemination—spills it in advance. . . . We return to it, rather as to the fold of the hymen, to the somber white of the cave or of the womb, to the black-on-white upon the womb, the locus of scattered emissions, of chances taken with no return, of separations."[16] For Derrida, dissemination cannot become an origin or source, nor an ultimate signified, the place of truth. Rather, it "represents the affirmation of this nonorigin, the remarkable empty locus of a hundred blanks no meaning can be ascribed to, in which mark supplements and substitution games are multiplied *ad infinitum*"[17] [Every form, the minimal unity of a letter, according to Derrida, is divided and divisible]. Lawlor puts this quite well in stating: "Like an atom, every text, every word, every letter, is out of our control. Made possible by the same, a roll of the dice gives a totally different idea, a totally other idea; lacking the arrow of meaning, the results for Derrida cannot be expected, foreseen, or anticipated."[18]

Derrida's interpretation of Mallarmé's genius as chance certainly marks a clean break with the Kantian tradition, which highlights genius as the life-giving principle in the creative imagination's production of a work. Here, we see the opposite, rather than creative imagination, the role of the roll of the dice, the dissemination from outside of the control of the subject, something that simply occurs.[19] The fuller context for this will be further considered and clarified in the next chapter with a fuller elucidation of language and living present, showing precisely how Derrida sees the play of chance. In the present context, the question that must be dealt with is whether it is possible to substitute this play of chance for the productive imagination, together with the play of reason. Is it not also necessary to subvert this play of reason, subordinating it to the play of chance? That these can be successfully integrated is obvious from the philosophy of Ricoeur, in which one sees explicitly the tension between a play of reason and a direct role of the play of the unconscious and the involuntary, in a sort of polemical unity. In Ricoeur's view there is likewise a certain decentering of the subject's role, placing some emphasis on the role of the unconscious and the involuntary in the constitution of meaning and discourse, but not yielding to them a priority proper to the conscious and the voluntary.

It is the empty space that Derrida's deconstruction employs with great skill. Again, Lawlor puts this well in saying: "The empty space between, in which writing zigzags like a drunk, is what provides the chances that cannot be imagined."[20] The move to chance as displacement of the subject is not meant to destroy the subject, but simply to put it in its place with a stress on syntax in a new sense. Thus some have in too strong a sense said that Derridean deconstruction is a perversion of philosophy,[21] instead of seeing it as philosophy at the limit in the sense that we have appropriated. To the extent that there is a role for the imagination, it serves to yield indeterminacy and ambivalence into discourse, moving away from logocentrism. It is interesting that the role of the creative imagination is completely subverted and buried by structuralism, and in a parallel way, by contemporary interpretations of psychoanalytic doctrine such as that of Lacan. For, in stark contrast to Ricoeur, for whom the Freudian unconscious and involuntary are inverted in their contributing to meaning constitution, these deconstructionists first give a strong priority to the structure and process of language. They thus subordinate the speech of the individual subject (*parole*) to the impersonal and quasi-absolute system of language as a whole, and the latter to the hidden structure of the unconscious, which has a similar role, each subverting creativity in meaning and action constitution. We will now turn to a different way of appropriating the productive imagination of Kant in a contemporary philosophy attuned to the same issues as postmodern deconstruction, that of Ricoeur.

RICOEUR AND IMAGINATION

Ricoeur's appropriation of the Kantian productive imagination, in stark contrast to the role of imagination in deconstruction, gives it a central place without jeopardizing the role of reason. The most intense role, continuous with that in symbols, is in the creativity of living metaphor, which is continued in narrative. Here we see Ricoeur extending and completing the role of the productive imagination beyond anything Kant conceived, and in a more integrated and whole philosophy than anyone else today. His view of imagination in these various roles and expressions allows him to interrelate any number of cognate disciplines, and to do so while preserving the fullness and mystery of human existence in its vital tension with the tendency toward rational ordering and expression. We must begin by looking at these various expressions of the productive imagination in Ricoeur's philosophy, which is so central as to lead to the whole gamut of his writings in the past five decades. We will focus therefore on those aspects that are directly related to our project of a dialogue with postmodern deconstruction, leading to our account of ethics at the limit. Thus, it will be necessary for us to focus on the productive imagination in the creativity of language, in action, and in distanciation-appropriation. This development will highlight the differences with other postmodern thinkers, especially deconstructionists, but must not be allowed to obliterate the basic common interests shared in these various enterprises.

A preliminary remark is in order about Ricoeur's placing ethics, or more precisely, an extended ethics, in a center of his entire philosophy. Such an extended ethics, with its role of evil in freedom and existence, gives rise to the view of hope and thus the necessity for speculative philosophy and its possibility as emerging from the innovation of meaning that is engendered by the productive imagination and its extension. Ricoeur's entire philosophy is thus bound to the interplay among imagination, understanding, and reason. For it is the imagination that is presented by reason with ideas. His philosophy recasts the Kantian view of the demand on the part of reason for totality as well as reason's placing of a limit on experience, in terms of his own development of a view of the quasitranscending of this limit through indirect expressions such as symbols and metaphors. Thus, in contrast to the position clarified above, Ricoeur's view goes beyond Kant's strict doctrine, while remaining as true to some of its essential tenets as possible for a post-Hegelian and contemporary philosophy.

Following Kant, Ricoeur speaks of the "the spirit" (*Geist*) in an aesthetic sense, as "the life-giving principle of the mind (*Gemut*)."[22] The ideas given by reason to the imagination assign a task to the interplay (game) between imagination and understanding, forcing the understanding to think more, as seen in the last chapter. Thus a more specific focus is obtained on how Ricoeur has opened up Kant's doctrine on several crucial points: first, the indirect expressions, symbols, metaphors, myths, and narrative discourse provide reason with an indirect access to the total and to the unconditioned; second, the illusion of reason in attempting to make its ideas an object of experience is overcome, not by denying the illusion, but by buying into another access; third, the speculative orientation of reason, rooted in the drive on the part of reason to unity and totality, is the outgrowth of the tendency to found, although in a limited way, the knowledge of understanding, but now nourished by means of the indirect expressions, presented to the understanding for thought, and demanding totality of reason from that thinking more of understanding. Thus, within that game between understanding and imagination, and the task assigned by the ideas of reason, the condition making speculative thought possible emerges. Yet the necessity of that thought arises from reason itself, in affording the life-giving principle to the mind, and, in so doing, producing the conditions that made possible what is necessary from reason, that is, speculative thought. This leads to a speculative discourse responding to and ontologically clarifying the postulate of reference within poetic discourse.[23]

Within the sphere of poetics, in metaphorical and narrative discourse, semantic innovation is placed in the extended role of schematism of the productive imagination, which for Kant, as seen in the last chapter, is symbolization. It is the work of the productive imagination to perceive resemblance in terms at first seen apart and then brought together by inaugurating the similarity between them. "This consists of schematizing the synthetic operation, of figuring the predicative assimilation from whence results the semantic innovation."[24] Ricoeur however, in this context wants to cut beneath the imaginative synthesis of providing schemata for the rules of understanding in unifying the manifold of sense for objective knowledge. This role of creative imagination cannot be separated from the connection between symbols and metaphors for Ricoeur, and the relation between the symbol and metaphor is essential regarding creativity in semantic innovation of the imagination. For symbols are bound to spirit and to desire. Continuous with symbols, metaphors stress the unbounded creativity in expressions with double meaning in the overall context of polysemy. Thus, looked at from that direction, the imagination in its role of schematism is the source of semantic innovation.[25] This, of course, entails both an extension of the Kantian role of schematism, and the collapse of the distinction between the determinative and the reflective judgments. And now following Kant more strictly, looked at from the perspective of reason, it is reason (spirit) that give to the imagination the ideas that stimulate the understanding to creative thought, which, in "thinking more," cannot ever be adequate to the idea. Thus, the demand for totality within the context of a bond to existence, through desire and spirit, allows a glimpse again at the infinite quest within a finite situation. It is beneficial to pursue this line of thought further in the direction of the productive imagination and its schematism, for it is here that we see Ricoeur's own philosophic framework, both as Kantian and as contemporary, undercutting and underlying all of his philosophy of the will and myriad excursions into dialogue with other philosophies.

In this context of the extended role of the productive imagination in schematism, Ricoeur compares the "grasping together" characteristic of the act of configuration to judgment as understood by Kant, reminding us somewhat of Heidegger's "gathering" of reason seen in chapter 2 above. Still following Kant, Ricoeur compares the production of the act of configuration to the work of the productive imagination understood as a transcendental, and not a psychological, faculty. And Ricoeur indicates, following the third *Critique* to some extent, that the productive imagination is not only rule-governed, but also constitutes the "generative matrix of rules."[26] Along this line, Ricoeur reminds us that in Kant's first *Critique*, the categories of the understanding are first schematized by the productive imagination, and that the schematism has this power because the productive imagination fundamentally has a synthetic function, connecting understanding and intuition by engendering syntheses that are intellectual and intuitive at the same time. Applying this creativity to his own project, we see that for him, emplotment,[27] too, engenders a mixed intelligibility between what he calls the point, theme, or thought of a story, and the intuitive presentation of circumstances, characters, episodes, and changes of fortune that make up the denouement. In this way, we may speak of a schematism of the narrative function. "This schematism, in turn, is constituted within a history that has all the characteristics of a tradition. Let us understand by this term not the inert transmission of some already dead deposit of material but the living transmission of an innovation always capable of being reactivated by a return to the most creative moments of poetic activity." In Ricoeur's understanding, traditionality enriches the relationship between plot and time with a new feature.

He says further: "However Kant only recognized those determinations of time that contribute to the objective constitution of the physical world. The schematism of the narrative function implies determinations of a new genre which are precisely the ones we have just designated by the dialectic of the episodic characteristics and the configuring of emplotment."[28] Thus, we see Ricoeur expanding on the Kantian determination of time to include, within the context of indirect expressions, the whole of the narrative function, which allows for expressing new worlds in texts. This in general is what he means, as seen in an early chapter above, when he says he denies the Kantian distinction between the determinative and reflective judgments in this context. Such expression is correlated to the other end of the hermeneutical arch as the original appropriation of the latent world of the text, expanding the world of the listener. Such ontic aspects of existence must be further investi-gated in terms of the ontic access to the Sacred explored in earlier works by Ricoeur, and culminating only now in his most recent works dealing with the world of the text and narrative discourse. In overcoming the supposed phenomenological subjectivism of Husserl, Ricoeur has refo-cused on the openness and rootedness of existence, and exposed the sig-nificance of the decenteredness of the Cogito in terms of its twofold dependence upon desire and spirit. This ontic existential dependence has its roots in a further dependence on the ultimate *telos* and *arché*, the Sacred, as the prelinguistic level subtending language. And, it is the metaphorical function that takes the ambiguity and polyvalence to the linguistic creative level.

Metaphoric function is not a part of conceptual thinking (IT, 57). As mentioned above, the theory of metaphor leads the theory of symbols into the neighborhood of the Kantian theory of the schematism and con-ceptual synthesis. Metaphor is the place in language, understood as dis-course, where this creativity comes about. It is distinguished from, but rooted in, the symbolic level of discourse and expression, and, as living metaphor, gives rise to conceptual thought.

Ricoeur expresses this insight in the following text, indicating the direction toward the logos of rationality: "Metaphor would be the place in discourse where this emergence may be detected because sameness and difference are in conflict. If metaphor can be treated as a figure of speech, it is because it overtly presents in the form of a conflict between sameness and difference the process which is covertly at work in the con-struction of all semantic fields, that is, *the kinship which brings individ-uals under the rule of a logical class.*"[29] However, Ricoeur also stresses the break, the discontinuity or *epoche* between the metaphoric and the speculative levels of discourse: "One passes from one discourse to the other only by an *epoche*"[30] But in spite of this rupture, speculative dis-course gets its possibility from the semantic function of metaphor in that the gain in signification is a demand in the concept but not a knowing by the concept.[31]

In two recent works,[32] Ricoeur brings together time with the seman-tic innovation of the productive imagination and schematism. Narrative fiction[33] takes on a central role because by means of it "we re-configure our confused, unformed, and at the limit mute temporal existence."[34] It is this that makes possible the "intersection" of the world of the text and the world of the reader, "wherein real action occurs and unfolds its spec-ified temporality."[35] The culmination, however, of the relation of time and narrative is reached within Ricoeur's project as a whole when the "refiguration of time by narrative" is achieved, when "referential inten-tions of the historical narrative and the fictional narrative *interweave.*

Our analysis of the fictive experience of time will at least have marked a decisive turning point in the direction of the solution to this problem that forms the horizon of my investigation, by providing something like a *world of the text* for us to think about, while awaiting its complement, the *life-world of the reader*, without which the signification of the literary work is incomplete."[36]

RICOEUR AND DISTANCIATION

We must turn now to the important role of distanciation in the philosophy and hermeneutics of Ricoeur, since, in this core element of his philosophy, we see his opposition to the linguistic view of postmodern deconstruction at its most intense point of divergence. For, according to the script of Derrida, Ricoeur's sense of distanciation is derivative, and on a level not allowing what Ricoeur sees in it, due to Derrida's differing view of language and the role of linguistic science, as will be seen in the next chapters.

Distanciation for Ricoeur begins even in the very act of meaning, with the structure of the noesis-noema, for the need for such a distinction is the demand to give an account of the meaning, the objectivity transcending the act that gives rise to it. Or as Merleau-Ponty puts it regarding the example of the Ninth Symphony of Beethoven, there is a distinction between what I experience and that I experience it.[37] This initial projecting of meaning is already a distanciation writ small, which gets more obvious as it runs the gamut and finally gets expressed in writing. To account for this full sweep of distanciation, we must view it in relation to its dialectic other, appropriation, and see this dialectic within the focus on the fourfold dialectic constituting the essential dimensions or moments of discourse. Thus it would be more precise to say that distanciation has its origin in the noema-noesis structure rather than emphasize its origin in productive imagination; semantic innovation is not irrelevant, in that the productive imagination is the activity, the noesis that brings the semantic innovation, the creation of new meaning, to light in its enigmatic activity. Thus, it is directly tied to distanciation in this basic sense, as shall be seen more clearly as distanciation is put into the broader context of discourse in opposition to *la langue* in the next chapter.

To say, as Lawlor does, that "because distanciation is defined by productive imagination, human experience can always transcend the limit" and that the "imagination's interplay between the finite and the infinite leads to distanciation's dialectical mixture,"[38] is quite misleading. For what is at stake are certain basic differences with Derrida about the nature of language, sign, and time, and certain priorities given in these contexts. To liberate Ricoeur's view from the possibility of misconceptions, a lengthy account of his view of distanciation and its general context must be understood before turning to the contrast between his view of sign and time and their roles in language. We cannot forget that for Ricoeur, discourse is understood as meaning, and actualized as event (IT, 12). And the break that occurs in taking the word in a sentence as a sign in a system of language (*la langue*) must not be allowed to truncate our view of language as discourse. Such a break comes in the shift of focus from the word in the sentence to the sign in a linguistic position. And this shift involves a break in continuity, but such a break is introduced from the outside, by the shift of focus by the investigator. It is this break, and the disregard for the presupposed and ignored semantic priority that Ricoeur emphasizes so much, that allows Derrida, together with structuralism and deconstruction in general, to invert this priority in favor of that of a syntactics, closure, and the flux. This can be seen to be the real point of difference between Ricoeur and Derrida.

There is a further point to be clarified in turning to Ricoeur's view of distanciation especially in relation to the dialectic of event and meaning. For from the priority and prejudice of the deconstructive perspective, this event is reduced to the temporal present and the Derridian priorities, leading to a distinctive misunderstanding of distanciation in this important and fundamental dialectic of event and meaning. And it must be kept in mind that for Derrida, this dialect and distanciation is overcome, but only by forfeiting the role of language that says something to someone, that is, with a viable semantic priority; and by jettisoning an approach to the lived present as containing a duration and a continuity, which was the original thrust of Husserl's investigation, for the sake of the regressive move to a Humean discreteness of time. And this view of time is not able to sustain anything meaningful, nor can it make any sense of our experience. Let us now turn to a full account of Ricoeur's view of distanciation and the dialectics relating to it as setting the stage for the treatment in the next chapter of language and sign, and lived time and the living present.

Discourse, Interpretation, and Meaning

Fundamental to Ricoeur's theory of language as discourse, with some modification and expansion in his latest works on narrative, is a fourfold dialectical structure of discourse: the dialectics between meaning and event, between sense and reference, between distanciation and appropriation, and between explanation and interpretation. These various considerations about language, experience, and discourse converge upon a theory of metaphor leading to narrative at the crossroads of various paths.

The dialectical structure of discourse is first constituted in the polarity of meaning and event. Meaning, as Husserl and Frege insisted, is distinguished from the event by its ideality that transcends the event. Another way of putting this is to note, as Ricoeur does, the ambiguity in this use of "meaning," including the utterer's meaning and the utterance meaning as what the noematic side says and means. Further, meaning, as the utterance (meaning) transcending the event and the utterer's meaning, is constituted by a further dialectic requiring a distinction between meaning and sense. This dialectic of meaning is in turn constituted by sense and reference. Thus, the ideality of meaning, transcending the event of discourse, includes the sense and reference. Meaning is broken down to sense and reference in discourse, to the "something said" and the "about something." The ideality of meaning involves "distanciation" in that it is "beyond" the concrete conditions from which it emerges.

Discourse as event is a necessary other pole to language as *langue*. But the event character must not be overextended to apply to the problematics of understanding. "If all discourse is actualized as an event, all discourse is understood as meaning" (IT, 12). This distinction between discourse actualized as event and understood as meaning preserves the ideality of meaning, not allowing it to be reduced solely to the conditions of the event that it transcends. On the other hand, reference is connected to the event side of discourse. That someone says something to someone about something, that is, "that someone refers to something at a certain time is an event, a speech event" (IT, 20). The reference points to two poles, the speaker and the world, not allowing for the closure of the language system: "Discourse refers back to its speaker at the same time that it refers to the world. This correlation is not fortuitous since it is ultimately the speaker who refers to the world in speaking. Discourse in action and in use refers backwards and forwards, to a speaker and a world" (IT, 22). The reference, as distinct and polarized from the sense, is connected to the event. In this way, the second dialectic (or one pole of it) goes back to the first dialectic. The reference pole of meaning does this precisely through the sense, giving a certain primacy to the sense dimension and a structure to the event. Ricoeur explains this correlation of the structure of sense, the structure of meaning, and the structure of the event in the following text:

> But the (speech) event receives its structure from the meaning as sense. The speaker refers to something on the basis of, or through, the ideal structure of the sense. The sense, so to speak, is traversed by the referring intention of the speaker. In this way the dialectic of event and meaning receives a new development from the dialectic of sense and reference. (IT, 20)

Ricoeur's reflection on the dialectical structure of discourse, beginning with the dialectics of event and meaning, and of sense and reference, leads to an analysis of the two other dialectics involved in discourse: the dialectic of distanciation and appropriation, and the dialectic
within appropriation (reading) as explanation and understanding. The
dialectic between distanciation and appropriation is polarized by writing and reading. Distanciation and its semantic autonomy allow appropriation in its own dialectic between explanation and understanding
[*erklaren* and *verstehen*]. The elements that need to be treated are integrated in the following passage (IT, 43):

> The problem of writing becomes a hermeneutical problem when it is
> referred to its complimentary pole, which is reading. A new dialectic
> then emerges, that of distanciation and appropriation. By appropria-
> tion I mean the counterpart of the semantic autonomy, which detached
> the text from its writer. To appropriate or to make 'one's own' what
> was 'alien.'

In the first pole of the dialectic of distanciation and appropriation,
the transition from speaking to writing brings to the fore the advent of
meaning in its transcendence and ideality. The dialectic of event and
meaning is not left behind, but instead is made more obvious and
explicit by writing. Further, "the semantic autonomy of the text which
now appears is still governed by the dialectic of event and meaning.
Writing is the full manifestation of discourse" (IT, 25).

In further drawing out the tension or polarity between the event of
discourse and its meaning, several traits of discourse can be contrasted.
Through this process the various aspects of distanciation emerge. In the
discourse as event, the present temporal flux is relevant. In the fixing of
discourse in writing, the event is surpassed by the meaning, including in
this broadened view of meaning, the analytic philosophers' threefold distinction: locutionary acts, illocutionary acts, and the perlocutionary acts
in the saying of the said (IT, 22).[39]

What the writing fixes, then, is not the event, but the noema of the
act of speaking, the meaning of the speech event (sense and reference)
(IT, 27). In the speech event, the subject speaking has a certain mediate
reference by the discourse. In the fixing of discourse in writing, there is
a certain autonomy of the text from the author. In the event of discourse
as dialogue what the speaker means to say or intends to say and the
actual meaning of what he says are almost the same. But in the discourse
of the text, there is such a distanciation that the intention of the author
might not be the same as the meaning fixed in the text. In fact, "Inscription becomes synonymous with the semantic autonomy of the text,
which results from the disconnection of the mental intention of the

author from the verbal meaning of the text, of what the author meant and what the text means" (IT, 29–30). This is the second mode of the surpassing of the event by the meaning.

For Ricoeur the third aspect or dimension of meaning surpassing the event has to do with the reference functions of discourse. The event of discourse has its reference or references that are immediate to the situation.[40] But the distanciation in the passage from speech to written discourse breaks or suspends that referential totality and allows the world as a referential totality in Heidegger's sense to emerge and to rejoin the theme of Being-in-the-world.[41] As Ricoeur states:

> My thesis here is that the abolition of first order reference, an abolition accomplished by fiction and poetry, is the condition of possibility for the liberation of second order of reference which reaches the world not only at the level of manipulable objects, but at the level Husserl designated by the expression *Lebenswelt* and Heidegger by 'Being-in-the-world.'

But what about the world of the text? For Ricoeur, what is to be interpreted is this Being-in-the-world, the world proposed by the text that I might inhabit and in which I might project my ownmost possibilities.[42] "Through fiction and poetry new possibilities of Being-in-the-world are opened up within everyday reality. Fiction and poetry intend being, but not through the modality of giveness, rather through the modality of possibility. And in this way everyday reality is metamorphized by means of what we could call the imaginative variations that literature works on the real."[43] The sense of "world" of the text is clarified in his own words in the following passage (IT, 37):

> We ought to enlarge our concept of the world, therefore, not only to allow for non-ostensive but still descriptive references, but also non-ostensive and non-descriptive references, those of poetic diction. The term 'world' then has the meaning that we all understand when we say of a new born child that he has come into the world. For me, the world is the ensemble of references opened up by every kind of text, descriptive or poetic, that I have read, understood, and loved. And to understand a text is to interpolate among the predicates of our situation all the significations that make a *Welt* out of our *Umwelt*. It is this enlarging of our horizon of existence that permits us to speak of the reference opened up by the text or of the world opened up by the referential claims of most texts.

Ricoeur has explicitly "rejoined"[44] Heidegger's sense of understanding as a structure of Being-in-the-world that projects our ownmost possibilities in situations in which we find ourselves. The proposed world is that which is to be interpreted in the text. This is the world of the text wherein one might project one's ownmost possibilities.[45] Whereas dialogical discourse is caught up in the interlocutory situation, with a particular audience of hearers, discourse fixed in writing becomes addressed to any reader. Thus there is a distanciation from the particular audience, and an address to any audience of readers,"[46] to an unknown reader and potentially to whomever knows how to read" (IT, 31). This is a further surpassing of the event of discourse in dialogue by the written discourse.

The context in which Ricoeur applies the categories of work to the distanciation of fixing the discourse in a text is that of interpretation. Structural analysis has yielded the important fruit of overcoming the too clear-cut distinction between explanation and understanding. Although hermeneutics is still the "art of discerning the discourse in a work,"[47] this discourse is only given within and through the structure of the work. Thus, interpretation or reading "is the reply to the fundamental distanciation which constitutes the objectification of man in works of discourse comparable to his objectification in the products of his work and art."[48]

The discourse as a work is a sequence longer than a sentence in that it presents a second-order organization that is the overall context in which each sentence is only a partial meaning in relation to the whole. It therefore can be considered a closed context for the interpretation of each sentence. "A text works as the first con-text for each partial meaning."[49] Thus, the interpretation of the text cannot be the construing of partial meanings added to one another. Rather, it must take into account the topic or topics, and the hierarchy of topics. Discourse as work follows certain rules of what is usually called literary genres. This element of composition as the rules of genre is a means of production and not a "means of classification" into kinds. In other words, these rules are for the performance of a competence rather than rules for classifying according to literary types.

The type of distanciation of the discourse as a work can be brought to the context of the polarity between the event and the meaning of discourse. The distanciation effected by the genre allows a structure for the discourse, which has as a characteristic that it is both open and closed. It is open in the sense that it is preserved by the genre from distortion, but because of that preservation, it is open to further new interpretations. It is closed in that it is not open for distortion. For Ricoeur, the instance of discourse *par excellence* is the individual work. For it is in the individual work of discourse that style, event, and individual come together and are correlated with genre or composition. The uniqueness of the work in its style, as bringing a context into existence, mediates the composition of the genre through which the work of discourse is organized and given structure. This allows for the passage from the structural aspect of the work to the understanding of its meaning in an appropriative interpretation. Thus explanation and understanding are brought together in an interarticulation rather than opposed and relegated to different realms of discourse or interpretation. In correlating the moments of explanation and appropriation in the discourse of the text, we have already to some extent brought forth the different modes of reading texts. Ricoeur explicitly interweaves the two modes, thus overcoming the dichotomy instituted between them by Dilthey. This dialectic between explanation and understanding leads to the heart of the pole of appropriation within the broader dialectic of distanciation and appropriation.[50]

Before the discourse of a text can be appropriated in new interpretations, the depth meaning must be attained. The acquisition of meaning is possible due to the way that meanings transcend the event of discourse. This distanciation, and the consequent autonomy of the text, allows for a twofold reading of the text; first a preliminary understanding, then an explanatory reading supporting an appropriative comprehension.[51] Although these two modes, understanding and explanation, are opposed, they can be interarticulated in such a way as to allow for arriving at the depth meaning of the discourse in the texts, and thus let the text itself interpret.

Interpretation thus *postpones* such an appropriation in order to *let the text speak*, to *allow the text* and its language to interpret itself originally. The concept of the first level of interpretation, then, is now an "objective interpretation"[52] that postpones the subjective or other end of the arch of hermeneutics. The reader must let the interpreting text have its say before too quickly appropriating it and reactualizing or enacting it. This structural analysis extends the initial (subjective) concept of interpretation, so as to admit a separation or bracketing of the reference of the supposed intentions of the author; the opportunity is then given for the reader to focus on and hear what the text itself wants to say and let it orient our thinking according to it and its direction. "The sense of the text is the direction which it opens up for our thought." Ricoeur goes on to underscore this crucial aspect of interpretation:[53]

> This concept of sense as direction for thought leads us to a new definition of interpretation which would be less a subjective operation than an objective process; less an act *on* the text, than an act *of* the text. This process of interpretation has something to do with the depth semantics of the text delivered by structural analysis; it is this depth semantics which is to be understood in dynamic terms; whereas the structure constitutes the statics of the text, the depth semantics is itself a process of meaning; it requires a fresh interpretation because it is itself an interpretation, this interpretation which I called the act of the text.

Ricoeur's account of interpretation does not eliminate the element of appropriation, but only postpones it until the end of the process. "It is the other end of what we have called the hermeneutical arch: it is the last pillar of the bridge, the anchor of the arch in the soil of lived experience."[54] The reader must enter into the development of the text, letting it first interpret and reveal the depth of meaning before undertaking its appropriation by "re-saying" as "re-enacting." Thus the objective interpretation necessitates postponing the subjective interpretation. Yet this way of balancing the subjective and objective poles of interpretation underscores the need to show how the work itself (i.e., the text), determines a context the scope of which is comparable to the concrete horizon that governs our everyday comportment, namely, the world.

In his recent writings, especially in *Time and Narrative*, Ricoeur further develops what he formerly called the subjective end of the hermeneutic arch in the analysis of reading in the context of the refiguration of time configured in narratives of history and of fiction. This context, however, requires further development of certain concepts mentioned above. The inadequacy of the terms "reference," and "redescription" requires adjustment in their use. Since the traditional distinction between the "reality" of historical narrative and the "unreality" of fictional narrative emerges as inadequate to deal with the interweaving of the time of history and the time of fiction, Ricoeur passes beyond these categories that he invoked in earlier works.[55] This move marks a transition from the epistemology of reference to the hermeneutics of refiguration. It is within the framework of joining the question of history's construction of a narrative as a reconstruction of something from the past with the question of the unreality of fiction that he wishes to address the problem of the "reality" and "unreality" in narrative. And it is within this framework that he examines the mediation achieved by reading between the world of the text and the world of the reader.

According to Ricoeur, reading involves a mediation of the world of the text and the world of the reader in which there is a passage from configuration to refiguration. This passage requires the confrontation between the world of the text and the world of the reader, involving the "dialectical structure of the operation of refiguration."[56] Ricoeur warns against giving too much room to the quasi-autonomy of the text accentuated by a structuralism that would emphasize the correlation between the implied author and the implied reader, both of which take on a role from indications offered within the text itself. It is, however, precisely this structural bracketing of the text that liberates the author's strategy of persuasion in poetic production from an "intentional fallacy" of a mere psychology of the author.[57] Just as writing requires a flesh and blood author, so too, reading requires a flesh and blood reader who actualizes and thereby transforms the role of the reader prestructured in the text. Likewise, the world of the text, although constituting "an absolutely original intentional object in relation it its 'internal' structure," requires a reader to become more than "a transcendence in immanence."[58] "Its ontological status remains in suspension—an excess in relation to structure, an anticipation in relation to reading. It is only in reading that the dynamism of configuration completes its course."[59]

Ricoeur develops his view of reading in *Time and Narrative* via the perusal of several theories of reading, gleaning from explicitly articulated and systemic views in several phases, and even going beyond a view of reading as merely appropriation. Such reading, in the context of "an aesthetic of reception," is received in two senses: in the sense of the individual in the act of reading, and in the sense of a hermeneutic of the public reception of a work.[60] Such a receptive reading in literary hermeneutics has a threefold task: primary understanding, explanation, and application or appropriation, where the application (or appropriation) is the goal, and primary understanding "guides the process from one stage to the next by virtue of the horizon of expectation it already contains."[61] This primary understanding allows the text to unfold its own expectations, and is the guideline for appropriation, bringing the expectations in the text to bear on the expectations within the reader's world—in the appropriation into that world. This brings together the expectations of both worlds.

But can the individual as interpreter simultaneously occupy both of these worlds, so that each of these become unified in the one world that the self uncovers in its everyday comportment? Put in other terms, where is the reciprocity between the quasi–self-contained structuring of meaning through language that the text provides and the preconceptual, prelinguistic background against which human existence first becomes comprehensible? Ultimately, the formulation of this question leads to the heart of the difference between Heidegger's and Ricoeur's hermeneutics, and a fortiori, the difference between Ricoeur's view and that of deconstruction, both within the postmodern context.

Ricoeur's manner of dealing with indirect language of images and the imagination differs radically from that of those who develop from Heidegger's finitization of reason. The postmodern and deconstructive critique of Heidegger transforms Heidegger's interpretation of the central role of the Kantian productive imagination by subordinating it to chance or to language itself. As seen above, for the deconstruction of Derrida, the closure results from the propensity to fixate on the effect within the flux of the *différance*, a fixation that prevents the transgressing of philosophy to *différance*, dissemination, and the "play of reason." And Lyotard, rendering the treatment of the sublime in the *Critique of*

Judgment as central and paradigmatic, seeking to displace any conceptual rule, thus supports invention that displaces the whole "game" over the innovation that makes new moves with the rules of the game. We have seen that thus, there is an attempt on the part of both to supplant the primacy of the Kantian theoretical understanding in its knowing function in favor of some priority of language that renders the human role (of imagination) passive and secondary to that of the "other." Further, language in their employ loses its semantic priority in favor of semiological priority.

What does this say about philosophy at its end? That its end as boundary is transgressed, and therefore, philosophy becomes thinking in its context of the whole or of completion. But, due to the limit of human experience, and to the quest for the total in thinking (and in action), philosophy will never be completed. Thus, one could perhaps say that philosophy culminates precisely in its attempt to stay attuned to its limited access to the total—to completion, and to "see" or to interpret at this point, its ultimate significance. And is this not what Ricoeur is attempting to do? We must attempt to come to grips now with precisely what the subordination of imagination means. Ricoeur's view of a central role of productive imagination, rooted in his interpretation of the priority of the semantic in language and the unity of language in the sentence, pulls the props out from under Derrida's reduction of the imagination and at once offers a richer and more viable view of language and semantic innovation at the center of his hermeneutic. As seen above and to be confirmed in the next chapters, if reason is not produced by imagination, then reason itself limits knowledge to experience from above, putting the imagination in a central position both in knowledge and in thinking, as it is for Ricoeur. This limit enacted by reason on human knowledge encompasses knowledge within the experience of reality itself, but allows reason to reach beyond the boundary to something of a more far-reaching significance.

CHAPTER 7

Sign, Time, and Trace: Semiotics and the Deconstruction of Presence

INTRODUCTION

Derrida's view of trace hinges on his critiques of Saussure's and Husserl's views of sign, as well as on his critique of Husserl's view of the living present, making trace central to language at the core of his deconstruction. It can be seen that Ricoeur's view of language, taking its point of departure from a more radical critique of Saussure and structuralism than that of Derrida, together with his radical critique of Derrida's deconstruction of Husserl's living present, pulls the props out from under Derrida's view of trace by offering a view of the living present and of time that is able to support a richer and more viable view of trace, language, and linguistics. Yet bringing to clear light Ricoeur's critiques of Derrida's understanding of the living present and of phenomenology's view of inner time will, at once, reveal his agreement with Derrida on essential points of a view of trace in a sign system, and with Husserl regarding the phenomenological primordiality of the living present. Although the following development regarding deconstruction's view of language, time, and the connection between them is critical regarding its interpretation of both time and sign, this positive element that must be gleaned from such a recent style of thinking about each emerges as something that cannot be avoided, and that must instruct any future development of thought today.

SEMIOTICS AND THE DECONSTRUCTION OF PRESENCE

Deconstruction today, emerging in response both to structuralism, which itself is spawned against the background of the linguistics of Ferdinand de Saussure and the structural anthropology of Claude Lévi-Strauss, and to Husserl's phenomenology of language, challenges any philosophy that makes central the semantic within semiotics[1] and the symbolic in human behavior. Thus deconstruction essentially cuts out the core of phenomenology for which a semantic fullness of signs is central and the symbolic in human behavior is distinctive. For phenomenology to survive this challenge it must adequately incorporate the essential dimensions of signs promulgated by deconstruction, while accounting for essential dimensions that it omits. Further, it must reject outright the discreteness of time required by such deconstruction of presence as inadequate to support a viable account of signs. Before turning to the task of establishing both of these points, this chapter will first attempt to present Derrida's view of language, sign, and time against the general backgrounds of the structuralism of Saussure and the phenomenology of Husserl, exposing a discreteness of time demanded by his rejection of presence; then it will attempt to present Ricoeur's view of language, sign, and time as a remedy for the deconstructive assumptions and resultant inadequacies. It is, however, to the challenge of semiology in general and to its positive contribution regarding sign theory that this discussion will first turn, before focusing explicitly on Derrida's understanding of sign and language.

The Challenge of Semeiology

Although radically different from one another in direction, structuralism and deconstruction share a certain philosophical viewpoint regarding sign theory, pitting them together in principle against a fuller view of signs and steering them into what has been referred to as "semeiological reductionism."[2] The philosophical presuppositions of semiological reductionism, for which, within language, the reference, fullness of sense, and subject are lost, challenge the very sense of any phenomenology of language, excluding its possibility and thus its survival as phenomenology. Saussure and Lévi-Strauss interpret signs as unities in relation to other signs in the whole system or network, resulting in a view of the constitution of signs (words) that precludes signification and a speaking subject and that completely excludes a phenomenology of speech.[3] Signification and a subject have little place in such a theory of language, thus, according to Ricoeur, levying a challenge to phenomenology: "The challenge consists in this, that the notion of signification is placed in a field other than the intentional aim of a subject."[4]

If structuralist and deconstructionist semiology and phenomenology entail antinomical views dealing with the same phenomenon, the confrontation between them cannot result merely in juxtaposition or an opposing of one to the other. In his own attempt to interarticulate semiology and phenomenology of language, Ricoeur says in opposition to Merleau-Ponty: "This reanimated phenomenology cannot be content with repeating the old descriptions of speech which do not recognize the theoretical status of linguistics, its view of sign constitution, and its first axioms, the primacy of structure over process,"[5] nor, it must be added, deconstruction and the primacy of flux over structure. The condition imposed by structuralist and deconstructionist semiology on phenomenology is such that it is "through and by means of a linguistic of language that a phenomenology of speech is today conceivable."[6] Thus, according to Ricoeur, the very possibility of such a phenomenology of speech has been challenged by the extreme philosophical presuppositions of any semiological reductionism. It is in a hand-to-hand struggle with the presuppositions of this semiology that it must reconquer the sense of a relation of transcendence in sign or reference, the sense of its relationship to the speaking subject and the origin of the symbolic function itself whereby man is a being-for-sense.[7] But, while demanding that phenomenology's theory of the constitution and the relation of signs account for a theory of structure and process, it is equally true that such semiology of both structuralism and deconstruction, must account for meaning or the semantic dimension of language that it fails adequately to recognize, as shall be seen. Before this struggle with semiology can begin, however, it is necessary to consider the positive contribution of the semiology of structuralism and deconstruction, which, in a specific sense, Ricoeur says makes phenomenology of speech possible.

The positive dimension of signs held in common by structuralist and deconstructionist semiology and Ricoeur is the recognition that signs, as distinguished from signals, stimuli, or causes, introduce a total network of meanings that separates humans from other creatures. This semiotic function captures the essential dimension of signs as standing in for, as taking the place of. "It belongs to the very structure of the sign to operate without fulfillment, in the absence of its object."[8] Further, signs separate human experience from the experience of pure presence as pure "unmediated immediacy." For Derrida, this indicates the downfall of presence, while for Ricoeur this points toward a new understanding of presence as mediated by meaning. The key to understanding why and how they part company on this pivotal issue lies in the different understandings by Derrida and Ricoeur of this essential separation effected by signs within language and the underlying and implicit view of time as discrete demanded by deconstruction's view of the relation between the instant and the living present.

Derrida's view of signs, springing from his analyses of Saussure and Husserl, considers signs to be separate from immediacy with things, as seen above, reflecting the Husserlian reduction that he carries further in the direction of Saussure. Derrida focuses on the initial distinction made by Saussure regarding the constitution of the sign into signifier and signified, analyses and disagrees with that interpretation of the relation between the signified and thought and consequently the relation between the signifier and the signified. For him, the signified is not to be equated with the concept, nor is the concept independent of the signifier, as he says in denying that a concept can be "simply present for thought, independent of a relationship to language, that is of a relationship to a system of signifiers."[9] Rather, the meaning of the sign emerges from its difference from other signs, and the signified can itself become a signifier, thus showing the collapse of the radical distinction made by Saussure between signifier as the material or physical image and signified as thought or concept expressed. "No element can function as a sign without referring to another element which itself is not simply present. This interweaving results in each 'element'—phoneme or grapheme—being constituted on the basis of the trace within it of the other elements of the chain or system."[10] The meaning of a sign, rather than immediately present as Husserl and Saussure thought, is constituted by a "tissue of differences," a network of referrals, and every so-called simple term is marked by the trace of another term. Hence, the "presumed interiority of meaning is already worked upon by its own exteriority. It is always already carried outside itself. It already differs (from itself) before any act of expression."[11] Thus, no particular sign can be considered to refer to any particular signified, a sign cannot have a unique meaning (it is undecidable), and the system of signifiers cannot be escaped. That we cannot escape the system of signifiers and that no particular sign can be considered to refer to any particular signified leads to the conclusion that there is no presence to meaning in the usual sense within language; no presence to consciousness or to things. Rather meaning transpires in the "play that is the web of language."[12] Thus, Derrida can be seen to deny the accessibility of the present and of presence. For everything transpires within language constituted by the network or system of signifiers, and is locked within that system. There is no escape from the system of signifiers. Since this is the case, there is no presence. This denial of presence reveals the priority of writing over speech. For speech is already bound into the network of signifiers, taking it beyond the so-called purity of its immediately present meaning. Instead of the meaning of a sign as immediately present, it is disseminated throughout the system of signifiers. Thus, since the priority that has been accorded to speech over writing, or phonocentrism, is a result of the view of presence and the present, with the denial of these, there is a concomitant denial of the priority of speech over writing.

In thus considering the signifier to be independent of a relation to any particular signified, but, rather, to be related to other signifiers in relations of difference, and in considering the system of signifiers as inescapable, Derrida has effectively cut off presence and the present now, moving instead to a view of language from which meaning, in a different sense from that of any usual semantics, emerges. For his deconstruction begins with the subordination of semantics in the traditional sense to syntax, and the development of a view of syntax quite different from its usual sense. From such a view of syntax, as the root of the formal dimension of language, the semantic dimension emerges. Thus, Derrida subscribes to a new and far more radical sense of syntax than that of syntax as form in contrast to content. Rather, for him, syntax is the condition making meaningful language possible, and at once, is itself productive of the semantic dimension of language. This has been referred to as a "syntax of syntax" from which the "formal syntactic properties can be syntactically composed and decomposed."[13] This reduction to syntax liberates the signifier from the "opressive regime"[14] of presence as immediacy, and at once ties it to the time flux over against structure or meaning. For, if syntax is prior to semantics and there is a "syntax of syntax,"[15] then the flux of syntax, the diachronic dimension, is in no way tied to or subordinated to semantics or to meaning, or to the structure of the system of language. Rather, it generates a kind of meaning in the very positioning of such words as "green is or,"[16] thus moving away from structuralism in favor of the flux underlying meaning and language. But it has lost the continuity, duration, and depth of lived time.[17] Thus syntax is the condition making meaningful language possible, and at once, for the deconstructionist, is productive of the semantic dimension of language. This recourse to the flux entails the centrality of time in relation to signs. What must be investigated further is the denial of presence and of the present-now in the deconstruction of Husserl's living present and that denial's latent view of time, resulting further in the deconstructionist view of signs and language.

Time and the Living Present

Some of the most scrutinized passages by deconstructionists in recent attention to Husserl's analyses of time are the passages where the distinction between the living present and the instant or the punctual now is made. What will be of importance to glean from Derrida's deconstruction, however, is his implicit understanding of time and the way in which his implicit point of reference structures his own deconstructionist position, for his approach here provides the basis from which he pulls the rug out from under not only the phenomenology of Husserl, but, indeed, all philosophy.

Husserl's account of internal time, it must be recalled, addresses the Humean problem of consciousness that is constituted by a flux of nows discrete from one another and that, as unidimensional, allows for no depth. Against this backdrop, Husserl specifically focuses upon the duration in consciousness of an object as the same from moment to moment. His analysis of the temporal constitution of consciousness reveals the object correlate within consciousness and the protentions or anticipations, and retentions or fundedness, which constitute a network of intentionalities. Thus Husserl's own focus in dealing with the living present is that of duration in the "sense of the continuation of the same,"[18] and in this context he insists on a non-atomistic interpretation of time. Just as objects are meaningfully perceived without explanation needing to collapse or decompose them into atomistic impressions, so too here, the living present is lived as a whole, an already given unity with a certain uniqueness to the status of protentions and retentions. For example, the loud sound of a ping, the kind a submarine makes in measuring distances, even though it might be heard as an instantaneous percussion, is grasped in an enduring and continuous consciousness. The sound resonates "in our ears," one might say. Husserl's treatment attempts to account for the "tempo-object"[19] as continuously present in some sense in duration. He describes the retentions and protentions as constitutive elements of consciousness, which show how the present moment endures or continues in consciousness even though it has receded into a deeper phase, and how anticipations grasp in some sense the upcoming moment. Retention as funded and protension as anticipatory reveal the depth of consciousness in its continuity and make presence of the object possible. It is precisely this continuity and oneness between the beginning of the tempo-object within consciousness, which Husserl calls the instant, and its duration that provide the context for his schema of retentions and protentions.

Husserl's account of the living present entails a thickness to the "now" containing retentions and protentions in a quasi-immediacy that does not require, and is to be radically distinguished from, a separate act of remembering, which would attempt to repeat and reproduce the occurrence. Rather, the retention and consequent endurance can be considered a kind of primary memory, a presence that is not the result of productive imagination yielding a separate act of repetition. Yet, for Husserl, retention is not incorporated in presence as the beginning of the object's presence in perception. Thus the living present is a sort of "thick now," including the retentions in a mode of presence not the same as that of the now in the narrow sense of the beginning in consciousness of an object. Yet the "thick now" is continuous with the "narrow now" and with it is already a unity, and thus does not require synthesis. These different modes must be made more explicit, for therein lies an ambiguity in Husserl's own account onto which Derrida latches.

Husserl's analysis of the beginning point or the narrow now of something appearing in time consciousness leaves a tension between it and the living present or thick now, thus lending itself to the interpretation of the "instant as a point."[20] But, for Husserl, the fact that the living present contains retention does not mean that it is past in the strictest sense. For the retention is past, but still as part of the living present, and thus is entirely different from the past in a strict sense as a repetition. To break this retention off from the living present is to render this phase of consciousness discontinuous and therefore discrete, a doctrine certainly alien to Husserl. Yet Husserl could be misinterpreted as not entirely ridding himself of the instant as discrete, which would make difficult his attempt to deal with experience as enduring within a continuum of duration. And, although it is explicitly clear that the now in Husserl's account cannot be collapsed into the point-like instant, the ambiguity of his treatment of the instant here gives rise to this tension between the instant or punctual now and the living present, which tension Derrida will be seen to exploit, thus losing the depth and thickness belonging to the living present (SP, 60).[21]

It is precisely in the duration of this "thick now" that Derrida wants to wedge a separation, making two alien and discrete parts. Derrida's deconstruction of the distinction between the living present and the instant or the punctual now reveals an alleged contradiction, based on the above tension, latent in Husserl's view of retentions and protentions in the living present. It is through Husserl's conception of the instant within the living present that Derrida identifies and deconstructs presence. The discussion will turn briefly to Derrida's interpretation of this correlation between the instant and the living present.

Derrida questions and deconstructs the privilege of this living present and its identity in the realization that, with a point "now," the presence of the perceived present can appear as such only inasmuch as it contains retention as a nonpresence and a nonperception. He acknowledges that Husserl's text shows that perceiving has retention as a modification of the present. He agrees that Husserl calls this a perception in the context of distinguishing retention from reproduction and imagination; that for Husserl the retention is considered part of the presentation, and primary remembrance is perception in distinguishing it from secondary memory and production of the imagination (SP, 64–65). Yet Derrida goes on to show that, for Husserl, "perception (impression) would be the phase of consciousness which constitutes the pure now, and memory every other phase of the continuity" (SP, 65). Thus, retention is considered nonpresence similar to the nonpresence of secondary memory.

According to Derrida's critique of Husserl, then, primary remembrance must be considered to be the "antithesis of perception" (SP, 64).

Using Husserl's own texts to show the contradiction with his own ear-lier assertions, Derrida remarks: "As soon as we admit this continuity of the now and the not-now, perception and nonperception, . . . in the pri-mordial retention, we admit the other into the self-identity of the *Augen-blick*" (SP, 65);[22] nonpresent and nonevidence are admitted into the thick now. This relation to nonpresence according to Derrida "radically destroys any possibility of a simple self-identity. And this holds in depth for the constituting flux itself" (SP, 66).[23] The fact that nonpresence and otherness are internal to presence strikes it down.

Derrida puts the nonperception and nonpresence of retention on the same side as that of reproduction, thus placing an alterity within the liv-ing present. "The difference between retention and reproduction, between primary and secondary memory, is not the radical difference Husserl wanted between perception and nonperception; it is rather a dif-ference between two modifications of nonperception" (SP, 65). For Der-rida, the presence of the present is the result of the "bending back of a return" (SP, 66) of repetition, of *différance* (SP, 142). Thus, for Derrida, as he says: "this pure difference, which constitutes the self-presence of the living present, introduces into self-presence from the beginning all the impurity putatively excluded from it. The living present springs forth out of its nonidentity with itself and from the possibility of a retentional trace. It is always already a trace" (SP, 85). And it is precisely in this dif-ference between the instant and the living present that the trace and lan-guage are appropriated, revealing another aspect of the living present more explicitly. In fact, it is the relation to nonpresence that actually "makes possible" (SP, 66) the presence of the perceived present. Even the instant gains its identity from its relation to nonpresence or nonper-ception.

The Trace

And this nonpresence is the place of the trace, for protention and reten-tion are traces that come to constitute the living present. The living pre-sent, then, springs forth out of this nonidentity with itself and from the sketched-out-ahead of the future and the retained sketch of the immedi-ate past, constituting what Derrida refers to as the intimate relation with its "outside" (SP, 86) as an openness to exteriority. The living present takes on the role of "power of synthesis" and of the "incessant gather-ing up of traces" (SP, 147). And it is *différance* that "makes the move-ment of signification possible only if each element that is said to be 'pre-sent,' appearing on the stage of presence, is related to something other than itself but retains the mark of a past element and already lets itself by hollowed out by the mark of its relation to a further element" (SP,

142). These traces then, of the future and of the past as protentions and as retentions, constitute the present by its relation "to what it is not" (SP, 143), that is, the trace constitutes the present by its relation to what it is not—as a future or past—and as such not even as a modified present. It is precisely this living present constituted as a nonsimple and derived effect, as a synthesis of traces, retentions, and projections, which Ricoeur refers to as losing phenomenological primordiality. And the use of language involves the play of differences, the play of traces of future and past to bring about the present and its presence. This play of traces is a "sort of inscription prior to writing, a protowriting without a present origin" (SP, 146). Thus, for Derrida, the trace is in some illusive sense the origin "of sense in general," it is the "*différance* which opens appearance [*l'apparaître*]."[24]

This deconstructive account of sign, trace, and the living present can now be discussed from a richer and more viable account of language and time, that of Ricoeur, the possibility of whose account rests on a completely opposed view of sign (language), time, and trace.

PAUL RICOEUR: SEMANTIC PRIORITY AND THE LIVING PRESENT

Ricoeur considers the project of the linguistics that leads to structuralism and deconstruction to be misdirected in that language as discourse, the saying of something to someone, is lost. Further, it often overlooks the fact that semiotics as sign theory cannot move to the sentence as the basic unit of meaning, as he says: "The sentence is not a larger or more complex word, it is a new entity. It may be decomposed into words but the words are something other than short sentences. A sentence is a whole irreducible to the sum of its parts. It is made up of words, but it is not a derivative function of its words. A sentence is made up of signs, but is not itself a sign."[25] Each stage, word, sentence, and text, are a new stage requiring a new structure and description.

Two insights distinguish Ricoeur's theory of meaning in language from many other theories: the relation between language and experience, and the relation between language and discourse. His view of the relation between language and experience springs from his agreement with Husserl in rooting meaning in intentionality that itself is grounded in lived experience. The theory of the functions of linguistic expressions, adapted mainly from Husserl's first logical investigation,[26] is crucial to Ricoeur's theory of language,[27] for these functions, the meaning function, the reference function, and the manifesting or indicating function, are essentially intertwined in the various dimensions of language. Furthermore, the investigation into linguistic expressions clarifies their relation to the variations, tensions, and polarities within the hierarchical levels of experience and language. It is the second insight within Ricoeur's theory of language that is particularly important in the context of structuralism and deconstruction due to its emphasis on the relation between language and discourse.

Ricoeur has constantly insisted on taking language as discourse in his attempts to interarticulate a phenomenology of language with a semiological approach. This insistence is based on a radical disagreement with Ferdinand de Saussure's fundamental distinction between *la langue* and *la parole* that does not leave room for language as discourse: "the withdrawal of the problem of discourse in the contemporary study of language is the price we must pay for the tremendous achievements brought about by the famous *Cours de linguistique generale* of the Swiss linguist Ferdinand de Saussure."[28] Ricoeur's disagreement with this distinction between *la langue* and *la parole*, more radical than the critique of Saussure by Derrida regarding signifier and signified, emerges in his attempt to go beyond the opposition between semiology and the phenomenology of language. He considers the unity of language (*le langage*) fundamental to both, unifying them in a hierarchy of levels: "To think language (*le langage*) should be to think the unity of that very reality which Saussure has disjoined—the unity of language (*la langue*) and speech (*la parole*)."[29] Thus, in order to overcome the opposition by an interarticulation in language, Ricoeur bases his view on a unity of language that does justice to both the semiology that takes *la langue* as an object, as well as to a phenomenology of speech. His intent is to avoid that initial separation between language (*la langue*) and speech (*la parole*) as a false dichotomy. The new unity must at the same time allow for the possibility of viewing language as an object of science and, at once, also allow for the event of communication. Consequently, he looks for a unity that surpasses the opposition between these aspects of language, thereby making possible an interarticulation between them.

The new unity of language, reaching the crux of the confrontation, is put on the side of semantics, and gives semantics, rather than semiology and syntax, the primordial role in language theory. There are several reasons for understanding this unity to lie on the side of discourse, function, and semantics. First, for Ricoeur, all roads lead from semantics in the sense that all sciences of language presuppose, at least implicitly, the semantic function. Further, by putting the unity on the side of semantics in the sentence, both sides of the antinomy or opposition can be articulated; and, finally, by putting the unity in the sentence, an articulation of the hierarchical levels of language is seen to make sense. "In short, the linking of methods, of points of view, of models, is a consequence of the hierarchy of levels in the work of language" (CI, 80). This hierarchy of levels, in spite of a break within them, makes possible the interarticulation of various approaches. As Ricoeur states: "My whole study will rest on the idea that the passage to the new unity of discourse constituted by the sentence or enunciation represents a break, a change, in the hierarchy of levels" (CI, 80). And to understand this hierarchy of levels, along with the break, it is necessary to consider the fundamental point at the center of Ricoeur's reflection that demands this change in the unity of language (*le langage*).

The strength of Ricoeur's position rests on the insight that the sciences of language presuppose a semantic function that they do not make thematic, but that, when excluded, give rise to the closed system of signs. This closed system of signs must be opened to bring to light what the sciences of language presuppose. Changing the unity of language to the semantic makes necessary a passage from structure to function.[30] It also makes apparent the semantic dimension of the sign, of which structuralists and deconstructionists alike have lost sight.

The heart of Ricoeur's consideration deals with putting together and selecting words. In order to put words together coherently, selecting them from the whole system, a delimitation is necessary. This means that the problem of polysemy has a place even in the sciences of language. It also means that polysemy and symbolism belong to both the constitution and to the function of every language. "So the possibility of symbolism is rooted in a function common to all words, in a universal function of language."[31]

For Ricoeur, the context acts as the sifter of which meaning is meant. "When I speak, I realize only one part of the signifying potential: the remainder is obliterated by the total significance of the sentence that operates as the unity of speech."[32] For structuralism, on the contrary, the meaning arrived at through or with this closed system of signs is not adequate because it does not do justice to the fullness of meaning. Rather, it yields only an abstract language and an abstract meaning constituting a symbolics without an underlying sense. As Ricoeur says later in *Interpretation Theory*, "At this extreme point language as discourse has disappeared."[33] In linking this objection with the unity of language and the interrelation between these two approaches to signs, he says:[34]

> *Parole*, as we said, is heterogeneous, besides being individual, diachronic and contingent. But *parole* also presents a structure that is irreducible in a specific sense to that of the combinatory possibilities opened up by the oppositions between discrete entities. My substitution of the term 'discourse' for that of '*parole*' (which expresses only the residual aspects of a science of '*langue*') is intended not only to emphasize the specificity of this new unit on which all discourse relies, but also to legitimate the dis-

tinction between semiotics and semantics as the two sciences which correspond to the two kinds of units characteristic of language, the sign and the sentence.

Since Ricoeur considers this distinction between semantics and semiotics to be the key to the problem of language, he based the four essays in the *Interpretation Theory* on what he calls "this initial methodological decision."[35] Within this decision, there are two ways of giving an account of symbolism: by that which constitutes it, the elements and structures, and by that which it wants to say or express. This marks the break in the hierarchy of levels. The break, constituted by the closed system of signs of semiology, reflects the different ways of considering the sign and the transition from semiology to semantics. This break and the transition are discussed in the following text:

> Moreover, these two sciences are not just distinct, but also reflect a hierarchical order. The object of semiotics—the sign—is merely virtual. Only the sentence is actual as the very event of speaking. This is why there is no way of passing from the word as a lexical sign to the sentence by mere extension of the same methodology to a more complex entity. The sentence is not a larger or more complex word, it is a new entity. It may be decomposed into words, but the words are something other than short sentences. A sentence is a whole irreducible to the sum of its parts. It is made up of words, but it is not a derivative function of words. A sentence is made up of signs, but it is not itself a sign.[36]

The same signs can be considered from two distinctively different points of view, so that it can be seen that there are not two definitions of sign. Rather, one point of view focuses on the relation of the sign to the system of signs, and the other point of view focuses on its function in the sentence (CI, 252).

> Opposing sign to sign is the *semiological* function; representing the real by signs is the *semantic* function, and the first is subordinated to the second. The first function serves the second; or, if one prefers, language is articulated for the purpose of the signifying or representative function.

The clarification of subordinating semiology and system to semantics and speech demands a deepening in the view of polysemy. Approaching this question of polysemy as the "pivot of semantics" (CI, 91) from the side of synchrony, we see what polysemy signifies in the system, that at any given moment, a word has many meanings which belong to the same state of the system. This view of polysemy misses the essential and crucial point, which is the process and history of usage (CI, 93). "Now the process of the transfer of meaning of metaphor presupposes new dimensions of meaning without losing the old ones. It is this cumulative, metaphorical process which is projected over the surface of the system as polysemy" (CI, 95).

However, this expansion and history of sense is limited by the return to the system. "Words have more than one sense, but they do not have an infinite sense."[37] Both limitation and expansion are processes: "regulated polysemy is of the panchronic order, that is, both synchronic and diachronic to the degree that a history projects itself into states of systems, which henceforth are only instantaneous crossections in the process of sense in the process of nomination."[38] Thus, the importance of the word as a sign in the articulation of structure and of function is clear. However, it is the context that brings about the univocity or plurivocity of words in use or in discourse. The extent of the limitation of the semantic depends on the context. If the structure of a discourse allows several frames of reference, themes, topics and isotopies,[39] then more than one interpretation of the multiple meanings is justified. But the crucial focal point is the word.

The word as the point of articulation of various levels of language calls for a distinction between the sign in semiology or syntax and the sign in semantics. On the one hand, the sign is "meaningless" in such semiology of structuralism and deconstruction. On the other hand, the sign is word in semantics. "Words are the point of articulation of the semiological and the semantic in each event of speech."[40] However, semantics cannot accept the closure of the sign system, which, as such, is the overextension of a method and theory. Semiology can be considered to reveal adequately the root of symbolic function and of polysemy, but an adjustment is required within semiology in interpreting the relation between diachrony and synchrony, due to the surplus or surcharge of sense and the semantic regulation of the context. Reflection on the closure of the sign system reveals how the meaningful use of signs as words does not allow for a closed system, but, rather, demands an openness of the sign system at a different but more essential level. At this level, signs have a reference function and a manifesting function, thus pointing to and standing for things.[41]

As expressions, they show or reveal the world, and, at once, manifest or posit the subject. The semiological sign system of structuralism and deconstruction cannot do adequate justice to this aspect of sign since, on the level of system, there is no saying of something about something, nor a positing of the I who appropriates language in speaking. The uniqueness of the I and of the situation or occasion of the speaker and of the speaking (e.g., tense, demonstratives) go beyond the limits of this level.

In thus favoring a diachronic process over synchronic structure, Ricoeur is somewhat in agreement with what has been seen in Derrida, for whom the movement of the play of differences entails the process, but for whom also the structural and process dimensions are equally derivative from *différance*. In order to further the dialogue between Ricoeur and Derrida, the discussion must now turn to the place of trace and time in Ricoeur's view of language in order to clarify how, for him, trace counters a phenomenology that "confuses the living present with the point-like instant,"[42] that is, that of Derrida. First, however, Ricoeur's own critique of phenomenology's internal time consciousness must be considered as the general context for his critique of Derrida's view of the living present and the now. Thus, attention must now be given to the aporia of lived and cosmic time that Ricoeur addresses in the three volumes of *Time and Narrative*.

Lived Time, Cosmic Time, and Historical Time

Ricoeur's *Time and Narrative* is constructed around the aporetic of time witnessed in the accounts of internal time and reaching an "extreme degree of aporia"[43] in phenomenology, a consideration raised initially by Augustine whose treatment of time presented the aporia of internal time, and later developed by Husserl and Heidegger.[44] Ricoeur is insistent on the inadequacy of this account to deal with cosmic time. And it is precisely this aporia between phenomenological time and cosmic time that history, with its manifold connections, brings together, bridging the gap between internal time and cosmic time.

Historical time, then, bridges the chasm between internal time and cosmic time by means of its connections, as seen in an earlier chapter: calendar time is the first of the connectors, joining astronomical time with human institutions, harmonizing "work with days and festivals with the season and the years. It integrates the community and its customs into the cosmic order."[45] The second connector, the notion of the sequence of generations, shown in the transmission of biblical curses and blessings from generation to generation, results from the connection between lived time and biological time that underlies it and connects it with astronomical time. This grounding of lived time on biological time "is thus added to the *inscription* of lived time upon astronomical time."[46] The third connector is implied by history's recourse to documents and monuments. Here Ricoeur appropriates the sense of trace employed by F. Simiand in defining history as knowledge by traces. Because of its mixed nature, the trace, according to Ricoeur, is a connector between lived time and physical time. The trace exists as such now, but it is a remnant or a vestige of something from another world as, for instance, documents or monuments. Further, it is a remnant, a vestige, a window to something that was in a past world. As Ricoeur says, "A trace, then, is a present thing which stands for (vaut) an absent past."[47] Or, it is also both "a remains and a sign of what was but no longer is."[48] For Ricoeur, the trace's double allegiance to different temporal orders is an original phenomenon that Heidegger's account, focusing on having-been of Dasein, does not adequately account for.

Ricoeur's strongest articulation of the critique of the phenomenology of time comes to grips with the primordial time of Heidegger. It might prove instructive to follow Ricoeur's critique of the phenomenology of time further, beginning with his perceptive insights on Augustine's analysis especially in relation to Husserl's phenomenology of time, and then turning to the limits of Heidegger's valuable contribution.

Although it is phenomenology that intensifies the aporia of time, it is in Augustine's *Confessions* that the aporetic of time in initially sketched in terms of the paradox of the triple present (present of the past, present of the future, present of the present)[49] in terms of the paradox of *distentio animi* and of the *intentio*; and in terms of the paradox of the originality of the present vis-à-vis the eternal present. Ricoeur considers Husserl's famous doctrine of time to prolong the Augustinian paradoxes. In the same vein Ricoeur extols the quality of achievements of *Being and Time* of Heidegger, that the principle of temporalization is sought out within the structure of care that allows for distinguishing time on different levels.

But by this very advance, phenomenology creates aporias. Ricoeur considers this failure to cover the problematic of time adequately in its entirety to have begun with Augustine's attempt to derive the Aristotelian cosmic time from "the simple distention of the soul hit up against the Aristotelian reef: referring time to movement and to the root of movement, the accomplishment of the unaccomplished of *phusis*."[50] Similarly, the Husserlian attempt to deal with time as a pure experience by putting aside objective time "strikes another reef, that Kantian one: it is from Kant that we learned that time as such is invisible, that it could not appear in any living experience, that it is always presupposed as the condition of experience, and from this fact could only appear indirectly on objects apprehended in space and according to the schemata and the categories of objectivity."[51] According to Ricoeur, it is this constraint that shows why internal time-consciousness borrows its structure from this objective time that the reduction holds in suspense. Even Heidegger's treatment of time with its levels of temporalization reveals most completely this inability. "But this very effort comes up against *the other* of phenomenological time: the 'popular' concept of time, made up of an infinite series of indifferent nows. Even the most decentered level of temporality—within-time-ness—where the 'in' of being in time is highlighted, never rejoins the 'ordinary' time which is simply removed from the phenomenological field by the allegation of an enigmatic leveling of the 'in' of 'within-time-ness.'"[52] Ricoeur considers Heidegger's attempt to include the history of time from Aristotle to Hegel in this ordinary time to be in vain. For Ricoeur, there is a disproportion between time that we unfold in living and time that envelops us everywhere.

Heidegger's account does not take into consideration the "heterogeneous temporal orders" to which the trace, as an original phenomenon, belongs. Ricoeur asks the crucial question of Heidegger's attempt to deal with this in terms of having been and within-time-ness: "For how does *Dasein* interpret its having-been-there if not by relying on the autonomy of marks left by the passage of former humans? Heidegger's failure to understand the phenomenon of the trace reflects the failure of *Sein und Zeit* to give an account of the time of the world which has no care for our care."[53] For no matter how much effort is exerted to consider the mode of Being of Dasein, and the past as derivative from the temporality or historicality of Dasein, the fact remains that there is still something past that is independent of human existence and Dasein's temporality and historicality—that other of which the trace serves as a trace of . . . as, for example, with the historical documents, monuments and implements that have no world remaining and no Dasein that is familiar with them. Ricoeur goes on to show how the trace, as an element with the history, crosses the gap between internal time and cosmic time. With this critique of the phenomenology of time in view, the discussion can now turn to his defense of Husserl's living present against the onslaught of Derrida in order to see what it means for him to say that he agrees with Derrida in a positive way about trace, but that his own view of trace, seen above, "can only counter a phenomenology which confuses the living present with the point-like instant."[54] The discussion will now turn to Ricoeur's reading of Husserl on time underlying signs.

Ricoeur's perceptive and penetrating reading of Husserl's account of internal time-consciousness focuses on two central points that are often overlooked in deconstructive interpretation:[55] first, that Husserl's inner time-consciousness is a continuum containing continuance, a fact that Ricoeur quite correctly makes central—and it is necessary to emphasize this point, since this character of Husserl's account has recently sunk into oblivion; and second, that the overall problem that is addressed and that retention solves is that of duration as such. Further, according to Ricoeur, the two of the "great discoveries of Husserlian phenomenology of time" are first the description of retention and protention; and second the distinction between retention and recollection (or between primary and secondary memory), both of which have been seen above.[56] With the reduction, objective time is bracketed, and the lived experience of time itself comes into focus. Ricoeur adds that: "it is the tempo-object as a reduced object that provides its telos to the investigation. And it is this tempo-object that indicates what has to be constituted in the sphere of pure immanence, namely, duration, in the sense of the continuation of the same throughout the succession of other phases. We may deplore the ambiguity of this strange entity, yet we owe it an analysis of time that is straightway an analysis of duration in the sense of continuation, of 'continuance considered as such' (*Verharren als solches*) and not simply of succession."[57]

Ricoeur insists throughout this account of Husserl that the "now" for Husserl cannot be considered a "point-like instant"[58] but rather, includes what Husserl calls longitudinal intentionality in contrast to transcendent intentionality. Ricoeur sees the phenomenological description shifting attention from the "sound that endures to the modes of its continuance"[59] precisely as the unity of duration (*Dauereinheit*). Thus, for Husserl, no synthetic function is necessary, since the unity is already there. Ricoeur keeps to a rather perceptive and true account of the sense of "the sound still resonates," emphasizing that the "still" implies both same and other; he quotes Husserl: "The sound itself is the same, but 'in the way that' it appears, the sound is continually different."[60] The reversal in perspective from the sound to the "mode of appearing" (*der ton "in der Weise vie"*)[61] brings the aspect of otherness into the foreground and transforms it into an enigma. Ricoeur, however, follows Husserl in that this otherness does not exclude identity. It is the longitudinal intentionality that ensures the continuity of the duration and preserves the same in the other and that marks the continuity of the whole or the totality of the continuous, which the term duration (*Dauer*) itself designates.[62] The identity resulting from this something that persists in change is an identity of temporal totality rather than one of logic.

According to Ricoeur's analysis of Husserl's texts, modification precedes difference. Husserl indicates by the term modification that the privileged status of each new now is shared by the series of instants that it retains. The difference is between the "recent present and the past properly speaking."[63] With the modification of the present into the recent present the "originary impression itself passes into the retention."

A second distinction proper to the phenomenology of internal time-consciousness is that between primary remembrance and secondary remembrance or recollection. "The break separating the presentation, which alone is an original self-giving act, from re-presentation further confirms the primacy of retention." For Ricoeur, highlighting this distinction, the question that haunts Husserl is this: "if the way in which recollection presentifies the past differs fundamentally from the presence of the past retention, how can a representation be faithful to its object?"⁶⁴ Thus Ricoeur's interpretation of Husserl recognizes and emphasizes the great difference between retention and recollection, which will become central to his pithy remarks on Derrida's interpretation (or misinterpretation) of this relation.

Ricoeur considers Derrida to stress the "subversive aspect of this solidarity between the living present and retention as regards the primacy of the *Augenblick*, hence the point-like present, identical to itself."⁶⁵ While Ricoeur takes into account Husserl's "strong sense" given to the distinction between the present and the instant, he is firmly opposed to placing the nonperception of retention on the same side of otherness as that of recollection, since retention is seen in phenomenological description to be essentially different from recollection. Retention is continuous with perception, while recollection is in the "strong sense" of the word a nonperception. A similar critique could be levied against Derrida's interpretation of retention as nonpresence. For Ricoeur's interpretation agrees that the nonpresence of retention is not to be equated with the nonpresence of second memory or recollection.

Thus, according to Ricoeur's interpretation, retention, rather than primarily a secondary memory in accordance with Derrida's "semiological reduction,"⁶⁶ essentially shares in primary memory and thus does not need repetition. Rather, it is retained and as such is present, although not absolutely intuited or identical with the beginning of the object in consciousness of which it is the endurance or retention in the mode of *continuing*. This beginning point must be interpreted as a thin now rather than as a pinpoint or an atom of time, for in the concrete flow of experience the instant point of time is an abstraction. This is precisely the element of the tension between the instant and the living present that Husserl's text obscures and that Derrida exploits. Husserl, however, as has been seen, focuses on duration with a view to accounting for continuance. Thus, in his phenomenology of internal time, he does not produce a view of consciousness or time constitution in which they are discrete.

Derrida, in picking up on the wrong side of this tension between the living present and the instant in Husserl's ambiguous treatment, has given rise to some equivocation regarding the "unity of a temporal present."⁶⁷ While for Husserl this unity involves the thick now, and thus also a continuity and depth to the living present, for Derrida's deconstructive interpretation it involves the now as an instant because of his own presupposition of the discrete view of time. Derrida's analysis entails this utilization of a discreteness of time, which leads him to consider the living present, the living now, within a discrete view of a flux with no depth, a pseudocontinuum of discrete points. Hence, for Derrida, Husserl's "thick now" or "big now"⁶⁸ collapses in the face of the alterity of past and future, revealing the failure of Husserl's time constitution.

In rejecting presence, Derrida has focused on the flux of time as discrete and represented or repeated. For Derrida "signification is formed only within the hollow of différance: of discontinuity and of discreteness, of the diversion and the reserve of what does not appear."[69] *Différance* can thus be seen to make signification possible because of the interval that separates the present from alterity. In this way nothing precedes *différance*.[70] What becomes clear is that if one begins with discreteness, the only alternatives are either pure identity or dire alterity. If one rejects, as Derrida rightly does, the alternative of pure identity, then his deconstructive stance is the logical conclusion.

What has been lost in favor of this superimposed discrete time is the lived time as the sense of human concrete existence, which, as such, is continuous, has duration, and moves as a whole. Derrida, exploiting the ambiguous status of the instant in Husserl's analysis, has excluded the living present as the focal point of sense, and has lost sight of the "unity of a temporal present" as precisely constitutive of the living present and not of an instant. For the instant as such does not exist since it is an abstraction from the continuum, or at best, as Husserl uses the term, merely the occasion within the continuum for the beginning or starting point of something in an experience. But, if the instant now is discrete and isolated, then the instant is a vacuous point discretely cut off from any other instant and the trace is separated from it. Indeed, all the elements at this instant are the constituted effects or products, none of which are present. And the system as a whole at any moment is constituted by the interrelation of all the elements. Protentions and retentions, since they are constituted effects, cannot bring about the required unity but, rather, presuppose it. How is the trace to cross over from one empty now point to another? It is not connected to any, except insofar as it is in the rich present state as a trace of a past with no present. Can such crossing over of the gaps or chasms between instants be allowed by the absolute presuppositions of this deconstructive view of the system of signs and trace? Since the trace is itself an effect, it cannot bring about a unity of instants except as itself an effected synthesis. Yet such a unity must pre-exist trace for its very possibility, for trace involves more than the instant.

A discrete instant is not sufficient to support any workable view of trace. Discreteness of the instant of time cannot support any connection between two times or two instants of time. For Derrida, there cannot be any such unity between two now points any more than for Hume could there be real connection or an identity established between two now points discretely cut off from one another. Thus, Derrida's view of the instant and the discreteness that it entails cannot support any viable trace, which is his main tool for any working role for signs. For trace must assume an already unified present entailing two times, the past somehow in the present. It must be present as a past that is no more and yet is really present, even if only as a trace of the past, but not as a constituted effect in an empty instant.

The notion of trace in this contemporary philosophy has taken on a role central both to language and to the living present, as well as to the relation between internal time consciousness and cosmic time. In Derrida's deconstruction traces are constitutive of the sign in the same way that the protentions and retentions as traces are constitutive of the living present. The prominence of trace in deconstruction follows largely from the loss of phenomenological primordiality of, and the decentering of focus from, the living present, presence, and things present as constituted to what constitutes them—the play of *différance* in the interplay of differences and of traces. Given the centrality of trace, we have had to clarify its role in the respective writings of Derrida and of Ricoeur, explicating what in Derrida's view of the living present and time renders it unable to sustain trace in contrast to Ricoeur's view of the living present and historical time that supports trace in its full sense.[71] These contrasting roles of trace highlight, in spite of a positive commonness, the vast chasm that separates the views of Derrida and Ricoeur, stretching even to all-pervasive metaphysical differences that require a decision in favor of one at the expense of the other.

Derrida's view of trace has been seen to hinge on his critiques of Saussure's and Husserl's views of sign, as well as on his critique of Husserl's view of the living present, making trace central to language at the core of his deconstruction. It has likewise shown that Ricoeur's view of language seen above, taking its point of departure from a more radical critique of Saussure and later structuralism than that of Derrida, together with his radical critique of Derrida's deconstruction of Husserl's living present, pulls the props out from under Derrida's view of trace by offering a view of the living present and of time that is able to support a richer and more viable view of trace, language, and linguistics. Yet bringing to clear light Ricoeur's critiques of Derrida's understanding of the living present and of phenomenology's view of inner time has, at once, revealed his agreement with Derrida on essential points of a view of trace in a sign system, and with Husserl regarding the phenomenological primordiality of the living present. In this regard, Ricoeur says that "Derrida is not mistaken in seeing in the trace, as early as the writing of *Speech and Phenomena*, 'a possibility which not only must inhabit the pure actuality of the now but must constitute it through the very movement of difference it introduces.' . . . And he goes on to add, 'Such a trace is . . . more 'primordial' than what is phenomenologically primordial,'"[72] a point with which he will disagree, holding rather that trace in his own appropriation will counter a "phenomenology that confuses the living present with the point-like instant."[73]

Thus, Ricoeur's alternative to Derrida's semiological reductionism and the flux of time as discrete on which it is founded provides a viable alternative that does not succumb to the facile distinction of Saussure, nor to Derrida's collapse of signs to the relations of differences within the system and the reduction of language to the play of *différance*. Rather, Ricoeur is able adequately to account for duration and continuity in the living present as the basis for language as discourse and for trace. And Ricoeur's account of the temporal context for understanding language undercuts Derrida's pseudo-alternatives of signs or presence, for the temporal span of the present is neither pure identity nor pure alterity. The present as thickened by retention and protentions "intends" the future in light of the past. Since the very function of the present is to mean and the very nature of presence requires signs, language and signs are inseparably intertwined with time. Thus, his theory of language as essentially discourse, his distinction between words and signs, and between signs and sentences, in the overall context of the unities of semiotics and of semantics, with the new unity of language in the semantics of the sentence, re-establishes some faith in philosophical analysis as having something worthwhile to say about something, even when it deals with an interpretation of language and of texts. While the positioning of signs, or the play of *différance*, can yield a productivity of some kind of meaning, it is not the replacement of the semantic dimension of language as primary. Syntax of any kind exists for the semantic. To invert this is to distort language, to make a mockery of meaning, to reduce meaning to an empty shell, as well as to render meaningless any attempt to communicate this message of inversion.

Yet, as we have constantly affirmed, something quite positive can be gleaned from the recent redirection of continental philosophy toward postmodern deconstruction considered in this chapter. In the attempt to articulate this dimension, let us first focus on the point of the deepening passage within the critique of Heidegger accused by Derrida of retaining a sense of the presence of Being in his efforts to overcome metaphysics. For Heidegger, in leading to a refocusing on the totality of the hermeneutical situation, or on the whole network of the presuppositional structure, has thrown into focus the sense of Being in its unity through which anything emerges into its Being. But according to deconstructionists, he fails to reach beyond this temporality structure and toward that from which it is the effect, the singularity of the flux. And just as Heidegger approaches Kant and the whole history of metaphysics with his own question of Being in order to see how Kant and others at least subliminally posed this question, so too, the critics of Heidegger, the post-Heideggerian deconstructionists, now bring their own pre-comprehension to their deconstruction of texts. And that which is in pre-comprehension precisely as other is not reachable as such, and everything in experience and awareness relates to it as other, both in the depth of the human and beyond.

It is precisely here that a positive message can be gleaned from deconstruction's reversal of language and philosophy. The "other" to which it leads can be interpreted in another way without going to such extremes, taking the example of lived time and cosmic time, which have been explored in some detail in this present chapter. In a sense lived time is part of cosmic time, because it is cosmic time in the lived experience of a cosmic, human being. What is clear is that the self-comprehension of lived time is at once a self-comprehension of cosmic time in that instance of the lived. And it must be seen that the "other" here is the cosmic in the lived, which is mediated, or expressed in the lived, which itself is experienced only in a quasi-unity of pre-comprehension. And by a certain extrapolation, we can see the characteristics of that other as cosmic, and of that cosmic precisely as other. This positive element fosters a move beyond a limited hermeneutic phenomenology of existence, a move that contemporary philosophy should foster in its manner of concrete reflection. And a parallel analysis holds true of language as that to which humans are receptive, and in terms of which they become decentered. Thus, deconstruction indicates for a philosophy at the limit of reason, more viable than deconstruction itself, a possible path for further inquiry. And it is precisely upon this Other, in a specific sense, that the following chapter must focus, taking account of the unique contribution of Levinas within postmodernity.

PART III

Ethics and Postmodernity

CHAPTER 8

Ricoeur and Levinas

INTRODUCTION

Paul Ricoeur's recent ethicomoral project, culminating in three of the last four chapters of *Oneself as Another*,[1] consists in polarizing the ethical philosophies of Aristotle and Kant, and integrating a critically adjusted version of each into a unique and encompassing ethical framework. Within this entire enterprise he likewise develops many opposing polarities that he similarly proceeds to interarticulate and appropriate into a coherent position. One such opposition is that between the exteriority at the heart of the ethical philosophy of Emmanuel Levinas and the interiority of Husserl's transcendental philosophy. And within this context he employs elements of Heidegger's existential analysis of Dasein to flesh out the way of a satisfactory interarticulation, from which he appropriates and develops his own position.

It is within this context that the accusation has been made that Ricoeur is too severe[2] in his critique of Levinas. Although we must concede to this accusation in a qualified way, such an admission must not prevent us from appreciating the fullness and the richness of Ricoeur's contemporary ethicomoral philosophy, especially in the light of the recent contrasting works on deconstruction and ethics.[3] I intend in this chapter to enter this present conversation on deconstruction and ethics by proposing a complex thesis: first, that Ricoeur's critique of Levinas is indeed a bit too severe, but when understood in his own context, the place of this critique in his overall project of an ethicomoral foundation and principle comes to light. It will be seen that Levinas' own position already contains in principle a fundamental dimension that Ricoeur wants to supply, even though it is in need of further development. This then becomes the context for adjusting Ricoeur's interpretation in deference to Levinas, but without altering Ricoeur's own position. Thus, after investigating Ricoeur's critique of Levinas and briefly defending Levinas' own position, I will attempt to work toward interarticulating the positions of Ricoeur and Levinas, incorporating both the solitude of interiority and the solicitude that Ricoeur incorporates from Heidegger. This leads into the second part of my thesis, arising from the treatment of the first: that Ricoeur, precisely by incorporating an essential element from Levinas, provides a viable ethics as an alternative to postmodern deconstruction.

At the outset, however, it must be admitted that Ricoeur's and Levinas' projects are entirely different and somewhat opposed. For, from Levinas' point of view, it could be claimed that Ricoeur's whole enterprise fits into the context of "totality," thus constituting precisely what Levinas intends to interrupt with infinity. Even in this apparent opposition, however, it must be admitted that Ricoeur's project, always considered to be ethical, has certain explicit affinities with that of Levinas. For Ricoeur has constantly adhered to the need in ethics precisely for Levinas' "face to face," even contending that ethics has its beginning in the second-person recognition of the other's will and freedom. And, on the other side, Ricoeur says that he has never assumed Levinas' ontology of totality, showing how Levinas restricts identity to the point that it "results that the self, not distinguished from the I, is not taken in the sense of the self-designation of a subject of discourse, action, narrative, or ethical commitment" (OA, 335). I believe it is here, with the notion of totality, that the difficulty between them is found. And Levinas' notion of totality in the context of the identity of the self needs to be extended, just as Ricoeur's interpretation of Levinas regarding the place within interiority for an encounter with the Other will be adjusted. It is to Ricoeur's critique that we must now turn.

RICOEUR BETWEEN LEVINAS AND HEIDEGGER: ANOTHER'S FURTHER ALTERITY

At the heart of today's postmodern conversation is the possibility of philosophy at new and provocative limits, involving seemingly disparate conversationalists. On the one hand, Levinas, whose later works have been at the heart of many postmodern deconstructive discussions, especially those focused on ethics, proposes a radical alterity of the Other, death, and time. This alterity cannot be voided of the ethical relation, as most deconstructive approaches attempt, without great loss in the conversation. On the other hand, Heidegger's work, often used today as a whipping post, and coming from the other direction, offers an account of coexistence, death, and time that Levinas radically opposes. We must confront this opposition to Heidegger in order to see to what extent Heidegger's thinking is reducible to the same and to totality as Levinas contends. In the context of this opposition, I consider Ricoeur's view to be in a position between Levinas and Heidegger, not merely an eclectic one, but rather, in his usual fruitful fashion of going the distance with each thinker, exposing his limits, and then appropriating each adjusted position in an interarticulation that becomes his own unique and ingeniously inclusive position, one that often gets too little attention among those who consider themselves today's avant-garde.

My thesis in this chapter is complex: first, that focusing on the respective critiques of Heidegger by both Levinas and Ricoeur allows us explicitly to see their differences with one another; that seeing these, we can move to relate them more clearly; and finally that we can come to understand, in the light of pursuing these differences, a final position that consists in somewhat adjusting Ricoeur's position enlightened by a rereading of Levinas. Before this final position emerges, however, I will test the contention of Kemp,[4] that Ricoeur is somewhat between Heidegger and Levinas, taking into account Ricoeur's perhaps too severe critique of Levinas.

Although Levinas continually affirmed the extreme importance of Heidegger's place in the philosophical tradition and in the twentieth century, his critique of Heidegger's work became more and more explicit. Yet it was obvious that Heidegger was one of the chief influences on his thought, which he openly admitted, and at once one of his main antagonists. This ongoing critique touches every main point of Levinas' developing position. Perhaps his most far-reaching critique is doubly aimed at the heart of Heidegger's writings. Levinas considers Heidegger to have failed to consider the transcendent Other; and to have failed to reach the unique and singular solitude of the existent. In fact, in spite of Heidegger's initial focus in *Being and Time* on the essence (*Wesen*) of Dasein as existence, he fails to consider the existent, thus missing his/her singularity and solitude. Rather, with his explication of coexistence as the *mit* or the *miteinander* or the *mitsein*, Heidegger has focused laterally within the Same. And in the other direction he has failed to reach toward the transcendence of the Other in a personal face-to-face relation, giving only a constitutive transcendence to the world as ultimate. Levinas, essentially focusing on this precise point, contends that transcendence to the Other is the ultimate constitution for the existent in its solitude. And it is within this general double critique that his manifold critiques of Heidegger can be seen. We must focus more on this overall double critique, investigating first the solitude of the singular existent, which itself comes to light in the context of exteriority and alterity.

For Levinas, alterity is the constitutive key to social life rather than some Heideggerian shared attribute such as coexistence as *mitsein* or *miteinander*. He obviously wants to separate himself from Heidegger, but he does not seem to want to make a clean break. I am inclined to interpret even his extreme remarks in this context to mean that he wants to extend beyond the coexistence or *mitsein* to exteriority as the ultimate constitution of the Other, which itself presupposes this coexistence, as indicated in the morality of nourishment, as will be seen. For Levinas, we must do full justice to the Other as alter ego. The Other, from a limited point of view, is indeed an alter ego as another myself or a coexistence or *mitsein*, but the Other is still *not me*, and thus is Other. Levinas wants to uproot the communion with the other as ultimately constitutive, showing that it is precisely only as transcendent that the Other is Other and not me; just as I am solitary and not the other: "the other is in no way another myself, participating with me in a common existence."[5] Yet, in any consideration of Levinas in the context of Ricoeur's critique, it is necessary to explicitly point out that Levinas finds a place for sympathy and pairing even though he rejects them as ultimately constitutive of the intersubjective relationship,[6] a point that Ricoeur seems to miss. Levinas says: "The other is known through sympathy, as another (my)self, as the alter ego. . . . But already, in the very heart of the relationship with the other that characterizes our social life, alterity appears as a nonreciprocal relationship—that is, as contrasting strongly with contemporaneousness. The Other as Other is not only an alter ego: the Other is what I myself am not. The Other is this, not because of the Other's character, or physiognomy, or psychology, but because of the Other's very alterity."[7] We see Levinas here developing the extreme separation between the exteriority of the Other and the solitude of the existent, which later becomes the focus throughout the whole of *Totality and Infinity*.[8] At this point we have seen explicitly the two sides of the double critique of Heidegger, that of the solitude of the existent and that of the Alterity of the separate Other. We have seen a twofold separation emerge in Levinas' treatment of totality and infinity: a separation of the personal Other from the intentional horizon of human existence; and the separation of the existent in his/her singular solitude from existence. In addition to what has been seen above, Levinas' critique of Heidegger's early basic ontological difference is also at the heart of the above double critique.

The fundamental critique of the ontological difference comes to light when Levinas indicates that for Heidegger the distinction between Being (*Sein*) and a being (*Seiende* or *Seiendes*) is a distinction, while for him it is a separation. For Heidegger, the two are always together, so that existing is always grasped in the existent and is "always possessed by someone. I do not think Heidegger can admit an existing without existents, which to him would seem absurd."[9] And closely tied with this difference regarding the interpretation of the ontological difference is Levinas' attitude toward Heidegger's sense of the disclosure constitutive of Dasein. For Levinas, it is precisely a breaking out of the context of Heideggerian disclosure that the exteriority of the Other and the separation of existents from their existence requires. The ultimate significance of the event of the face to face and of the work of justice does not lie in disclosure as Heidegger contends, but rather lies beyond any intentional structure and are constituted outside of representation and knowledge. "No prior disclosure illuminates the production of these essentially nocturnal events. The welcoming of the face and the work of justice—which condition the birth of truth itself—are not interpretable in terms of disclosure. . . . The relation between the same and the other is not always reducible to knowledge of the other by the same, nor even to the *revelation* of the other to the same, which is already fundamentally different from disclosure."[10] And an extension of this critical stance toward Heidegger is constituted by Levinas' basic ethics as one involving ethical relation. For it is here that he accuses Heidegger of a downfall that is unforgivable.

Heidegger has missed completely the sense of ethics, especially in his very response to Jean Beaufret regarding an originary ethics rooted in the truth of being. For it is here that his ethics emerges as impersonal and ontological, and it is an "ontology without morals," an "ontology of the Neutral."[11] As indicated above in Levinas' critique of Heidegger, Dasein is closed in on itself in the sense that it is not related to infinity or to the Other. Its deficiency or inauthenticity must consist in some relation to itself, resulting in the diminuated and defective ethics mentioned above. This is not a personal ethics, nor one that reaches the Other, but rather a dimension of Dasein's relation to Being in the emergence of the truth of Being for Dasein—at most an originary ethics within that relation. As Peperzak so eloquently and precisely expresses this:

> The idea of a debt or guilt toward others than the self is excluded from this thought. By the absence of a true alterity that could question and accuse *Dasein*'s freedom, that is, by the absence of an ethical 'principle,' the Heideggerian perspective belongs to a tradition the barbarous depths of which were shown by Nazism. When Heidegger criticizes the essence of technology, he forgets that the source of modern evil, such as it was manifested in Nazism, is found at a depth that lies deeper than the realm of technology. Alluding to certain expressions found in Heidegger's later works, Levinas sketches the portrait of a pagan existence rooted in mother earth and prone to exploitation—very different from the sober existence of availability for the needs of others. The individuals are immersed in the *physis* that encompass them like elements of its unfolding. The intoxication of a polytheistic enthusiasm renewed by Heidegger through his interpretation of Hölderlin and the Presocratics shows by exaggeration what inspiration is hidden at the bottom of the 'lucid sobriety' of philosophers.[12]

Related to the above critique regarding the failure to get out of the subjectivity is Levinas' critique of Heidegger's view of time in relation to exstasis, which does not break out of the subjectivity of Dasein. Perhaps, I might add, the closest the later Heidegger comes to such a breakout is the time of Being, which is somewhat independent of Dasein and is emitted in events. But this still misses essentially what Levinas indicates, even though it could be claimed that the time of the other person appears somewhat on the horizon of worldly time, ecstatic temporality.[13] It is here that one can see Levinas' critique of the Heideggerian Being toward death, for Levinas considers death to be an alterity related to time. For Heidegger, death is the possibility of no longer having possibilities, or the impossibility of possibility.[14] What strikes Levinas about Heidegger's account of death is that it shatters "inauthentic possibilities"[15] rather than existence itself. For Levinas, rather, "Death in Heidegger is an event of freedom, whereas for me the subject seems to reach the limit of the possible in suffering. It finds itself enchained, overwhelmed, and in some way passive."[16] For Levinas, Heidegger does not go far enough regarding time. Levinas considers time as radical alterity connected to the alterity of the Other. But this alterity of time of the Other is not simultaneous with the time of the subject, which is the time of knowledge and representation, so that the other and the subject do not meet at the same time. As Cohen puts it so well, the "time of the Other disrupts or interrupts my temporality. It is this upset, this insertion of the Other's time into mine, that establishes the alterity of veritable time, which is neither the Other's time nor mine."[17] It must be remembered that for Levinas death is never a present,[18] for if death is, then the subject is not, and if it is not, then the subject is. In this way the tie among death, time, and the other, all as alterity, is traced. We see again in these themes that Levinas' critique of Heidegger is carried further. For rather than death serving to make a Dasein authentic or individuated or open to Being, Levinas sees the other, death, and time[19] as radical alterity. Likewise with the fundamental modes of being in relation to Dasein, especially the ready-to-hand, as we shall now see.

One of Levinas' constant themes leading to the heart of his ethical relation is the reconsideration of our relation to an object, which should not be reduced to Heidegger's ready-to-hand (*zuhandenheit*). It can be seen that enjoyment is a mode that cuts beneath the ready-to-hand and that Heidegger overlooks this phenomenon entirely. Levinas has stated: "This relationship with an object can be characterized by enjoyment (*jouissance*). All enjoyment is a way of being, but also a sensation—that is, light and knowledge. It is absorption of the object, but also distance with regard to it." Levinas goes on a few sentences later to add an important insight presupposed by and prior in some sense to the ethical relation. This point will have a significant role in Ricoeur's critique of Levinas' lack of reciprocity for the ethical relation. He states that: "The

morality of 'earthly nourishments' is the first morality, the first abnega-
tion. It is not the last, but one must pass through it."[20] And it is this
notion of nourishment that is at the heart of his critique of Heidegger
regarding enjoyment, for Levinas contends that "prior to being a system
of tools, the world is an ensemble of nourishments. Human life in the
world does not go beyond the objects that fulfill it. . . . These are the
nourishments characteristic of our existence in the world. It is an ecstatic
existence—being outside oneself—but limited by the object."[21] And it is
precisely this relation with an object that Levinas wants to characterize
as enjoyment (*jouissance*), a way of being prior to the ready-to-hand. I
will now turn to Ricoeur's critiques of Heidegger's thought, which is not
as extreme as that of Levinas, in order to integrate the two critiques into
a viable position emerging from the fundamental insight of both Ricoeur
and Levinas.

It can be seen that Ricoeur's fundamental critique of Heidegger in
Oneself as Another presupposes the earlier critiques made years ago.[22]
Although Ricoeur has been critical of Heidegger from the beginning of
his work decades ago, even before it was fashionable, he employs far
more of Heidegger's analyses than Levinas.[23] The points of his critiques
that interest me for our present discussion are those complex and central remarks in the essay "Existence and Hermeneutics" and remarks in
Fallible Man[24] and *Time and Narrative*.[25] It is against the backdrop of
these critiques that *Oneself as Another* must be read to avoid interpreting Ricoeur's critique of Heidegger as not going far enough.[26] For it is
there that we see his critique center on Heidegger's "short way" to
ontology in contrast to Ricoeur's own "long way"; and at the heart of
this critique is the other regarding Heidegger's premature projection of
an ontological unity of Dasein, which unity of the human Ricoeur insists
is a limit concept, something toward which we as human aim, and which
cannot be affirmed as given to existence. And also equally relevant to
this double critique is the radical difference is their appropriations of
Kant's role of reason. For Heidegger, Kant is approached as laying the
foundation of metaphysics, looked at from his own hermeneutical situatedness of posing the Being question. In this endeavor, human Being is
interpreted as essentially finite, so that human reason is brought down
to earth and sensibilized, with the imagination as the central place of origin, following the interpretation of the romantics in the late eighteenth
century and early nineteenth century. Ricoeur ardently opposes this rendition of reason, one that Cassirer calls an "iron-wood" or a contradiction in terms.[27] And in addition, we should look briefly at Ricoeur's critique of Heidegger's treatment of time in order to find a further place of
affinity with Levinas. Before turning to Ricoeur's treatment of Heidegger in *Oneself as Another* leading to his appropriation of Levinas' basic

insight, it will prove fruitful to cast this later against the backdrop of a further understanding of these earlier stances against Heidegger.

In his pivotal essay "Existence and Hermeneutics," Ricoeur contrasts his own "longer way" for reaching ontology, taking hermeneutic phenomenology as the proper vehicle, with Heidegger's "shorter way" of re-asking the question of Being by assuming the intimacy between the inquirer and the Being of the inquirer. Ricoeur does not want to jeopardize the advantage from his longer way, that it dwells on the ontic level in order to resolve the conflicts and to solve problems often overlooked in attempting to trace the most direct route to the question of Being. Ricoeur's basic objections to Heidegger's short way, as mentioned above, is that it too quickly reaches a unity of Dasein that Ricoeur does not consider to be forthcoming, and that remains for him problematical in that the unity of man is a regulative idea and not one that an ontology of Dasein can reveal.[28]

Ricoeur emphasizes the conflict of interpretations as revealing differing aspects of existence that ontically found various hermeneutic methods.[29] Further, on this ontic level and in an extended ethics, he has focused pointedly upon the problem of the place of evil in freedom within human existence and upon the ontic relation of human existence to the Sacred that is central to his whole philosophy. Thus, for Ricoeur, pausing to dwell on the ontic has fostered an integration or a dialectizing of the symbols that support a phenomenology of spirit and a psychoanalysis of desire, with their respective orientations to teleology and to archeology. And both of these prepare for the relation to the Sacred within a phenomenology of religion and its eschatology. These advantages of the long way for Ricoeur militate against Heidegger's short way.

The fundamental justification of the long way over the short way to ontology is the underlying difference in the fore-comprehension of human existence. For Ricoeur, as mentioned, the unity of man as a regulative idea cannot be achieved in existence and is not easily accessible to an ontology worked out too quickly. He says: "moreover, it is only in a conflict of rival hermeneutics that we perceive something of the being to be interpreted: a unified ontology is as inaccessible to our method as a separate ontology. Rather, in every instance each hermeneutics discovers the aspect of existence which founds it as method."[30] Thus, at the very outset, Ricoeur has challenged Heidegger's view of care in a fundamental ontology emerging from an existential analysis of Dasein properly grasped in the fore-comprehension. In addition, his view of the fallenness of human existence, in avoiding the ontologization of fault by placing evil in the disproportionate synthesis between the infinite and the finite, militates against the quick move from the concrete existence of man to conditions of possibility of that everyday existence.

Thus a great impasse is evinced in the differing passages from existence to ontology by Ricoeur and by Heidegger. Heidegger does not share Ricoeur's view of a broken existence as fallen, nor does he dwell on the founding in ontic existence of the conflict of interpretations and questions of method that arise from that conflict. Although Ricoeur's position could be somewhat mitigated here by softening the effect of the existential place of evil, the difference can be breached only by a radical adjustment in hermeneutics of existence, one closer to the general context of Levinas than to that of Heidegger. In our present context, this becomes another advantage of Ricoeur's approach, that it allows somewhat of a rapport with Levinas' insistence on the singularity and solitude of the existent, as will become clearer later.

Ricoeur's philosophy recasts the Kantian view of the demand on the part of reason for totality as well as reason's placing on knowledge a limit to experience in terms of his own development of a view of the quasitranscending of this limit through indirect expressions such as symbols, metaphors, and narrative. In addition, for Ricoeur, such a demand for totality in a philosophy of limits requires that ethics be extended beyond the Kantian formal ethic of law and freedom to an ethics of the actualization of freedom in the act of existing. Such an extended ethics reorients the place of radical evil in existence and freedom, to the synthesis between the infinite and the finite as the existential structural place for the possibility of evil, allowing for a natural tendency to good but a mere proclivity toward evil. From that view of evil in freedom and existence emerges the view of hope and thus the necessity for speculative philosophy and its condition of possibility from the innovation of meaning engendered by the productive imagination in affording schemata for the rules of understanding, and the extension of this function.

This broadened ethics, later to be seen as not incompatible with Levinas' ethics, is understood as a philosophy that leads from alienation to freedom and beatitude, attempting to grasp the "effort to exist in its desire to be,"[31] and opposing any reduction of reflection to a simple critique or to a mere "justification of science and duty as a reappropriation of our effort to exist; epistemology is only a part of this broader task: we have to recover the act of existing, the positing of the self, in all the density of its works."[32] Hence, it can be seen that Ricoeur has corrected Kant's view of the place of evil in freedom. He has, however, considered the locus of evil to stem from the disproportion in the synthesis between finitude and infinitude on the theoretical, practical, and especially affective levels that come to expression in the fullness of symbolic language. It is from the symbols of evil that thought reaches the notion of the servile will or the will in bondage. We have seen, then, that the advantages of the "long way" militate against the Heideggerian "short way." For, although his work on hermeneutics of existence and on the conflict of interpretations seems to founder in dwelling on the ontic level before reaching the promised land of ontology, the resolution of the conflict indicates the importance of considering the ontic level further than Heidegger does.[33]

Thus, at the very outset, Ricoeur has challenged Heidegger's view of the explicitly temporal unification of Dasein's Being as care. Here, with the consideration of the conflicts in interpreting existence, Ricoeur's two objections to Heidegger's short way converge. For differing methods of interpretation are rooted in the different and polemically synthesized dimensions of human existence that they respectively reveal. Now, it can be seen that this earlier twofold critique of Heidegger must be integrated with Ricoeur's own later critiques regarding the comprehension of Being. And these critiques must be brought together with Levinas' critique regarding the need for the injunction of the face to face and with his critiques of Heidegger seen above. With this in view, I will now turn to Ricoeur's recent critique of Heidegger's view of time, temporality, and history.

Heidegger wants to ground every understanding of real historical time on the comprehension of historicality in such a way that the written history of historical sciences is derived from the understanding of history. Ricoeur claims that Heidegger does not give us any "way to show in what sense the real historical understanding, properly speaking, is derived from this original understanding,"[34] explicitly bringing into play the critiques analyzed above. Heidegger fails to show how historical sciences are dissociated from natural sciences and how one can arbitrate conflicts between competing interpretations, often inside even the same science. It is in this context that Ricoeur accuses Heidegger of not resolving, but rather dissolving, problems of the conflicts of interpretation. Ricoeur, however, in his later criticism, focuses again on a central point in Heidegger's whole philosophy, that of temporality, time, and history. And, indeed, it is Heidegger's failure to address sufficiently the ontic and the sciences that prevents him from adequately dealing with the alterity of time or the alterity of the Other, something to which Ricoeur can be seen to be open without too much adjustment in his own position. For, in both "Existence and Hermeneutics" and in *Time and Narrative*, Ricoeur shows the need to pass through, on this level from which Heidegger's reflection begins but too quickly escapes, indirect language of narrative, earlier focusing on symbols and metaphors, now on narrative history and fiction. Reflection becomes an interpretation of language to decipher the meaning of my existence, even of myself, acces-

sible in depth only in such indirect accesses. This view of Ricoeur culminates in the studies in *Oneself as Another*. And it is in this later focus
that narrative, or more precisely, the story, can constitute or determine
time in a way not envisioned by Kant or allowed for by Heidegger or
Levinas. This move represents Ricoeur's continual expansion or completion of the work of Kant and Heidegger, here with regard to the constitution of time, the productive imagination, and the reflective judgment, all expanded into a coherent picture of a philosophy of action and
ethical regeneration. In this context we can see that historical or human
time, with its three connectors, the calendar, the sequence of generations, and the trace, all constitute historical time "through which we join
not only our predecessors, contemporaries and successors, but also the
universe and cosmological time."[35] Thus, Ricoeur's criticism, which
begins by reproaching Heidegger for wanting to derive an understanding of history from an understanding of Dasein's existence, ends in
reproaching Heidegger for an incapacity to think historical time itself.
We must turn to Ricoeur's fuller critique of Heidegger's category of temporality.

Ricoeur's strongest articulation of the critique of the phenomenology of time comes to grips with the primordial time of Heidegger, as
seen in the last chapter. This critique of Heidegger's limitations regarding time is a serious one that cannot be ignored, in spite of the fact that
Ricoeur extols the achievements of *Being and Time*, that is, that the
principle of temporalization is sought out within the structure of care
that allows for distinguishing time on different levels. Nevertheless, even
with its levels of temporalization, Heidegger's treatment of time reveals
most completely an inability to incorporate a certain sense of time. For
it is from Kant that we learned that time as such is invisible, that it could
not appear in any living experience, that it is always presupposed as the
condition of experience, and from this fact could only appear indirectly
on objects apprehended in space and according to the schemata and the
categories of objectivity. According to Ricoeur, it is this constraint that
shows why even internal time-consciousness borrows its structure from
this objective time that the reduction holds in suspense. And even Heidegger's inclusion of the levels of temporalization fall before this objection: "But this very effort comes up against *the other* of phenomenological time: the 'popular' concept of time, made up of an infinite series of
indifferent nows. Even the most decentered level of temporality—
within-time-ness—where the 'in' of being in time is highlighted, never
rejoins the 'ordinary' time which is simply removed from the phenomenological field by the allegation of an enigmatic leveling of the 'in'
of 'within-time-ness'."[36] Ricoeur considers Heidegger's attempt to
include the history of time from Aristotle to Hegel in this ordinary time

to be in vain. For Ricoeur, there is a disproportion between time that we unfold in living and time that envelops us everywhere.

Heidegger's account does not take into consideration the "hetero-geneous temporal orders" to which the trace, as an original phe-nomenon, belongs, as seen in the last chapter. Ricoeur asks the critical question of Heidegger's attempt to deal with this in terms of having been and within-time-ness: "For how does *Dasein* interpret its having-been-there if not by relying on the autonomy of marks left by the passage of former humans? Heidegger's failure to understand the phenomenon of trace reflects the failure of *Sein and Zeit* to give an account of the time of the world which has no care for our care." [37] Ricoeur goes on to show how the trace, as an element with a history, crosses the gap between internal time and cosmic time.

This critique parallels the broader critique of Heidegger's hermeneutic considered above. Although Ricoeur is exemplarily respect-ful of Heidegger's hermeneutic ontology and primordial time that it reveals, he must supply a hermeneutic that does more than that of Hei-degger. In allowing the text a certain distanciation from its situation of origin, and focusing on it in a quasi-independence of the reader, Ricoeur has pointed out in hermeneutics something similar to what he is point-ing out here regarding time, that is, the need adequately to deal with that which is not reducible to the having been of Dasein in the temporal ecstases. For no matter how much effort is exerted to consider the mode of being of Dasein, and the past as derivative from the temporality or historicality of Dasein, the fact remains that there is still something past that is independent of human existence and Dasein's temporality and historicality—that other of which the trace serves as a trace—as, for example, with the historical documents, monuments, and implements that have no world remaining and no Dasein that is familiar with them. This requires, in fact, demands a reconstruction by imagination and intelligent interpretation and explanation, before being appropriated into familiarity of human existence. This is the same domain that is entered through a critique of Heidegger regarding the inadequacy of the internal time of phenomenology and his own primordial time that can-not encompass cosmic time. This critique of Heidegger shows clearly how Heidegger's perspective must be recognized in its limits regarding time and hermeneutics, especially concerning that which is not reducible to care. The primordial relation of Dasein to Being is inadequate to deal with the otherness of cosmic time and of texts.

Further, for Heidegger, the drive for Being within his hermeneutical situatedness, the absolute status of the Being-question constitutive of Dasein, leads Heidegger further into a pitfall regarding history. In the *Rule of Metaphor* Ricoeur turns against "the manner in which Heidegger opposes all other ontologies by confining them inside the bounds of 'the' metaphysical."[38] Continuing with Kemp, we see that "[t]his 'destruction of metaphysics' signifies in Ricoeur's eyes an 'unacceptable claim . . . [to put] an end to the history of being,'[39] a claim which is no more legitimate than the Hegelian attempt to demonstrate the closing of history."[40] Rather than support such a destruction or, today, deconstruction, of metaphysics, Ricoeur asks: "Which resources of ontology are capable of being reawakened, liberated and regenerated by coming in touch with a phenomenology of self?"[41] One can see in this criticism of Heidegger's destruction of the history of metaphysics a latent critique of historical time.

Now that we have seen the fundamental critiques made by both Levinas and Ricoeur of Heidegger, we can contrast them with a view toward bringing their differing ethical orientations together, and in the process, see if situating Ricoeur between Levinas and Heidegger allows for a further development of his position in the light of that of Levinas. We have seen that Levinas reveals a twofold separation that Heidegger does not develop: the separation between communal existence or coexistence (*mitsein*) and the singularity and solitude of the existing existent; and the separation between the Other and Being in the world. Taking into account Ricoeur's critiques of Heidegger, we can see first that Ricoeur's insistence on remaining on the ontic level gives his initial philosophical focus a basic affinity with that of Levinas, for the ethical relation emphasized by Levinas takes place between two concretely singular persons existing in some sense in separation and external to one another. Although Ricoeur himself does not agree with the intense separation, he does allow for a certain alterity that is not so far removed from that of Levinas as to prevent an ethical relation of Levinas' kind. It is precisely Ricoeur's alterity of time that allows a further extension of his philosophy in the direction of Levinas, and, picking up on a theme of the ethical freedom in the second person as not too far from the face to face, we can develop his position in a greater affinity for a positive contribution from Levinas, while leaving his overall ethical framework and principle in tact. And it is this general context of the ethical framework and principle, bringing an adapted Aristotelian teleology and Kantian deontology in a coherent ethics that serves as a critique and an extension beyond Levinas.

While Levinas has been seen to critique Heidegger's treatment of time as not reaching time's alterity, especially in relation to death, Ricoeur's critique centers around cosmic time as external to and other than internal time, thus tying time to the cosmic rather than the Other as Levinas does. They both, however, have recognized the insufficiency of Heidegger's temporality of Dasein in relation to some other as the failure to break out of subjectivity or of Dasein. Now, time as other for both Levinas and Ricoeur can be brought together, since the cosmic is definitely other than temporality of Dasein, as seen earlier, and thus overlaps with Levinas' view. The cosmic time of Ricoeur certainly must be admitted in a full treatment, and just as the cosmic time includes any singularity (me) independently of the time of Dasein, that is, it is the time that pre-exists us and surrounds us, and into which we are incorporated, it likewise is the time in which the Other is included, and in which the Other participates. Just as my time shares in the cosmic insofar as I am of the cosmic, so too for the other. Thus the alterity overlaps in time, and the alterity of time of the other reveals again the alterity of the other. Thus, Ricoeur's alterity of time of the cosmic can be brought to Levinas' alterity of the Other. And this Other is the place of the injunction or call to responsibility. We must reflect further on the other separation that Levinas includes against Heidegger, the separation between communal existence or coexistence (*mitsein*) and singularity of the existent. We must see if there is a connection with Ricoeur in spite of his critique of Levinas. The question concerning Ricoeur is whether he really accounts for a "singularity" or an overcoming of Heidegger on this point to the extent that Levinas does so. Ricoeur does seem to include the singularity in the face to face, but the question as posed leaves open the extent to which he has explicitly incorporated it.

SOLICITUDE IN RECIPROCITY
AND SOLITUDE IN EXISTENCE

Ricoeur contends that Levinas, with his powerful message of responsibility elicited within the face-to-face epiphany of the other, describes the other as so separate, isolated, and solitary that no real encounter is possible without a supplementary dimension to give a basis for a response of responsibility, one that makes it possible. In spite of an intense respect for Levinas, Ricoeur has found the account of the face to face incapable of establishing the relation required for such a response. He, rather, sees Levinas's entire philosophy as resting "on the initiative of the other," but this initiative establishes no relation. According to Ricoeur's terse formulation, "E. Levinas' entire philosophy rests on the initiative of the other in the intersubjective relation. In reality this initiative establishes no relation at all, to the extent that the other represents absolute exteriority with respect to an ego defined by the condition of separation. The other, in this sense, absolves himself of any relation. This irrelation defines exteriority as such" (OA, 188–189). It is this lack of relation that defines exteriority. It seems that even in the contention by Levinas that escaping the solitude of existence, in the face-to-face encounter, involves a glimpse of the infinite, its trace in the face, there is no possibility for such a response, because there is no possibility of a relation that would allow it or elicit it.

Ricoeur's reading of Levinas involves a move from *Totality and Infinity*[42] to *Otherwise than Being*,[43] showing the development of his point in Levinas to the point of exaggeration. This reading interprets the role of the self before the encounter with the other face to face as "a stubbornly closed, locked up, separate ego" (OA, 337);[44] the Other is an "ab-solute exteriority which can present itself to the separate ego by the epiphany of the face."[45] This hyperbole of the separation is carried further in the notion of the "the substitution" in *Otherwise than Being*. Ricoeur contends that here Levinas' hyperbole reaches the point of paroxysm when "Levinas speaks about responsibility which 'under accusation by everyone' goes to the point of substitution of the I for the Other. Here the other is no longer, as in *Totality and Infinity*, the master of justice, he is 'the offender, who, as offender, no less requires the gesture of pardon and expiation'"[46] (OA, 338). In this later account a subject becomes a hostage.[47] In spite of Peter Kemp's criticism of Ricoeur's reading of Levinas from *Otherwise than Being* to *Totality and Infinity*, it seems that Ricoeur's reading of Levinas in terms of the later work is justified, in that Levinas' thought should be assumed to develop and become more mature so that the later thought is contained in the earlier at least in some form.[48] According to Richard Cohen's view of the progression of Levinas' view of alterity, Ricoeur is not wrong in interpreting back to *Totality and Infinity* from *Otherwise than Being*. What is wrong, however, is that Ricoeur overlooked something in *Totality and Infinity* presupposed by the epiphany of the face: that is the role of other people in interiority, with its economy, enjoyment, and hospitality. The face to face, even in *Totality and Infinity*, presupposes this life with others. The precise point for Levinas is that the face to face goes beyond this—and so does the epiphany in *Otherwise than Being*. And, for the face-to-face encounter, the two, the Same and the Other, must be separate and exterior to one another or there is no infinite beyond the totality.

In an attempt to do justice to Levinas' position, independent of Ricoeur's critique, two basic points need to be explicitly laid out: first, transcendence in Levinas' sense requires that the two terms (persons) be external to each other, or there is no real transcendence in the face to face; and second, that interiority or totality in Levinas' sense already contains a capacity for relation with the Other, as mentioned above. There is an exteriority already there that makes the exteriority of transcendence possible, without jeopardizing the transcendence of the latter. In addition, the two-sided dimension of desire further illuminates these two issues.

Even if a place is stressed for the possibility of an encounter, the two terms dealt with in *Totality and Infinity* must be external to one another *in the strong sense*. Otherwise, there is only all-encompassing totality at the expense of exteriority. To obliterate this is to destroy the possibility of any relation between the totality and the face of the Other. Levinas has correctly indicated, then, that we cannot characterize the Other as a reality that can be "integrated or 'sublated' into any consciousness, spirit, or other form of interiority."[49] Yet Levinas admits the transitive relation in which we live, but indicates that: "I *am* not the Other, I am all alone. It is thus the being in me, the fact that I exist, my *existing*, that constitutes the absolutely intransitive element, something without intentionality or relationship. One can exchange everything between beings except existing."[50] In developing his view of solitude of existing, Levinas is pitting himself against Heidegger, for whom Dasein is transcendence and Being-in-the-world with others, but, from Levinas' point of view, all within totality. Further, when Phillipe Neno asked Levinas regarding the ethical relation making us escape this solitude, Levinas shot back immediately regarding the infinite that, "I am not afraid of the word God, which appears quite often in my essays. To my mind the infinite comes to the signifyingness of the face. The face *signifies* the Infinite." This infinite is insatiable, it is the "exigency of holiness."[51] Thus, it can be seen that Levinas, with his complex statements of solitude and infinity, is clear in emphasizing that solitude is a mark of the fact of being, and being, rather than solitude, is what one must escape.[52] He further affirms that *Time and the Other* represents an attempt to escape from this isolation of existing, as the preceding book, *Existence and Existents* signifies an attempt to escape from the "there is."[53] And it is precisely this "escape" character of Levinas that must not be lost. For Levinas, the fact of being is private, and existence alone cannot be communicated, cannot be shared as such. "Solitude thus appears here as the isolation which marks the very event of being."[54] And we come back to the affirmation of the transitive dimension. We can indeed be with others through sight, touching, sympathy, and so on. Yet, although these are all transitive, we cannot be the other. The pivotal question for the present discussion is whether saying that solitude is a mark of existence, and that it is being that we must escape can give a proper possibility for a response of responsibility to the other, in alterity. Is the Other so other that a relationship is impossible? Must something further be supplied to Levinas' view to make the face to face possible?

Ricoeur of course does not exclude the fact that the two terms, the Same and the Other, or interiority (totality) and exteriority (infinity), must be external to each other, even though at times he seems to be oblivious to this point. For he cannot employ Levinas' face to face with the Other in his own polarization of Levinas and Husserl unless he maintains the exteriority of the terms as the main point of Levinas' *Totality and Infinity*, before he integrates these oppositions within his own developed position. It is in this general movement that Ricoeur is certainly not oblivious to the required exteriority of the Other. His critique challenges the other main point, claiming that interiority or the totality includes no base for being called by the epiphany of the face of the Other. The positive contribution of Ricoeur is that he expands Levinas in a needed direction to round out and render explicit the place in the subject for such a response as solicitude and self-esteem, as will be seen. These, however, from Levinas' point of view remain within the context of totality of the subject. And likewise, Ricoeur's fundamental point in *Oneself as Another* presents a complex identity not found as such in Levinas, a point to which Ricoeur explicitly adverts in his comments on Levinas. Let us now turn to the second point of Levinas' view mentioned above.[55]

Ricoeur's omission mentioned above is precisely what Kemp indicates in accusing Ricoeur of having missed an equilibrium among the levels of analysis that allows *the Totality and Infinity* to make sense out of a separation. This equilibrium allows for the separation between ethical existence and pre-ethical life to be without contradiction. In *Totality and Infinity*, according to Kemp, there are three levels of description of existence none of which excludes the others: "that of enjoyment and habitation (called 'Interiority and Economy'); that of the face (called 'Exteriority and the Face'); and that of love and fecundity (called 'Beyond the Face')." Kemp goes on to show on the first level how the other is included in the enjoyment of life, but not strictly as face. The other is seen to be "present in intimacy and sweetness, in familiarity and femininity."[56] He goes on to say the same about the analysis by Levinas of the economy of labor in the home, which can become a home of hospitality. But the hand may be "a manipulator, and one may close one's house instead of opening it to the poor and the stranger."[57] In these cases, the Same closes in on itself, "so that interiority and the economy of the home cannot constitute an ethics. Indeed, it is only the face entering from the exteriority which assigns us to responsibility."[58]

Even in the preface of *Totality and Infinity* Levinas has already set the stage for this insight in the context of eschatology, where a continuity between totality and that which is outside the totality can be clearly seen. Levinas says explicitly that "this 'beyond' the totality and objective experience" is "reflected *within* the totality and history, *within* experience. . . . The eschatological, as the 'beyond' of history . . . arouses them, (beings) in and calls them forth to their full responsibility."[59] Yet, in the very context of establishing the connection, Levinas is quick to indicate that the seeds of a break are already within this totality. For, as he says: "The first 'vision' of eschatology . . . reveals the very possibility of eschatology, that is, the breach of the totality, the possibility of a *signification without a context*."[60]

Levinas, in preserving this distinctness or separation between totality and infinity, has overstressed the identity of the Same or interiority at the expense of what Ricoeur has always supported as the alterity within an identity of a self. Levinas consequently passes over the twofold sense of identity in Ricoeur's account of the identity of the Same and the identity of the self: *idem identity* and *ipse identity*. Although his recent *Oneself as Another* is his most explicit and best development of this break within the reflecting existent, Ricoeur has been articulating in one way or another this view since the beginning of his writings, coming to emphasize this aspect of reflective philosophy in the Yale Terry Lectures followed by the book on Freud.[61] Here in *Oneself as Another*, he has developed explicitly the alterity within oneself, which, in our present context, allows a mediation between oneself and the Other. It is true that Levinas would certainly consider this whole project of reflective philosophy of Ricoeur to be a matter of totality and identity of Self, but in doing so he would indeed sell Ricoeur short, for Ricoeur is quite correct in stating that Levinas has no such dual sense of self-identity, but a rather simple Same. This, even for Ricoeur, does not preclude the need for the exteriority of the Other mentioned above in order to have a transcendence in the call of the other in the face-to-face epiphany. And that is perhaps the point that Ricoeur most admires in Levinas, the transcendence of the face to face that entails an encounter between two independent and solitary existents. In this sense, Ricoeur does not want to exclude the solitude of each individual, a solitude that cannot be overcome. Yet that is not the end of the issue. For he considers the solicitude of which Levinas' position does not take account to be equiprimordial. In defense of Levinas, in spite of what has been said, perhaps one could stretch the point and consider both of Ricoeur's senses of identity to be collapsed in Levinas' Same, which must be somehow identical with itself independently of an encounter with the Other. This point is possibly borne out by Peperzak's observation that this "self-identity of Me is . . . the concrete activity of self-identification through which I establish myself as inhabitant and owner of my world."[62] The point to be emphasized is that the very project of *Totality and Infinity* attempts to establish the separation and difference between totality as Same and the infinity as Other, thus refusing to encompass them both within the same horizon of totality.[63] It is precisely this point that Ricoeur tends to over-interpret when looking to the interiority's inability to respond, missing something of that dimension in Levinas' own *Totality and Infinity*.

Ricoeur and Levinas both similarly take a positive attitude toward desire that requires a transformation of the treatment of Kant. First, in liberating the will from its identity with the Kantian pure practical reason, overcoming Kantian epistemological priority, they both give a more positive place for desire. Desire is thus redeemed from its role of pollution and defilement and rather takes on a positive role in the activity of the will and in action in general. It is in this context that the double-sidedness of desire must be considered in the face-to-face transcendence.

It is the double-sidedness of desire that indicates the transcendence in the epiphany of the face and the possibility within interiority for the epiphany of exteriority. On the first side of desire, the satisfaction of needs stands within the economy of totality. Levinas employs the experience of enjoyment as a fulfilled need on the affective level to highlight the isolation of the enjoying subject. Someone else cannot feel my pleasures and pains, which confirms the enjoying subject in its identity with itself. Such being at home with oneself separates from all others as a unique and original substance not absorbed by the continuity of the universe. The opposition between the interior and the exterior must not be interpreted in terms of the traditional opposition between the ego and its world or between subject and object. "Through its needs and its enjoyment but also through representation and objectifying knowledge, the solitary ego is related to the 'exteriority' of elements, equipment, things, and objects, but *this* 'exteriority' cannot resist the ego's encompassing capacity of appropriation and integration. The exteriority revealed by the face is that by which the alterity of the Other escapes from the dimension where interiority and exteriority, subject and object, mind and matter, traditionally are opposed and put into contradiction or mediated dialectically as moments of a differential whole."[64] The face of the Other is an expression that cannot be reduced to my world or to the task of self-realization; "it is the interdiction of killing this vulnerable defenseless, and naked other in front of me."[65]

On the other side of desire is the concrete way of transcendence to the Other, but this is not a desire that satisfies a need, for that remains within the context of totality and focuses on relations with others that do not yet involve transcendence in the fullest sense. This whole phenomenon is recast in relation to desire that is not the satisfaction of needs.[66] Rather than grasped in fulfilled satisfaction, this aspect of desire cannot be integrated, and thus is transcendent and exterior. Hence, the Other, not represented or comprehended, does not become something that is mine. Thus, for Levinas, this desire does not have the structure of intentionality. "It is, thus, neither the natural tendency that was thematized in Aristotle's ethics as a teleological striving for self-realization nor a nostalgic 'eksisting' toward a contentment that—although delayed—could fulfill the longing subject and bring it to its rest."[67] In a sense, the will and desire reach out toward an object or person as it is, while cognition brings something into the subject, into interiority. The desired thus remains transcendent and, as such, exterior. This is an essential point of Levinas.

The crucial aspect of this side of desire is the fact that it shows an essential impossibility of fusion or union. The desired has one thing in common with death, that both are absolutely other, so that neither death nor the Other can take place within the unfolding of my possibilities. This is because desire and the desired are insatiate and insatiable, so that the distance separating them cannot be abolished. It is precisely this double-sidedness of desire as separation and relation that, preserving the exteriority of the two terms and thus allowing for transcendence in the epiphany of the face, opens the space for an analysis of human existence as two-dimensional reality. Here we follow Peperzak, who agrees in substance with the point made above from Kemp. First, "as separated individuals, we are independent and egocentric, centers and masters of an economy that is also an egonomy." Second, "as transcending toward the Other, we live in a different dimension, the structure of which is made of transcendence, alterity, and the impossibility of totalization and identification." The difficulty of Levinas's enterprise, especially in this context of Ricoeur's interpretation, "lies in the task of showing—in the form of a thematic, and thereby necessarily gathering, discourse—that gathering, coherence, and unity do not constitute the ultimate horizon of such a discourse, and that otherness, separation, and transcendence are irreducible to any unity."[68]

From what has already been considered above about the exteriority within interiority, Ricoeur's main point of critique of Levinas, that there is no place within interiority for a response to the face of the other, must be mitigated in the light of what has been seen in Levinas' own view. Ricoeur's critique overemphasizes the exteriority at the expense of this very possibility of relation to the transcendent Other as within interiority. Again, it must be emphasized that *Totality and Infinity* was written to emphasize the exteriority of the face of the Other precisely as a break with interiority. This however does not necessarily preclude some place within totality for the experience of the face of the other. In a sense, the Other is already included in the enjoyment of life, in economy, and in hospitality, but not strictly as face, which remains transcendent. But here we have a place to anchor such an epiphany of the face. And it is only the face entering from the exteriority that "assigns us to responsibility."[69] For Levinas, the face breaks with the usual cultural meaning and hence calls into question the horizon of the world. As Bernasconi observes: "'no face can be approached with empty hands and closed home,' is Levinas's way of saying that the relation with the absolutely Other who paralyzes possession presupposes economic existence and the Other who welcomes me in the home. Thus in the movement parallel to that found in the account of representation and enjoyment, Levinas reverses the movement by which it seemed that the face of the Other was being made an ultimate ground. Hence the intimacy of the home is the 'first concretization.'"[70]

The only adequate response to the revelation of the absolute in the face is respect, generosity, and donation. It is because the Other's face is naked, that it commands and obligates. The other's emergence is the "refutation of my egoism and therewith the fundamental dispossession that is needed for the possibility of universalization and objectification by putting the world of things in common. . . . The face-to-face of a living discourse is the concrete way in which the fundamental relation is practiced. It is neither mediated nor otherwise preceded by an original 'we' or 'being-with': on the contrary, all forms of association or community are founded in the relation of the Same and the Other."[71] Thus the tension between the views of Levinas and Ricoeur comes to the fore, for it is to this very Heideggerian context castigated by Levinas that Ricoeur wants to turn for his expansion upon Levinas' doctrine. Thus, Ricoeur has to adjust Levinas here, since he advocates Heidegger's solicitude and also self-esteem and need of others as the place of the possibility for a response that is supposedly cut off by the lack of relation due to separation, isolation, and solitude of the Same. We must turn back now to Ricoeur's critique in the light of this further development of Levinas' thought in order to see what legitimacy his remarks have, and then to see how Ricoeur, enlightened by Levinas, proffers a more viable ethics than that of postmodernists, who are influenced by Levinas, yet want to divest his ethics of any real ethical relation.[72]

Ricoeur's critique of Levinas regarding the separation and exteriority of the other and the initiative from the other as incapable of establishing the relation allowing a response of responsibility takes place within the context of bringing two entirely different directions of movement together: the movement from the Other (exteriority) to me (interiority); and the movement of inwardness toward the other. Ricoeur admits having to adjust each of these views. But what cannot be overlooked is that for Levinas the relation is between two which are external to one another, and not reducible to the totality of the Same. The stress on the separation, isolation, solitude, exteriority keeps the distance between the two as other than a mere opposition within the context of totality. Further, it must be kept in mind that Ricoeur is not entirely oblivious to this, since his negative comment on Levinas' view of "totality" shows that he sees the alterity between the infinite and totality not to require such an interpretation of totality as so closed up.

Ricoeur, in interpreting the face as the "master of justice," since, as Levinas says, it forbids murder and commands justice, and is thus the source of the injunction, immediately contrasts its dissymmetry with the reciprocity of friendship. Although not mentioned here, his own view puts justice consequent upon friendship in the formation of communities following Aristotle. Perhaps Levinas would respond that the face to face does not require friendship, and his alterity as a call elicits the response of responsibility. But it must be admitted that these are two different contexts of discourse: one of transcendence; the other of the framework of ethics. And within the first context of discourse, Ricoeur questions whether the injunction, to be heard and received, must not call first for a response that compensates for the dissymmetry of the face-to-face encounter without which the exchange would be broken off. In other words, the other's initiative, to be reciprocated, must somehow free the capacity for giving (OA, 189). He suggests that goodness could spring forth in a being who does not detest himself to the point of being unable to hear the injunction from the other. And the goodness, for Ricoeur, is connected to the aim at the good life, which is often tied to doing for others out of regard for them.

In the context of Ricoeur's own conviction of the priority of the ethical over the moral, Levinas's language of summons and injunction seems already too moral in a way similar to Kant in relation to Aristotle: that is, the ethical is the foundation of the moral, and the injunction, duty, and the law should not arise on the ethical horizon too soon. Ricoeur delves below moral duty to find a latent "ethical sense" (OA, 190) that can be invoked in cases of "undecidable matters of conscience" (OA, 190). It must be remembered that Ricoeur, in the Seventh and Eighth Studies of Oneself as Another, polarizes Aristotelian ethics of virtue and Kantian morality of obligation, showing all the while the more fundamental dimension of the ethical aiming at or seeking of the good life. It is clear, then, why solicitude of the ethical is presupposed for the injunction: the critique seen of Kant in the Eighth Study could well be applied to Levinas, that the injunction is invoked too soon, even with the substitution of the face and the infinite for the Kantian pure rational moral law. Thus, in this present context, it is clear why Ricoeur shows that Levinas needs the ability to respond and the ability for some kind of reciprocity based on solicitude, which itself is caught up in seeking the good life or human good. But one has to admit that, in defense of Levinas, even Ricoeur has recognized the basic dimension of the face to face for ethics. And earlier in Oneself as Another, before confronting the position of Levinas, Ricoeur has already laid bare the notion of self-esteem latent within and intrinsic to the ethical aiming at the good life, from which he now extracts, or within which he interprets, a basic solicitude having the status of a "benevolent spontaneity" (OA, 190). Such benevolent spontaneity is the bases of a receiving at the same level as being called to responsibility in acting in accordance with justice, which is presupposed by any response of responsibility. This reciprocity, or receiving and reaching, is not the same as the equality of friendship, but it does compensate for the dissymmetry. Although the whole of the Aristotelian framework eventually comes to light in reflection as the pre-required framework for morality, it does not necessarily get the first focus within a philosophical reflection. And even for Ricoeur, as has been seen, it is freedom in the second person or the face of other in the personal relation that begins ethics and takes on the connotation of transcending the values of our culture and times.[73] Further, it is violence and evil that demand that the limit of the Aristotelian framework be recognized.

Ricoeur contends that it is the search for equality across inequality that establishes the place of solicitude in ethics. Solicitude bespeaks a lack belonging to self-esteem, as the reflexive moment of the wish for the good life, constituted with a lack evolving with a need, a need for friends, and giving rise to the awareness of the self among others. Thus it is seen that solicitude is not external to self-esteem, but is constituted as a moment of self-esteem in its lack and need.

Ricoeur sees another inequality emerging from the figure of the other as master of justice in suffering, which takes the form not merely of pain, but of reduction or destruction of the power for acting or being-able to act. Again, the other seems to be reduced to receiving, and the self who responds is again the one who gives. Ricoeur, however, sees a subtle form of giving emerging from the very weakness of the one suffering. "A self reminded of the vulnerability of the condition of mortality can receive from the friend's weakness more than he or she can give in return by drawing from his or her own reserves of strength" (OA, 191). Here magnanimity enters. On this phenomenological level, feelings must be considered as affects that enter into motivation. This is in Aristotle's context of "disposition." And it is feelings (here as affects) in solitude that are revealed in the self by the other's suffering and by the moral injunction (OA, 191). For Ricoeur, "this intimate union between the ethical aim of solicitude and the affective flesh of feelings seems to me to justify the choice of the term 'solicitude'" (OA, 192). Thus, it is seen that, between the extreme poles in the call to responsibility, the initiative comes from the other, and in sympathy for the sufferer, the initiative comes from the living self, where a quasifriendship appears as a midpoint in which the sufferer and sympathizer share the same wish to live together (OA, 192).[74]

In the Tenth Study, in accord with his own dialectic procedure, Ricoeur polarizes the most extreme positions, finds a crack by means of which to open them, and brings out something implicit that allows a rapprochement, or better put, an interarticulation that, as he works it out fully, becomes his unique position. His own position is constituted from elements of opposing positions that he critiques, adapts, and then creatively appropriates in a new and better integration. And it is noteworthy that the "analogical transfer" considered in the context of Husserl, not Heidegger, is somewhat independent of the movement from the Other toward me, even though it intersects with it. Neither Husserl's nor Heidegger's accounts get to the necessary point of addressing the Other's movement toward me, and that is precisely why they need the movement of Levinas' analysis. In Ricoeur's own appropriation of this opposition, Levinas' account must be opened to allow to a limited extent for this ability of myself to receive and to approach the other; and that the accounts of both Husserl and Heidegger must be opened to allow for a place for encountering the other as such before their analysis closes themselves off from such an encounter. "It is here that the analogical transfer from myself to the other intersects with the inverse movement of the other toward me. It intersects with the latter but does not abolish it, even if it does not presuppose it" (OA, 335).

Ricoeur says: "At the origin of this movement (of the other toward me) lies a break. And this break occurs at the point of articulation of phenomenology and of the ontology of the 'great kinds,' the Same and the Other" (OA, 335). It misses the twofold sense of identity as idem identity and ipse identity. This is precisely the place where Kemp's remarks are relevant. The question for us is the status of this break, since Levinas does allow for it in principle as seen in the reading of those sections of *Time and Infinity* mentioned above. Ricoeur considers Levinas' account to so radically oppose the Other and the Same as to exclude his own twofold sense of identity, that of ipse and idem, so central to his position and to this *Oneself as Another*. This exclusion is the result of Levinas' ontology of totality that houses his view of the identity of the Same. And this ontology of totality "results that the self, not distinguished from the I, is not taken in the sense of the self-designation of a subject of discourse, action, narrative, or ethical commitment" (OA, 335). It is the case that, even after the attempt made above to mitigate the point Kemp makes concerning the pre-ethical levels that are not exclusive of the ethical and its exteriority, they indeed still can be seen not to supply adequately this twofold sense of identity in which the self, considered as another, has a bridge across the gap between the self and the other. We have found, however, that there is a place at the point of the exteriority within interiority to graft Ricoeur's double view of the self, inclusive of the ipseity of the self as well as idem identity, mentioned above.

Ricoeur considers both the break effect of Levinas and the reduction to ownness in Husserl to stem from the use of hyperbole as the "systematic practice of excess" (OA, 337). In Ricoeur's mind this hyperbole is precisely the closing up of the inwardness of immanence of transcendental phenomenology. And Ricoeur sees Levinas' hyperbole to reach both the Same and the Other, so that first the closed, locked up separate ego, before the Other is spoken of hyperbolically as absolute exteriority. Ricoeur goes on to interpret the even greater hyperbole of *Otherwise than Being* in the development about "substitution of the I for the Other" (OA, 338–341). The conclusion to this section on Levinas returns to the confrontation between Husserl and Levinas. He again emphasizes that there is no contradiction in the dialectically complementarity between the two movements: that of the Other toward the Same, and that of the Same toward the Other. These two movements do not annihilate one another "to the extent that one unfolds in the gnoseological dimension of sense, the other in the ethical dimension of injunction. The assignment of responsibility, in the second dimension, refers to the power of self designation, transferred, in accordance with the first dimension, to every third person assumed to be capable of saying 'I'. Was not this intersecting dialectic of oneself and the other than self anticipated in the analysis of the promise? If another were not counting on me, would I be capable of keeping my word, of maintaining myself?" (OA, 340–341). This is at the heart of Ricoeur's ethicomoral position.

In taking Ricoeur to task for a too severe criticism of Levinas, Kemp admits that Ricoeur's critique is not too severe if one agrees with Ricoeur that "grounding ethics requires one to ascribe to solicitude a more fundamental status than obedience to duty."[75] This is a critical point, for it focuses precisely on Ricoeur's basic aim: to provide a quasi-Aristotelian ethical framework and an adjusted Kantian deontological principle. The total backdrop and context for this critique of Levinas is Ricoeur's own efforts to critique and open up Kantian ethics of duty or obligation to its proper grounding in an ethics or an ethos, coming from the opposed direction. And in this Ricoeur's critique makes sense. But both Ricoeur and Levinas disagree with Kant to the extent that they each remove the priority to the absolute a priori moral law given to pure practical reason; and each opens the way to the fundamental role of desire, liberated from the Kantian interpretation, as seen above. While Ricoeur wants to ground the obligation to law in the ethics of teleology, and in this context we could fix solicitude of our present context, Levinas wants to bring obligation alive in the concrete situation of the face to face, thus breaking out of totality, including even breaking out of the framework that Ricoeur is so careful to provide. Ricoeur's criticism of Kant can well be leveled at Levinas in that Levinas could be considered to bring up the injunction too soon, but Ricoeur now has to supply for Levinas what he supplies for Kant, a foundation and a framework for ethics, which is precisely what he has intended all along. Although in a full reflection that focuses on the moral situation one might first begin with the transcendence of the "face to face," this beginning does not supply an adequate foundation for ethical life, which has transpired at a basic level long before this reflection catches it in the act, so to speak. And this is precisely where Ricoeur incorporates a quasi-Aristotelian teleological dimension into the ethicomoral situation. And while Ricoeur might want to add this to Levinas, and rightly so, it can be found that in the context of totality, Levinas has already to some extent included the situation that makes the "face to face" possible within totality.

Retaining Levinas' responsibility within Ricoeur's ethicomoral integration allows Ricoeur's place of receptivity to be integrated with an element of Levinas' view of totality, the latent exteriority. But this must preclude any subordination of Levinas' exteriority of the face and infinity to the totality, which he so consistently and rigorously avoids, and which would falsify or remove precisely the uniqueness of his view of alterity. In accepting the role of solicitude in human existence, Ricoeur has developed a place within interiority that really allows a response to the face of the Other. And in doing so, he has accounted for a central, indeed, the central point of Levinas, that a breakthrough—a breakout—of the "totality" of traditional philosophy is necessary for there to be a face-to-face encounter. This is precisely what Ricoeur has done in inter-articulating the two movements of Husserl and Levinas. And incorporating this alterity of the Other is not entirely alien to Ricoeur's previous work, as seen in earlier chapters, for he has encountered similar elements within his recent philosophy. For instance, in his development of time in *Time and Narrative*, he has focused upon and accounted for the alterity of cosmic time. So too here, the exteriority of the Other is outside the domain of the Heideggerian or Husserlian world, and of Levinas' totality. This is precisely the element of Levinas that must not be jeopardized in our present expansion of Levinas' view in order to clarify how a relation is possible within interiority. And, I daresay, Ricoeur seems to want to embrace this face to face in indicating it as the place where ethics really begins. And it is precisely in accepting the alterity of the Other that he has taken a positive element in agreement with Levinas, a point that even deconstruction likes. But this affinity with deconstruction cannot be exaggerated, for, in this context of even a mitigated deconstruction, Levinas' account of the ethical relation is lost to the deconstructive process, so that what remains is only the obligation of deconstructing. And nothing of Ricoeur's undertaking as a project of ethicomoral philosophy, except this same alterity that he shares with Levinas, can survive this deconstructive process.[76]

Hence, by bringing the opposing movements of Heidegger and Levinas together, Ricoeur is able to adhere to a positive contribution of postmodern deconstruction without succumbing to the allure of its plunge into the abyss, forsaking the priority of the enterprise of reason. Thus, by focusing on both Levinas' and Ricoeur's critiques of Heidegger, we have been able to find the common ground of alterity between them, which, in spite of the distance that separates them, allows an integration that supports Ricoeur's ethicomoral position.[77]

Ricoeur adopts a version of Levinas' view to provide an ethics of responsibility and obligation as an alternative to postmodern deconstructive writings on/against ethics. In this, he has a basic rapport with the position of Levinas, which can be seen from what has been said. Due to his critique of and expansion on the Kantian philosophy, Ricoeur is able to interarticulate the ethical as encompassing the aim of an accomplished life with the moral as encompassing the actualization of the ethical aim in norms that are characterized at once by "claims to universality. and by an effect of constraint" (OA, 170). Following from his critique of Kant's practical reason and freedom, and from the expansion of Kantian themes, Ricoeur is able to turn in a positive way to a priority of the teleological, putting into place the evaluative element of Aristotelian ethics to subtend the moral imperative of Kant, Levinas, and deconstruction. As to the positive element of deconstruction, Ricoeur's recent dwelling on alterity of cosmic time and his addressing the alterity of the Other of Levinas in the tension that he sees between Husserlian inwardness and Levinas' exteriority reveals the alterity that the face to face manifests beyond interiority. He has clearly appropriated a certain positive element from Levinas in terms of the alterity of the other, the epiphany of the face, and its assignment of responsibility. Ricoeur and Levinas, against the so-called deconstructive ethics that deconstructs the ethical relation, both invoke the face to face of the personal other at the heart of ethical response.[78] Ricoeur's rich and full treatment of ethicomoral philosophy entailing the points above, because of his positive relation to Levinas, emerges as one of the most viable ethics today in contrast to deconstructive ethics, which is hardly an ethics.

CHAPTER 9

Ethics and Postmodernity

INTRODUCTION

We can now turn to the contemporary conversation regarding ethics in an attempt to go beyond the impasses presented by recent postmodern deconstruction. This opposition is essentially intertwined with the deconstructive interpretation of the role of imagination, language and sign, and lived time, as seen above. Continuing along these lines, the further investigation of the contemporary scene of ethical discussion will allow us to grasp the significance of the relation between reflective and determinative judgments in the emergence of a viable context for seriously reflecting upon and conversing about ethics and morality today.

The vast conversation today concerning ethics entails a tension between certain poles around which similar types of discussion take place. For, on the one hand, we see Alasdair MacIntyre's critique of the western tradition, and a concomitant return to a quasimedieval Aristotelian ethics.[1] And, following Caputo, we can place Heidegger's originary ethos in the same camp, since both of these entail an eschatological element. Also, in this context Ricoeur's allegiance to an eschatological element at the heart of his ethics would place him in this same group. In extreme opposition to these variations in the eschatologically oriented ethics, the postmodern deconstructionists proclaim that all ethics of value and moral intelligibility, even that of MacIntyre and Heidegger, have not gone far enough in their respective critiques, and yet have gone too far in the direction of closure. Thus they require a deconstructive (clotural) reading bringing to light a latent dislocation in terms of limit and end in their formulations of an ethical position. And included within this latter context is the somewhat mitigated deconstructive account of John Caputo, with its own latent tendency beyond an originary ethos, even in invoking a quasi-Rortian term.[2] In the spirit of carrying further this latter project, the question arises whether ethics today can be seen in a viable relation to the tradition or, more generally, whether there is any viable ethics today worth speaking about.

Caputo responds deconstructively to that question by replacing ethics with a poetics of obligation. Similarly, Critchley contends that

Derridian deconstruction should be understood as an ethical demand, as long as ethics is understood in the sense that Derrida has taken from Levinas, who has influenced Derrida greatly over the years. This places an ethical demand on what Critchley wants to develop as "clotural reading," the significance of which we have seen above. Can the ethical demand of deconstruction, interpreting ethics in the way of Levinas, be what Caputo sanctions in invoking Levinas in *Against Ethics*?

Before focusing more specifically on any author, it is necessary to recall once again the importance of the role of the hermeneutic situation for each as the context from which reflection emerges and, in a way, to which it returns. Heidegger, in refocusing on the totality of the hermeneutical situation or on the whole network of presuppositional structures, has thrown into focus the sense of Being in its unity through which anything emerges into its Being. It must become clear that for the deconstructionist this is still a mediation of something not present, and as such is an effect, which means that Heidegger does not go far enough. This finite Being-temporality structure must be superseded, not by a move above it or below, but rather, by seeing its derivative nature as not far enough into the singularity of the flux. This Being-temporality is an effect, and can at best mediate the flux, whose singularities cannot be adequately encompassed by Being, which must be gone beyond. And just as Heidegger approaches Kant with his own question of Being in order to see how Kant at least subliminally posed the question, so too, the post-Heideggerians are now approaching authors and texts with their own pre-comprehension of the flux and singularity that they allege Heidegger does not ever really get hold of.

Heidegger can be seen to replace typical, traditional discussions about ethics, including the displaced ethics of modernity, ethics of values (Scheler), and Ricoeur's position, with his "originary ethos" and the truth of Being. From that situated point of view, ethical discussion, even those of the types of Ricoeur and the tradition, take place at a second level in contrast to Heidegger's originary level. Further, Heidegger has cut deeper to an ontological level more fundamental than any other ethical consideration. If one invokes the distinction between the ontic and the ontological, Heidegger's "originary ethos" clearly reflects the ontological level. And for Heidegger, this ontological dimension is the precondition for any ontic occurrence. One can possibly look at the lived experience on the ontic level as having a certain priority, even though it is not foundational in Heidegger's sense. This approach does allow, however, for the concrete influences in our concrete institutions, communities, and families to emerge as important within the sweep of history and of the tradition. Although the claim cannot be made for the same radicality as Heidegger's *Being and Time* or "Letter on Humanism," it does allow discussion concerning the conditions of ethics, indeed somehow rooted in the Being of humans, but without succumbing to Heidegger's quasi-absolute presuppositional stance in his own depiction of the hermeneutical situation only in terms of the Being question, which he developed from Kant's notion of the natural disposition to metaphysics. This is not meant to demean Heidegger's attempt to put derivative ethical discussion in their place. Rather, it opens Heidegger's too narrow articulation of the problem in a possible direction that needs to be aired today, especially in the light of the criticism of Heidegger's thinking (and ethics) as inadequate to deal with, and perhaps even conducive to, the types of extremes emerging from Nazi Germany and the undertaking of genocide. For Heidegger, it is Being that issues the directive, not man, whose task is "to become responsive to the nomos sent his way, not to be a legislator of universal imperatives." Does this nomos sent his way emerge from the Being of this particular epoch, at this time, and is it so different from time to time? Is it dependent on or issued from Being in the sense of the historical Being of this community or Dasein? Is there no universal imperative above and beyond the Being of a particular Being of an epoch and hence of this people?

These questions, it seems to me, approach the recent deconstructive position, according to which the flux is the pervasive feature underlying even Heidegger's truth of Being, and in terms of which deconstructing or clotural reading produces a dislocation of any second-level fixations, revealing the limit of any such articulation. This is the direction of Caputo's recent works, from *Radical Hermeneutics* to *Against Ethics*, both going beyond Heidegger as well as appropriating a postmodern deconstructive stance regarding ethics, and proposing in its stead a poetics of obligation. It is to this mitigated deconstructive stance that the discussion will now turn, for, what applies to this ethics as mitigated deconstruction, applies a fortiori to the rest.

CAPUTO'S ETHICAL MINIMALISM

Caputo seems to make good sense out of deconstructive ethics, retaining reason in play instead of casting it out as the usual Heideggian legacy.[3] The recognition that reason's main or only role is not the "normal" situation of system, law, science, or even philosophy, all of which need the authoritarian posture of reason and its supporters in that status for its reign. Rather its more important role is that of discovery, creativity, disruption, revolution against those solidifications and their pretentiousness in view of their own contingency. This revolutionary move involves a reorientation (regrouping) to deal with the ongoing flux with which this new orientation has come to grips.

It was Heidegger's undertaking to delimit reason, to reveal the epochal-historical limits (RH, 223) of reason, which eventually allow more and more room for the play of reason. Caputo shows in the following text this relation of reason thus limited to its alternative: "The poet lets the rose be, lets it rise up and linger for a while in its own emergent *physis*. But letting-be is what *legein* and *logos* mean, and *ratio* is the romanized, de-cadent, fallen-off derivative sense of the original Greek experience, which gives it a treacherous twist that sets in motion the medieval scholastic and early modern Latinization of *logos*, which leads to Leibniz (SG, 67ff.)" (RH, 224).[4] This exposes the "rule of the principle of reason to its *other*, to the thinking which has the boldness and the audacity not to demand reasons. . . . Poetic thinking . . . achieves a relationship with the world which is more simple and primordial than reason; it is in touch with things long before the demand for reason arises and, indeed, is so deeply tuned to things that the need for reasons never arises" (RH, 224). This puts the poet in the context of the flux. And it is the point at which Caputo wants to disagree with Heidegger: Heidegger puts the poetic play outside the realm of the principle of reason, while Caputo wants to bring the play of reason precisely within poetic dwelling and activity. Or, more precisely, he wants to put play directly within reason instead of cutting reason off from play as alien to it, as he sees Heidegger doing. Thus, poetizing is brought home to reason.

Heidegger's gradual move away from the principle of reason's reign is heralded on stage mainly due to his destruction (deconstruction) and retrieval of Kant, stemming from his initial centralization of imagination at the expense of reason in general, and the resultant loss of the infinite. If one jumps thus into the flowing waters of flux, destroying that rational aspect of human experience, existence, being, and activity, then the role of poetizing and thinking is limited. My project in this entire present study has been to challenge precisely this interpretation and leveling down of limit. If someone jumps in a river, there is a someone who goes with the current, instead of merely melting down into the texture of the river.

Caputo wants to keep reason in play, or rather, to put play into reason, rather than to find a field of play outside of reason precisely because it is such serious business. Thus, Caputo, rather than escaping and moving beyond reason, reviews the notion of reason, finding at its core the play that too often is relegated to another domain. This of course involves a radical change in the normal or traditional view of reason, because this precisely addresses the question of the fuller scope of the "normal" or traditional as it is forced to the limit in the context of revolution or rediscovery or attunement to the flux, from which that "normal" originates and comes to dominate precisely as the "normal." This view highlights not merely the establishing of another "normal" in contrast to that first one, nor is it merely a looking at the process of its emerging. Rather it brings into focus and highlights that mode of play which then becomes the most important aspect of the whole process, one not ever to be lost sight of, once it merges into light, since it puts all principles, truth, doctrines, and so forth in their place. And one of these doctrines is metaphysics, which, once revealed in this new light, is transgressed leading into a so-called postmetaphysical era. This postmetaphysical era cannot, however, be interpreted as though it has completely freed itself of metaphysics, for this very articulation and play is related directly to that metaphysics and cannot ever completely escape it. And, although Caputo uses the term "postmetaphysical," his aim chiefly is to get beyond the metaphysics of presence. Yet any approach to the flux in radical hermeneutics must admittedly involve metaphysics in some way, at least to the extent that the flux is a way of characterizing a new era of metaphysics even if it is considered a postmetaphysics.

This play of reason in relation to the flux overcomes such metaphysics of presence that has become institutionalized. And Caputo is quick to agree that we cannot escape either one. Institutions facilitate, get things done, and are inevitable (RH, 235). But one cannot avoid the obvious fact that today the deconstructive and antimodern style or movement has become a force to be reckoned with, has dominated some circles, and has gotten full sway and support from some groups who identify themselves with it. This is precisely the institutionalization that cannot be avoided. But what must be maintained to be consistent is the attitude of play of reason in the flux, of reason at play in the flux without buying into the violence necessary to the institution to preserve its dominance. This is of course difficult to achieve, even for this postmodern movement, as is obvious from the fact that the very institutionalization of this movement has made it a force on the contemporary scene. Thus the inevitable role of the institution must be seen as an essential dimension of the revolution—that is, revolutions can become the vogue. This is not quite the same as the static and categorical institutionalizations of the tradition, for these are intrinsically and essentially pitted against the interpretation of the flux as their substrate, since the tendency is to move into that grounding of reason at the expense of the play of reason and the attunement to the flux. We will see the essential role of institutionalization in a more positive light later in the context of interpreting the originary ethos from the ontic perspective.

Ethics of Dissemination

What is left of ethics after a postmetaphysical critique? It is clear that for Heidegger the discourse on originary ethos in relation to the truth of Being is the primary place for any ethical discourse, cutting below the various ethical positions to their origin in the relation of Dasein to the truth of Being. Caputo wants to uncover precisely the ethics that arises from the ashes of metaphysics, from the very foundering of metaphysics, as the ethics of dissemination or of *Gelassenheit*. "It is precisely from the breakdown of standpoints and resting points of all sorts that we begin to act. If radical hermeneutics wants to expose us to the flux, then I want to show that this does not therefore leave us in the lurch. On the contrary I will argue that this in fact liberates action—from subjugation to metaphysical principles on the one hand and eschatological dreaming on the other hand" (RH, 238). And it is the ethics of dissemination that brings us to act on the margins of metaphysics and of eschatology after their foundering.

The tendency among deconstructive thinkers is to derive an ethics of obligation directly from the foundering of metaphysics, which, according to Caputo, gives rise to some idea about how to dwell with one another (RH, 257), and also leads to responsibility and obligation in clotural reading according to Critchley. Such a radical hermeneutics or clotural reading is a lesson in humility for reason itself at the heart of its most rational yearning, for it involves facing up to the limited claims of any knowledge, truth, or account of science, metaphysics, and ethics.

Caputo means by an ethics of dissemination, "an ethics bent on dispersing power clusters, constellations of power which grind us all under" (RH, 260). And in *Against Ethics*, he works out the details of this project as a poetics of obligation that he pits against ethics as such, manifesting a great respect for the other and for the contingency entailed in the flux: "an ethics of dissemination is an ethics of thereness, an ethics aimed at giving what is other as big a break as possible. . . . Hence, the ethics of dissemination begins by systematically reversing these oppositional schemes, reversing the discrimination strategically, in order finally to displace oppositional arrangements in favor of the open and nonexclusionary. . . . Its model is the Socratic work of showing up the contingency of every scheme. It delimits the authority of all programmers, planners, managers, and controllers of all sorts" (RH, 260). It accomplishes this by letting the system unravel, "letting the play in the system loose."

Mitigated deconstruction, especially that of the Caputo and the like, does not attempt to extricate reason from the flux, separating it from what is left for deconstructive work. Rather, it incorporates play at the heart of reason, and reason at the core of play, as shown above. The enterprise of reason is loosened up so to speak. This is perhaps one mode of philosophy at the limits of reason.

Caputo, rather than allow for pressing for standards and criteria in this play, considers the playing out of the ethicopolitical reason to be along the lines of fair play" (RH, 261). "It means that we keep the debate fair and free from manipulative interests" (RH, 262). This does not entail a rational play free from interests, for that is impossible to achieve. Rather, it means a play of reason that keeps competing interests in play in the game, requiring a fair competition and respect for the interested competitors that play the game. Caputo wants to replace the *phronésis* of the Aristotelian *polis* (as the skill to apply the agreed-upon paradigm), with the requirement of *civility* (as a kind of meta-*phronésis*), on the part of the modern mega-*polis*. This "civility is the virtue of knowing how to like and live with the dissemination of *ethos*" (RH, 262). What this ethics of dissemination warrants is the constant caution vis-à-vis institutions and organizations, so that they do not become solidified, which, in principle, is the tendency of anything dwelling in the mode of presence. Thus, the task of such an ethics is to keep the flux and its ambiguity in view and keep it in play, in the play of reason, rather than allow a false fixation "above" it, so to speak. Thus, it goes hand in hand with the interpretation of suspicion, as a "genealogy of suspicion" (RH, 263). It also can be formulated as letting the play be, reminiscent of Heideggerian *Gelassenheit*. This character of ethics of dissemination puts it in opposition to teleological ethics as that which puts the play out of play in favor of subordination to a *telos*, rather than in the spirit of *Gellasenheit* as letting the play play. The highest form of this latter is love according to Meister Eckhart (RH, 265). "For remember that in Eckhart, to whom we owe this idea, *Gelassenheit*, letting-be, meant love, *caritas*. That is why the ethics of dissemination belongs together with an ethics of *Gelassenheit*, and both are united in the Augustinian formula '*dilige, et quod vis fac*'" (RH, 266). This of course entails letting be, not in the restricted interest of Heidegger, concerning things, but the respect and reverence that the other commands.

Caputo assures us, however, that dissemination does not reject outright reason, morals, and faith; it simply gives a "more humble account of their provenance" (RH, 273). This is perhaps one mode of philosophy at the limit of reason. Caputo's mitigated deconstruction really is less offensive than extreme deconstruction, since it simply returns to lived experience and its constitutive flux, adverts to its unfathomable richness, and allows for the fact that there is always a residue requiring a constant attunement as a source for any closure. Thus, any closure must be adamantly attuned to the flux that underlies it as militating against the very closure that gives rise to that return.

Suffering such as that caused by earthquake, sickness, etc. exposes the vulnerability of human existence, its lack of defense against the play of the flux. "It takes a good earthquake to make a scholar appreciate the contingency of things, Johannes Climacus said (even though he writes well about modal logic). . . . [N]othing demonstrates more forcefully the limitation of the 'conscious subject' and human powers than blind and fortuitous violence" (RH, 278). This illustrates yet another vantagepoint of deconstruction—or rather, here, radical hermeneutics insofar as it is a mitigated deconstruction, in proffering access to the "other." We have seen this in our example of lived time. With the encounter of the face we can see the other in a new way. And, likewise, with suffering by myself or another whose face—or suffering—I witness first hand, the suffering presented in the visage, both concealing and revealing its enigmatic depth and contingency, thus shows the limitation of human experience and existence.

Continuing the line of development, it is worth a look at the Acknowledgments page, where Caputo says, concerning the publication of "Donner la mort":[5] "this deferred gift, which also instructs Levinas on how to read Kierkegaard, confirms my premonition that for Derrida, as for Kierkegaard, ethics ought to be sacrificed in the name of obligation." One thing noteworthy in this is the overcoming of ethics in Kierkegaard in favor of obligation. This overturn of ethics is not what I find stymieing: rather, it is the deference to obligation in Kierkegaard. Where does this come from? This is playing rather freely with Kierkegaard, for he wants to replace ethics with faith (or love), replace the whole way of actualizing one's existence in terms of the law (to which one is obligated) by faith in a personal God. Even in his pseudonymous stance of Johannes de Silentio, whose point of view is that of the ethical looking into the religious and Christian faith, which act he cannot yet make—it is a gift of God (he does cross the ethical without even thinking in deference to faith). And Kierkegaard has Johannes think in terms of the perspective within which Johannes acts, of the "teleological suspension of the ethical." For Kierkegaard, behind the scene so to speak, this teleological suspension of the ethical is a necessity for the faith he attempts to promote, which entails an intense personal relation to a personal God, the relation which the Hebrew account of Abraham has always fostered, and to which St. Paul adhered. But Kierkegaard, faithful follower of Luther on this point in spite of his many critiques of Luther, makes an option for faith, and thus sees the need to abrogate reason and its entire domain, that of philosophy. Now, following Heidegger, if one wants to overcome reason, abrogate philosophy, then this move is acceptable. But Caputo has explicitly stated, as seen above, that he wants to maintain a play of reason, instead of putting reason out of play, so to speak. And although Kierkegaard moves to faith and thus abrogates reason for the most part, on reading his works, and not merely the pseudonymous works, one finds a refined activity of reason in play within his faith-theological reflections. That is, *Purity of Heart*, as an edifying discourse, is in Kierkegaard's own voice, and thus does not represent a point of view outside his faith commitment, as do his works constituting his aesthetic authorship reflecting the aesthetic and ethical modes of actualizing freedom. Yet this work, though a work that could well be studied as ascetic theology totally within the personal faith commitment espoused by Kierkegaard, largely entails a specific interpretation of Platonic doctrine, baptized in this treatment for this religious perspective.

Caputo wants to leave reason in play in much the same fashion, and now to serve a postmetaphysical purpose in relation to the flux. Of course, even Derrida will admit that this still has a relation to metaphysics, which cannot be entirely left behind. We come back to the question concerning Caputo's attempt to keep the so-called Kierkegaardian element of obligation, but outside of ethics.[6] Kant did that, insofar as his deontological moral philosophy left ethics and the whole Aristotelian ethical reflection in a second, inferior, and polluted position, in deference to an a priori pure will, relating to the moral law given by pure reason, which, as entirely pure and practical, has allegiance only to that law. And it is in this latter context that Kant extols the quality of the role of obligation to this law. Caputo, following and transgressing Heidegger's move to the flux, simply buries this obligation in the flux, outside the realm of metaphysical pitfalls and illusions, below ethics, and before any structures have emerged from the flux as its effects. Pulling together Caputo's thesis (and summary), "My project is more Thought-less and Latinate, conducted in good English, with the help of Romance tongues—but it is not, I trust, too romantic. On the contrary, it is part of my present heretical state of mind to think that the Big Story, the *grand récit*, of Being's bends and turns, the *Seinsroman* of the great Beginnings, which assure us of Something Saving, is where romanticism makes its nest" (AE, 3). The allusion, by way of exemplification, immediately preceding this self description, refers to his situation as: "to be compared to a man who discovers that the ground he hitherto took to be a *terra firma* is in fact an island adrift in a vast sea, so that even if he stands absolutely firm he is in fact constantly in motion. Add to this the thought that the sea is endless, the sky starless, and the island's drift aimless, and you gain some measure of the level of my consternation" (AE, 3). Reflecting back to the occasion on which Merleau-Ponty reports and critiques both Einstein's and Bergson's views of time, to the critique by Bergson of Einstein: Bergson was concerned to make Einstein take into account the primordial reference to lived time, rather than to the abstract plurality to which Einstein refers in his own work. According to Merleau-Ponty, neither of them really had a proper view of lived time, although Bergson is the one who first set us on the way to a reflective grasp of lived primordial time. This whole account is quite to the point of Caputo's *petit récit* in our context, for in pulling the ground out from under the ones who think themselves to stand on *terra firma*, he has switched the focus to the motion, even of this "island adrift in a vast sea," where the "sea is endless, the sky starless, and the island's drift aimless," which allows us to glimpse Caputo's consternation. Is it not the case that jumping into the abyss or dwelling only on the flux could be considered the same as Einstein's move into the abstraction of his plurality of temporal references, without any deference given to the primordial lived time, but now a jump in the opposite direction? While it may be true that the abyss is there, that the island is floating in motion, the prime reference for us humans is and always will be the lived, in reference to which we move at will to extremes in either direction, to that above (Einstein's); or to that below, the flux. So, whether it is Einstein's derivative time or deconstruction's derivative space (or time), the prime reference for humans is the lived time and lived space, in terms of which all else can be grasped. Admitting the drift or the move in either direction, although valid, does not obfuscate the lived precisely as lived, from which awareness of either emerges. But is that all that is being said here? Are the lived merely effects of something more primordial? And the term primordial is not quite right either, because it itself is supercharged and derivative as an effect. So which is the derivative?

Perhaps a further simple example from another attempt to see experience as derivative will clarify the issue. Hume and modernity manifest a penchant for dealing with sense experience in terms of decomposing it into impressions, overlooking the fact that sense experience, or perception, as Merleau-Ponty so emphatically affirms, is first experienced as a whole before it is brought under the microscope and seen in terms of its parts, impressions. "The whole is prior to the parts" is the way Merleau-Ponty put this, "and the whole is not a conceptual whole," but, rather, one of perception. Hume, however, is not entirely wrong. For, although his account of perception by reducing it to sensation and impressions presupposes the second level and scientific perspective, and its abstract, quantitative orientation, his account is true on that level that presupposes such a scientific orientation. It simply is not primordial as is the lived perception. Although it may have merit from a derived point of view, the fact remains that it does not tell us what experience is about. It misses the point. And is that not what deconstruction is doing here?

It misses the point in reference to the lived space and time in terms of which other accounts are derivative, even their own. So, picking up on an old theme, let's get back "to the things themselves," in this case, time and space as first lived. It is naive to think otherwise, even though it is a sophisticated naiveté.

What kind of poetics can one have on this level vis-à-vis obligation and flux? Retelling beautiful stories about obligation, the context of Johnnes de Silentio's treatment of Abraham and the suspension of the ethical, and of the poetics of obligation: "Then it would turn out that obligation does not oblige us to renounce poetics, but to poetize differently" (AE, 10).

Caputo wants to add Kant's voice to this eulogy given to Abraham, even though Johannes de Silentio has pitted Abraham against a very Kantian version of the Law. Caputo maintains that Kant's categorical imperative is the "closest Abraham ever gets to wearing philosophical robes (almost)." According to Caputo, "Kant set sail in the turbulent straits that flow between obligation and ethics, between the Law and autonomy, between Jew and Greek. His 'metaphysics of morals' is the work of an *Aufklarer* who also loves father Abraham, who loves the Law more than God" (AF, 12).

Caputo has a rather intriguing and insightful rendition of the significance of Johannes de Silentio's interpretation of Abraham, the reason for heralding Abraham as their paradigm of faith. It centers on the notion of the impossible, that Abraham was willing to sacrifice, murder from the ethical point of view, in spite of his faith in God's word to bring forth generations from his son. Thus he, in this willingness, did not falter in faith in God, even though it required the impossible looked at from reason's point of view. From this religious, as *religare,* Caputo moves to the notion of *obligare*; re-ligare and ob-ligare come from the same root word, "bond." "But the impossible is the religious, the *re-ligare*, which means the one-on-one bond of the existing individual with the Absolute, the absolute relation to the Absolute. The *religare* is the *ob-ligare*, the absolute bond, the obligation, but without the shelter afforded by the universal, the rational, the eternal. In short, Johannes de Silentio writes a eulogy to obligation without ethics" (AE, 18). Then, Caputo moves to distance himself from Levinas' notion of the infinite emerging from the encounter with the face of the other, where he himself wants to distinguish his and Levinas' notions of the flesh. For Levinas, the "flesh" is the surface of the infinite. And rather than forfeiting ethics, Levinas puts it in the primary place of first philosophy.[7] For Caputo, in contrast, it is at best the hyperbolical (AE, 19). It is now necessary to relate obligation in deconstruction to the broader context of certain findings of the previous chapters.

The Es Gibt *and Obligation*

Deconstruction seems, at least to some extent, to have realized that the very grammar, syntax, and semantics of one's own language, whichever it might be, presupposes or assumes a logic and metaphysics, and when contrasted with those of other languages, leads to the flux beneath them all, which none of them can adequately express. But, rather than lead only in that direction, should not these be seen to lead to something that they all have in common, as for instance, the simple effort toward discourse?

Caputo is quite correct, and Derrida has concurred precisely on this point throughout *Positions*, that metaphysics is in some sense unavoidable. And in fact even the effort to neutralize metaphysics is caught up in metaphysics, as can be seen in Kant's efforts to ground metaphysics in terms of his critique and limit, and in Husserl's attempt to establish consciousness as able transcendentally to neutralize real being. We have seen Ricoeur's analysis above where he has revealed this shortcoming of Husserlian phenomenology. And Caputo's insight, that it is time to "overcome the 'overcoming of metaphysics'" makes sense, but not quite the sense that he intends, which needs to be recontextualized and reappropriated so that it can be refigured for philosophy for the future. This admittedly goes in a different direction than he envisions or wishes.

To admit with Caputo that events are "indefinitely redescribable" or "indefinitely reconfigurable" as embracing a polyarch is not to add anything substantial to the contemporary discussion concerning a serious consideration of configuration and the richness of the source from which it arises. Nor does it justify, merely because of that wealth or richness at its source, taking a stand favoring the flux alone as all that is admitted at drawing one's attention and commitment, as against the tendency to that very source as a constant feeder and nourishment. Thought is in need of constantly returning to the richness of the lived, whether it is thought of the concrete, or thought that attempts to move toward the speculative, to characterize that flux in whatever view and slim categories it can. To be in need of such constant openness, the need to maintain that openness in opposition to any closure as ending the openness or closing it often does not require a jump or perverbial leap into the abyss. As seen in chapter 1, being aware of, and open to, such an abyss, listening carefully and looking carefully, not in a glance, but rather in a penetrating and searching gaze, does not necessarily prevent using that very openness to move on to further activity, to configuration and to reconfiguration. Caputo is correct to keep the eye of the law on the withered "It" behind the *es gibt*. Yet such obligation happens in a void, attempting to get beyond Heidegger's famous *es gibt* where the *es* is Being. Even with proper names one (i.e., a good deconstructionist) finds that if probed far enough, one will find the improper beneath the proper, that if it were truly proper it would not happen. There is an anonymous element lurking there, the "pseudonymous is the mask of the anonymous" (AE, 226).

Thus Caputo is using the account of *es gibt*, its anonymity, flux, and chaos to eradicate any trace of the eschatological, which he has found even in Heidegger's account of Being and the event, as mentioned earlier. Caputo's minimalism means that events, though they might or might not give joy, simply happen without any meaning or direction to the whole (AE, 233). He summarizes his position as follows: "While there are numerous meanings *in* events, there is no meaning *to* events overall, no overarching Meaning which is their point, their *logos* or *telos*, their sum and their substance. The sum and substance of events is nothing other than the events themselves" (AE, 234–235). This central point of Caputo reveals that, even if there were such a meaning, this closure of attitude would not allow it to penetrate. So this doctrine about closure and the attempt to remain in the flux contain a certain closure to anything contrary to its own absolute, which itself must be seen in relation to that (i.e., absolute!) of Heidegger, as already seen.

One of the many redeeming features of Caputo's thought is that it is adamantly attuned to those who are in the throes of some kind of breakdown and who are "so exposed to the abyss by which events are inhabited that they cannot get as far as ordinary life and its ordinary joys and sorrow" as, for instance, someone who has suffered ignominiously (AE, 235). But this account simply draws out the consequences of the point made above about a lack of cosmic meaning to the whole. His way of being attuned to these, however, is not the only one possible, and the jump into their abyss with them is not necessarily the answer. Even for the greatest evils, such as the Holocaust, all he can offer is that: "we must confess to having no cosmic backups for our condemnation of Auschwitz. That is our embarrassment and scandal. We have to live with the anonymity that insinuates itself into obligations. But if it is not possible to expel anonymity with infinity, it is at least possible to *defy* the anonymity of the *es gibt* and its cosmic dice game and to attach oneself, almost blindly, with a hypervalorization, with a hyperbolic valorization, to proper names" (AE, 236–237).

The bottom line in all of this is that obligation is simply there. It does, however, need simple proper names. Yet Caputo contends that the needs of the flesh are all that is required for obligation. In this context, the impersonal, rather than the opposite of the personal, is the "encompassing matrix and ever-present horizon of the personal" (AE, 238). And by this personal is not meant some metaphysical gesture or point.

He says, in perhaps one of the passages that is of utmost importance for understanding this (his) position: by the personal, "I am happy enough to grant that it is mostly a matter of grammar; I do not feel the need for a grand metaphysical backup. I mean, very minimalistically, something that is mostly a matter of phrasing[:] 'you' say; 'we' or 'I' hear; 'he,' 'she,' or 'they' are spoken about. Personal phrases happen. There are happenings of a personal kind" (AE, 238). And he rounds out this affirmation: "By a person I do not mean an autonomous metaphysical subject, but a subject of obligation, something that makes demands on me, that asks for a hand, for the flesh of my hand. A person is a place where obligations happen, where 'someone' says 'I' to 'me,' where 'you' call upon 'me,' where 'they' call upon 'me' or 'us.' A person is a place where the eyes of the other come over me, overtake me, pulling me up short. From obligations a whole network of interpersonal relation springs up; in persons a whole network of obligations takes root" (AE, 238). And he goes on in this context: "Obligation spring up in a void, like grass in the cracks of sidewalks. The personal is a web woven over the impersonal, a filmy, gossamer surface across a dense mass. A name in the midst of namelessness. A bit of light and warmth in the midst of a surrounding darkness and cloud, like the window of the house in Trakl's *Winterabend*, lit up within and come on by the weary traveler or stranger. The person is always the wayfarer, the stranger, like Abraham or Ishmael" (AE, 238). Caputo seems to move in the direction of Derridian deconstruction in reducing all, even the personal, to grammar, but he seems to slip back into the "subject of obligation," where "you" call upon "me."

Caputo is yet again to be commended for adverting to something that too many philosophers have ignored, tragedy. At least here we have an attempt to directly face and deal with evil and tragedy. And it is precisely this that can keep the concrete actualization of freedom from becoming absorbed in a system, a closure that ignores the fulness and wealth of that which serves it as fodder and context. But this attempt to give the tragic sufficient place does not necessarily have to go to such extremes.

> Ill health, a sudden and irrevocable reverse of fortune, or even ordinary misfortunes that other people deal with handily, can send one spinning into the abyss. There are disasters that drive one to the limit, *in extremis*, beyond the bonds and boundaries of ordinary life. The abyss peers out from behind the cracks of daily life, the way a great ravine becomes visible between the tracks of a railroad if we let ourselves look down. There is nothing deep and firm to sustain us, not if we look down, not if we ask *why?* and demand an ultimate response, a final answer. What sustains the elements of life is only their internal connectedness and inherent worth. (AE, 242)

Two things come to mind in this context: the numerous people to whom one could refer over the past few decades who have had break-downs (nervous or otherwise); and the Holocaust. Is it really the case that all that can be said regarding these two cases is that there is obligation, and the personal involvement is limited basically to that of grammar? Even if this is meant to open the path to religious faith, does this do justice to the human situation, prescinding from faith? And does it not lead to somewhat of a misconstruing of faith? While it is true that the Judeo-Christian traditions have harkened to respond to this predicament of humans, is this the best interpretation of the human situation? It is almost as though we need another existentialist movement to reintroduce the genuinely and radically personal, which no continentalist should ever again allow to lie fallow. And we also again need a counter-reformation to show that our essential being is not intrinsically corrupt to the core, or that the human heart is not dirty and perverse by nature.

For Caputo, life is healed only by life, and even faith approaches and takes root in life if it is to help. Such a person of faith "is not one who knows nothing of the abyss but rather one who has looked down this abyss and construed it in terms of the traces and stirrings of a living hand, who finds in the abyss of suffering an infinity, who sees the Other as the trace of the Infinite. Faith is a matter of a radical hermeneutic, an art of construing shadows, in the midst of what is happening" (244–245).[8]

After this lengthy analysis and critique of Caputo's poetics of obligation, we can now turn back to the fuller current of deconstruction and ethics.

Ethical Demand of Deconstruction (Derrida)

We can now return to the question of a Derridian ethical element, invoking Levinas' view of ethics in the context of double reading and closure. Critchley refers to what he calls an "unconditional ethical imperative" as the source of the "injunction that produces deconstruction and is produced through deconstructive reading." He also shows "how the 'concept' of general text and *différance* can be articulated within an ethical problematic,"[9] the central element of which entails the concept of the closure of metaphysics, a concept already seen above. Critchley contends, against a too typical tendency to consider all ethics to presuppose the metaphysics that deconstruction deconstructs, that there is an ethic at the heart of deconstruction.

Thus, it becomes clear that Caputo, and from the chapter above, Cornell and Critchley, all attuned to the Derrida-Levinas dialogue, put obligation at the heart of deconstruction. Caputo, however, following

Derrida's hesitance, rejects ethics in favor of a poetics of obligation, while Critchley and Cornell, following Levinas, hang onto the term in their own rejection of virtually the same ethics that Caputo rejects. This is certainly fair game, and his move is a respectable and laudable one. For my part, I would agree with their efforts here, appropriating a positive contribution of deconstruction. Then, I would indicate that they have pointed to something essential to any responsible reading today, even of a hermeneutic nature rather than that of deconstruction, and go onto a further extension of ethics following Ricoeur, who is influenced by their same source, Levinas, but in an entirely different way. For Ricoeur, there is an opening back to the tradition, rather than a cutting away toward a deconstructive clotural reading. We will see that this obligation or duty at the heart of the deconstructive enterprise is not something to be lost sight of, even if it requires an extension beyond the usual sense of ethics. But is it not to be seen as self-sufficient, and as tied to something that would best be brought into a more positive frame of philosophical mind.

Critchley's argument, then, would put an ethical duty at the heart of the deconstructive enterprise: "Rather, I hope to demonstrate that the pattern of reading produced in the deconstruction of—mostly, but by no means exclusively—philosophical texts has an ethical structure: deconstruction 'is' ethical; or, to formulate the same though less ontologically . . . , deconstruction takes place (*a lieu*) ethically, or there is duty in deconstruction (Il y a du devoir dans la deconstruction)" (Critchley, 2).

Critchley's main point about Levinas' ethics in relation to a more traditionally oriented ethics, is that it reveals a level of primordial ethical experience that is more primordial than, and is presupposed by, those ethical considerations that attempt to reflect on maxims or judgments in relation to social action and civic duty, and that are derived and distinct from that primordial level. Levinas himself does not see his task as one of constructing an ethics. He says, rather, "I only try to seek its meaning (*sens*)."[10] This primacy for Levinas means the primacy of the interhuman relation, the seeing of the face to which one says something.

All of the commentators of deconstruction considered here, Caputo, Cornell, and Critchley, report on Derrida's ethics by entering the discussion between Derrida and Levinas. It seems that Derrida has dialogued with and deconstructed Levinas' ethics in coming to a deconstructive ethics of his own, if the term "ethics" can even be retained. Caputo, in his *Against Ethics*, has opted to stress the "other" to ethics. Ethics presupposes the very metaphysics that deconstruction must deconstruct, which requires the deconstruction of even Heideggian "originary ethos." Yet, although they agree for the most part on the essential points toward an ethics of deconstruction, Cornell and Critchley do not abrogate the term "ethics" or "ethical," they simply transform the word, or deconstruct it. Further, for all of them, and for Derrida, this sense of ethics at the heart of the deconstructive enterprise is a philosophy of limit, but not necessarily a philosophy that is critical philosophy, which itself would need deconstructing.

All three of the authors above introduce a new sense of ethics at the heart of the deconstructive enterprise. For Drucilla Cornell this ethical impulse can be easily seen at the heart of her interpretation of this enterprise as a philosophy of limit.[11] As has been seen, Caputo, deconstructing the ethics and the metaphysics on which it is built, reveals the poetic obligation at the heart of deconstruction. And Critchley sees a primordial importance to ethics at the heart of deconstructive reading, or clotural reading. And for all three, it is the role of Levinas's reflections on the ethical relation that takes on significance, especially in the light of the discussion between him and Derrida. For my part, the one problem that I have is that Levinas does not seem to enclose all this in terms of language, and that taken to be a system of signs, each has the function of a trace. Caputo seems to address this head on when he discusses the sense of self in terms of personal pronouns. One can deconstruct ethics, arriving thereby at an ethical demand placed on deconstruction itself. That is precisely what emerges in raising the question of ethics in the context of deconstruction in relation to any philosophy of limit: that there is some serious and sincere ethical obligation or responsibility at the heart of the enterprise, already envisioned by Derrida, especially as he deconstructs Levinas.

CONCLUSION

The positive element of deconstruction mentioned throughout these chapters must not obscure its failures as a philosophy of limit that must be brought to light. The limit keeps the deconstructive process open at the closure by serving to check any structure and any sense, making it recoil onto the abyss from which it arises. And it allows obligation and responsibility to the Other to emerge. We have tried to maintain both a yes as well as a no to deconstruction. The yes: to alterity, to the "other" to which any phenomenological heritage must be opened. And the no: to any return to a reduction to a naive view of time, sign, and language that this position requires in all its articulations.[12] A brief development and review of this critique is necessary before turning to Ricoeur alternative ethics.

Further, I must make clear the latent contradiction in deconstruction between the positive element and the negative element, which needs critique: the positive element reintroduces with force the "other"; but its account of the flux, of time, of sign, of consciousness, and of language eliminates any possibility of experiencing or accessing that other.[13] This deconstructive consideration, however, leading to alterity, is similar to the modern account of sense experience in cognition, as mentioned above. Perception was broken down to sense experience, which was further decomposed into impressions within a conscious flow considered to be discrete because of the point like instant now. Against this reductionistic view, the philosophical return to lived experience brought back the holistic human perspective. We must now return to a reconsideration of sign, time, and trace to make clear how this claim is justified.[14]

In Derrida's deconstruction traces are constitutive of the sign in the same way that the protentions and retentions as traces are constitutive of the living present. The prominence of trace in deconstruction follows largely from the loss of phenomenological primordiality of, and the decentering of focus from, the living present, presence, and things present as constituted to what constitutes them—the play of *différance* in the interplay of differences and of traces. Derrida's view of the living present and time, however, renders it unable to sustain trace in contrast to Ricoeur's view of the living present and historical time that supports trace in its full sense, as seen in an earlier chapter. These contrasting roles of trace highlight, in spite of a positive commonness, the vast chasm that separates the views of Derrida and Ricoeur. This chasm stretches even to all-pervasive metaphysical differences that require a decision in favor of one at the expense of the other kind of philosophizing at the limit, with each able to accuse the other of closure. Thus, as already seen in chapter seven, Ricoeur's view of sign, trace, semantics, and the flux of time as discrete on which they are founded provides a viable alternative that does not succumb to the facile orientation of Saussure's basic distinction between *la langue* and *la parole*. Nor does it succumb to Derrida's collapse of signs to the relations of differences within the system or to his reduction of language to the play of *différance*.

Considering such limits of sign, trace, and time, it is not surprising that with the loss of the semantic, there is likewise a loss of ethics. Ricoeur's ethics, by contrast, is an attempt to interarticulate an ethics of the good and a morality of right, bringing the Aristotelian and Kantian traditions together by his critique of Kant and providing a framework from the teleology of desire. And in doing so, he does not jettison the personal relation. Rather, he leans heavily on Levinas' view of the face to face, and the personal relation.

Due to his expansions on the Kantian philosophy at the limit, Ricoeur is able to interarticulate the moral as encompassing the articulation or actualization of the ethical aim in norms that according to Ricoeur are characterized at once by "claim to universality and by an effect of constraint" (OA, 170) with the "ethical" as encompassing the aim of an accomplished life. Following from his critique of Kant's practical reason and freedom, and from the expansion of Kantian themes, Ricoeur is able to turn in a positive way to a priority of the teleological, putting into place the evaluative element of Aristotelian ethics to subtend the moral imperative of Kant and deconstruction.

As to the positive element of deconstruction, Ricoeur's recent dwelling on alterity of cosmic time and his addressing the alterity of Levinas in the tension that he sees between Husserlian inwardness and Levinas' exteriority reveal the alterity that the face to face actualizes beyond interiority. Thus, he has clearly appropriated a certain positive element of deconstruction, but without succumbing to its closure, its limited treatment of limit without a concomitant focus on the positive element of opening, and on the extensions beyond limit. Ricoeur's rich and full treatment of ethicomoral philosophy, entailing the points above, emerges as an ethics viable for today.[15]

CHAPTER 10

The Ethics of Good and the Morality of Obligation

INTRODUCTION

The failure of postmodern deconstruction to give a viable account of time and the living present, sign and trace, and philosophy at the boundary of reason as context for a viable ethics prompts us to turn to the philosophy of Paul Ricoeur as an alternative, since all along the way his philosophy has been seen as a corrective force. We find his ethicomoral philosophy to be fundamentally attuned to the whole western tradition and sensitive to the ethicomoral dimensions of human life, as well as to those of the political, the legal, and the religious. His challenging writings on ethics afford the most encompassing and viable ethical framework and principle for facing up to problems in ethics today.

Ricoeur's ethics can be seen to revolve around the intersecting of two axis: the first entails the "dialogical constitution of the Self"[1] as the horizontal axis of his twofold sense of human identity, the *ipséité* that Ricoeur opposes to the *mêmeté*. The second axis is that of the "hierarchical constitution of the predicates that qualify human action in terms of morality" (LJ, 14). This dialogical constitution of the self along the first axis entails a twofold sense of the "other," or other person.[2] The French language has two words for "other," *autrui* and *autre*, but the first means the personal Other. This personal Other is the Other in the personal relation of the I-thou encounter of the face to face, while the second sense of other entails a distance, or a less personal other. The personal relation entails the virtue of friendship, which is a virtue on a much smaller scale than that of its correlate, justice that obtains in the distant interrelations of larger groups. And this latter relation to the other is mediated by the institution. "The Other according to friendship is the 'you,' the other according to justice is the 'each one,' as it is signified by the Latin adage: *suum cuique tribuere*, to each his own" (LJ, 14–15).

It is particularly with the second axis that one can truly speak of the conceptual dimensions of moral philosophy that Ricoeur has developed at the end of his *Oneself as Another*. It is along the lines of three levels of predicates that Ricoeur has divided his treatment in that work. The first is that of the "good," which gives rise to the definition of ethics as "the desire (wish) (*souhait*) of a good life" (LJ, 16). This level is constituted as the basis of morality by the bond among life, desire, lack, and accomplishment. And this is the teleological dimension of Aristotle, according to which the good indicates a whole life seeking accomplishment in a fulfilling happiness, and, as such, is the teleological level of moral action. Ricoeur centers its focus on the formula: "the desire for an accomplished life with and for others in just institutions" (LJ, 17), showing, contrary to many moralists today, that the basic question on this level is: how do I live my life, and not what ought I to do. And such living of one's life can be accomplished, as Aristotle shows, in living together (*interesse*) in the community or city. "It is as citizens that we become human. The wish to live in just institutions signifies nothing else" (LJ, 17).

In contrast to this first teleological level of predicates, the second level, the deontological, entails the predicate, obligation. This is the level of the norm, duty, and interdiction. And it must be stated that what requires the transition from the teleological to the deontological is the violence that humans perpetuate on one another. Yet this fact does not give a priority to this second level since the teleological is the proper foundation of the deontological. For the deontological, as including norm, duty, and imperative, arises out of the primitive soil of desire and seeking of the good life with and for others in just institutions.

The level of the moral norm produces conflicting situations, requiring practical reason to return to the ethical aim of the good life, reminiscent of, but not equivalent to, Hegel's concrete actualization of meaningful action. This recourse to Hegelian actualization of freedom precisely situates Ricoeur's critique of Kant's formal and abstract treatment of freedom. Moral judgment in situation requires conviction, a judgment in situation adequate to deal with its singularity in aiming at the good life, thus developing further the dialectic of the moral norm and the ethical aim, and supplying the third predicate, "equitable." Such moral judgment in situation and its conviction are what Ricoeur calls practical wisdom, reminiscent of Aristotle's book VI of the *Nicomachean Ethics*. We turn now to the first of these ethical predicates, the good, and to the teleological foundations that it entails.

AIMING AT THE GOOD LIFE

An ethics such as this, although emerging from a philosophy of action, is not limited to deciphering the ethical dimensions of human acts. It rather extends to the whole ethical attitude, and focuses at first primarily upon the fundamental ethical intention. "Let us define 'ethical intention' as *aiming at the 'good life'* with and for others, in just institutions" (OA, 172). The first essential element of this account is the "good life" as the object of the ethical aim or the ultimate end of action that Ricoeur aligns with Aristotle's notion of "living well." And, of course, Aristotle's notion of the good for us and not as such in any particular thing, as Ricoeur states this, "the good is rather that which is lacking to all things. This ethics in its entirety presupposes the nonsaturable use of the predicate 'good'" (OA, 172). We learn from Aristotle that: "Every art (*tekhné*) and every inquiry (*methodos*), and similarly every action (*praxis*) and pursuit (*proairesis*, preferential choice) is thought to aim at some good; and for this reason the good has rightly been declared to be that at which all things aim" (OA, 172).[3] This sets up the good life in terms of practice, the teleology internal to which is the structuring principle for the aim of the "good life" (OA, 172–173). Ricoeur sees a difficulty in Aristotle's view that such an action has itself as end and yet has the further end, happiness, as ulterior. I am not sure that Aristotle is as unclear and difficult as Ricoeur makes him out to be in this context of deliberation over means. It seems that the action is its own end, as is the case in the action of intellect, the end of which is to understand; and similarly with willing. But there is in Aristotle enough to warrant saying, following his biological model, that the ulterior end of humans is the fulfillment of the being of humans as such, which he later calls happiness. Aristotle spends some effort to clarify the preferential choice and deliberation, stating that we do not deliberate about ends, but rather only about the means to the end. Aiming at certain ends is for Aristotle a wish (*boulesis*, 3.3a2). But does the reflection on a life's profession or plan make one deliberate about an end?

It is at least questionable whether Aristotle considers all means as merely instrumental in the strict sense of today. Aristotle, it seems, can consider the life choices of a profession as that which will bring an individual happiness, and in that sense, as a means to the end. And if one questions his/her own professional commitment with a view toward a possible change, this is a deliberation of means to end. This interpretation does not mitigate the point at stake for Ricoeur, for whom the question is one of what will count for an individual as a "adequate description of the end" of his/her life (OA, 174). For Ricoeur such questioning and deliberation aim to specify and make more determined the sense of the "good life."

According to Ricoeur, book VI on the dianoetic virtues rather than the virtues of character discussed in books II-V, offers a more complex model of deliberation as the path followed by *phronésis*, practical wisdom, and, more precisely, the path that the man of *phronésis*—the *phronimos*—follows to guide his life. Ricoeur emphasizes that the greatest lesson here is the close tie between practical wisdom and the wise man, between *phronésis* and the *phronimos*. The question in this context regards the specification best suited to the ultimate ends pursued. Ricoeur now invokes his hierarchizing of the concept of action in such a way as to carry it to the level of the concept of praxis, thus placing practices and life plans on different levels of the scale of praxis. He considers this same hierarchy of praxis now from the point of view of its ethical integration under the idea of the "good life" (OA, 175). On the first level, that of practices, he invokes MacIntyre's term "standards of excellence," in the evaluation of doing something well, which allows us to characterize a doctor, an architect, a painter, or a chess player as "good." This involves rules of comparison shared by a given community of practitioners and internalized by the masters and virtuosi of the practice considered. When posed in reaction to self-esteem, this aspect prevents a closure into solipsism. Thus, it can be seen, somewhat following MacIntyre, that practices are cooperative activities the constitutive rules of which are established socially; with the standards of excellence originating from a communal source or institution. According to Ricoeur (OA, 176) these standards of excellence relate to the ethical aim of living well by providing us with a sense for the idea of internal good immanent to a practice, thus constituting the teleology of action "as is expressed on the phenomenological plane by the notions of interest and satisfaction, which must not be confused with those of pleasure." Ricoeur considers this dimension of the internal good, following MacIntyre, as providing an initial support for the reflexive moment of self-esteem, in that in appraising our actions we come to appraise ourselves as their author. And further, this concept of the internal goods will be reconsidered within the properly normative conception of morality, where a context must be provided for the empty form of the categorical imperative. Thus, as shall be seen, in the rearticulation of the categorical imperative (in terms of the golden rule), Ricoeur picks up again this notion of goods, recasts them as human goods, as content for the categorical imperative, but which itself is seen as rooted in the broader ethical orientation or intention.

Now, extending our consideration from practices to the broader notion of a life plan where partial actions are integrated into a broader unity of life likewise extends the notion of goods internal to practice. On this level we revisit the problem mentioned above regarding deliberation, preferential choice, and means to ends. I consider this so-called ambiguity to be settled, as seen above, simply by indicating that in this case the actual choice of a way of life, a profession or vocation, is a choice of a means, in a broad sense, to a more ultimate end, or even, finally, the most far-reaching end, happiness (*eudiamonia*) as a fulfillment of the properly human function, and everything concomitantly required for it. This, along the lines of the biological model that Aristotle followed, is the fulfillment of the formal dimension, the properly human element or function, as its perfection. But Ricoeur contrasts *tekhné* and practical wisdom (*phronésis*). So, for him the means-end model is no longer sufficient, for it is a question of making rather specific the vague ideals of what is considered to be a good life for the person as a whole, making use of the *phronésis* that has been shown to escape the means-ends model.

The life plan focuses on the person as a whole in contrast to the more narrow focus of practices. This is the context of Aristotle's inquiry into the specifically human function or work (*ergon*). In this present context, writers such as Ricoeur and many others, in referring to life, are reflecting on that specifically human work or function, reason. Aristotle, of course, attempts to spell out the virtue that is specifically human, reason functioning at its best, according to excellence as that which perfects humans as such, similar to the good shoemaker, the doctor, the musician. These latter are said to be good when they function well or with excellence (*areté*). Ricoeur wants to tie practices to life plan, as included within its scope, in that once chosen, the life plan supplies the end and finality for practices, giving ends in themselves for which practices become means with subordinate ends. But the question to be posed here is precisely how he finds that in Aristotle. Aristotle moves quickly to the final human end as their ultimate good, as their fulfillment and perfection, which is correlated to virtue (*areté*). Thus, when humans function well or excellently in that properly human function, reason, they are virtuous, and such virtue leads to happiness as the fulfillment of the specific being of humans as uniquely human. However, we do have to incorporate the intellectual (dianoietic) virtues with the virtues of character for fuller happiness or finality, which opens the door for a deeper and broader consideration. Does all this have relevance for ethics today? It seems so! The virtues of character (moral virtues) build up character or producing a morally prudent person, who has the habits becoming to excellence (virtue) and happiness.

The very choice of a vocation that sets the practices in motion and gives them an end in itself is able to be adjusted, in which case deliberation is again involved, but now in relation to *phronésis* "in which the *phronimos* is no less at issue than the *phronésis*" (OA, 178). In expanding further, we come to what today has come to be called the "narrative unity of life" (OA, 178), which includes the Aristotelian "living well" mentioned above.

But what is the "good life" referred to above? "[T]he nebulus of ide-als and dreams of achievements with regard to which a life is held to be more or less fulfilled or unfulfilled. It is the plane of 'time lost' and of 'time regained'" (OA, 179). In this sense, according to Ricoeur, the "good life" is basically the finality in terms of which all these actions are done or directed, which actions are said by Aristotle to be done for themselves. Once their end has been posited, these practices do not lose their self-sufficiency. For Ricoeur this opening and closedness of prac-tices maintains a tension between them and the more inclusive orienta-tion of the "good life" within the more total structure of praxis (OA, 179). This is sort of a horizon or limit idea for Ricoeur that turns between *phronésis* and *phronimos*.

> In more modern terms, we would say that it is in unending work of inter-pretation applied to action and to oneself that we pursue the search for adequation between what seems to us to be best with regard to our life as a whole and the preferential choices that govern our practices. There are several ways of introducing the hermeneutical point of view at this final stage. First is that between our aim of a 'good life' and the most impor-tant decision of our existence (career, loves, leisure, etc.). This can be likened to the text in which the whole and the part are to be understood each in terms of the other. Next, the idea of interpretation adds to the simple idea of meaning that of a meaning for someone. For the agent, interpreting the text of an action is interpreting himself or herself. . . . By the same token, our concept of the self is greatly enriched by this relation between interpretation of the text of action and self-interpretation. On the ethical plane, self-interpretation becomes self-esteem. In return, self-esteem follows the fate of interpretation. Like the latter, it provokes con-troversy, dispute, rivalry—in short, the conflict of interpretations—in the exercise of practical judgment. This means that the search for adequation between our life ideals and our decisions, themselves vital ones, is not open to the sort of verification expected in the sciences of observation. The adequation of interpretation involves an exercise of judgment which, at best, can aspire to plausibility in the eyes of others, even if, in the eyes of the agent, his or her own conviction borders on the sort of experiential evidence which, at the end of book VI of the *Nichomachean Ethics*, made *phronésis* comparable to *aisthesis*. This experiential evidence is the new figure in which *attestation* appears, when the certainty of being the author of one's own discourse and of one's own acts becomes the conviction of judging well and acting well in a momentary and provisional approxima-tion of living well. (OA, 179–180)

With and for Others

Within the horizon of the good life, solicitude or being with others must be linked as essential to the dialogical dimension of self-esteem, which will emerge at the heart of the ethical orientation. It is necessary at the outset to note, as Ricoeur does (OA, 180), that first and foremost it is self-esteem that is first considered, before even focusing upon the esteem of "myself": "To say self is not to say myself." It seems to me that this distinction takes into account the path from Kant to Heidegger, and the fact that the constant backdrop in such a focus is Kant's second formulation of the categorical imperative where the human person as such is the focus, while for Heidegger, from the very beginning of the first chapter of *Being and Time*, existence is *mine*, *jemeinikeit*, so that the *Sein* as *mitsein* is mine (*jemeinikeit*) and has mineness as essential to it, where the *je* indicates "in each case" (OA, 180). But Ricoeur refers to Heidegger here as indicating that mineness or self is "in each case" mine. And Ricoeur, going somewhat beyond Heidegger's sense, considers the base of this "in each case" to the "unexpressed reference to others."

Ricoeur wants, in this context of solicitude, to glean something from Aristotle's treatment of the ethics of "reciprocity, of sharing, of living together" (OA, 187)[4] opposing the too strong role given to the other by Levinas, whose "other" places a demand from the outside strictly as such. Ricoeur, it seems to me, is correct in emphasizing that it takes a self to have an other than self, and it is this self that in self-esteem emerges within the reflexive moment of the aim at (for) the good life. We shall see that here we are referred back to Aristotle's treatment of friendship that focus us on the reciprocity in the give and take of selves who esteem themselves. And it will be seen that to the extent that friendship raises the question of equality, it puts us in the direction of justice in an Aristotelian sense, thus leading to the third element, that of the third person and of institutions within the ethical life.

It is necessary to see that the worthiness of self-esteem rests in human capacities and not mainly in their accomplishments. In this context capacity means the fundamental pragmatic dimension of human existence. In contrast to this context of ethics as such, philosophical anthropology reveals capacity as a pervasive and essential dimension of concrete human existence and being. On the ethical level of consideration, the "I can" brings to the fore the evaluation central to the practical that Aristotle so emphasized. The relevant question here that Ricoeur articulates so well, is "whether the mediation of the other is not required along the route from capacity to realization" (OA, 181). This mediating role of others is certainly not foreign to the existential-ontological tradition that has for so long considered coexistence to be central to human being, and as such, required on the ontic and concrete level. The question focuses specifically on the ontic level of this phenomenon, on the concrete need for others, ontologically constitutive, and ontically lived out in many concrete forms and manifestations, but showing this concrete need. What is not so clear and obvious, however, is the specific and concrete (ontic) need for the other for the actual process of actualizing the capacities.[5] But we can go back to Aristotle to find the involvement of the other in the actualization of capacities, contrary to those who want to interpret him as dealing with a quasi-isolated individual to whom he wants to add the dimension of justice as living in society.

To see Aristotle's focus on the need of the other as this mediating role in today's context of coexistence, we can again follow Ricoeur in his analysis of friendship in Aristotle's ethics. Ricoeur considers friendship "to serve for Aristotle as a transition between the aim of the 'good life,' which we have seen reflected in self-esteem, apparently a solitary virtue, and justice, the virtue of human plurality belonging to the political sphere: . . . friendship is a virtue—an excellence—at work in deliberative choices and capable of being elevated to the rank of *habitus*, without ceasing to require actual exercise, without which it would no longer be an activity" (OA, 182). Aristotle ends up with the notion that the happy man or woman needs friends (EN, 9.9).[6]

The analysis of the term friendship reveals it to have several senses that must be distinguished according to the object loved, the (*phileta*), for the sake of the good, of utility, or of pleasure (OA, 182). And it can be seen that self-love itself is mediated to the extent that the predilection of one self is desire oriented in reference to the good. Further, friendship presents itself as a mutual relationship, with reciprocity as part of its most basic definition. So, friendship, belonging essentially to the ethical as the first unfolding of the wish to live will, brings to the fore the problematic of reciprocity.

> The idea of mutuality indeed has its own requirements which are not eclipsed by either a genesis based on the Same, as in Husserl, or a genesis based on the Other, as in Levinas. According to the idea of mutuality, each loves the other *as being the man he is* (8.3.1156a18–19). This is not the case in a friendship based on utility, where one loves the other for the sake of some expected advantage, and even less so in the case of friendship for pleasure. We therefore see reciprocity imposing itself already on the ethical plane. This reciprocity, on the plane of morality, at the time of violence, will be required by the Golden Rule and the categorical imperative of respect. This 'as being' (as being what the other is) averting any subsequent egoistic leanings, is constitutive of mutuality. And mutuality, in turn, cannot be conceived of without the relation to the good in the self, in the friend, in friendship. Thus, the reflexivity of oneself is not abolished but is split into two by mutuality, under the control of the predicate 'good,' applied to agents as well as to actions. (OA, 183–184)

It is this mutuality, and the addition of the notion of equality, which borders on justice, as the mutual rendering of equal amounts, in giving and receiving. Friendship properly belongs to the interpersonal relations (with intimacy), while justice belongs properly to institutions (as third person). Thus, justice is seen to encompass many citizens while friendship is limited to a few.

But before leaving the context of the second person, the personal interpretation, and friendship, we should see that Aristotle says things about friendship that influence later ages, especially the medieval; but it is better to consider these points in Aristotle before they are recast into any other appropriation. Here we can follow the discussion by Ricoeur loosely, but only to a limited extent since his interest, while that of ethics, is cast within the broader problematics of the self as oneself and another, thus focusing on that correlation in friendship more than anything else.

The sum and substance of the point for our interest made by Aristotle is the affirmation that his own existence is desirable for the good man, at the heart of which is a certain lack entering into the essential dimensions of friendship, in spite of the stability that is at once presupposed. In order to deal with this lack leading to the need for friends on the part of the happy person, Aristotle has recourse to the fundamental metaphysical distinctions underlying his ethics: that of act and potency (power is the word used here by Ricoeur), and, not invoked by Ricoeur, the formal and final causes. For it is within the relationship between the formal and final causes, as relating to human being and nature, that is revealed the fulfillment or perfection that Aristotle calls happiness as *eudaimonia*, the actualization of potentiality to its fullest finality. The relation between the becoming of a being toward its finality, or the relation between *energeia* and *entelechia*, is precisely that: the potency or potentiality, actualized through the process of the form at work,[7] in the sense of *energeia*, reaches perfection or fulfillment as *entelechia* or finality. Friendship would than be an activity as a becoming, or the process of actualization, all of which indicate *energeia* that is still lacking with regard to the full actuality or fulfillment or perfection of the thing as *entelecheia*. Ricoeur says concerning this point: "Under the aegis of need, a link is made between activity and life and, finally, between happiness and pleasure. Friendship, therefore, works toward establishing the conditions for the realization of life, considered in its intrinsic goodness and its basic pleasure" (OA, 186). Ricoeur goes on to add that: "to the notions of life and activity, we must add that of *consicousness*" of perception and activity as well as of consciousness of life. He continues:

> So, to the extent to which the consciousness of life is pleasant, one can say that the profound meaning of *philautia* is that, *desire*: the good man's own being is desirable to him; given this, the being of his friend is then equally desirable to him. Having thus joined together activity

and life, the desirable and the pleasant, the consciousness of existing and the joy of the consciousness of existing, Aristotle can then posit, as a partial conclusion to his complicated reasoning: 'If all this be true, as his own being is desirable for each man, so or almost so, is that of his friend' (9.9.1170b7–8). And the argument can spring back: 'Now his being was seen to be desirable because he perceived his own goodness, and such perception is pleasant in itself. He needs, therefore, to be conscious of the existence of his friend as well' (1170b9–11). And this can be realized only in 'living together' [*suzen*]. (1170b11)

Returning to the term solicitude, we can see more clearly how the value whereby each person is irreplaceable in our affection and our esteem can be derived from this solicitude. "In this respect, it is in experiencing the irreparable loss of the loved other that we learn, through the transfer of the other onto ourselves, the irreplaceable character of our own life. It is first for the other that I am irreplaceable. In this sense, solicitude replies to the other's esteem for me. But if this response were not in a certain manner spontaneous, how could solicitude not be reduced to dreary duty?" (OA, 193). For Ricoeur, similitude is the "fruit of the exchange between esteem for oneself and solicitude for others," which exchange allows us to realize that I cannot have self-esteem unless I have esteem for others as myself, attesting to the belief of worth, thus bringing together as equivalent the esteem of the other as a oneself and the esteem of oneself as an other (OA, 193–194).

We have already intimated that justice is latent in the friendship mode of interpersonal encounters in the second-person face to face since the other is also third person and thus leads to institutions. Turning to justice in third-person relations in institutions brings ethical features to the fore not yet found in concentrating on second-person relations, such as the requirement of equality, that is, to each person his or her rights.

The basic sense of institution places it in the context from which the name of ethics derives. For institutions are characterized by "the bond of common mores, and not that of constraining rules," which put us in the context of the basic ethos in the sense of the fundament mores as consisting in customs, habits, values, and so on, showing the source of both words, ethics, and morals. This third-person dimension includes such a plurality that there cannot be personal or face to face or second person, precisely as a plurality. And the acting together or living together is spread over a length of time instead of being limited merely to instantaneous acting together. The power of this group has its own fragility, lasting only as long as people act together, and vanishing when they disperse. It thus manifests the fragility of power as the "second-order fragility of institutions and of all the human affairs gravitating around them" (OA, 196). Furthermore, there is the public space or publicness to this living and acting in concert "within which the activities we have termed practices come to light" (OA, 196).

Ricoeur, following to some extent Hannah Arendt, states that "it is power, as wanting to live and act together, that brings to the ethical aim the point of application of its indispensable third dimensions: *justice*" (OA, 196). In taking up this discussion of justice in institutions (of third-person relations), Ricoeur distinguishes justice as it is related to the *good* "with respect to which it marks the extension of interpersonal relationships to institutions." That sense of justice is distinguished from justice in relation to the *legel*, "the judicial system conferring upon the law coherence and the right of constraint" (OA, 197). We shall continue here in the context of the first, leaving the second aspect for the next section of our study.

We have already seen, on the level of interpersonal relations in the second person, that the concept of equality, and therefore of justice, has already arisen subliminally. Ricoeur sees now that the transition from this interpersonal level to the societal level, both within the ethical aim, requires justice, equality, and especially distribution as considered by Aristotle. On this level the sense of justice is closer to the fundamental notion of ethos than to the idea of justice (*jus*). It is clear that the passage on this level to the institution as part of the ethical aim has been necessary, reveals the cohesion existing among the components, the individual, interpersonal, and societal, within the ethical aim. For Ricoeur, "equality, however it is modulated, *is to life in institutions what solicitude is to interpersonal relations.* Solicitude provides to the self another, who is a face, in the strong sense that Emmanuel Levinas has taught us to recognize. Equality provides to the self another who is an *each*" (OA, 202). Thus, the sense of justice presupposes rather than takes away from solicitude, in that it holds persons to be irreplaceable. And justice, as applicable to all humanity, adds to solicitude.

In the move from the ethical to the moral, the ethical aim must be reconsidered in the light of the moral norm, thus marking the move from the teleological foundation to the deontological principle. As far as Ricoeur is concerned, this move to the moral norm reveals conflicts provoked by the formalism of the deontological moment, leading us back to an ethics in a given situation (OA, 203). Three stages in this consideration must be passed through: first, the aim of the "good life" will be tested by the norm; second, the dialogical structure of the norm must be considered, bringing solicitude to the fore as the primary dimension of the relation of self to the self's other on the ethical level; finally, the investigation into the sense of justice is continued, moving from the sense of justice to the rule of justice, extending from interpersonal relations to social relations and to the institutions that underlie them. In this consideration the connection between self-esteem on the ethical level and self-respect on the moral level, are clarified (OA, 203). For Ricoeur self-respect is self-esteem under the reign of moral law.

The Aim of the Good Life and Obligation

Ricoeur develops the elements of the deontological by contrasting each of its phases with each corresponding phase of the teleological as: "aiming at the good life with and for other in just institutions." The parallel and essential first element of the moral phase is: good will as determining the good without qualification, the criterion of universalization, legislation by form alone, and autonomy, manifesting the opposition between autonomy and heteronomy as constitutive of moral selfhood (OA, 210). The abstract character of autonomy is tied to the universality of this level, escaping the alternatives of monologue and dialogue, and establishing both its grandeur and its lack. Kant says that he progresses from this universal as form, to matter in which persons are grasped as ends in themselves, and to the "complete determination of all maxims" following the notion of the kingdom of ends (OA, 211).[8] "A progression," Kant adds, "may be said to take place through the categories of *unity* of the form of the will (its universality); of the *multiplicity* of its matter (its objects, that is, its ends); and of the *totality* or completeness of its system of ends" (OA, 211).[9] Ricoeur reminds us about these points that unity, multiplicity, and totality are categories of quantity. But it is only in a certain sense that the *unity* of the form is distinguished from the *plurality* of matter; it is the unity of universality of willing grasped in the abstract moment when it is not divided among the plurality of persons, rather than that of a solitary ego.

In moving to the universal level, an abstract level that is not the personal you or me and thus cannot be reduced to an egological stance or solipsism, it is necessary to note that it is precisely this abstract character that will later require the second configuration of the norm. It is beneficial to indicate, without denying the break Kantian formalism makes with the teleological, the features by which this deontological conception of morality remains in some sense attached to the teleological conception of ethics, just as it was possible for us to see above that the teleological conception of ethics, by reason of its universality, was in some way attached to the deontological conception by way of morality. As Ricoeur so well puts this: "Now if ethics points toward universalism through the features we have just recalled, moral obligation is itself not without some connection to the aim of the 'good life.' The anchoring of the deontological moment in the teleological aim is made evident by the place occupied in Kant by the concept of good will at the threshold of the *Groundwork of the Metaphysics of Morals*: 'It is impossible to conceive anything at all in the world, or even out of it, which can be taken as good without qualification [*ohne Einschrankung*], except a *good will*'" (OA, 205).[10]

The universalism implicit in the teleological perspective, with its middle term (*mesotes*), or the intermediate, can be considered a beginning of universality. Ricoeur points out that to posit, as the object of self-esteem, capacities such as the initiative of acting, implicitly gives a universal sense to these capacities, as being that by virtue of which we hold them to be worthy of esteem, and ourselves as well. And when we appropriated the Heideggerian *Jemeinikeit* as mineness, in each ease assigned to the self, that and all the existentialia can be seen to be universal.

Kant has taken out of play anything that might qualify the will as not good, both internally and externally, which is recognized through its relation to the law. The will takes the place in the Kantian morality that rational desire, recognized through its aim, occupied in Aristotelian ethics. What allows Kant to make this move is his famous distinction between *der Wille* as the will mentioned above, and *die Willkür*, which brings into play the aim in practical reason. It is here that Ricoeur has ingeniously interwoven the elements allowing the two frameworks to be interarticulated in his own typical fashion of seeing the positive elements of each in looking at mutually exclusive positions, and then working toward an ingenious interarticulation. Ricoeur adds to the above the following: "In a vocabulary closer to our own, one could say that will is express'd in the speech acts belonging to the family of *imperatives*, whereas the verbal expressions of desire—including happiness—are speech acts in the *optative* mode" (OA, 206). It is precisely here that in adjusting each position we can continue to follow Ricoeur's manner of bringing the two traditions together into an ethicomoral philosophy viable today in spite of the many attacks launched against any sort of ethics or moral philosophy.

Tied to universality in the moral orientation is the dimension of constraint belonging to the idea of duty. The will, which is practical reason, is characterized as finite in humans and as such is empirically determined by sensible inclinations. The tie between the notion of the good will and the notion of an action done out of duty is so close that they become substituted for one another. Ricoeur interprets: "A good will without qualification is, in the first instance, a will that is constitutionally subject to limitations. For it, the good without qualification has the form of duty, the imperative, moral constraint. The entire critical process aims at moving back from this finite condition of the will to practical reason, conceived as self-legislation, as *autonomy*" (OA, 206–207).

What Kant is indicating by the "concept of a will [*der Wille*] estimable in itself and good apart from any further end,"[11] is the pure will oriented to the law of reason, the moral law given from reason, but considered here independent from any input from a rational end (teleology of any kind) or from inclinations. Kant continues here in the *Groundwork*, as Ricoeur states it: "one has to 'take up the concept of *duty*, which includes that of a good will, exposed, however, to certain subjective limitations and obstacles. These, so far from hiding a good will or disguising it, rather bring it out by contrast and make it shine forth more brightly.'" It is here that the break between the critique and the ordinary moral sense occurs according to Ricoeur (OA, 206, fn. 5).[12] By a strategy of purifying, excluding, placing at a distance, this morality of obligation arrives at good without qualification as equaling the "self-legislating will, in accordance with the supreme principle of autonomy" (OA, 207). Ricoeur adds, bringing this into the context of the *Oneself as Another*, that of the identity of the self as ipse and as idem: "The entire critical process aims at moving back from this finite condition of the will to practical reason, conceived as self-legislation, as *autonomy*. Only at this stage will the self find the first support for its moral status, without any influence from the dialogic structure which, while not being added on from outside, unfolds its meaning in the interpersonal dimension" (OA, 207).

Ricoeur makes an astute observation about Kant's setting aside the empirical impurity in inclination. He considers this to be the case because of its inadequacy with respect to the criterion of universality in distinguishing the empirical impurity in inclination and separating it from recalcitrance, and hence from virtual disobedience, "which take into account the constraining character of the moral imperative. The two problematics, that of universality and that of the constraint, are without doubt difficult to distinguish because of the finite constitution of the will" (OA, 207). Ricoeur points out that one can at least conceive of a mode of subjective determination that would not bear the mark of the antagonism between reason and desire. Ricoeur is alluding to his eidetic of will, which revealed the coming together of the finite and infinite in the practical synthesis not to be essentially flawed or faulted. Thus it is conceivable that freedom is harmonious in such a way as not to be tarnished by any blemish arising from a flaw in the relation between desire and reason. This removes the polluting effect of inclination on the will in isolating the empirical from the harmony between desire and reason. This for Ricoeur corresponds to the step of submitting the maxims of action to the *rule of universalization*, precisely as the process of testing the maxims to see if they are adequate to the absolute esteem of good will—can the maxim of my action be universalizable?

Two further points in Ricoeur's analysis are important for us: first, that it is precisely this notion of maxim that is unprecedented in the teleological tradition, in spite of its own claim to universality seen above; the maxim is manifest as containing an inadequation in its claim to universality, in terms of the universality inscribed within practical reason. At this point, the recalcitrance of inclination is not regarded, but rather an inadequation in the claim to universality attached to the maxim.

Ricoeur notes a new difference between the moral norm and the ethical aim in the relation between commanding and obeying, which in Kant's consideration internalizes in one person or actor what usually is taken to be between two different people. Now, for Kant, there are two within the same person, the one who commands, reason, and the one who obeys or disobeys, inclinations or desire. For Kant the imperative takes the form of a categorical imperative instead of a hypothetical imperative, which latter posits first the end. The categorical imperative is the only one that meets the requirement of universalization. Regarding maxims that are subjective: "All material practical rules place the ground of the determination of the will in the lower faculty of desire, and if there were no purely formal laws of the will adequate to determine it, we could not admit (the existence of) any higher faculty of desire."[13] Ricoeur understands this consideration of maxims to cross a second threshold of formalism: "mediation by maxims is not forgotten, but subjective maxims are carried back en mass to their single source, the 'faculty of desiring' and the objective maxims to the simple (blosse) form of legislation" (OA, 210).

In this analysis of Kantian morality, indeed, one of the most insightful readings of Kantianism today, Ricoeur focuses on the split and opposition between autonomy (self-legislation), and heteronomy. Ricoeur sees freedom as denoting will (*der Wille*) in its fundamental structure and no longer in terms of its finite condition (*die Willkür*). In the "Dialectic" of the first *Critique* Kant was able to establish a freedom as conceivable.

> Here freedom is justified practically: first in the negative terms, by its total independence with respect to 'all determining grounds of events in nature according to the law of causality'[14] and then positively, as the self-givenness of the law (Theorem 4). With *autonomy*, the split . . . reaches its most radical expression: to autonomy is opposed the *heteronomy* of the arbitrator, in virtue of which the will gives itself only 'directions for a reasonable obedience to pathological laws' (Theorem 4, p. 34). With this opposition—this *Widerstreit*—between autonomy and heteronomy, formalism reaches its apex; Kant can then proclaim that morality resides where 'the mere legislative form of maxims is the sole sufficient ground of a will' (p. 28).

For Ricoeur this involves a sublimation of the imperative, that is, when autonomy substitutes obedience to oneself for obedience to another, obedience has lost all character of dependence and submission. True obedience, one could say, is autonomy: "good will as determining the good without qualification, the criterion of universalization, legislation by form alone, and, finally, autonomy" (OA, 210).

In turning to certain "potential aporia" (OA, 212) in Kantian morality itself, Ricoeur makes the following remark about this split in affectivity between a feeling imprinted in the human heart by reason alone as the mark of reason in feeling, and those that belong to the pathology of desire: "This split, which breaks affectivity in two, cannot help but concern our investigation into the tie—never severed, in my opinion—between the moral norm and the ethical aim. If self-esteem is indeed, as we have admitted, the reflexive expression of the aim of the 'good life,' it seems to fall under the Kantian knife, which casts it over onto the other side of the dividing line" (OA, 214). Ricoeur goes on to affirm that the "question for us has never been, however, making the Kantian tone harmonize with the Aristotelian tone. Actually, the real question is not that at all. For it is perfectly legitimate to see in Kantian respect the variant of self-esteem that has successfully passed the test of the criterion of universalization. Anticipating what we shall say later concerning the place of evil in our deontological conception of morality, we can state that what is 'knocked down' and 'humiliated' is the variant of self-esteem that Kant calls *Selbstliebe* and that constitutes the always possible and in fact, most ordinary perversion of self-esteem" (OA, 214–215). Ricoeur quotes Kant's *Critique of Practical Reason* (OA, 214, n. 24): "This propensity to make the subjective determining grounds of one's choice [*Willkür*] into an objective determining ground of the will [*Wille*] in general can be called self-love; when it makes itself legislative and an unconditional practical principle, it can be called self-conceit."[15] Ricoeur admits that what we have called self-esteem does not appear to escape this condemnation: "All claims of self-esteem [*Selbstschatzung*] which precede conformity to the moral law are null and void."[16] Ricoeur's use of and development from Kant here is quite ingenious, reaching a crucial point in the development of his own way of proceeding vis-à-vis Aristotle and Kant: he considers this placing of love of self out of bounds as playing a critical function with regard to self-esteem and a purgative function with regard to evil. "Self-love, I shall venture to say, is self-esteem perverted by what we shall later call the penchant for evil. Respect is self-esteem that has passed through the sieve of the universal and constraining norm—in short, self-esteem under the reign of the law. This conjunction with respect between self-positing and self-affection authorizes us to question, in the following

study, the independence of the principle of autonomy— . . . —in relation
to the teleological perspective, in other words, to doubt the autonomy of
autonomy" (OA, 215).

Ricoeur indicates that in the *Religion within the Limits of Reason
Alone* Kant tends to exonerate desire and inclination, and to make free
choice the source of all the splits, situating evil, rather than in innocent
desire, on the level of the formulation of the maxims. "Evil is, in the lit-
eral sense of the word, perversion, that is, a reversal of the order that
requires respect for the law to be placed above inclination. It is a matter
here of a misuse of (free) choice and not of the maleficence of desire
(nor, moreover, is it a matter of the corruption of practical reason itself,
which would make humankind diabolical and not simply . . . bad"
(OA, 215–216). In the primordial maxim, serving as the grounding for
all bad maxims, consists the propensity (*Hang*) for evil, which in turn is
to be distinguished from the predisposition (*Anlage*) to good, which
Kant considers to be inherent in the condition of a finite will, and "consequently, to affirm the contingency of this propensity on the scale of
human history" (OA, 216). This propensity for evil affects the

> use of freedom, the capacity for actually being autonomous. This is the
> true problem for us. For this affection of freedom, even if it does not
> strike the principle of morality, which continues to be autonomy, does
> put into question the exercise, the realization of freedom. This uncom-
> mon situation opens, moreover, a place for religion that is distinct from
> that of morality—religion, according to Kant, possessing no theme
> other than the *regeneration* of freedom, that is, restoring to freedom
> the control over it of the good principle. In addition, this consideration
> of the capacity—lost and to be recovered—of freedom brings back to
> the forefront the problem of good and evil, which the strictly deonto-
> logical version of morality had relegated to a subsidiary level. (OA,
> 216)[17]

Ricoeur goes on to state in a footnote:

> In carrying the question of evil to the level of 'predispositions' (*Gesin-
> nungen*), Kant links up with the teleology of the *Critique of Judgment*.
> He reviews the degrees of this teleology applied to human nature at the
> start of the essay on radical evil: the disposition to *animality*, to
> *humanity*, to *personality*.[18] To the extent that the concept of predispo-
> sition belongs to teleology, the vocabulary of good and evil returns in
> the present context, in an entirely different sense, it is true, than the one
> rejected in the *Critique*, in chapter 2 of the 'Analytic.' It is, in fact on
> the level of the third predisposition that the propensity for evil is exer-
> cised, a predisposition defined here as 'the capacity for respect for the
> moral law as *in itself a sufficient incentive of the will*' (pp. 22–23). We
> are reminded that 'all of these predispositions are not only *good* in the

negative fashion (in that they do not contradict the moral law); they are also predispositions *toward good* (they enjoin the observance of the law.) They are *original*, for they are bound up with the possibility of human nature.'[19] It is on this predispositional terrain—steeped in finality!—that the notion of *propensity* to evil takes its place: 'By propensity (*propensio*) I understand the subjective ground of the possibility of an inclination . . . so far as mankind in general is liable to it' (pp. 23–24). The propensity to evil is therefore inscribed in the most general theory of predispositions, as a sort of second-order predisposition, a predisposition deeply rooted in the formation of maxims that deviated from those of the moral law. This is why one can speak of them only in terms of *subjective ground*. (OA, p. 217, fn. 29)

Thus, for Kant the problem of good and evil entails the subjective ground of the use of freedom (considered above in footnote 29) and directly concerns the status of autonomy. The question focuses on autonomy in relation to feeling, what Kant singles out as the feeling of respect, which opens up a certain passivity or receptivity at the heart of freedom. Ricoeur says that "we thus have to admit that the penchant for evil affects free choice on the very level where respect is itself the specific affection that has been stated, the affection of freedom by the law. And it is as such that evil is radical (and not original): 'This evil is *radical*, because it corrupts the ground of all maxims; it is moreover, as a natural propensity, *inextirpable* by human powers'" (p. 32). Ricoeur shows how Kant retains an element of both Augustine and Pelagius in his view of a penchant for evil as "a quasi nature. . . . Evil, in a certain sense, begins anew with each evil act, although, in another sense, it is always already there" (OA, 217–218, fn. 31).

In thus radicalizing evil, Kant also has radicalized the idea of free choice by putting it "at the very source of the formation of maxims" (OA, 218). Evil is thus considered to reveal an essential dimension of free choice, in that it carries an "original wound" affecting its capacity for determining itself for or against the law. There is thus an enigma of the actual exercise of freedom that sheds light on the origin of evil. "The fact that this penchant is always already present in every opportunity to choose but that it is at the same time a maxim of (free) choice is no less inscrutable than the origin of evil" (OA, 218). In the light of this role of evil in relation to free will, Ricoeur indicates the need for submitting the aim of the good life to the test of moral obligation, which he describes in a paraphrase of the categorical imperative as follows: "Act solely in accordance with the maxim by which you can wish at the same time that what *ought not to be*, namely, evil, will indeed *not exist*" (OA, 218). This formulation reveals the precise reason that the teleological dimension of ethics needs the deontological dimension of morality.

Solicitude and the Norm

Respect for persons is not external to the Kantian moral principle. Rather, it develops in an implicit dialogic structure on the plane of obligation or rules. And it can be shown that there is a tie by which the norm of respect for persons is connected to solicitude within the dialogic structure of the ethical aim. This respect for persons is, on the moral plane, in the same relation to autonomy as solicitude is, on the ethical plane, to the aim of the good life. This relation demands a clarification of the transition in Kant to the second formulation of the categorical imperative. Ricoeur takes as his point of departure for this project the Golden Rule, interpreting it as part of the "*endoxa* acclaimed by Aristotle's ethics, one of those received notions that the philosopher does not have to invent, but to clarify and justify" (OA, 219). Ricoeur is not oblivious to the fact that Kant would not have such a sympathetic reading of the Golden Rule.

Ricoeur invokes a formula from Hillel and from one of the Gospels: the negative one from Hillel, "Do not do unto your neighbor what you would hate him to do to you. This is the entire law; the rest is commentary." And from the Gospels: "Treat others as you would like them to treat you" (Luke 6:31). This positive formulation spotlights benevolence leading directly to the formulation: "love your neighbor as yourself" (Matt. 22:39), making more obvious the connection between solicitude and the norm, according to Ricoeur. The earlier formulations from Hillel and the Gospel, however, better reflects the norm of reciprocity.

Ricoeur is quick to add, however, that this reciprocity stands out against the background of an initial dissymmetry between the actor as protagonist of the action and the patient. It is from this basic dissymmetry that all the evil offshoots of interaction spring, from small to great, such as murder and torture. Violence can be seen to be power of one will exerted over on other, all the way from holding power over someone by torture, an extreme form of abuse. Such violence is the diminution or the destruction of the victim's power-to-do. And in torture the torturer sometimes succeeds in destroying the victim's self-esteem, which our present analysis by way of the norm has elevated to the level of self-respect. "What is called humiliation—a horrible caricature of humility—is nothing else than the destruction of self-respect, beyond the destruction of the power-to-act. Here we seem to have reached the depth of evil" (OA, 220). Anticipating his later turning to promise, Ricoeur indicates the kind of violence that can be concealed in language as a "act of discourse, hence as action" (p. 220). He mentions that the "betrayal of friendship, the inverse figure of faithfulness," indicates something of the malice of which the human heart is capable. The counterpart to these figures of evil in the intersubjective realm can be seen in the prescriptions and prohibitions stemming from the Golden Rule: you shall not lie, steal, kill, torture: as replies by morality to violence. Morality responds to all of the figures of evil with a *no*. Ricoeur refers to this negative form of prohibition as inexpugnable, because of the recourse of moral philosophy to the primacy of the ethical. The negative formulation of the rule seems to be appropriate to this situation of recourse from the ethical to the moral rule, now seen in this negative prohibition (OA, 221). For solicitude on the ethical level as the mutual exchange of self-esteems is seen to be thoroughly affirmative, where this original affirmation is the "hidden should of the prohibition" (OA, 221).

In the second phase of the argument, the respect owed to persons on the moral plane is in the same relation to autonomy as solicitude on the ethical plane was seen to be to the aim of the "good life." Ricoeur recalls at this point the price paid to move to solicitude as the second moment of the ethical phase, a break with the so-called "separation" of the ego. In Kant the second phase, the second formulation of the categorical imperative, is seen to be a direct development from the first. Ricoeur sees in the second formulation the "seat of a tension" between two terms, that of humanity and that of the person as an end in himself or herself. "The idea of humanity as a singular term is introduced in the context of an abstract universality that governs the principle of autonomy, without the consideration of persons. The idea of persons as ends in themselves, however, demands that one take into account the plurality of persons, without allowing one to take this idea as far as the concept of otherness" (OA, 222). Ricoeur indicates, however, that Kant seems to argue in favor of the priority of the continuity assured by the idea of humanity with the principle of autonomy, at the expense of the discontinuity marking the introduction of the idea of an end in itself and of persons as ends in themselves. To bring out this tension in Kant's formulation, a discussion returning to the Golden Rule is opportune, thus allowing the possibility of treating the Kantian imperative as the formalization of the Golden Rule.

Ricoeur sees the Golden Rule as imposing a new ground upon which formalism can be seen to impose itself. "What Kant termed *matter* or *plurality* is quite precisely this field of interaction where one will exerts a power over another and where the rule of reciprocity replies to the initial dissymmetry between agent and patient" (OA, 222). This rule of reciprocity is what makes patient and agent equivalent. And it is this process of formalization, applied to this very rule of reciprocity, that tends to repeat the test of the rule for universalization in this context of plurality. And it is precisely this test of the rule for universalization that guarantees the principle of autonomy, bringing into play the notion of *humanity*. "In this regard, the notion of humanity can be considered the plural expression of the requirement of universality that presided over the deduction of autonomy, hence taken as mediating term between the diversity of persons, the notion humanity is at the root of this diversity, otherness which is dramatized in the dissymmetrical relation of the power one will holds over another, opposed by the Golden Rule" (OA, 222–223). The test of universalization is still operative, eliminating anything that does not measure up. Thus, love and hate as subjective principles of maxims that are empirical are not adequate to this requirement of universality. Further, love and hate, as potential desires, are hostile to the rule and so enter into the conflict between the subjective principle and the objective principle. No direct tie, other than that between the self and the other than self, can be established unless something is named, in my person or in that of others, as worthy of respect. And that is humanity, in the "comprehensive or fundamental sense of that by reason of which one is made worthy of respect," and that is nothing other than "universality considered from the point of view of the multiplicity of persons: What Kant termed 'object' or 'matter'" (OA, 223). Ricoeur observes in a footnote that:

> This shift from unity to plurality finds a basis in the teleology of the *Criqique of Judgment*, as we recalled earlier at the time of the discussion of radical evil, which placed the predisposition to personality, considered as a reasonable and responsible being, above the predisposition of man as a living being to animal nature (*Religion*, p. 21). This teleology, based upon the notion of original predisposition to the good in human nature, is not easy to dissociate entirely from the Aristotelian-style teleology that remains rooted in an anthropology of desire. In this respect, the Kantian break is perhaps not as radical as Kant had wanted and believed it to be. Our critique of the *Critique* finds one of its points of application here. It will be one of the effects of the crisis provoked by moral formalism to reintroduce, on the level of the conditions of the actualization of freedom and of the moral principles that govern it, something like 'generic goods' and 'social goods.' Without this addition of plainly teleological concepts, one does not see what the 'material' idea of humanity contributes to the 'formal' idea of universality. (OA, 224, n. 35)

If I follow Ricoeur correctly, the idea of humanity supplies a rule of universalization in the passage from the ethical aim to the moral norm, and acts as a guide for the principle of autonomy, leading from unity that does not take persons into account to plurality. "In so doing, this pluralization, internal to the universal, retrospectively confirms that the self, reflexively implied by the formal imperative, was not monologic in nature but simply indifferent to the distinction of persons and, in this sense, capable of being inscribed in the field of the plurality of persons" (OA, 224). Ricoeur sees the notion of person as an end in itself as coming to balance that of humanity in that it introduces in the formulation of the imperative the distinction between "your person" and "the person of anyone else," thus bringing plurality to the fore. He thus sees something new being said in the notions of "matter," of "object," and of "duty" as identified with those of end-in-itself. The newness expressed is what the Golden Rule says on a popular level prior to being subjected to the critique. "What indeed is it to treat humanity in my person and in the person of others as a *means* if not to exert *upon* the will of others that power which, full of restraint in the case of influence, is unleashed in all the forms that violence takes, culminating in torture?" (OA, 225) Both the Golden Rule and the imperative of respect for persons aim to establish reciprocity where it is lacking or infringed upon. Ricoeur makes an interesting observation, keenly noting that in Kant's *Groundwork of the Metaphysics of Morals*, autonomy (moral law) and the notion of person as an end in himself are confirmed directly in the same way. Consciousness of autonomy is a "fact of reason," the fact that morality exists; and morality exists because the person himself exists (*existiert*) as an end in himself, so that we have always known the difference between persons and things. Kant himself stresses this point: "The ground of this principle is: *Rational nature exists as an end in itself.* This is the way in which a man necessarily conceives his own existence [*sein eignes Dasein*]."[20] This is only put forward as a postulate at this point in Kant's development, and only later is its ground given in the final chapter.[21] "But since the belonging of reasonable being to the intelligible world is in itself not the object of any knowledge, it adds nothing to the connection postulated here between the status of the person and existence as an end in itself: 'By *thinking* itself into the intelligible world, practical reason does not overstep its limits in the least: it would do so only if it sought to *intuit or feel itself* into that world'"[22] (OA, 226).

From the Sense of Justice to the "Principles of Justice"

The rule of justice, as a deontological conception, can be seen in relation to the sense of justice, to belong to the ethical aim, in that the rule develops from the sense. This development requires clear justification, since, when the deontological must have recourse to the sense of justice due to the conflicts it produces, a recourse to the sense of justice must be understood (OA, 227).

With regard to the sense of justice, we have already seen that by "institutions" is meant the diverse structures of wanting to live together for secure duration, cohesion, and distinction; from which was developed the notion of distribution, which we found in the *Nichomachean Ethics* of Aristotle as distributive justice, and which concept can now be seen at the point of intersection of the ethical aim and the deontological perspective, the main thrust of these pages. The ideas of just division and just share still belong to the ethical aim under the guise of equality. Ricoeur concluded his reflections on the sense of justice by saying that it tended both toward the sense of mutual indebtedness and toward that of disinterested interest. The "normative viewpoint gives precedence to the second sense, which leans toward individualism, over the first sense which can be said to be more openly communitarian" (OA, 227).

Ricoeur considers the principle legacy of ethics to morality to lie in the very idea of the *just*, which looks both ways: in the direction of the "good" as the extension of solicitude to "each one" of the faceless members of society; and in the direction of the "legal," to such a degree does the prestige of justice appear to dissolve into that of positive law. The following pages are concerned entirely with the process of formulation of a purely deontological interpretation of justice. "The deontological approach was able to gain a foothold in the institutional domain, where the idea of justice applies only by joining with the contractualist tradition, more precisely, with the *fiction* of a social contract. . . . The aim and the function of the fiction of a contract is to separate the 'just' from the 'good,' by substituting the procedure of an imaginary deliberation for any prior commitment to an alleged common good. According to this hypothesis, it is the contractual procedure that is assumed to engender the principle or principles of justice" (OA, 228).

Ricoeur engages in a detailed reading and critique of John Rawls, *Theory of Justice*,[23] presenting the difficulties tied to this unparalleled situation in moral theory giving rise to the question of the principle of determining whether the deontological theory of justice does not in a certain way call upon the ethical sense of justice. That is, does a purely procedural conception of justice succeed in breaking all ties to a sense of justice that precedes it and accompanies it all along? Ricoeur's basic thesis is that at best, this conception provides the formalization of a sense of justice that it does not ever cease to presuppose.[24] He contends that Rawls himself admits that this procedural conception is based on an argument which rests upon a "pre-understanding of what is meant by the unjust and the just" (OA, 237). "In truth, Rawls never repudiates his ambition to give an independent proof of the truth of his principles of justice, but in a more complex way, demands for his theory what he calls a *reflective equilibrium* between the theory and our 'considered convictions' (ibid.). . . .Theoretical arguments then play the same role of examination that Kant assigned to the rule of universalization of maxims" (OA, 237).

Thus it is that the full sense of the attempt to free the deontological view of morality from the teleological perspective of ethics stands out; and, in addition, the limits of such an attempt have become clear (237–238). The deontological view is founded three times over on a principle that provides its own legitimization: autonomy in the first sphere, the positing of the person as an end in himself in the second, and the social contract in the third. And the inherent limits of such an enterprise can be seen from the increasing difficulties encountered by the sort of self-foundation presupposed by this liberation. Going back to the beginning, with the principle of autonomy, it "draws its legitimacy solely from itself, whence the difficult status, in the *Critique of Practical Reason*, of the famous "fact of reason" (OA, 238). Ricoeur considers the contract to occupy on the plane of institutions a place parallel to that of autonomy on the plane of morality. But this contract draws its legitimacy from "a fiction—a founding fiction":—"Is it because the self-foundation of the political body lacks the basic attestation from which good will and the person as end in himself draw their legitimacy?" Once the crude condition of enslavement, as well as the awareness of their own sovereignty arising from the will to live together, has been forgotten, this fiction can give the contract a place parallel to that of the principle of autonomy and of the person as an end of himself. "If now, by moving backward, we carry this doubt affecting the fiction of the contract back to the principle of autonomy, does not the latter also risk finding itself a fiction intended to compensate for forgetting the foundation of deontology in *the desire to live well with and for others in just institutions*?" (OA, 239) This is the basic critique of Kant levied here, which establishes the priority of the ethical over the moral, since the moral can be seen, as we did above, to presuppose and be founded upon the ethical desire to live will. . . . Thus, the sense of justice is presupposed. And it is to this sense of justice, and to the concrete situation of ethics, that a return must be made because of the inadequacies of the deontological to serve as an ethics by which to live. For it produces conflicts that can only be resolved by such a return to the concrete situation of judging, close to the Aristotelian phronésis, but now enlightened by the critical phase of deontology. For this deontology is not at all abrogated, but, rather, due to its shortcomings, supplemented by the recourse to the concrete situation of actions for which it is meant to legislate.

CHAPTER 11

Judging in Concrete Situations: The Equitable

FROM ETHICAL FOUNDATIONS
TO MORAL PRINCIPLES AND BACK AGAIN

The last of Ricoeur's three chapters on "little ethics" (OA, 190), in which solicitude plays a central role, returns to an Aristotelian practical wisdom (*phronésis*), purified and filtered through Kant's moral obligation.[1] Between the naive phronésis and the critical *phronésis* of this last phase is the required passage through the region of Kantian obligation and duty. These demand that what ought not be, not be, that is, evil; and that the suffering inflicted on humans by the other humans be abolished. This level, however, leads to intense conflicts on several fronts in the return to actions in a concrete situation, indicating a serious inadequacy of deontology. On this return, Ricoeur considers it to be "through public debate, friendly discussion and shared conviction that moral judgment in situation is formed" (OA, 290–291).

And, due to these conflictual situations, that is, due to the conflicts arising out of the deontological ethics in its path to concrete actions, practical wisdom must now return to the initial ethical framework of moral judgment in situation, to the aim of the good life with and for others in just institutions. Such a passage from the Kantian general maxims of action to moral judgment in concrete situation simply requires the "reawakening of the resources of singularity inherent in the aim of the true life" (OA, 240). Failure to pass through these conflicts that shake us lose from a strict allegiance to a morality constituted only by principles, and failure to have such a recourse back to the concrete situation and to a critical *phronésis*, allow us to succumb to the seduction of a moral situationism and arbitrariness. Conviction thus takes on a central role in judgment in situation. On this level of the concrete situation, if moral judgment develops the dialectic to be brought forth, conviction is the only way out, in Ricoeur's view. Conviction of moral judgment thus shows that there is no need to posit a constitution of a "third agency" (OA, 240) to be added to the ethical aim and the moral norm. We must now focus on the conflicts arising from the moral level and on the critical conviction entailed in judging in the concrete situation. Moral judgment in situation and its convictions are what Ricoeur calls practical wisdom, reminiscent of Aristotle's book six on practical wisdom and deliberation.

In first turning to the place of conflict arising from the turn to concrete action in moral philosophy, Ricoeur takes up first the pre-philosophical or non-philosophical contribution to practical wisdom from Greek tragedy, using as an exemplary case the Greek play, *Antigone*. Such tragic wisdom, he finds, brings practical wisdom back "to the test of moral judgment in situation alone" (OA, 241). It is from the recognition of the aporia-producing limit experiences in tragedy that tragic wisdom can instruct practical wisdom. In the case of Antigone herself, she narrows the laws to focus specifically on funeral demands, invoking themes to ground her conviction. Thus in a way she points to the human character of every institution. The legacy of tragedy, however, is less a teaching than a conversion of the manner of looking, which ethics needs to appropriate. The final word or appeal to practical wisdom is to deliberate well (OA, 246).

Before ending this enlightening section on tragedy, Ricoeur points out that tragedy does not teach moral philosophy as much as it evokes a gap between tragic wisdom and moral wisdom by highlighting the conflicts as aporia in the concrete situation of moral life. It thus "condemns the person of practice to reorient action," indeed, a risky business, responding to tragic wisdom (OA, 247). The facing of conflicts inevitable in the moral life, exposed by tragic wisdom, brings about the transition from catharsis to conviction.

What makes ethical conflicts inevitable for Ricoeur lies not only in the one-sidedness of the characters, but also in the one-sidedness of the moral principles confronting the complexities of concrete life (OA, 249). In response to these conflicts in action, Ricoeur attempts to have recourse to the ethical ground in concrete situations of judgment giving rise to the wisdom of judgment in situations. And this is what sets him on his course to outline the various conflicts arising within the principles of deontological moral philosophy.

CONFLICT AND INSTITUTION

Ricoeur begins this discussion by invoking again the three categories behind the three formulations of the categorical imperative: the universal self, the plurality of persons, and the institutional environment. He begins with the third, thus moving in a backward direction, turning first to the institution and thus to the concrete situation of ethics or to *Sittlichkeit*. Such a backward movement allows him to bring to the fore the most intense conflict on the level of autonomy at the end of the treatment. This is the cornerstone of Kantian morality, as Kant himself defended it.

But beginning on the level of institution makes it necessary for us to revisit the rule of justice in that it already contains the seeds of conflict in the equivocal character of its notion of distribution. In exposing this equivocalness, Ricoeur poses the question: "Does it aim at separating out the interests of mutually disinterested individuals or at reinforcing the bond of cooperation?" (OA, 250). The words "share" and "sharing" carry the same equivocalness, in that, for instance, they each relate to what is mine and not yours, as well as to a cooperative sharing in a greater whole. In this context, Ricoeur employs the Hegelian notion of right in relation to the actualization of freedom to counter the Kantian view of right that is limited to separating what is mine from what is another's. Ricoeur buys into Hegel's project in the *Philosophy of Right* to the extent that it opposes political atomism. It is only in institutions that distinctively human capacities and predispositions distinguishing human action as such can come to maturity. Thus, for Ricoeur, there is an obligation to support and serve these very institutions in order for the development to continue (OA, 254). In this direction of Ricoeur's thought the central question is whether or not there is a different and higher obligation to serve the state than that of the rule of justice or the sense of justice. Ricoeur certainly, and correctly, I might add, separates himself from the Hegelian ontology of *Geist* as rendering the state as something "capable of thinking of itself by itself" (OA, 255). In this way, the treatment of concrete moral life (*Sittlichkeit*) does not legitimate a judging agency that is superior to moral consciousness. One does not have to consider institutions, that is, the state, to have a self-knowledge and spirituality distinct from that of individuals just to admit that they are derived from previously existing institutions. This does not mitigate the impact of Hegel's condemnation of a moral consciousness that understands itself as a "supreme tribunal," in ignorance of the *Sittlichkeit* that embodies the "spirit" of a people. When the morality of a community (Nazi Germany, for instance) becomes perverted, and permeates the spirit of a people, the real spirit of the people "takes refuge" in the moral consciousness of a small number of individuals. Any conflict between the moral consciousness and the spirit of the people testifies to the tragedy of action considered above in the context of *Antigone*. Ricoeur, however, finds that investigating political practice is the best way to counter or demystify the Hegelian state, and, in the process, preserving some of the richness of the Hegelian analysis. Thus he turns first to the conflicts given rise to in political practice, showing the importance of the relation between power and domination, which, when misunderstood or misused, leads to the emergence of conflicts. It is the virtue of justice that has been considered to balance this relation, keeping domination at bay by shared power. He sees this endless task as central to democracy.

Ricoeur considers the gap between power and domination, constitutive of the political, to be the base of the definition of the political as the "set of organized practices relating to the distribution of political power, better termed domination" (OA, 257). Proper to the spheres of these practices are three radical dimensions of conflict. The first of these levels of conflict entails the ordering of priorities in establishing or coming to agreement about the primary goods. In this context, that of a "state of law" (OA, 258), deliberation coincides with public discussion. And here the judgment in situation takes the form of free elections in Western democracies. Equivalent to "good deliberation" recommended by the chorus in *Antigone*, as seen above, is the enlightened judgment that hopefully arises from public debate (259). This is the manner in which democracies deal with the conflicts arising from practices. Thus, a decision can be reached, but not in such a way as to be conclusive. It is an ongoing process.

The second radical level of conflict in the spheres of political practice leads to debate concerning the ends of good government in the choice of a democratic constitution. This entails a long-term discussion, not reducible to an ideology, as an "integral part of the political mediation through which we aspire to a full life, to the 'good life'" (OA, 258), and expressing a certain form of state as preferable. That is why it is encountered, according to Ricoeur, along the return path from morality to ethics within the framework of political judgment in situation. Since the end of good government sanctions one set of values at the expense of another, it is perhaps impossible to arrive at such a point definitively. They are undecidable. Yet the choice of a good constitution is an example of judgment in situation, at a particular time and place, when such a constitution is in demand.

The third level of conflicts arising out of political practice, bringing to a high pitch the difference between power and domination, entails the process of legitimation of a democracy under its various guises. Ricoeur contends that this legitimation is a more radical choice than that of a democratic constitution, for here there is some basis in the will of the people, wanting to live together, to legitimate the political practice or government by some latent, tacit, or implicit contract agreement, revealing in an acute way the relation between domination and power. Although the basis of democracy involves a certain indeterminacy, there are still reasons that such a democracy is preferred over a totalitarian system. Thus, although the foundation of its legitimacy is uncertain, its reasons are constitutive of the desire to live together. And one of the ways of becoming aware of these reasons is the projection of what Ricoeur calls the "fiction of the social contract." In response to the legitimation crisis, Ricoeur contends that there "is nothing better to offer, in reply to the legitimation crisis . . . , than the memory of an the intersection in the public space of appearance of the traditions that make room for tolerance and pluralism, not out of concessions to external pressures, but out of inner conviction, even if this is late in coming" (OA, 260). Such inner conviction can be seen to be in relation to a rather public *phronésis* "resembling the debate itself" (OA, 261). At this point Ricoeur invokes the Aristotelian notion of equity as an instance of *phronésis* addressing the singular in contrast to the universality of the law, thus acting as a corrective of the law. He tenuously ties this notion of equity to the legitimation crisis by seeing it as applied in the public debate and ensuing decision making as the only agent qualified to correct the legitimation crisis. Equity can now be seen to be another name for the sense of justice "when the latter traverses the hardship and conflicts resulting from the application of the *rule* of justice" (OA, 262).

CONFLICT AND RESPECT

We come to the second category behind the second formulation of the categorical imperative, the plurality of persons, putting into stark contrast and eventual conflict this plurality and the universality of the law. In the formulation, so act as to treat humanity in your own person as well as in the person of others, always as an end and not merely as a means, Ricoeur sees this conflict first emerging from the tension that can be drawn out between the universalist version of the imperative centered on the idea of humanity as universal, and the pluralist version centered on the idea of persons as ends in themselves. Kant sees no opposition to the extent that humanity designates the dignity by reason of which persons deserve respect, in spite of their plurality. The conflict and tension arise between the universality of the rules as such and the solicitude toward others. This conflict results from the incompatibility between that universality and the otherness of persons. Because of the multiplicity of rules generated by the categorical imperative, the universalism of these rules can collide with the demands of otherness inherent in solicitude.

One of the better examples for reflection in this context is that of the duty to keep one's promises. The duty results from the universalization of the general maxim, which itself arises from experiences of life, becoming a subjective maxim to be universalized.[2] It is clear that the "other" is taken fully into account only on the return path from universalization to application in the concrete situation, and not on the first path toward universalization. This second path entails the test of circumstances and consequences, where a face, a countenance, of genuine otherness of persons can make each one irreplaceable, singular, and thus an exception. In thus reflecting on the keeping or not of one's promises, as true and false promises, the focus is taken away from concern for personal integrity and redirected to the rule of reciprocity of the Golden Rule, "since the latter takes into account the initial dissymmetry of agent and patient, with all the effects of violence that result from this dissymmetry" (OA, 265). For Ricoeur, a false promise is already a figure of the evil in using language, something about which he has written a great deal over the years.[3]

Ricoeur considers the obligation to keep one's promises to be constituted by the principle of fidelity, the dialogical structure of which is the place for grafting the conflicts of duty. Also, this dialogical structure consists in a dual or dyadic structure involving two persons, the one who promises and must keep it, and the one to whom it is made. Besides this dyadic structure, there is the plural structure arising from adding a witness before whom the promise is made, and, behind the witness, the language that one pledges to safeguard. This plural structure renders the promise indistinguishable from the rule of justice. Thus, we must limit the consideration here to the dyadic structure of the fidelity in making a promise. And, it must be mentioned, this dyadic structure is often overlooked, as with Kant, who sees only the person involved with the testing of the maxim.[4] Ricoeur emphasizes the role of self-constancy belonging to ipse identity that is involved in keeping one's promise, highlighting the "dialogic-dyadic structure" of this self-constancy in its moral significance. Rather than consider this form of self-constancy as closed in on oneself, a problem confronted and solved by Gabriel Marcel, Ricoeur, following Marcel, sees that it is to the other that I wish to be faithful, here referred to as availability[5] in the Marcelian sense of *disponibilité*. Thus it is seen that availability is the key that opens self-constancy to the dialogic structure established by the Golden Rule, bringing reciprocity back into the picture, so that the other can count on me. This "counting on" connects self-constancy to the principle of reciprocity founded in solicitude. Failure to keep one's promises betrays both the other's expectation and the institution that mediates the mutual trust of speaking subjects. This analysis of keeping and failing to keep promises reveals the huge gap in Kant's analysis, which ignores the direction from the rule to the concrete situation of application, and the conflicts between the very rule and the respect to the other person as such. Ricoeur's suggestion is one of the finest in ethical theory today: "Practical wisdom consists in inventing conduct that will best satisfy the exception required by solicitude, by betraying the rule to the smallest extent possible" (OA, 269). Respect for the other in the concrete situation might require a course of action that would contradict the absolute demand of duty to the law, but the respect for the person of the other takes precedence, not to the extent of defying the law, but simply in recognizing the exception in this case required by a higher value.[6]

The respect considered in these various cases as examples of conflict refers to the solicitude toward the otherness of persons, including potential persons. This very solicitude is precisely what gives rise to the conflicts, but now it is no longer the naive solicitude considered in the previous chapters, but rather a critical solicitude that has been tested both by the moral conditions of respect and the conflicts generated by that very test. This critical solicitude is the form of practical reason in dealing with interpersonal relations (OA, 273).

CONFLICT AND AUTONOMY

Since autonomy is the pivot of Kantian moral philosophy in that it defines the moral self, the conflicts in this realm take on a special significance. And it must be remembered that it is this deontological morality itself that leads to these conflicts in the context of application to the concrete situation of institutions, persons, and autonomy of persons. In the present case of autonomy, it is the confrontation between the universality proper to the rules in relation to the principle of morality and the positive values in the concrete situation and context of community in which these rules are supposedly applied or realized (OA, 274). It should not be surprising that in this context of the conflicts in the realm of autonomy, we find the focal point of the conflicts in the other two realms discussed above, since the demand for universalization "finds its privileged field of manifestation in interpersonal relations governed by the principle of respect owed to persons and in institutions governed by the rule of justice" (OA, 285).

Ricoeur proposes a threefold revision of the Kantian heritage to bring out the full force of this antagonism between the principle and the concrete context of values. In this context he picks up on three aporias at the heart of autonomy of the self-legislation in Kantian moral philosophy. First, there is the self-affection proper to the will giving to itself the moral law from reason, the *factum rationis*, undeniably entailing a certain receptivity and passivity to the will; second, there is the affection by the otherness of motive entailing a certain passivity, even though this motive of respect is brought about by pure reason itself in relation to the law (OA, 275); and third, there is the radical affection of the propensity to evil, "which, without destroying our predisposition toward the good, affects our capacity to act out of duty" (OA, 275). The most important aspect of this threefold decentering of autonomy is the insight that autonomy can no longer be considered self-sufficient. "Dependency as 'externality,' related to the dialogic condition of autonomy, in a sense takes over from dependency as [interiority] revealed by these three aporias" (OA, 275). Autonomy can now be seen as dependent on heteronomy in the threefold sense of other mentioned above. And this threefold sense of otherness joins the dialogic otherness making autonomy part and parcel of and dependent on both the rule of justice and the rule of reciprocity, bringing to the fore the other stages of Ricoeur's reversal of order regarding the categories underlying the three formulations of the categorical imperative. This critique and revision of Kant can be seen to fill out the critique considered in part I regarding Kantian practical reason, a critique that in large measure Ricoeur was seen in the last chapter to have in common with Levinas.

Ricoeur, in developing this level of conflict, attempts to reformulate the ethics of argumentation in an effort to center it on the antagonism between it and convention. He proposes to substitute for this antagonism the dialectic between argumentation and conviction having a practical outcome of arbitrating moral judgment in situation (OA, 287). It is in this way that argumentation becomes the "critical agency operating *at the heart* of convictions" thus "assuming the task not of eliminating but of carrying them to the level of 'considered convictions,' in what Rawls calls a *reflective equilibrium*" (OA, 288). Conviction is so important here because it expresses the positions "from which result the meanings, interpretations, and evaluations relating to the multiple goods that occupy the scale of praxis, from practices and their immanent goods, passing by way of life plans, life histories, and including the conceptions humans have, alone or together, of what a complete life would be" (OA, 288). It is in this context that we discuss and reinforce articulations between deontology and teleology, finding its highest and most fragile expression in "*the reflective equilibrium between the ethics of argumentation and considered convictions*" (OA, 289). The notion of "universals in context or of potential or inchoate universals is" a notion that accounts for this reflective equilibrium sought here between universality and historicity. A discussion in which convictions are elevated above conventions allows alleged universals to become universals recognized by all. This allows the conclusion that Ricoeur has been pursuing, that one of the faces of practical wisdom is "the art of conversation, in which the ethics of argumentation is put to the test in the conflict of convictions" (OA, 290). This completes our journey in the effort to show how *phronésis* becomes critical, as indicated in the beginning of this chapter.

CONCLUSION

My working hypothesis for this entire study has been that, by understanding deconstruction as a philosophy of limit and taking into account its positive element, it is possible to advance an alternative, more viable ethics at the limit-boundary that both takes into account deconstructive reading and passes beyond it. And it is precisely the tension between limit and extension that allows a revived ethics, cast against the backdrop of Kantian limits and the extensions beyond them, to take place within the polarity between ethical foundations and moral principle of obligation. In this context, it has been necessary to confront deconstruction's critique of any such philosophy as a closure that requires deconstruction. We have, indeed, found that, at least in a sense, this very critique of closure can be turned back on deconstruction itself, and that the heart of deconstruction as a philosophy of limit essentially entails a misunderstanding of time, sign, and trace.

Further, as part of our hypothesis about a better alternative path, we have found it necessary to make clear the latent contradiction in deconstruction between the positive element, which we have stressed throughout this work, and the negative element that needs critique: the positive element reintroduces with force the "other"; but its account of the flux of time, of sign, of consciousness, and of language eliminates any possibility of experiencing or accessing that other. For such a deconstructive consideration, leading to alterity, is much like the modern reductionistic account of sense experience in cognition, as mentioned above. Against this reductionistic view, the philosophical return to lived experience brought back the holistic human perspective.

The positive element of deconstruction mentioned throughout these chapters must not obscure its failure as a philosophy of limit that has been brought to light. This sense of limit serves to check any structure and any sense, making it recoil onto the abyss from which it arises. And it allows obligation and responsibility to the Other to emerge, keeping the deconstructive process open at the closure. We must keep in mind, however, that we have maintained both a yes as well as a no to deconstruction: the yes to alterity, to the "other" to which any phenomenological heritage must be opened; and the no to any return to a reduction to a naive view of time, sign, and language that this position requires in all its articulations. It is precisely this failure of postmodern deconstruction to give a viable account of time and the living present, sign and trace, and philosophy at the boundary of reason as context for a viable ethics that has prompted us to turn to the philosophy of Paul Ricoeur as an alternative, since all along the way his philosophy has been seen as a corrective force. We find his ethicomoral philosophy to be fundamentally attuned to the whole western tradition and sensitive to the ethicomoral dimensions of human life. It likewise includes in its sweep the dimensions of the political, the legal, and the religious. His challenging writings on ethics provide the most viable integration of an ethical framework and moral principle in ethics today, thus setting the stage for facing up to problems in ethics today.

It is precisely Derrida's view of the living present and time that has been seen to render it unable to sustain trace in contrast to Ricoeur's view of the living present and historical time that supports trace in its full sense. These contrasting roles of trace highlight, in spite of a positive commonness, the vast chasm that separates the views of Derrida and Ricoeur. This chasm stretches even to all-pervasive metaphysical differences that require a decision in favor of one at the expense of the other kind of philosophizing at the limit, with each able to accuse the other of closure.

Thus, Ricoeur's alternative to Derrida's semiological reductionism, and the flux of time as discrete on which it is founded, provide a viable position that does not succumb to the facile distinction of Saussure between *la langue* and *la parole*, nor to Derrida's collapse of signs to the relations of differences within the system and the reduction of language to the play of *différance*. Rather, Ricoeur is able adequately to account for duration and continuity in the living present as the basis for language as discourse and for trace. And Ricoeur's account of the temporal context for understanding language undercuts Derrida's pseudo-alternatives of signs or presence, for the temporal span of the present is neither pure identity nor pure alterity. The present, as thickened by retention and protention, "intends" the future in light of the past. Since the very function of the present is to mean and the very nature of presence requires signs, language and signs are inseparably intertwined with time. Thus, his theory of language as essentially discourse, his distinctions between words and signs and between signs and sentences, in the overall contexts of the new unity of language in the semantics of the sentence, re-establishes some faith in philosophical analysis as having something worthwhile to say about something, even when it deals with an interpretation of language, of texts, and of ethical praxis. While the positioning of signs, or the play of *différance*, can yield a productivity of some kind of meaning, it is not the replacement of the semantic dimension of language as primary. Syntax of any kind exists for the semantic. To invert this is to distort language, to make a mockery of meaning, to reduce meaning to an empty shell, as well as to render meaningless any attempt to communicate this message of inversion.

Considering such limits of sign, trace, and time, it is not surprising that with the loss of the semantic, there is likewise a loss of ethics. Ricoeur's ethics, by contrast, is an attempt to interarticulate an ethics of the good and a morality of right, bringing the Aristotelian and Kantian traditions together by his critique of Kant and providing a framework from the teleology of desire. And in doing so, he does not jettison the personal relation. Rather, he leans heavily on Levinas' view of the face to face, and the personal relation.

In dwelling further on the contemporary conversation regarding ethics in the context of the dialogue between Levinas and Derrida, several distinctive accounts of deconstructive ethics can be seen. In our treatments in the chapters above, we proceeded from an analysis and critique of Caputo's poetics of obligation and moved to the consideration of the fuller current of deconstruction and ethics. It has been seen that Caputo, Cornell, and Critchley all, attuned to the Derrida-Levinas dialogue, put obligation at the heart of deconstruction, but Caputo, following Derrida's hesitance, rejects ethics in favor of a poetics of obligation, while Critchley and Cornell, following Levinas, hang onto the term in their own rejection of virtually the same ethics that Caputo rejects. For my part, first recognizing a positive contribution of deconstruction, I have proceeded to a further extension of ethics following Ricoeur, who has been seen to be likewise influenced by Levinas, but in a way entirely different from deconstruction. For Ricoeur, there is an opening back to the tradition, rather than a cutting away toward a deconstructive clotural reading. We have seen that this obligation or duty at the heart of the deconstructive enterprise is not something to be lost sight of, even if it requires an extension beyond the usual sense of ethics. But is it not to be seen as self sufficient. And it is tied to something which would best be brought into a more positive frame of philosophical mind.

Critchley's argument, then, would put an ethical duty at the heart of the deconstructive enterprise: "Rather, I hope to demonstrate that the pattern of reading produced in the deconstruction of—mostly, but by no means exclusively—philosophical texts has an ethical structure: deconstruction 'is' ethical; or, to formulate the same thought less ontologically . . . deconstruction takes place (*a lieu*) ethically, or there is duty in deconstruction (*Il y a du devoir dans la déconstruction*)."[7] Critchley's main point about Levinas' ethics in relation to a more traditionally oriented ethics, even such as that of Ricoeur, is that it reveals a level of ethical experience that is more primordial than, and is presupposed by, those ethical considerations that attempt to reflect on maxims or judgments in relation to social action and civic duty, and that are derived and distinct from that primordial level. Levinas himself does not see his task as one of constructing an ethics. He says, rather, that "I only try to seek its meaning (sens)."[8] This primacy for Levinas means the face-to-face personal relation.

All of the commentators of deconstruction considered here, Caputo, Cornell, and Critchley, report on Derrida's ethics by entering the discussion between Derrida and Levinas. It seems that Derrida has dialogued with and deconstructed Levinas' ethics in coming to a deconstructive ethics of his own, if the term "ethics" can even be retained. Caputo, in his *Against Ethics*, has opted to stress the "other" to ethics. Ethics presupposes the very metaphysics that deconstruction must deconstruct, which requires the deconstruction of even Heideggian "originary ethos." Yet, although they agree for the most part on the essential points toward an ethics of deconstruction, Cornell and Critchley do not abrogate the term "ethics" or "ethical." They simply transform the word, or deconstruct it. Further, for all of them, and for Derrida, this sense of ethics at the heart of the deconstructive enterprise is a philosophy of limit, but not necessarily a critical philosophy, which itself would need deconstructing.

All three of the authors mentioned above introduce a new sense of ethics at the heart of the deconstructive enterprise. For Drucilla Cornell this ethical impulse has been seen at the heart of her interpretation of this enterprise as a philosophy of limit.[9] As has been seen, Caputo, deconstructing the ethics and the metaphysics on which it is built, reveals the poetic obligation at the heart of deconstruction. And Critchley sees a primordial importance to ethics at the heart of deconstructive or clotural reading. And for all three, it is the role of Levinas' reflections on the ethical relation that takes on significance, especially in the light of the discussion between him and Derrida. Levinas, however, by contrast, does not enclose all this in terms of language taken to be a system of signs, with each sign functioning as a trace. Caputo seems to address this directly when he discusses the sense of self in terms of personal pronouns. One can deconstruct ethics, arriving thereby at an ethical demand placed on deconstruction itself. That is precisely what emerges in raising the question of ethics in the context of deconstruction understood as a philosophy of limit: that there is some serious and sincere ethical obligation or responsibility at the heart of the enterprise, already envisioned by Derrida, especially as he deconstructs Levinas. We have already demonstrated the failures in the context of deconstruction's positive contribution mentioned throughout our studies, as well as the extent to which we can even speak of this as ethics.

We have found it necessary to invoke the ethicomoral philosophy of Paul Ricoeur that takes account of these positive elements of postmodern deconstruction, but does not succumb to its failures. Paul Ricoeur's recent ethicomoral project, culminating in three of the last four chapters of *Oneself as Another*,[10] and extended in *Le Just*,[11] consists in polarizing the ethical philosophies of Aristotle and Kant, and integrating a critically adjusted version of each into a unique and encompassing ethical framework. Within this entire enterprise he likewise develops many opposing polarities that he similarly proceeds to interarticulate and appropriate into a coherent position. One such opposition is that between the exteriority at the heart of the ethical philosophy of Emmanuel Levinas and the interiority of Husserl's transcendental philosophy. And within this context he appropriates elements of Heidegger's existential analysis of Dasein to flesh out the way of a satisfactory interarticulation, from which he develops his own position.

Although Ricoeur's critique of Levinas has been seen perhaps to be a bit too severe, once placed in his overall project of an ethicomoral foundation and principle, one can see how much of Levinas' position he retains, precisely what he rejects. And one can also see a misunderstanding of Levinas. It was seen that a fundamental dimension that Ricoeur wants to supply to Levinas' own position is already contained in it, even though it is in need of further development. This then becomes the context for adjusting Ricoeur's interpretation in deference to Levinas, but without any need to alter Ricoeur's own position. Thus, after investigating Ricoeur's critique of Levinas and briefly defending Levinas' own position, I attempted to work toward interarticulating the positions of Ricoeur and Levinas, incorporating both the solitude of interiority and the solicitude that Ricoeur incorporates from Heidegger. This leads to the second part of my thesis in reading the relation between Levinas and Ricoeur, arising from the treatment of the first: that Ricoeur, precisely by incorporating an essential element from Levinas, provides a viable ethics as an alternative to postmodern deconstruction. For Ricoeur has constantly adhered to the need in ethics precisely for Levinas' "face to face," even contending that ethics has its beginning in the second person recognition of the other's will and freedom. And, on the other side, Ricoeur says that he has not ever assumed Levinas' ontology of totality, showing how Levinas restricts identity to the point that it "results that the self, not distinguished from the I, is not taken in the sense of the self-designation of a subject of discourse, action, narrative, or ethical commitment" (OA, 335). It is here with the notion of totality that the difficulty between them was seen. And Levinas' notion of totality in the context of the identity of the self needed to be extended, just as Ricoeur's interpretation of Levinas regarding the place within interiority for an encounter with the Other was adjusted.

In addition, by retaining Levinas' element of responsibility within Ricoeur's ethicomoral integration, Ricoeur's place of receptivity was able to be integrated with an element of Levinas' view of totality, the latent exteriority. But this must preclude any subordination of Levinas' exteriority of the face and infinity to the totality, which he so consistently and rigorously avoids, and which would falsify or remove precisely the uniqueness of his view of alterity. In accepting the role of solicitude in human existence, Ricoeur has developed a place within interiority that really allows a response to the face of the Other. And in doing so, he has accounted for a central, indeed, the central point of Levinas, that a breakthrough—a breakout—of the "totality" of traditional philosophy is necessary for there to be a face-to-face encounter. This is precisely what Ricoeur has done in interarticulating the two movements of Husserl and Levinas. And incorporating this alterity of the Other is not entirely alien to Ricoeur's previous work, as seen in earlier chapters, for he has embraced similar elements within his recent philosophy. For instance, in his development of time in *Time and Narrative*, he has focused upon and accounted for the alterity of cosmic time. So too here, the exteriority of the Other is outside the domain of the Heideggerian or Husserlian world, and of Levinas' totality. This is precisely the element of Levinas that must not be jeopardized in our present expansion of Levinas' view in order to clarify how a relation is possible within interiority. And, I daresay, Ricoeur seems to want to embrace this face to face in indicating it as the place where ethics really begins. And it is precisely in accepting the alterity of the Other that he has taken a positive element in agreement with Levinas, a point that even deconstruction likes. But this affinity with deconstruction cannot be exaggerated, for, in this context of even a mitigated deconstruction, Levinas' account of the ethical relation is lost to the deconstructive process, so that what remains is only the obligation of deconstructing. And nothing of Ricoeur's undertaking as a project of ethicomoral philosophy, except this same alterity that he shares with Levinas, can survive this deconstructive process.

Hence, by bringing the opposing movements of Heidegger and Levinas together, Ricoeur is able, as already mentioned, to adhere to a positive contribution of postmodern deconstruction without succumbing to the allure of its plunge into the abyss, forsaking the priority of the enterprise of reason. Thus, by focusing on both Levinas' and Ricoeur's critiques of Heidegger, we have been able to find the common ground of alterity between them, which, in spite of the distance that separates them, allows an integration that supports Ricoeur's ethicomoral position.

Ricoeur's use and adjustments of Levinas in a dialectic with Heidegger-Husserl provides an ethics of responsibility and obligation as an alternative to postmodern deconstructive writings on/against ethics. In this, he has a basic rapport with the position of Levinas, which can be seen from what has been said. Due to his critique of and expansion on the Kantian philosophy, Ricoeur is able to interarticulate the ethical as encompassing the aim of an accomplished life with the moral as encompassing the actualization of the ethical aim in norms that are characterized at once by "claims to universality and by an effect of constraint" (OA, 170). Following from his critique of Kant's practical reason and freedom, and from the expansion of Kantian themes, Ricoeur is able to turn in a positive way to a priority of the teleological, putting into place the evaluative element of Aristotelian ethics to subtend the moral imperative of Kant, Levinas, and deconstruction. As to the positive element of deconstruction, Ricoeur's recent dwelling on alterity of cosmic time and his addressing the alterity of the Other of Levinas in the tension that he sees between Husserlian inwardness and Levinas' exteriority reveals the alterity which the face to face manifests beyond interiority. He has clearly appropriated a certain positive element from Levinas in terms of the alterity of the other, the epiphany of the face, and its assignment of responsibility. Ricoeur and Levinas, against the so-called deconstructive ethics that deconstructs the ethical relation, both invoke the face to face of the personal other at the heart of ethical response. Ricoeur's rich and full treatment of ethicomoral philosophy, in part because of his positive relation to Levinas, emerges as a contemporary ethics capable of addressing concrete ethicomoral problems and conflicts in everyday life in contrast to deconstructive ethics.

As stated just above, the positive element of deconstruction must not obscure its failure to offer any real extension beyond the limit. It only deconstructs. And it allows obligation and responsibility to the Other to emerge. By contrast, Ricoeur's manner of dealing with the "Other" of deconstruction is through indirect language, such as symbols, metaphors, and narrative; and through historical time, including calendar time, generation, and the trace. And this ethics at the limit takes limit to be boundary and the poetic narrative, as having determinative status in the Kantian sense, due to Ricoeur's overcoming the distinction between determinative and reflective judgments, thus allowing ethical action creatively to express new possibilities for existence. Is not this a ray of hope even for those individuals who are marginalized? Does it not do justice to their plight without making the suffering and evil, the violence and the injustice the only consideration for ethics, as deconstructive does? And does this not afford more than merely doing violence to the structures that are? Certainly such a poetic narrative and its

244 ETHICS AND POSTMODERNITY

role in ethical action does not succumb to the dominance of structures since it is essentially poetic. And finally, the effect of such a monumental event as the Holocaust should not be a proclamation that "it happens," as at least some deconstructionists say, but rather, a vehement "never again," with all the hope that this entails, in spite of the realization that it could happen again. At the end of our whole project of philosophy at the limit of reason, with constant reference to ethics and postmodernity, we must assess the limits of what we have found.

In this final point of the conclusion of this lengthy study I want to draw out the dimensions of certain unresolved paradoxes, especially concerning the limit that has been the focus of this study, and imagination. For limit and imagination are at the very core of any philosophy today, as has become evident in this study proposing Ricoeur's ethicomoral philosophy, taking account of certain deconstructive elements, as viable for our times. And, although we have shown this adequately, the fuller implications of limit and imagination, due to these studies, have emerged as requiring further investigation. For philosophy today at the limit/boundary intimately entails the imagination. The status of the second element of limit based on Peirce's secondness is often interpreted as an idealism because of the proximity between his secondness and Kant's noumenal realm. How is this limit really two directional? Further, Ricoeur's view of indirect expressions, limit experiences, limit expressions, and limit concepts, seems to entail some difficulty, as does the view of deconstruction as a philosophy of limit. For deconstruction has been seen not to offer any viable view of extensions beyond Kant's limit, in spite of its recourse to Peirce's secondness. Its view of limit as maintaining the process of deconstructing as a dynamic process is a further contribution. It is not, however, viable within deconstruction's view of language and the living present. Thus we are left with the need to further develop a view of philosophy at the boundary/limit that is able adequately to address the overcoming of the phenomenal-noumenal distinction, as supposedly evinced in twentieth-century phenomenology and pragmatism. This study has successfully gone the distance, but has raised to a heightened level the guideline of philosophy at the limit/boundary.

And if this problem or aporia is to be further pursued, it has become apparent that the role of the imagination is paramount in continuing to pursue the course of thought as a philosophical activity at the limit. For, as seen in the two decades after Kant's publication of his third *Critique*, with romanticism and idealism, leading ultimately to Hegel, it is precisely how one addresses the role of the imagination that allows a viable possibility of philosophical discourse for our future. Thus the thematic aporias of the next two studies have come into focus, and the present work has become the first word, and not the last, on these issues.

NOTES

PREFACE

1. Patrick L. Bourgeois, "The Limit of Ricoeur's Hermeneutic of Existence," in Lewis Edwin Hahn, editor, *The Philosophy of Paul Ricoeur: The Library of Living Philosophers*, vol. 22 (Chicago and La Salle, Ill.: Open Court, 1995), pp. 549–567.

2. There is an ambiguity in the way in which we use the term limit, limit-boundary, and boundary. Some deconstructionists, as we will see in the first chapter, speak of a philosophy of limit, but in the strict Kantian context, this is more precisely called a philosophy of boundary or bounds. Hence the title of this present study. Until we treat the strict Kantian sense of these terms, I will take some latitude in using them but attempt to remain faithful in most cases to Kant's strict distinction. The notion of limit for Kant is that within which something is circumscribed or contained. One can stand at this limit (*die Schranke*) as a boundary (*die Grenze*), which has a positive dimension of the "beyond" added to limit as *die Schranke*. Thus, from the vantage point of the limit as boundary one can advert to both sides, while the limit confines one to what is within the limit. For Kant the limit, in the sense of boundary, can be transgressed, but not as knowledge. It must be pointed out, however, that, although Kant is extremely consistent in his use of *die Schranke* and *die Grenze*, his translators are not. And sometimes, the translation from French to English has allowed Ricoeur's references to *Grenze* to be translated as limit instead of boundary. Thus, to some extent, this ambiguity will be present in the first few chapters of this work.

3. The recent development of Paul Ricoeur's ethical position is the best model of this for our enterprise.

4. Kevin J. Vanhoozer, "Philosophical Antecedents to Ricoeur's Time and Narrative," in *On Paul Ricoeur*, edited by David Wood (London and New York: Routledge, 1991), and *Biblical Narrative in the Philosophy of Paul Ricoeur: A Study in Hermeneutics and Theology* (Cambridge: Cambridge University Press, 1990).

5. It will remain, however, for a second volume of this present work to fully investigate the broader role of the Kantian productive imagination, its appropriation by his immediate followers and its evolving development in the twentieth century, with an intense study of its significance on the contemporary scene.

6. Martin Heidegger, *Kant and the Problem of Metaphysics*, translated by James S. Churchill (Bloomington: Indiana University Press, 1962).

7. In the context of Levinas' work, it should be assumed that when "Other" is capitalized, it translates the French "*autrui*," the personal Other; and when "other" is not capitalized, it translates the French "*autre*." [See the translator's footnote in *Totality and Infinity*: Emmanuel Levinas, *Totality and Infinity* (Pittsburgh: Duquesne University Press, 1969), p. 24.] In quoting other authors in their use of Levinas' works, I have followed their capitalization, but they seem to follow this note also.

8. Simon Chritchley, *The Ethics of Deconstruction* (Oxford: Blackwell, 1992), p. xi.

9. Chritchley, *The Ethics of Deconstruction*, p. 2.

10. Emmanuel Levinas, *Ethique et infini*, p. 85, quoted in Critchley, *The Ethics of Deconstruction*, p. 4.

11. Drucilla Cornell, *The Philosophy of Limit*, pp. 8–9.

12. Paul Ricoeur, *Oneself as Another*, translated by Kathleen Blamey (Chicago: The University of Chicago Press, 1992). Henceforth, *Oneself as Another* will be referred to within the text as OA, and likewise in the notes.

13. Paul Ricoeur, *Le Just* (Paris: Editions Esprit, 1995).

14. It is my contention, not to be developed here, that Ricoeur's ethics, instructed by Aristotle, Kant, and the entire tradition of philosophy, even postmodern deconstruction, proffers a very viable contemporary ethics. This would contrast his work with that of postmodern deconstruction especially that of Derrida. Some recent secondary literature to which this relates by contrast are the following: John D. Caputo, *Against Ethics* (Bloomington: Indiana University Press, 1993); Drucilla Cornell, The *Philosophy of Limit* (New York and London: Routledge, 1992); and Simon Critchley, *Deconstructive Ethics: Derrida and Levinas* (Oxford: Blackwell, 1992). These works all respond to the dialogue between Levinas and Derrida. Cf. especially Jacques Derrida's "Violence and Metaphysics: An Essay on the Thought of Emmanuel Levinas," in *Writing and Difference* (Chicago: The University of Chicago Press, 1978). It is this essay by Derrida that in some measure put Levinas' work on ethics in the heart of postmodern discussions.

CHAPTER 1. ETHICS AT THE LIMIT OF REASON

1. Alasdair Macintyr, *After Virtue: A Study in Moral Theory* (Notre Dame, Ind.: University of Notre Dame Press, 1984).

2. John D. Caputo, *Radical Hermeneutics: Repetition, Deconstruction, and the Hermeneutic Project* (Bloomington and Indianapolis: Indiana University Press, 1987), chapter 9.

3. This term will be dealt with shortly.

4. Caputo, *Radical Hermeneutics* and *Against Ethics: Contributions to a Poetics of Obligation with Constant Reference to Deconstruction* (Bloomington and Indianapolis: Indiana University Press, 1993).

5. I will use the term limit in this context, since some deconstructionists do use the term in this way. It would be more precise, however, to use the term boundary or bound in this context, since usually there are two sides to the limit in the way that we will see deconstructionists use it.

6. This challenge to ethics is specifically summed up in the title of one of the main texts that is a product of the ongoing deconstructive tradition: *Against Ethics: Contributions to a Poetics of Obligation with Constant Reference to Deconstruction.* Jack Caputo, the author of this recent work, is the best writer of English in this style of thinking today, and is emerging as one of its leading voices in this country. And likewise, Simon Critchley's *The Ethics of Deconstruction* challenges any too typical ethics today as within a closure. Simon Critchley, *The Ethics of Deconstruction: Derrida and Levinas*, (Oxford: Blackwell, 1992).

7. The recent development of Paul Ricoeur's ethical position is the best model of this for our enterprise.

8. The treatment of these themes, time, sign and trace, will be taken up in ensuing chapters.

9. It is worth noting here that for Kant the limit is from an act of reason, limiting knowledge to experience and preventing any transcendent use of categories of understanding. However, it is also necessary to remember that for Kant metaphysics is possible in general by focusing on the limit concepts and not going beyond that: for example, his use of theology. Thus, with Ricoeur, such a metaphysics gets new life through the semantic structure of the symbol, and indirect expressions, also cast within a Kantian framework. But now in this case ethics at the limit gets a full sense, and can actually do something more than deconstruct. It is indeed a philosophy, an ethics, at the limit of reason. Ricoeur's view will emerge in its central importance throughout the following studies.

10. Drucilla Cornell, *The Philosophy of Limit* (New York and London: Routledge, 1992) p. 1. Cornell's interest in renaming deconstruction a philosophy of limit is not the same as ours, for she is primarily interested in deconstruction, thus renamed, in its relation to law: "Indeed, the significance of understanding justice as the limit to any system of positive law is the first reason I am renaming deconstruction as the philosophy of the limit," p. 2.

11. Cornell, *The Philosophy of Limit*, p. 70

12. As Caputo puts it so well, "Cornell has laid to rest, definitively I would say, the popular nonsense . . . that deconstruction is some sort of skepticism or even a pernicious nihilism." Caputo, on blurb of Cornell's book.

13. It should be noted that something more than the Kantian distinction between limit and boundary is involved here. For we are not merely speaking of a boundary, but rather of a limiting role coming from two directions; one from reason, the other from the given.

14. Simon Critchley, *The Ethics of Deconstruction*, p. 87. Bernasconi agrees with Critchley here, emphasizing that Derrida, in 1967 prefers closure to end, since, for him, there is no "sudden passage" beyond philosophy.

15. Ibid., p. 87.

16. Ibid., pp. 88–89

17. Ibid., p. 89.

18. In this investigation, my working hypothesis will emerge, that is, that the philosophy that helps most in terms of these questions, without succumbing to their allure uncritically, is that of Paul Ricoeur. His philosophy is indeed a philosophy of limit, and must be confronted with and distinguished from, and

then perhaps even expanded in terms of, the deconstructive style of thinking precisely as a philosophy of limit. And since Ricoeur considers himself a post-Hegelian Kantian at least in some small sense, and since Kant epitomizes the very enlightenment of modernity that both deconstruction and Ricoeur oppose, this present work must reach back to that great philosophy which initially posited this philosophy of limit.

19. William James, "The Will to Believe," in *Pragmatism: The Classic Writings*, edited by H. S. Thayer (New York: New American Library 1970), pp. 186–209.

20. It might be worth recalling the role, for Kant, of the *Critique of Judgment* in establishing a strictly limited basis of the Critical philosophy in reflective judgment in purposiveness and all to which that leads—all outside any knowledge claims. And this is the presupposed element for all empirical science, the transcendental conditions have been established in the *First Critique*.

21. William James, *The Varieties of Religious Experience* (New York: Collier Books, 1961), pp. 397–401.

22. Robert Bernasconi, "Deconstruction and the Possibility of Ethics," in *Deconstruction and Philosophy: The Texts of Jacques Derrida*, edited by John Sallis (Chicago: The University of Chicago Press, 1987), p. 135.

23. "As Derrida explains: 'There is *no* beyond-the-undecidable, but this beyond nevertheless remains to be thought from this 'somewhat more reliable point of "reference"; and one can only be involved there in a promise, giving one's word on the subject, even if one denies it by signing ironically.'" Cornell, p. 85, quoting Derrida, "Acts," p. 137.

24. Cornell has gone beyond this point, establishing that such a philosophy of limit, as ethics, and in the context of a feminist contribution, can be seen to offer a "'new,' 'different' ethical configuration." *The Philosophy of the Limit*, p. 170.

25. Stated by Philippe Nemo in Emmanuel Levinas, *Ethics and Infinity: Conversations with Philippe Nemo*, translated by Richard A. Cohen (Pittsburgh: Duquesne University Press, 1985), p. 90.

26. Adriaan Peperzak, *To the Other: An Introduction to the Philosophy of Emmanuel Levinas* (West Lafayette, Ind.: Purdue University, 1993), pp. 53–54. For a very fine treatment of this element of Heidegger, where he in his later work is seen to shuck off any trace of the Judeo-Christian tradition in favor of the pagan Greek and German traditions, as Peperzak states here so well, see John D. Caputo, *Demythologizing of Heidegger*, (Bloomington: Indiana University Press, 1993).

CHAPTER 2. DEATH, END, AND LIMIT OF PHILOSOPHY

1. I do not pretend to treat exhaustively the problem of philosophy at its limit, closure, or interruption, but merely to shed light on the problem in order to show how the positions of postmodern deconstruction and Ricoeur fit into that context, thus contrasting these two recent efforts toward ethics or against ethics. Any extensive study of limit, boundary, end, rupture, and closure would

require a thorough study not only of what we cover in these first four chapters, but also in the history of philosophy from Kant up until and through the present time. The extensions beyond the limits initiated by Kant and brought to culmination by Ricoeur will be seen in the chapter 4. A complete study of philosophy at the limit will make up a future volume.

2. Martin Heidegger, *Nietzsche*, vol. 4: *Nihilism*, translated by Frank A. Capuzzi, edited, with notes and an analysis by David Farrell Krell (San Francisco: Harper & Row, 1982), p. 148.

3. Ibid., p. 148.

4. Robert Bernasconi, "Levinas and Derrida: The Question of the Closure of Metaphysics," in *Face to Face with Levinas*, edited by Richard A. Cohen (Albany: State University of New York Press, 1986), p. 182.

5. John Sallis, "End(s)," *Research in Phenomenology*, vol. 13 (1983), p. 87, quoting Heidegger, "The End of Philosophy and the Task of Thinking," in *On Time and Being*, translated by Joan Stambaugh (New York: Harper & Row, 1972); *Zur Sache des Denkens* (Tubingen: Max Niemeyer Verlag, 1969), p. 61.

6. Sallis, "End(s)," p. 88; in German, p. 63.

7. Sallis, "End(s)," p. 91.

8. Ibid., pp. 91–92.

9. Martin Heidegger, *Kant and the Problem of Metaphysics*, 4th ed., enlarged, translated by Richard Taft (Bloomington and Indianapolis: Indiana University Press, 1990).

10. Heidegger, "The End of Philosophy and the Task of Thinking," p. 55.

11. See *Kant and the Problem of Metaphysics*, p. xv: "The Kant book (*Kant and the Problem of Metaphysics*), written immediately after the conclusion of the second Davos Hochschule course, March 17–April 6, 1929, was based on the preparatory work for that course."

12. Immanuel Kant, *Prolegomena to Any Future Metaphysics*, edited by Lewis White Beck (New York: Bobbs-Merrill, 1950), p. 114.

13. Heidegger, *Kant and the Problem of Metaphysics*, p. 3.

14. Ibid., appendices, p. 171.

15. Ibid.

16. Heidegger, "The End of Philosophy and the Task of Thinking," p. 55.

17. Ibid., p. 56.

18. Ibid., p. 57. I will not address the absurd claim that Heidegger makes in this essay at this point of development: "The end of philosophy means: the beginning of the world civilization based upon Western European thinking" (p. 59). Caputo has a very good critique of Heidegger's self-limitation in his later narrowing down of the question of the origins of philosophy in the early tradition and throughout the Western tradition. This present claim of the Western European basis of thinking is equally narrow and stupid, and comes under the same kind of critique. See John D. Caputo, *Demythologizing Heidegger* (Bloomington and Indianapolis: Indiana University Press, 1993).

19. Heidegger, "The End of Philosophy and the Task of Thinking," p. 73.

20. Ibid., p. 71.

21. Ibid., p. 69.

22. Ibid., p. 68.

23. John D. Caputo, *The Mystical Elements in Heidegger's Thought* (New York: Fordham University Press, 1986), p. 2.

24. Ibid., p. 4, Caputo quoting Heidegger's "Letter on Humanism," translated by E. Lohner, In *Philosophy in the Twentieth Century*, edited by W. Barrett and H. Aiken, vol. 3: *Contemporary European Thought* (New York: Harper & Row, 1971), p. 224.

25. Heidegger here is vastly at odds with postmodern deconstructionists regarding language in this remark in that he does not give the same quasi-autonomous role to language as postmodern deconstruction does.

26. Martin Heidegger, *What Is Philosophy?*, translated with an introduction by William Kluback and Jean T. Wilde (New Haven, Conn.: College & University Press, 1956), p. 93.

27. One must go beyond the limitations of this English translation, which freely translates Sagen and Sprache as "language," without distinguishing between them. This leads to a complete misreading of some of the central passages in this text, as will be seen in the case of one of the most important sentences in the book correlating being with speaking and Being with saying.

28. Heidegger, "What Is Philosophy?," p. 95. The English translates *Sagens* here as "language."

29. Ibid., pp. 94, 95.

30. Ibid., pp. 76, 77. I have substituted "The being" for "Being," which is capitalized as the first word in the sentence, and thus misleading, translating "Das seiende."

31. I have again translated *das Sagens* as "saying" instead of as "language."

32. All one has to do in this context is invoke the best treatment of this in Heidegger, that by William Richardson, in *Heidegger: Through Phenomenology to Thought*: "During the course of Heidegger's development, he uses the word 'philosophy' sometimes in the narrow sense, by which it is identified with metaphysics, sometimes in the broad sense, as a response to Beings's appeal. In the first case, it shares the same destiny as metaphysics and must be overcome. In the second, it is a consummation devoutly to be wished." (The Hague: Martinus Nijhoff, 1963), p. 23.

33. Bernasconi is interested in the question of whether philosophy suffered "a sudden death, or is it suffering a lingering one." "Levinas and Derrida: The Question of the Closure of Metaphysics," p. 181. Is it still dying and, if so, has it always been dying, a real possibility that would be interesting to explore. The real question for Bernasconi, getting this from Derrida, is the relation of the future of philosophy to thinking. And I do think that this is a critical issue for philosophy, especially in its recent European vintage.

34. Robert Bernasconi, "Levinas and Derrida," p. 181 ff.

35. Ibid., p. 182.

36. Jacque Derrida, *Positions*, translated and annotated by Alan Bass (Chicago: The University of Chicago Press, 1981), p. 12.

37. In fact, some contend that Derrida here is correcting some contrary interpretations of Heidegger that claim an end of philosophy. Critchley, *The Ethics of Deconstruction*, p. 80: Bernasconi, "Levinas and Derrida," p. 183. Thus, Derrida's break with Heidegger is not with relation to this closure and end

of philosophy, but rather, as Critchley argues, it is with the project of eschatology and the unity of the history of metaphysics (Critchley, ibid., p. 86).

38. Critchley, *The Ethics of Deconstruction*, p. 73.

39. Bernasconi, "Levinas and Derrida," p. 183. Footnote 9 refers to Heidegger's *Identity and Difference*, p. 73.

40. Ibid., p. 184.

41. Before turning to Levinas and end on p. 185, Bernasconi says: "If we turn now to Levinas, we find a tendency—not wholly absent from 'Violence and Metaphysics'—to associate him with the early Heidegger, who announced 'the destruction of the history of ontology,' rather than the later Heidegger, the Heidegger of the history of being, whom we have been considering in relation to Derrida" (184). It is interesting, as Bernasconi notes, that Derrida does not mention the passage in *Totality and Infinity* where Levinas specifically confronts those thinkers who announce the end of philosophy, especially Hegel and Heidegger.

42. Bernasconi goes so far as to raise the question of whether Derrida's reading of Levinas is "innocent," and whether he therefore does justice to Levinas, suggesting that perhaps Derrida is guided by the same kind of necessity as Rousseau in wanting the absolute origin of language to be from the south.

43. Emmanuel Levinas, *Otherwise than Being or Beyond Essence*, translated by Alphonso Lingis (The Hague: Martinus Nijhoff Publishers, 1981), p. 20; Bernasconi, "Levinas and Derrida," p. 185.

44. We will confront Ricoeur's too extreme critique of Levinas in chapter 7, appropriating more of Levinas for our purposes than Ricoeur is able to do in his extreme formulation of opposed polarities between Levinas and Husserl.

45. This dimension of Levinas' position will be fully explored and defended in a chapter 7.

46. Levinas, *Totality and Infinity*, p. 39.

47. Ibid., p. 281.

48. Perhaps it is necessary to think Kant here, regarding the infinite, and the critique of Cassirer and Ricoeur regarding the cutting off of the infinite in Heidegger's *Kant and the Problem of Metaphysics*. The infinite and reason must be reintroduced, and at once, somehow integrated with the move beneath the subject-object dichotomy that Heidegger initiated, and of which Levinas is not oblivious. Is it not significant that Levinas refers to the idea of the infinity in terms of the transcendental method, that perhaps this is the condition making possible the exteriority of the other, so that there is not first, foremost, and only exteriority? For he has said "The rigorously developed concept of this transcendence is expressed by the term infinity [24–25]. . . . For the way we are describing to work back and remain this side of objective certitude resembles what has come to be called the transcendental method (in which the technical procedures of transcendental idealism need not necessarily be comprised) [25]."

49. Levinas, *Totality and Infinity*, p. 41.

50. Ibid., p. 24.

51. Robert Bernasconi, "Levinas and Derrida," p. 195.

52. Ibid.

53. Ibid., p. 198.

54. Bernasconi seems to plant the seed for this point in the context of dealing with the two sources of language in Levinas as depicted in Derrida's "Violence and Metaphysics." There he defends two senses of Levinas.

55. Peperzak, Adriaan, *To the Other: An Intrduction to the Philosophy of Emmanuel Levinas* (West Lafayette, Ind.: Purdue University Press, 1993), p. 120ff.

CHAPTER 3. LIMIT, CRITIQUE, AND REASON

1. Kevin J. Vanhoozer, *Biblical Narrative in the Philosophy of Paul Ricoeur* (Cambridge and New York: Cambridge University Press, 1990); and Kevin J. Verhoozer, "Philosophical Antecedents to Ricoeur's *Time and Narrative*," in *On Paul Ricoeur; Narrative and Interpretation*, edited by David Wood, pp. 34–55.

2. Immanuel Kant, *Prolegomena to Any Future Metaphysics*, with an introduction by Lewis White Beck (Indianapolis: Bobbs-Merrill, 1950), p. 114. Hereafter cited within the text as PFM, first in English and second, when necessary, in to the following German text: *Prolegomena zu einer jeden kunftigen Metaphysik: Die als Wissenschaft wird auftreten konnen* (Stuttgart: Philipp Reclam, 1989).

3. "In our reason both are comprehended, and the question is, How does reason proceed to set boundaries to the understanding as regards both these fields? Experience, which contains all that belongs to the sensible world, does not bound itself; it only proceeds in every case from the conditioned to some other equally conditioned object. That which bounds it must lie quite without it, and this is the field of the pure beings of the understanding. But this field, so far as the *determination* of the nature of these beings is concerned, is an empty space for us; and apart from dogmatically defined concepts, we cannot pass beyond the field of possible experience. But as a boundary itself is something positive, which belongs to that which lies within as well as to the space that lies without the given content, it is still an actual positive cognition that reason only acquires by enlarging itself to this boundary, yet without attempting to pass it because it there finds itself in the presence of an empty space in which it can conceive forms of things, but not things themselves. *But the setting of a boundary to the field of the understanding by something which is otherwise unknown to it is still a cognition which belongs to reason even at this point, and by which it is neither confined within the sensible nor strays beyond it, but only limits itself as befits the knowledge of a boundary, to the relation between that which lies beyond it and that which is contained within it*" (PFM, 109).

4. "When I compare all the transcendental Ideas, the totality of which constitutes the proper problem of natural pure reason, compelling it to quit the mere contemplation of nature, to transcend all possible experience, and in this endeavor to produce the thing (be it knowledge or fiction) called metaphysics, I think I perceive that the aim of this natural tendency is to free our concepts from the fetters of experience and from the limits of the mere contemplation of nature so far as at least to open to us a field containing mere objects for the pure understanding which no sensibility can reach, not indeed for the purpose of specula-

tively occupying ourselves with them (for there we can find no ground to stand on), but in order that practical principles [may be assumed as at least possible]; for practical principles, unless they find scope for their necessary expectation and hope, could not expand to the universality which reason unavoidably requires from a moral point of view" (PFM, 111).

5. Kant here refers to the *Critique of Pure Reason*, "Regulative Use of Ideas of Pure Reason" for the treatment of the solution to these questions.

6. "[U]nd das ist auch der Zweck und Nutzen dieser Naturanlage unserer Vernunft, welche Metaphysik, als ihr Lieblingskind, ausgeborfen hat, dessen Erzeugung, so wie jede andere in der Welt, nicht dem ungefahren Zufalle, sondern einem ursprunglichen Keime zuzuschreiben, ist, welcher zu gorssen Zwecken weislich organisiert ist" (PFM, p. 102/131).

7. Heidgger, *Kant and the Problem of Metaphysics*, 4th ed., appendices, pp. 170–171.

8. Ibid., p. 171.

9. Ibid.

10. Ernst Cassirer, "Remarks on Martin Heidegger's Interpretation of Kant," in *Kant; Disputed Questions*, edited and translated by Moltke S. Gram (Chicago: Quadrangle Books. 1967), p. 143.

11. Ibid., p. 145.

12. Ibid., pp. 147–148.

13. "A Discussion between Ernst Cassirer and Martin Heidegger," translated by Francis Slade, in *The Existentialist Tradition*, ed. Nino Languilli (Garden City, N.Y.: Doubleday, 1971), p. 193.

14. Ernst Cassirer: "Remarks on Martin Heidegger's Interpretation of Kant," p. 149.

15. For example, epistemic dimensions that are latent in Heidegger's efforts toward developing a fundamental ontology emerge in the realization that to investigate the pre-reflective level of any knowledge is largely to investigate the epistemic substrate for knowledge, even if it involves the explication of the structures and process of the Being of the knower. In this shift of focus from strictly ontological to epistemological considerations, the perspective upon the schemata is no longer limited to the context of the Being of entities encountered in Being-in-the-world. Rather, the fore-understanding grasps the schemata from the point of view of any possible cognitive access to these same entities, coming to grips, from the cognitive point of view, with how they are meaningfully grasped. The epistemic focus changes the attitude toward the schemata, but retains the legacy of existential phenomenology as the deepening of intentionality, in one way or another, below that of acts of awareness to the underlying structure, which includes schemata and schematization and to its root in transcendence.

Thus, Ricoeur is correct in indicating that Heidegger has overcome the aporia in the modern epistemological controversies over the methods of the sciences by delving to their presupposed foundation in ontology.

16. "A Discussion between Ernst Cassirer and Martin Heidegger," p. 193.

17. Cf. Charles M. Sherover, "The Question of Noumenal Time," *Man and World*, vol. 10, no. 4 (1977), pp. 411–434. Also see Heidegger, *Vom Wesen der menschlichen Freiheit*, pp. 231–236.

18. Paul Ricoeur, *Fallible Man*, p. 67.

19. Paul Ricoeur, *The Rule of Metaphor* and *Time and Narrative* (cf. vol. 1 of *Time and Narrative*, p. ix. *The Rule of Metaphor: Multi-Disciplinary Studies of the Creation of Meaning in Language*, translated by Robert Czerney with Kathleen McLaughlin and John Costello, S.J. (Toronto and Buffalo: University of Toronto Press, 1977); *Time and Narrative*, vol. 1, translated by Kathleen McLaughlin and David Pellauer (Chicago and London: The University of Chicago Press, 1984); vol. 2, translated by Kathleen McLaughlin and David Pellauer (Chicago and London: The University of Chicago Press, 1945); vol. 3, translated by Kathleen Blamey and David Pellauer (Chicago and London: The University of Chicago Press, 1988).

20. Regarding "fictional narrative" Ricoeur remarks: "Remaining faithful to the convention concerning vocabulary I adopted in my first volume, I am giving the term 'fiction' a narrower extension than that adopted by the many authors who take it to be synonymous with 'narrative configuration.' . . . I am reserving the term 'fiction' for those literary creations that do not have historical narrative's ambition to constitute a true narrative. If we take 'configuration' and 'fiction' as synonyms we no longer have a term available to account for the different relation of each of these two narrative modes to the question of truth. What historical narrative and fictional narrative do have in common is that they both stem from the same configurating operations I put under the title mimesis 2. On the other hand, what opposes them to each other does not have to do with the structuring activity invested in their narrative structures as such, rather it has to do with the 'truth-claim' that defines the third mimetic relation."

21. Ricoeur, *Time and Narrative*, vol. 1, p. xi. It is this that makes possible the "intersection" of the world of the text and the world of the reader, "wherein real action occurs and unfolds its specified temporality."

22. Ibid., vol. 2, p. 160. It is in volume 3, which constitutes part IV of *Time and Narrative*, on "Narrated Time," that this project is culminated.

23. *Time and Narrative*, vol. 1, p. 84. "It might already be objected with respect to my thesis about the universally aporetic character of the pure phenomenology of time that Heidegger's hermeneutics marks a decisive break with Augustine's and Husserl's subjectivist hermeneutics. By founding his phenomenology on an ontology of Dasein and of Being-in-the-world, is Heidegger not correct in affirming that temporality, as he describes it, is 'more subjective' than any subject and 'more objective' than any object, inasmuch as his ontology is not bound by the subject/object dichotomy? I do not deny this. The analyses I shall devote to Heidegger will do full justice to the originality that a phenomenology founded upon an ontology and that presents itself as a hermeneutics can boast of."

24. Ibid.

25. Ibid., vol. 1, p. 85.

26. Ibid.

27. Ibid., vol. 1, p. 87.

28. Paul Ricoeur, "Narrated Time," *Philosophy Today*, vol. 29, no. 4/4 (Winter 1985), p. 261. This article is a good summary of the third volume of *Time and Narrative*.

29. For a fuller account of the aporetics of temnporality, see part IV of *Time and Narrative*, vol. 3, section 1. The first statement of the aporia marks the very beginning of *Time and Narrative*, vol. 1, part I.

30. Ricoeur, "Narrated Time," p. 263. For a clear and full account of historical time and these connectors, see: *Time and Narrative*, vol. 3, pp. 104–126.

31. Ricoeur, "Narrated Time," p. 264.

32. Ibid.

33. Ricoeur, *Time and Narrative*, vol. 3, p. 5. For his complete account, see Ricoeur, *Time and Narrative*, vol. 1, pp. 5–30.

34. Ricoeur, "Narrated Time," p. 261.

35. Ibid., p. 262.

36. Ibid. For Ricoeur's lengthy treatment and critique of Heidegger on temporality, see *Time and Narrative*, vol. 3, pp. 60–96.

37. Ricoeur, "Narrated Time," p. 265.

38. Paul Ricoeur, "Kant and Husserl," p. 181. For this present discussion, this article will be referred to in the text as KH, followed by the pages.

39. B 275–276; see also the note to the preface of the second edition of B xi.

40. Ricoeur is first quoting Kant here: "Kant and Husserl," pp. 187. This paragraph analyzes these pages 187–188 of Ricoeur's interpretation of Husserl.

41. Ricoeur, "Kant and Husserl," pp. 187–188.

42. But Heidegger goes too far in this regard. Yet it is necessary to ask, does Ricoeur and do the French in general in approaching this question within phenomenology have the same hermeneutical situational presupposition that Heidegger does? that is, the question of Being as the only one essentially consuming Dasein, and the most pervasive question, missed by the history of metaphysics before Heidegger? that is, is Heidegger correct in focusing first on the preconceptual self comprehension of being as the basic structural dimension of human being? And further, if we once focus on that question and explicate its relevance and its priority, does everything else fall out of the picture so that there is no longer, on this level anything which needs to be explicated, any need . . . relevance . . . advantage . . . interest to pursue anything else? for example, ethics? philosophical anthropology?

43. Ricoeur, "Kant and Husserl," p. 176.

44. Paul Ricoeur, "New Developments in Phenomenology in France: The Phenomenology of Language," *Social Research*, vol. 34 (1967), p. 7.

45. My emphasis.

46. Ricoeur, "Kant and Husserl," pp. 190–191.

47. Even in this context, however, it must be remembered that Husserl wants to bracket and separate off any use of being, reality, or existence within the purity of phenomenological reduction. He does not put what is bracketed out of operation. It is not disconnected in the sense of radically cut off, but left operative, even though it cannot be used in phenomenological analysis.

48. This translation of *Grenze* is an instance of the ambiguity in English translation of *Grense* and *Schranke*, for, in English, they overlap, allowing the translations "limit" for both. Kant however is absolutely consistent in the Prolegomena, and as far as I know, everywhere else, in the use of *Grenze* as bound-

ary, bound, and the use of *Schranke* for limit. Here it is necessary to put "boundary" here even though the translator of Ricoeur has put "limit." This follows for the whole present context.

CHAPTER 4. LIMIT AND GROUND
IN PRACTICAL REASON

1. Immanuel Kant, *Fundamental Principles of the Metaphysics of Morals*, translated by Thomas K. Abbott (Indianapolis and New York: Bobbs-Merrill, 1949), no. 12.

2. Immanuel Kant, "On the Typic of Pure Practical Judgment," pp. 70–74. *Critique of Practical Reason*, translated, with an introduction, by Lewis White Beck (Indianapolis: Bobbs-Merrill, 1956), pp. 70–74. This important section is immediately followed, in chapter 3, by the section on incentives: "The Incentives of Pure Practical Reason," p. 74. This work will be cited in the text as CPrR followed by the page number.

3. This entire discussion of Kant is extremely important for working though the critique of Kant by Ricoeur to be seen later in this chapter, and in a later chapter regarding Ricoeur's interarticulation of Kant's moral philosophy with Aristotle's ethical philosophy.

4. Relevant to his own later development in the third *Critique*, and to a later chapter for us, is Kant's remake regarding the determination from a priori concepts the relation of cognition to the felling of pleasure or displeasure: "Here we have the first and perhaps the only case wherein we can determine from a priori concepts the relation of a cognition (here a cognition of pure practical reason) to the feeling of pleasure or displeasure." *Critique of Practical Reason*, p. 75.

5. Kant's following treatment of duty and obligation rooted in respect will be taken up in a later chapter to the extent necessary, when Ricoeur's own critique of Kant is brought forth for consideration.

6. Kant, *Critique of Practical Reason*, p. 81.

7. Ibid., p. 88.

8. Kant, *Critique of Judgment*, p. 16.

9. Ibid., p. 230.

10. Ibid.

11. Kant, *Critique of Practical Reason*, p. 114.

12. We must not confuse this motive in the context of the object of the will with what Kant calls a "rational motive," which is the "condition that the maxim have universal validity as a law" (Kant, *Fundamental Principles of the Metaphysics of Morals*, p. 75).

13. Ibid., pp. 75–76.

14. Ibid., p. 76.

15. Ibid., p. 75.

16. Ibid., 76.

17. Kant, *Critique of Practical Reason*, p. 4.

18. Kant says: "Nevertheless he does actually take an interest in it, the basis

of which in us we call the moral feeling, which some have falsely assigned as the standard of our moral judgment, whereas it must rather be viewed as the *subjective* effect that the law exercises on the will, the objective principle of which is furnished by reason alone." GMM, Abbot, p. 77.

19. Paul Ricoeur, "What Does Humanism Mean?" in *Political and Social Essays*, edited by David Stewart and Joseph Bien (Athens, Ohio: Ohio University Press, 1974), pp. 85–87.

20. See "Reply to Patrick L. Bourgeois," in *The Philosophy of Paul Ricoeur*, The Library of Living Philosophers, volume 22, edited by Lewis Edwin Hahn (Chicago and La Salle, Ill.: Open Court, 1995), p. 567

21. There is a third important extension for Ricoeur not able to be treated here: "one would have to specify in what sense the philosophy of religion, without in any way enlarging the critique . . . proposes a sort of enlargement under the heading of the regeneration of moral will and hence under that of the restoration of the power of free action." Ricoeur refers here to the function of limitation exercised in this work, which continues within the limit of reason alone, yet the limitation exercised here is said to be in a "different manner from that of the three *Critiques*."

22. Ricoeur, "Reply to Patrick L. Bourgeois," p. 568. Ricoeur is here referring to his critique of Kant in terms of the latent receptivity in the structure of human action with which he has so ardently disagreed since the unity and antinomy articles and the *Freedom and Nature: The Voluntary and the Involuntary* and *Fallible Man* and which he develops so well in *Oneself as Another*. Paul Ricoeur, *Freedom and Nature: the Voluntary and the Involuntary*, translated by Erazim V. Kohak (Evanston, Ill.: Northwestern University Press, 1966); Fallible Man, revised translation by Charles A. Kelbley (New York: Fordham University Press, 1986); *Oneself as Another*, translated. by Kathleen Blamey (Chicago: The University of Chicago Press, 1992).

23. Paul Ricoeur, *The Voluntary and the Involuntary*, p. 131.

24. Paul Ricoeur, *Husserl: An Analysis of His Phenomenally*, translated by Edward G. Ballard and Lester Embree (Evanston, Ill.: Northwestern University Press, 1976), p. 199.

25. Ricoeur develops these points throughout *The Voluntary and the Involuntary* and recently, more clearly in *Oneself as Another*, throughout study 3.

26. Ricoeur, "Reply to Patrick L. Bourgeois," p. 568

27. Ibid.

28. Ricoeur's own extension of Kant's productive imagination in semantic innovation, and his dissolving of the distinction between the determinative and reflective judgments will be pursued further in the ensuing chapters.

29. Paul Ricoeur, "Biblical Hermeneutics," *Semeia* IV, 1975, p. 142.

30. Ricoeur, *Semeia* IV, 1975, p. 142.

31. Paul Ricoeur, *Oneself as Another*, p. 17

32. He may be too severe in his critique of Levinas.

33. For a full treatment of these points, see Patrick L. Bourgeois, "Trace, Semiotics, and the Living Present: Derrida or Ricoeur," *Southwest Philosophy Review*, vol. 9 (August 1993); "Semiotics and the Deconstruction of Presence: A Ricoeurian Alternative," *American Catholic Philosophical Quarterly*, 1993; and

"The Instant and the Living Present: Ricoeur and Derrida," *Philosophy Today*, 1993.

34. Nowadays, following Lingis' translation of *Totality and Infinity*, Other with a capital O translates *Autrui* (the personal other, the you) and other translates *autre*. See Emmanuel Levinas, *Totality and Infinity*, translated by Alphonso Lingis (Pittsburgh: Duquesne University Press, 1969), pp. 24–25, translator's note

35. We must further consider Kant's strict use of limit and going beyond it as such. The notion of limit for Kant is that within which something is circumscribed or contained. One can stand at this limit (*die Schranke*) as a boundary (*die Grenze*), which has a positive dimension of the "beyond" added to limit as *die Schranke*. Thus, from the vantage point of the limit as boundary one can advert to both sides, while the limit confines one to what is within the limit. For Kant the limit, in the sense of boundary, can be transgressed, but not as knowledge. It this context, we can remember that it is precisely here that both Cassirer and Heidegger, in spite of their essentially different reading of Kant, agree on the fact of a positive reading given to the transcendental dialectic of Kant, placing them both close to our project here. It is perhaps here with the combined notions of limit-boundary, that even Kant himself allows a bit of an opening to the limit's closure.

36. Cf David Wood, "Introduction: Interpreting Narrative," in *On Paul Ricoeur: Narrative and Interpretation*, edited by David Wood (London and New York: Routledge, 1991).

37. See note 12 above.

38. These topics of time, sign, language, and others mentioned in this section will be the focus of ensuing chapters.

39. Caputo, *Against Ethics*, passim.

CHAPTER 5. IMAGINATION AT THE BOUNDARY

1. Martin Heidegger, *Kant and the Problem of Metaphysics*, translated by James S. Churchill (Bloomington: Indiana University Press, 1962).

2. The scope of the present study only allows us to delve into those interpretations of the Kantian imagination close to us in our time, requiring that we pass over those arising immediately following Kant's publication of his third *Critique*. It will be the task of the next volume of this study thoroughly to investigate the imagination in great depth, including essential developments within the history of post Kantian thought.

3. Ricoeur, *Husserl: An Analysis of His Thought*, p. 191.

4. Kant, *Critique of Practical Reason*, pp. 71–72.

5. Kearney, *The Wake of the Imagination: Toward a Modsmodern Culture* (Minneapolis: University of Minnesota Press, 1988), p. 171. Kearney, here, however, is wrong, simply falling under the influence of Heidegger's interpretation-retrieval of Kant. Kearney, in a footnote in his section on Kant, admits that he has fallen under Heidegger's interpretation here.

6. This role in narrative's "semantic innovation" becomes central as giv-

ing to (feeding) the imagination . . . for action to "regenerate"—for example, what inspires the young explorer, warrior . . . or image of Christ.

7. Kearney, *The Wake of the Imagination*, pp. 5–6 notes.

8. See Kearney, *The Wake of the Imagination*, p. 178ff. This again is an area that will be studied in depth in a future volume on the imagination at the limit of reason.

9. Innanuel Kant, *Anthropology from a Pragmatic Point of View*, translated, with an introduction and notes, by Mary J. Gregor (The Hague: Martinus Nijhoff, 1974).

10. John Sallis, *The Gathering of Reason* (Athens, Ohio: Ohio University Press, 1980), p. 156.

11. Ibid.

12. Kant, B 151, quoted in Sallis, *The Gathering of Reason*, p. 156.

13. Of course, it is clear that this does not respond to the claiim of Heideggerians that Heidegger does not necessarily dispute that point, since his "interpretation" is a destruction and a repetition or retrieval, and from the hermeneutical situatedness of the question of Being.

14. Kant, *Critique of Judgment*, p. 82.

15. Ibid.

16. Ibid., p. 85.

17. Kearney, *The Wake of the Imagination*, p. 174.

18. Immanuel Kant, *Kritik der Urteilsdraft* (Stuttgart: Philipp Reclam, 1966), p. 235.

19. This remark regarding chance can help to clarify Derrida's effectively scuttling the creativity of imagination in favor of this chance.

20. Kant, *Kritik der Urteilsdraft*, p. 246.

21. Ibid., p. 247.

22. Here I follow the recent translation of Kant's *Critique of Judgment: Including the First Introduction*, translated, with an introduction by Werner S. Pluhar (Indianapolis & Cambridge: Hackett, 1987), pp. 183–184.

23. We must remember that empirical concepts have intuitions that Kant calls examples. Cf. 198.

24. One must note the similarity between this "supersensible ground" as the "common . . . yet unknown" bond between the theoretical and the practical faculties. This reminds us of the text at the end of the introduction to the *Critique of Pure Reason* made famous by Heidegger. Is it not perhaps possible that Kant, even as early as this first *Critique*, was previewing such a rational ground, and not one in sensibility, in the imagination, even the transcendental imagination? He has stated there: "by way of intoduction or anticipation we need only say that there are two stems of human knowledge, namely, *sensibility* and *understanding*, which perhaps spring from a common, but to us unknown root." *Critique of Pure Reason*, p. 61.

25. It will remain, however, for a second volume of this present work to fully investigate the broader role of the Kantian productive imagination, its appropriation by his immediate followers and its evolving development in the twentieth century, with an intense study of its significance on the contemporary scene.

CHAPTER 6. IMAGINATION

1. See the following articles for these two points of Derrida concerning the living present and sign in language: Patrick L. Bourgeois, "Semiotics and the Deconstruction of Presence: A Ricoeurian Alternative," *American Catholic Philosophical Quarterly*, vol. 46; and Patrick L. Bourgeois, "Trace, Semiotics, and the Living Present: Derrida or Ricoeur," *Southwest Philosophy Review*, vol. 9 (1993).

2. Richard Kearney, *The Wake of Imagination: Toward a Postmodern Culture* (Minneapolis: University of Minnesota Press, 1988), p. 96, Quoting Jacques Derrida, *Dissemination*, translated by Barbara Johnson (Chicago: The University of Chicago Press, 1981) p. 93.

3. It will be seen shortly that the distinction between reproductive and productive imagination in the Kantian context is dissolved by deconstruction.

4. These specific points will be taken up in the ensuing chapters.

5. The translator's note at the beginning of "The Double Session" to the word "lustre" states: "'A decorative object, as a chandelier having glass pendants' (American Heritage Dictionary)."

6. Kearney, *The Wake of Imagination*, p. 290

7. "The Double Session," p. 177

8. Kearney, *The Wake of Imagination*, p. 290. He quotes Derrida, "The Double Session," in *Dissemination*, translated by Barbara Johnson (Chicago: The University of Chicago Press, 1981), p. 223.

9. Kearney, *The Wake of Imagination*, p. 290.

10. Derrida, "The Attending Discourse," in *Dissemination*, p. 325, quoted by Kearney, *The Wake of Imagination*, pp. 290–291.

11. This is the fundamental thesis of Leonard Lawlor in *Imagination and Chance: The Difference between the Thought of Ricoeur and Derrida* (Albany: State University of New York Press, 1992).

12. Lawlor, *Imagination and Chance*, p. 105, quoting Derrida, *Edmund Husserl's Origin of Geometry: An Introduction*, translated by John P. Leavey Jr. (Lincoln, Nebraska: University of Nebraska Press, 1989); Jacques Derrida, *L'Origine de la geometrie, traduction et introduction*, (Paris: Presses Universitaires de France, 1974 [1962]), p. 149/166.

13. Lawlor, *Imagination and Chance*, p. 109.

14. Ibid., p. 121, and quoting Derrida, *Dissemination*, p. 279/312.

15. Jacque Derrida, *Dissemination*, p. 277.

16. Ibid., pp. 268–269/300.

17. Ibid., p. 268, n. 67.

18. Lawlor, *Imagination and Chance*, p. 122.

19. "Dissemination implies for Derrida that every form, every letter, every atom of language, air, is divided and divisible" (Lawlor, *Imagination and Chance*, p. 125). "Derrida, therefore, is quite explicit in 'The Double Session': dissemination does not project a horizon. Referring only to white spaces, a trace lacks the direction of meaning. Lacking the direction of sense, its trajectory is unexpectable. It neither moves ahead and fulfills a desire nor does it renew what we already believed. It neither answers a question nor does it keep a promise.

No one can predict into which constellation an atom will fall. No matter what we wish, a letter can institute a revolution within the tradition. When it does, this can only be called a surprise, a surprise so wonderful that it cannot be packed into the baggage of experience, a surprise so divine that it is totally other" (Lawlor, *Imagination and Chance*, pp. 127–128). Consistent with his view of chance, (according to Lawlor's interpretation) Derrida says that "The empty space between, in which writing zigzags like a drunk, is what provides the chance that cannot be imagined" (Lawlor, *Imagination and Chance*, pp. 108–109).

20. Ibid., p. 129

21. If this is truly the case, one might consider the very affirmation of this nihilist position to present serious difficulties for itself precisely as expressed in intelligible terms. Yet this last difficulty can be adequately dealt with, for, to paraphrase William James, what distinguishes us as nihilist and non-nihilists is a postulate, a will to believe based in the human, volutional, passional nature, which, although accepted on the basis of such an option, has its truth claim from within the very claim itself in terms of whether it makes the most sense among possible interpretations. The question at stake is whether one can express intelligibly a move away from intelligibility toward that abyss of which the intelligible is wont to be about. And certainly, from a space within that position, the account of nihilism can be claimed to make sense in affirming the illusion of sense.

22. Paul Ricoeur, *The Rule of Metaphor*, translated by Robert Czerny with Kathleen McLaughlin and John Costello, S.J. (Toronto: University of Toronto Press, 1977), p. 303: *La Metaphore vive* (Paris: Editions du Seuil, 1975), p. 383.

23. Ricoeur, *The Rule of Metaphor*, p. 303: *La Metaphore vive*, p. 383.

24. Paul Ricoeur, *Time and Narrative*, vol. 1, translated by Kathleen McLaughlin and David Pellauer (Chicago: The University of Chicago Press, 1984), p. x: *Temps et récit* (Paris: Editions du Seuil, 1983), p. 12.

25. "But if we follow Kant rather than Hume, I mean the theory of schematism and that of productive imagination, we have to look at imagination as the place of nascent meanings and categories, rather than as the place of fading impressions. . . . And could we not say by anticipation that imagination is the emergence of conceptual meaning through the interplay between sameness and difference? Metaphor would be the place in discourse where this emergence may be detected because sameness and difference are in conflict." Paul Ricoeur, "Creativity in Language," *Philosophy Today*, vol. 17, no. 2 (Summer 1973), p. 109.

26. Paul Ricoeur, *Time and Narrative*, vol. 1, p. 68, *Temps et récit*, p. 106.

27. Although he denies this Kantian distinction, Ricoeur contends that the kinship between emplotment and the reflective judgment that Kant opposes to the determinant judgment, in the sense that it reflects upon the work of thinking at work in the aesthetic judgment of taste and in the teleological judgment applied to organic wholes. One could say that the act of emplotment has a similar function inasmuch as it extracts a configuration from a succession.

28. Ricoeur, *Time and Narrative*, p. 244, fn. 18: p. 106, fn. 1.

29. Paul Ricoeur, "Creativity in Language: Word, Polysemy, Metaphor," *Philosophy Today*, vol. 17 (1973), pp. 109–110.

30. Paul Ricoeur, *The Rule of Metaphor*, translated by Robert Czerny et al. (Toronto: University of Toronto Press, 1977), p. 300. Hereafter cited within the text as RM. Although the citations are from the English edition, some of the translations from the original French are my own. *La Metaphore vive* (Paris: Editions du Seuil, 1975).

31. Ricoeur, *The Rule of Metaphor*, pp. 296–297.

32. *The Rule of Metaphor* and *Time and Narrative* (cf. vol. 1, p. ix.)

33. Regarding "fictional narrative" Ricoeur remarks: "Remaining faithful to the convention concerning vocabulary I adopted in my first volume, I am giving the term "fiction" a narrower extension than that adopted by the many authors who take it to be synonymous with "narrative configuration. . . . I am reserving the term 'fiction' for those literary creations that do not have historical narrative's ambition to constitute a true narrative. If we take 'configuration' and 'fiction' as synonyms we no longer have a term available to account for the different relation of each of these two narrative modes to the question of truth. What historical narrative and fictional narrative do have in common is that they both stem from the same configurating operations I put under the title mimesis 2. On the other hand, what opposes them to each other does not have to do with the structuring activity invested in their narrative structures as such, rather it has to do with the 'truth-claim' that defines the third mimetic relation."

34. Ricoeur, *Time and Narrative*, vol. 1, p. xi.

35. Ibid.

36. Ibid., vol. 2, p. 160. It is in volume 3, which constitutes part IV of *Time and Narrative*, on "Narrated Time," that this project is culminated.

37. Merleau-Ponty, *The Primacy of Perception*,

38. Lawlor, *Imagination and Chance*, p. 83.

39. Therefore it is necessary to understand by the meaning of the speech-act, or by the *noema* of the saying, not only the sentence, in the narrow sense of the propositional act, but also the illocutionary force and even the perlocutionary action in the measure that these three aspects of the speech-act are codified, gathered into paradigms, and where, consequently, they can be identified and re-identified as having the same meaning. Therefore I am here giving the word "meaning" a very large acceptance that covers all the aspects and levels of the intentional exteriorization that makes the inscription of discourse possible. Paul Ricoeur, "The Model of the Text: Meaningful Action Considered as a Text," *Social Research*, vol. 38 (1971), p. 534; this article appears later in *Hermeneutics and the Human Sciences* (London: Cambridge University Press, 1981), p. 200, corresponding to the above citation.

40. It is important to note that in his recent work on narrative, especially in *Time and Narrative*, Ricoeur speaks of surpassing the language of reference. This development will be dealt with in the next section on reading and narrative. Cf. especially, Ricoeur, *Time and Narrative*, vol. 3, pp. 5–6; and p. 156ff.

41. Ricoeur, "The Hermeneutical Function of Distanciation," *Philosophy Today*, vol. 17 (1973), p.140.

42. Ibid. p. 141.

43. Ibid.

44. Ibid., p. 140.

45. "I want to take this idea of the 'projection of our ownmost possibilities' from his analysis and apply it to the theory of the text. Actually, what is to be interpreted in a text is a proposed world, a world that I might inhabit and wherein I might project my ownmost possibilities. This is what I call the world of the text, the world properly belonging to this unique text."

46. Ricoeur, "The Hermeneutical Function of Distanciation," p. 135; "The Model of the Text," pp. 536–537.

47. Ricoeur,"The Hermeneutical Function of Distanciation," p. 139.

48. Ibid.

49. Ibid., p. 135.

50. "With the dialectic of explanation and understanding, I have to provide my interpretation theory with an analysis of writing which will be the counterpart of that of the text as a work of discourse. To the extent that the act of reading is the counterpart of the act of writing, the dialectic of event and meaning, so essential to the structure of discourse . . . generates correlative dialectic in reading between understanding or comprehension (the *verstehen* of the German hermeneutical tradition) and explanation (the *erklaren* of the same tradition)" (IT, 71).

51. "For the sake of a didactic exposition of the dialectic of explanation and understanding, as phases of a unique process, I propose to describe this dialectic first as a move from understanding to explaining and then as a move from explanation to comprehension. The first time, understanding will be a naive grasping of the meaning of the text as a whole. The second time, comprehension will be a sophisticated mode of understanding, supported by explanatory procedures. In the beginning, understanding is a guess. At the end, it satisfies the concept and appropriation, which was described in the third essay as the rejoinder to the kind of distanciation linked to the full objectification of the text. Explanation, then, will appear as the mediation between two stages of understanding. If isolated from this concrete process, it is a mere abstraction, an artifact of methodology" (IT, 74–75).

52. Ricoeur, "What Is a Text?" p. 149.

53. Ibid., p. 148.

54. Ibid., p. 150.

55. Ricoeur, *Time and Narrative*, vol. 3, pp. 5–6, 156ff.

56. Ibid., p. 177.

57. Ibid., p. 160.

58. Ibid., p. 158.

59. Ibid., pp. 158–159.

60. Ibid., p. 167.

61. Ibid., p. 174.

CHAPTER 7. SIGN, TIME, AND TRACE

1. It should be noted that this term is used differently by Europeans and by Americans. In large measure, what Ricoeur wants to include in language, and accuses Saussure of separating out of language, the American philosophers retain in a fuller semiotics, which is not reductionistic.

2. This term "semeiological reductionism" is taken from Martin Dillon, *Merleau-Ponty's Ontology* (Bloomington: Indiana University Press, 1988), p. 178.

3. Martin Dillon contends that Saussure does not himself exclude the extralinguistic, but is compatible with that development, which his followers do take. See *Merleau-Ponty's Ontology*, p. 181.

4. Paul Ricoeur, "The Question of the Subject: The Challenge of Semeiology," *The Conflict of Interpretation: Essays in Hermeneutics*, edited by Don Ihde (Evanston, Ill.: Northwestern University Press, 1974), p. 246.

5. Paul Ricoeur, "New Developments in Phenomenology in France: The Phenomenology of Language," *Social Research*, vol. 34 (1967), p. 19.

6. Ricoeur, "New Developments in Phenomenology in France," p. 19.

7. Ibid.

8. John Caputo, "The Economy of Signs in Husserl and Derrida: From Uselessness to Full Employment," in *Deconstruction and Philosophy: The Texts of Jacques Derrida*, edited by John Sallis (Chicago: The University of Chicago Press, 1987), pp. 103–104.

9. Jacques Derrida, *Positions*, translated by Alan Bass (Chicago: University of Chicago Press, 1981), p. 19.

10. Derrida, *Positions*, pp. 26–27.

11. Ibid., p. 33.

12. Hilary Lawson, *Reflexivity: The Post-modern Predicament* (La Salle, Ill.: Open Court, 1985), p. 100.

13. Rodolphe Gasche "Infrastructures and Systematicity," in *Deconstruction and Philosophy: The Texts of Jacques Derrida*, pp. 11–12.

14. John Caputo, "The Economy of Signs in Husserl and Derrida," p. 105.

15. Rodolphe Gasche, "Infrastructures and Systematicity," p. 12.

16. "The expressions 'green is or' and 'abracadabra'" are but "isolations of this structure and hence a welcome *liberation* from the rule of intuitionism, a liberation which is in fact made possible by the reduction of the rules of a priori grammar. . . . This reduction . . . *liberates* the signifier from the opressive regime of intuitionism and its unfair demand that every signifier lead to intuitionism and its unfair demand that every signifier leads to Being, presence, objectivity, even when such demands cannot be met. Intuitionism exacts a tax which no one can pay." John Caputo, "The Economy of Signs in Husserl and Derrida," p. 105.

17. Cf. Caputo in his essay in Sallis, speaks of representation (also in RH), and Sallis, in chapter on presence in *Delimitations*, refers to it as repetition.

18. Paul Ricoeur, *Time and Narrative*, translated by Kathleen Blamey and David Pellauer (Chicago: University of Chicago Press, 1988), vol. 3, p. 26.

19. Ibid.

20. Derrida considers Husserl's view of this instant as a point to be a pivotal concept for his phenomenology, as he says: "we cannot avoid noting that a certain concept of the 'now,' of the present as punctuality of the instant, discretely but decisively sanctions the whole system of 'essential distinctions.' . . . This spread is nonetheless thought and described on the basis of the self-identity of the now as point, as a 'source-point'." Jacques Derrida, *Speech and Phenomena: And Other Essays of Husserl's Theory of Signs*, translated by David B. Alli-

son and Newton Bercer (Evanston, Ill.: Northwestern University Press, 1973), p. 65. This work will be referred to within the text as SP.

21. Although Derrida exploits this latent tension within Husserl's account between the "instant as a point" (ibid., p. 60) and the thickness and depth of the present, he is aware that, in spite of this tension, Husserl himself is explicitly convinced that no "now" can be isolated as a pure instant, a pure punctuality (ibid., pp. 61–62).

22. It is to be noted this is not the "point" now, which, even for Derrida, has not lost its identity.

23. He goes on: "This point strikes down the very root of the argument for the uselessness of signs in the self-relation."

24. Derrida, *Of Grammatoloty*, translated by Gayatri Chakravorty Spivak (Baltimore: Johns Hopkins University Press, 1976), p. 65.

25. Ricoeur, *Interpretation Theory*, p. 7.

26. Edmund Husserl, *Logical Investigations*, translated by J. N. Findlay (New York: Humanities Press, 1970). Cf. Patrick L. Bourgeois, *Extension of Ricoeur's Hermeneutic* (The Hague: Martinus Nijhoff, 1975). In the *Investigations*, the meaning and reference functions are manifest as central to Ricoeur's thinking from the beginning of his writings. Also see Paul Ricoeur, *Freedom and Nature*, p. 15 and *Symbolism of Evil*, p. 17 and footnote 12; *Husserl: An Analysis of His Phenomenology*, passim; "Structure-Word-Event," *Philosophy Today*, vol. 12 (Summer 1968), pp. 114–129. These are only some of the more explicit references to Husserl. Many more could be given, specifically referring to the relation between meaning and reference functions of linguistic expressions. Ricoeur makes a particularly astute analysis of linguistic expressions in Husserls early writings in: "Husserl and Wittgenstein" in *Phenomenology and Existentialism*, edited by Edward Lee and Maurice Mandelbaum (Baltimore: Johns Hopkins University Press, 1967), pp. 207–217.

27. Ricoeur, *Interpretation Theory: Discourse and the Surplus of Meaning* (Fort Worth: The Texas Christian University Press, 1966), p. 89. Hereafter this book will be referred to within the text as IT.

28. IT, 2–3.

29. Ricoeur, *The Conflict of Interpretations*. Hereafter cited within the text as CI.

30. Ricoeur, "The Hermeneutical Function of Distanciation," *Philosophy Today*, vol. 17 (1973), p. 134. This article also appears in the anthology of Ricoeur's articles, *Hermeneutics and the Human Sciences* (Cambridge: Cambridge University Press, 1981).

31. Ricoeur, *Conflict of Interpretation*, p. 77.

32. Ibid., p. 71.

33. Ricoeur, *Interpretation Theory*, p. 6.

34. Ibid., p. 7. See also Paul Ricoeur, "What Is a Text? Explanation and Interpretation," an article at the end of David M. Rasmussen, *Myhthic-Symbolic Language and Philosophical Anthropology* (The Hague: Martinus Nijhoff, 1971), p. 148. This article also appears in the recently published anthology of Ricoeur articles, *Hermeneuitics and the Human Sciences* (Cambridge: Cambridge University Press, 1981).

35. Ricoeur, *Interpretation Theory*, p. 8.
36. Ibid., p. 7.
37. Ricoeur, *Time and Narrative*, vol. 3, p. 93.
38. Ibid., p. 94.
39. Ibid., pp. 94–95.
40. Ibid., p. 93.
41. In taking discourse, the semantic and symbolic as that distinctive level of human behavior and lived language as fundamental, Ricoeur has still preserved the positive contribution from semiology about the reduction, admitting the separation in language. According to Ricoeur, semiology presents the condition making language possible evinced in the view of the separation, distance, difference as the origin and commencement of a language, which, in other words, is the reduction. However, such a view, in cutting off signification and the subject, retains only the negative and first aspect of reduction. Nevertheless, insofar as it adheres to or guards this distance or separation, semiology can be considered "as the condition of possibility of sign as such," giving rise to the transcendental character of the symbolic function (Ricoeur, "Philosophy of Language," 28–29). Ricoeur considers the positive side of the reduction to be the condition of possibility of the reference, and of signification, to the saying of something about something. And the third aspect of reduction, the subjective aspect, is "the possibility of an ego to designate itself in the instance of discourse. Positivity and subjectivity go together, in the measure that the reference to the world and the reference to self . . . the showing of a world and the positing of an ego, are symmetrical and reciprocal" (Ricoeur, *Conflict of Interpretation*, p. 256). Thus the reduction in its fuller sense is this return to the self departing from its other which makes the transcendental not only of signs, but of signification. (For a fuller account of Ricoeur's view of these points, see Patrick L. Bourgeois, *The Extension of Ricoeur's Hermeneutic* [The Hague: Martinus Nijhoff, 1975], chapter 7).
42. Ricoeur, *Time and Narrative*, vol. 3, p. 283, n. 12.
43. Paul Ricoeur, "Narrated Time," *Philosophy Today*, vol. 29, no. 4/4 (Winter 1985), p. 261. This article is a good summary of the third volume of *Time and Narrative*.
44. For a fuller account of the aporetics of temporality, see part IV of *Time and Narrative*, vol. 3, section 1. The first statement of the aporia marks the very beginning of *Time and Narrative*, vol. 1, part I.
45. Ricoeur, "Narrated Time," p. 263. For a clear and full account of historical time and these connectors, see *Time and Narrative*, vol. 3, pp. 104–126.
46. Ricoeur, "Narrated Time," p. 264.
47. Ibid.
48. Ricoeur, *Time and Narrative*, vol. 3, p. 5.
49. Ricoeur, "Narrated Time," p. 261. For his complete account, see Ricoeur, *Time and Narrative*, vol. 1, pp. 5–30.
50. Ricoeur, "Narrated Time," p. 262.
51. Ibid.
52. Ibid. For Ricoeur's lengthy treatment and critique of Heidegger on temporality, see *Time and Narrative*, vol. 3, pp. 60–96.

53. Ricoeur, "Narrated Time," p. 265.

54. Ricoeur, *Time and Narrative*, vol. 3, p. 283, n. 12.

55. Ricoeur makes clear that the general context for his treatment of Husserl's focus on internal time-consciousness is primarily that of objective or world or cosmic time (Aristotle) in contrast to the time of the soul of Augustine or of time-consciousness . . . in the sense of internal (*inneres*). This context for Ricoeur contains the positive discovery and the aporia of phenomenology of time-consciousness, and the suspension of objective or cosmic or world time in order to change focus to inner time-consciousness itself (*Zeitbewusstsein*). Ricoeur, in the context of indicating a "homonymy," makes a statement that fixes his focus on the central tenet coming out of Husserl's descriptive account of internal time-conscisousness: "that the phenomenologist cannot avoid admitting, . . . a certain homonymy between the 'flow of consciousness' and the 'Objective flow of time'; or, again, between the 'one after the other' of immanent time and the succession of objective time; or yet, again, the continuum of the one and that of the other" (*Time and Narrative*, vol. 3, p. 24).

56. Ibid., pp. 24, 26–27.

57. Ibid., pp. 24, 26.

58. Ibid., p. 26.

59. Ibid., p. 27.

60. Ibid., pp. 27–28.

61. Ibid.

62. Ibid., p. 29.

63. Ibid., p. 30.

64. Ibid. p. 34.

65. Ibid., p. 283, n. 12.

66. John D. Caputo, "The Economy of Signs in Husserl and Derrida: From Uselessness to Full Employment," in *Deconstruction and Philosophy: The Texts of Jacques Derrida* edited by John Sallis (Chicago: The University of Chicago Press, 1987), p. 101.

67. John D. Caputo, "The Economy of Signs in Husserl and Derrida," p. 60.

68. Ricoeur, *Time and Narrative*, vol. 3, p. 28.

69. Jacques Derrida, *Of Grammatology*, translated by Gayatri Chakravorty Spivak (Baltimore: John Hopkins University Press, 1976) p. 69.

70. Jacques Derrida, *Positions*, translated by Alan Bass (Chicago: University of Chicago Press, 1981), p. 28.

71. It will be seen that Derrida's deconstructionist position is in fact a throwback to the use of alternatives and dilemmas beyond which phenomenology long ago moved. Phenomenology offers a shattering attack on virtually all the assumptions governing the philosophical tradition and the kinds of alternatives and dilemmas to which they gave rise, as well as similar assumptions presented in seemingly new linguistic garments, of what is often considered mainstream philosophy today. Ironically, it is the alternatives and dilemmas operative within Derrida's deconstruction itself that best brings to clear light the way in which Ricoeur's recent writings provide the way out of the impasses presented by deconstruction and the solutions for moving beyond it.

72. Ricoeur, *Time and Narrative*, translated by Kathleen Blamey and David

Pellauer (Chicago: University of Chicago Press, 1988), vol. 3, p. 283, n. 12. Ricoeur here quotes Derrida's *Speech and Phenomena*, p. 67.

73. Ricoeur, *Time and Narrative*, translated by Kathleen Blamey and David Pellauer (Chicago: University of Chicago Press, 1988), vol. 3, p. 283, n. 12.

CHAPTER 8. RICOEUR AND LEVINAS

1. Paul Ricoeur, *Oneself as Another*, translated by Kathleen Blamey (Chicago: The University of Chicago Press, 1992). Henceforth, *Oneself as Another* will be referred to within the text as OA, and likewise in the notes.

2. Peter Kemp contends that while Ricoeur's critique of Levinas is too severe, his critique of Heidegger is not severe enough. I will follow Kemp to some extent in the development of this chapter, but differ from his critique on some points. See Peter Kemp, "Ricoeur between Heidegger and Levinas: Original Affirmation between Ontological Attestation and Ethical Injunction," in *Philosophy and Social Criticism*, vol. 21 (1995).

3. It is my contention, not to be developed here, that Ricoeur's ethics, instructed by Aristotle, Kant, and the entire tradition of philosophy, even postmodern deconstruction, proffers a very viable contemporary ethics. This would contrast his work with that of postmodern deconstruction especially that of Derrida. Some recent secondary literature to which this relates by contrast are the following: John D. Caputo, *Against Ethics* (Bloomington: Indiana University Press, 1993); Drucilla Cornell, *The Philosophy of Limit* (New York and London: Routledge, 1992); and Simon Critchley, *Deconstructive Ethics: Derrida and Levinas* (Oxford: Blackwell, 1992). These works all respond to the dialogue between Levinas and Derrida. Cf. especially Jacques Derrida, "Violence and Metaphysics: An Essay on the Thought of Emmanuel Levinas," in *Writing and Difference* (Chicago: The University of Chicago Press, 1978). It is this essay by Derrida that in some measure put Levinas' work on ethics in the heart of postmodern discussions.

4. See Kemp, "Ricoeur between Heidegger and Levinas."

5 Emmanuel Levinas, *Time and the Other*, translated by Richard A. Cohen (Pittsburgh: Duquesne University Press, 1987), p. 75.

6 Richard A. Cohen, footnote 63, p. 83 of Levinas, *Time and the Other*.

7. Levinas, *Time and the Other*, p. 83.

8. *Totality and Infinity: An Essay on Exteriority*, translated by Alphonso Lingis (Pittsburgh: Duqesne University Press, 1969).

9. Levinas, *Time and the Other*, p. 45.

10. Levinas, *Totality and Infinity*, pp. 27–28.

11. Stated by Philippe Nemo in Emmanuel Levinas, *Ethics and Infinity: Conversations with Philippe Nemo*, translated by Richard A. Cohen (Pittsburgh: Duquesne University Press, 1985), p. 90.

12. Adriaan Peperzak, *To the Other: An Introduction to the Philosophy of Emmanuel Levinas* (West Lafayette, Ind.: Purdue University, 1993), p. 54. For a very fine treatment of this element of Heidegger, where he in his later work is seen to shuck off any trace of the Judeo-Christian tradition in favor of the pagan

Greek and German traditions, as Peperzak states here so well, see John D. Caputo, *Demythologizing of Heidegger* (Bloomington: Indiana University Press, 1993).

13. Richard A. Cohen, introduction to Emmanuel Levinas, *Time and the Other*, p. 7.

14. Levinas, *Time and the Other*, p. 70.

15. Cohen, introduction to *Time and the Other*, p. 8.

16. Levinas, *Time and the Other*, pp. 70–71.

17. Cohen, introduction to *Time and the Other*, p. 12.

18. Regarding the "present" here, Cohen makes a good point in indicating that in both French and English "the present" can mean both a gift or the present time.

19. There is another essential aspect of Levinas' thought, but not necessary for the full development of my own thesis. That is the role of the will, which as desire that is not the satisfaction of a need, and one that is not to be satisfied, carries to transcendence. Cohen focuses on Levinas' passivity of will that emerges here. In the face to face, in the seeing the offense of the offended, the good will is "elected to its moral status," so that the other counts more than I do: "The irreducible alterity of the Other, the time of the Other, impinges on the subject's temporal syntheses from the outside, disrupting its unity with another time, the time of the Other or ethics, the command which comes from on high. And in the same extraordinary moment, the Other's command calls forth a subjectivity for-the-Other, that is to say, a subjectivity which fears murder more than death,' which recognizes itself as murderous and the Other as vulnerable or destitute, the object of the subject's actual or potential violence, the object of irresponsibility and injustice." This quote of Cohen is in *Time and the Other*, p. 17: see pages 16–17 for the sentence before this.

20. Emmanuel, *Time and the Other*, pp. 63–64. Cohen tells us in a footnote to this text of Levinas, also develops the notion of enjoyment in *Existence and Existents*, pp. 37–45; *Totality and Infinity*, pp. 127–139, 143–151; and *Otherwise than Being*, pp. 72–74. See also R. Cohen, "Emmanuel Levinas; Happiness Is Sensational Time," *Philosophy Today*, vol. 25, no. 3 (Fall 1981), pp. 196–203.

21. Levinas, *Time and the Other*, p. 63.

22. Paul Ricoeur, "Existence and Hermeneutics," in *Conflict of Interpretation: Essays in Hermeneutics*, edited by Don Ihde (Evanston, Ill.: Northwestern University Press, 1974).

23. I do not mean here to imply that Levinas has less respect for Heidegger than Ricoeur does, for his famous statements about Heidegger being one of the five great philosophers throughout the ages cannot be forgotten, nor his contention that one must encounter in depth Heidegger's thought in order to surpass it. Levinas' entire effort is tied to this surpassing of Heidegger's initial ontology and later thought of Being, not that Heidegger is the only thinker with this profound an influence on Levinas in his attempt to account for the transcendence to the Infinite Other. One need only to remember his critiques of Husserl, as well as his espousal of Rosencranz.

24. Paul Ricoeur, *Fallible Man*, translated by Charles A. Kelbley (Chicago: Henry Regnery Company, 1965), especially p. 67.

25. Paul Ricoeur, *Time and Narrative*, translated by Kathleen Blamey and David Pellauer (Chicago: University of Chicago Press, 1988), vol. 3.

26. As mentioned in note 2, Peter Kemp contends that while Ricoeur's critique of Levinas is too severe, which is at least in part true, his critique of Heidegger is not severe enough. Kemp wants to tie this accusation to a reading of Heidegger's notion of authenticity. As will be seen later, this is not so simply true. See Kemp, "Ricoeur between Heidegger and Levinas."

27. Ernst Cassirer, "Kant and the Problem of Metaphysics," in *Kant: Disputed Questions*, edited with an introduction and new translations by Moltke S. Gram (Chicago: Quadrangle Books 1967), pp. 131–158.

28. It can be admitted at this point that perhaps Ricoeur stresses too much the broken aspect of human being and the truncated dimension of human existence. His account, especially the later ones, does ring true. Further Heidegger shows the advantage of passing to the originary level in an ontology that provides a more comprehensive and foundational unity below the broken existence that supports the conflict of hermeneutics of existence that has preoccupied Ricoeur for so long. Heidegger, however, as will be seen, has had to lop off the entire Kantian reason and the infinite, as well as the function of understanding in relation to such a reason driven to totality, completeness, and the unconditioned. Thus, although Heidegger is useful in helping to get Ricoeur from fixating on his earlier interpretation of the existential role of evil, Ricoeur, even in his later somewhat mitigated appropriation of Kant's view of the tendency to the good and the proclivity to evil, Ricoeur cannot ever go the distance with Heidegger's diminuated role of Kantian reason.

29. Ricoeur, "Existence and Hermeneutics," pp. 6–11.

30. Ibid., p. 19.

31. Paul Ricoeur, *Freud and Philosophy: An Essay on Interpretation*, translated by Denis Savage (New Haven: Yale University Press, 1970), p. 45.

32. Ibid.

33. Ricoeur, *The Conflict of Interpretation*, p. 19. He says: "Moreover, it is only in a conflict of rival hermeneutics that we perceive something of the being to be interpreted: a unified ontology is as inaccessible to our method as a separate ontology. Rather, in every instance each hermeneutics discovers the aspect of existence which founds it as a method."

34. Ibid., p. 10. See Kemp, "Ricoeur between Heidegger and Levinas," p. 47.

35. Kemp, "Ricoeur between Heidegger and Levinas," p. 47.

36. Paul Ricoeur, "Narrated Time," *Philosophy Today*, vol. 29, no. 4/4 (Winter 1985), p. 262. For Ricoeur's lengthy treatment and critique of Heidegger on temporality, see *Time and Narrative*, vol. 3, pp. 60–96.

37. Ricoeur, "Narrated Time," p. 265.

38. See Kemp, "Ricoeur between Heidegger and Levinas," p. 48. The focus of our discussion here is from the end of the *Rule of Metaphor*: Paul Ricoeur, *The Rule of Metaphor: Multi-Disciplinary Studies of the Creation of Meaning in Language*, tranlated by Robert Czerny with Kathleen McLaughlin and John Costello, S.J. (Toronto: University of Toronto Press, 1975), especially p. 311.

39. Kemp, "Ricoeur between Heidegger and Levinas," p. 48, quoting Ricoeur, *The Rule of Metaphor*, p. 312.

40. Kemp, "Ricoeur between Heidegger and Levinas," p. 48.

41. Ibid., p. 49.

42. Emmanuel Levinas, *Totality and Infinity: An Essay on Exteriority*, translated by Alphonso Lingis, (Pittsburgh: Duquesne University Press, 1969).

43. Emmanuel Levinas, *Otherwise than Being or Beyond Essence*, translated by Alphonso Lingis (The Hague: Martinus Nijhoff, 1974).

44. See Kemp, "Ricoeur between Heidegger and Levinas," p. 56. See OA, 337 (French ed., 337).

45. Kemp, "Ricoeur between Heidegger and Levinas," p. 54.

46. See also ibid., p. 55. SO, 390.

47. Levinas, OB, 112 (French ed., 142). Kemp, "Ricoeur between Heidegger and Levinas," p. 55.

48. It is clear from reading the introduction by Cohen to *Time and the Other* that the later thought is contained in the earlier. Following Cohen's view of the progression of alterity, Ricoeur is not wrong in interpreting back to *Totality and Infinity* from *Otherwise than Being*. Kemp, on the other hand, makes a point of indicating that one should read Levinas in such a way as to give more importance to *Totality and Infinity* rather than to *Otherwise than Being*.

49. Adriaan Peperzak, *To the Other: An Introduction to the Philosophy of Emmanuel Levinas* (West Lafayette, Ind.: Purdue University Press, 1993), p. 120.

50. Levinas, *Time and the Other*, p. 42. Quoted, too, in *Ethics and Infinity*, p. 59.

51. Levinas, EI, p. 105.

52. Ibid., p. 59

53. Ibid., p. 57

54. Ibid., pp. 57–58.

55. It is not possible here to do an in depth study, but only to indicate certain focal points. An in-depth study would require a rather lengthy work.

56. Kemp, "Ricoeur between Heidegger and Levinas," p. 56.

57. Ibid., p. 55.

58. Ibid., p. 57.

59. Levinas, *Totality and Infinity*, p. 23.

60. Ibid.

61. Paul Ricoeur, *Freud and Philosophy: An Essay on Interpretation*, translated by Denis Savage (New Haven and London: Yale University Press, 1970), *De l'interpretation: Essai sur Freud* (Paris: Éditions du Seuil, 1965).

62. Peperzak, *To the Other*, p. 136.

63. Ibid., p. 138.

64. Ibid., p. 161.

65. Ibid., p. 164.

66. Ibid., p. 133 .

67. Ibid., p. 134.

68. Ibid., p. 135.

69. Kemp, "Ricoeur between Heidegger and Levinas," p. 56.

70. Robert Bernasconi "Rereading Totality and Infinity," pp. 33–34. Quoting Leivinas (TI, 172; Tel 147; and TI 153; Tel 126).

71. Ibid., p. 145.

72. Robert Bernasconi, "Deconstruction and the Possibility of Ethics," in *Deconstruction and Philosophy: The Texts of Jacques Derrida*, edited by John Sallis (Chicago: The University of Chicago Press, 1987), especially p. 135. Bernasconi admits that deconstruction (at least Derrida in "Violence and Metaphysics") does seem to preserve the ethical relation, but only in the sense of the thought of the ethical relation, not yet a practice, in its insistence that the logos of it is the impossible-unthinkable-unsayable. This for Bernasconi, is deconstruction's rigorously holding to the limits of thinking. In this context, the ethical enactment lies especially in the refusal of deconstruction to take on the standpoint of critique, thus not passing judgment in its own voice on its own behalf. So understood, deconstruction as such cannot accept anything of the ethical, even the ethical relation as Levinas had it, and must deconstruct it in terms of the non-logocentrism, the ellipsis, of its own view. The only ethical relation allowed here is the impersonal deconstructive process itself.

73. Paul Ricoeur "The Problem of the Foundation of Moral Philosophy," *Philosophy Today*, vol. 28 (1978), pp. 178, 182–184.

74. Levinas does not give such a positive or prominent place to sympathy in his critique of Husserl. Richard Cohen points out that "it is at the level of the 'decency' of 'everyday life' then, that Levinas finds a place for the sympathy and pairing that he has rejected as ultimate constitutive of the inter-subjective relationship" (in Cohen's footnote 62, p. 83 of *Time and the Other*). Alterity is precisely what Levinas wants to emphasize, while Ricoeur is trying to round it out and make it more viable in taking Husserl's direction into account.

75. Kemp, "Ricoeur between Heidegger and Levinas," p. 55.

76. See note 28 above.

77. See note 28 above.

78. Although some deconstructionists such a Critchley and Cornell advance a deconstructive ethics, and hold onto the term, the ethics they allow amount to no more than the responsibility in the process of deconstruction.

CHAPTER 9. ETHICS AND POSTMODERNITY

1. Jack Caputo, *Radical Hermeneutics*, pp. 240–244.

2. Shaun Gallagher, "The Place of Phronesis in Postmodern Hermeneutics," *Philosophy Today*, vol. 37 (Fall 1993), pp. 298–305.

3. Following Caputo in *Radical Hermeneutics*, chapters 8 and 9. Hereafter cited in the text as RH.

4. Caputo quotes here from SG, that is, *Der Satz vom Grund*, 3rd ed. (Pfullingen: Neske, 1965).

5. In *L'Ethique du don: Jacques Derrida et la pensée du don* (Paris: Metailie, 1992), which appeared after the completion of his own book, *Against Ethics*.

6. It is clearly becoming necessary for me to deal with the Kierkegaardian input into contemporary ethics, since Caputo has used his writings, especially *Repetition* and now the pseudonymous author Johannes de Silentio, the name under which *Fear and Trembling* was published.

7. We will see Levinas' ethics in the following chapter.

8. Caputo's footnote 29 is quite revealing regarding the ultimate intent of this work: "In my view, Levinas describes the dynamics of faith as well as anybody. Indeed, I think that what Levinas provides is above all a metaphysics of the religious, of faith, which organizes faith around the trace of the Infinite Other. I myself take the present work to be, among other things, a background for a possible account of faith and I take the notion of *différance* as a propaedeutic to a theory of faith; see chapter 2, note 21." This note reads: "There is, I think, an important (quasi) philosophy of religious in deconstruction; for a little start on it, see Charles E. Winquist and John D. Caputo, 'Derrida and the Study of Religion,' *Religious Studies Review*, vol. 16 (January 1990), pp. 19–25.

9. Critchley, *The Ethics of Deconstruction*, p. xi.

10. Emmanuel Levinas, *Éthique et infini*, 85, quoted in Critchley, *The Ethics of Deconstruction*, p. 4.

11. Cornell, *The Philosophy of Limit*, pp. 8–9.

12. For a full elaboration of this critique of deconstruction's view of sign, time, language, and trace, see Patrick L. Bourgeois, "Trace, Semiotic, and the Living Present: Derrida or Ricoeur, " *Southwest Philosophy Review*, vol. 9 (August 1993); see also, "Semiotics and the Deconstruction of Presence: A Ricoeurian Alternative," *American Catholic Philosophical Quarterly*, 1993; and finally, "The Instant and the Living Present: Ricoeur and Derrida," *Philosophy Today*, vol. 37 (1993).

13. For a full treatment of these points, see Bourgeois, "Trace, Semiotics, and the Living Present"; Bourgeois, "Semiotics and the Deconstruction of Presence"; and "The Instant and the Living Present."

14. Please see the note above for references where this critique is carried out more fully. Here, all that can be given is a summary of points.

15. He many be too severe in his critique of Levinas.

CHAPTER 10. THE ETHICS OF GOOD

1. Paul Ricoeur, *Le Just* (Paris: Editions Esprit, 1995), pp. 13–14. This work will be cited in the text as LJ.

2. Note that the same procedure of capitalization will be followed here in the Ricoeurian context of using the French "*autrui*" and "*autre*" as used in the context of Levinas. We will thus capitalize "Other" when the personal other is meant [*autrui*], and the lower case for the translation of the less personal "other" [*autre*].

3. Ricoeur, quoting Aristotle in footnote 1 (1.1.1094a1–3).

4. Cf. Aristotle's treatment of intimacy in book 9.12.

5. Perhaps it is Merleau-Ponty who best shows the personal, human, and cultural dimension of human existence in a world where the personal dimension, developed somewhere about the third year for the child manifest in the appropriation of the correct use of personal pronouns (cf. "The Child's Relations with Others" in Pr.P). His phenomenology of perception shows the pre-personal—personal dimensions of human existence, and how, although the pre-personal is

never left behind, the personal dimension of our coexistence is presupposed for the full development of a human as a human.

6. Ricoeur mentions in a footnote here that power and act come up here, and that he will treat this in the tenth study: "One will see in E.N.9.9 the analysis of friendship run up against the difficult problem of power and act, of activity (*energeia*) and of act in the strong sense (*entelekheia*), which we shall take the risk of confronting directly in the tenth study, sec. 2." OA, 182 footnote 13.

7. This term "for at work" is taken from Gary B. Herbert, whose section on Aristotle gives its background, in *The Philosophical History of Right*, copyright 1997, Loyola University, unpublished manuscript.

8. Ricoeur quoting Kant, *Groundwork*, pp. 103–104.

9. *Groundwork* 4.436, p. 104, quoted by Ricoeur, OA, 211.

10. Ricoeur, quoting Kant, *Groundwork*, p. 61, his edition.

11. Kant, *Groundwork*, Ricoeur's edition, pp. 64–65.

12. Ricoeur's edition of Kant's *Groundwork* is quoted here, pp. 64–65.

13. CPrR, no. 3, Theorem 2, Corollary, p. 21.

14. Ricoeur referring to (CPrR, no. 3, Theorem 2, Corollary, p. 21).

15. Ricoeur, quoting CPrR, p. 77.

16. Ricoeur, quoting CPrR, p. 76.

17. *Critique of Practical Reason*, "Analytic," chap. 2. In other works, the question of good and evil returns with the question of 'the subjective ground of the use of freedom'" (OA, 217, footnote 29.

18. Ricoeur, quoting Kant's *Religion*, p. 21.

19. Ricoeur, quoting Kant's *Religion*, p. 23.

20. Ricoeur, referring to Kant, GMM, 4.429, p. 96.

21. Ricoeur, referring to Kant, GMM, 4.429, p. 96.

22. Ricoeur, referring to Kant, GMM, 4.458, p. 126.

23. See Ricoeur's footnote no. 54 of OA, which is a good critique, quoting an article that he wrote in *Esprit*, 1988, no. 2.

24. Cf. fn. 54, critiquing circularity of Rawls.

CHAPTER 11. JUDGING IN CONCRETE SITUATIONS

1. In a recent conference on Ricoeur's ethics, sponsored by the Divinity School of the University of Chicago in October 1999, Ricoeur indicated a shift in the way in which he would approach the treatment of ethics and moral philosophy. He would now focus first on the moral, with its attempt to universalize or test the moral norms by means of the categorical immperative. This initial focus would then lead from the moral in two directions: toward the ethical foundation, the *archai*, the *Ursprung*; and also toward applied ethics, as *phronésis* or paractical wisdom, and as judgment in the concrete situation. I understand this to be a shift in approach and not in content or doctrine of ethicomoral philosophy as we have been pursuing it throughout our studies.

2. There are two things that Ricoeur points out here about Kant's treatment: first that his test for universalization by way of contradiction is quite limited; and that the first challenge to this duty comes by was of the agent making

an exception for her/him self in the process of testing by universalizing. OA, 263–264.

3. For example, see "Violence et langage," in *Lectures I: Autour du politique* (Paris: Éditions du Seuil, 1991), pp. 131–140.

4. It is less relevant for our purposes here, but certainly important for Ricoeur's entire project in *Oneself as Another* that he relates the self-constancy to the ipse identity in contrast to that of idem identity: "Have we not ourselves made self-constancy through time the highest expression of the identity of *ipse* in contrast to that of *idem*, that is, in opposition to the mere permanence or perseverance of things (a permanence that is found on the plane of selfhood only in character). There is nothing to repudiate in these analyses." (OA, 267).

5. It is generally known that Marcel considered availability to be manifest in the way one can listen, as available to another, or in a closed sort of way, as not available. Thus availability connotes an openness to the other and a willingness of be there for him/her.

6. The two examples that Ricoeur invokes here are at the "beginning of life," and at the "end of life." The latter deals with the difficult question of telling the truth to the patient who is dying in relation to the dire consequences of doing so; and the former deals with the problem of the state of the unborn life. Ricoeur takes an interesting angle in each of these considerations. For with regard to the end of life, the first conflict is the telling of the terminal sentence that could be an agony and torture for the sick. On the other hand, it could be the occasion for a real good on a level above the level of material good, allowing the dying person, with death already accepted, to have the opportunity for "exchange in giving and receiving under the sign of death accepted" (OA, 270). Regarding the beginning of life, Ricoeur cuts beneath many of the traditional arguments, yet keeping them in view while remaining faithful to his views of identity of sameness and identity of as selfhood, suggesting that respect must be accompanied "by a minimum ontology of development that adds to the idea of capacity, belonging to a logic of all or nothing, that of aptitude which admits of degrees of actualization. . . . Such identification of thresholds and degrees marking the appearance of properties of personal being is dependent on science alone. But the ontological tenor assigned to the predicate 'potential' in the expression 'potential human person' is perhaps not separable from the manner of 'treating' beings corresponding to these various stages. Manner of being and manner of treating would seem to be mutually determined in the formation of prudential judgments occasioned by each advance in the power that technology confers today on humankind over life in its beginnings. Once again, if science is alone competent to describe the thresholds of development, the appreciation of rights and duties relative to each of them belongs to a genuine moral invention that will establish, following a progression comparable to that of the biologic thresholds, qualitatively different rights: the right not to suffer, the right to protection (this notion itself presenting several degrees of 'force' or 'emphasis'), the right to respect, once something like an exchange, even asymmetrical, of preverbal signs is begun between the fetus and its mother. It is this give-and-take between the description of thresholds and the appraisal of rights and duties, in the intermediary zone between things and persons, that justifies classifying bioethics in the

zone of prudential judgment. . . . It is part of that practical wisdom required by conflictual situations resulting from respect itself in an area in which the dichotomy between persons and things is akimbo" (OA, 272).

7. Critchley, *The Ethics of Deconstruction*, p. 2.

8. Emmanuel Levinas, *Ethique et infini*, 85, quoted from Critchley, *The Ethics of Deconstruction*, p. 4.

9. Drucilla Cornell, *The Philosophy of Limit*, pp. 8–9.

10. Paul Ricoeur, *Oneself as Another*, translated by Kathleen Blamey (Chicago: The University of Chicago Press, 1992). Henceforth, *Oneself as Another* will be referred to within the text as OA, and likewise in the notes.

11. Paul Ricoeur, *Le Just* (Paris: Éditions Esprit, 1995).

INDEX